NEGOTIATING WITH EVIL

NEGOTIATING WITH EVIL
WHEN TO TALK TO TERRORISTS

MITCHELL B. REISS

OPEN ROAD

INTEGRATED MEDIA

NEW YORK

Copyright © 2010 by Mitchell B. Reiss
Cover design by Elizabeth Connor
Book design by Danielle Young

ISBN: 978-1-4532-0070-4

Published in 2010 by Open Road Integrated Media
180 Varick Street
New York, NY 10014
www.openroadmedia.com

To Elisabeth

CONTENTS

INTRODUCTION

MAPPING THE CHALLENGE

Drinking champagne and balancing hors d'oeuvres on paper napkins, the two hundred guests appeared not to have a care in the world. They had accepted the invitation of the American consul general in Northern Ireland to celebrate America's Independence Day at the official residence, Ardnavalley, just outside of Belfast. The guests included the good and the great from across the six counties—politicians, business leaders, artists, and athletes. Also at the party, but less noticeable, lurked a handful of ex–paramilitary leaders and former terrorists.

As the afternoon wore on, I noticed that some of the guests who had lost family and friends during the Troubles were quietly huddling among the garden flowers and fountains with the former members of paramilitary or terrorist organizations accountable for their loss. Both parties were deep in thoughtful conversation, oblivious to the other guests. The scene struck me as something completely unexpected: people who had suffered unfathomable sorrow showing extraordinary self-control, even grace, with former enemies.

This spectacle made a powerful impression on me. How could people who had suffered so much behave this way? Over 3,700 people had been killed and 30,000 more wounded during the Troubles; one of every five people in Northern Ireland had a family member killed or injured. Comparable figures for the United States would have translated to 600,000 dead and 6 million wounded. I imagined how I would feel if I had experienced the same anguish, and traveled to a much darker place—a deep desire for revenge. I simply did not possess the inner strength of these people, and as I watched them speaking quietly to one another, I silently gave thanks I did not need to.

As I stood there, I wondered how democratic states might make the same journey. Engaging with mortal enemies, with terrorists, with evil, raised questions of national security, morality, and the social contract between the state and the people. How could governments go from vilifying those intent on their destruction to making a complete U-turn and negotiating with them? What concerns must governments weigh, from the dangerous precedent that "violence pays" to the charges of appeasement to the betrayal of the memory of those who made the ultimate sacrifice defending the state?

Finally, how should a government move forward once this difficult decision is made? Obviously, it is not simply a case of bumping into one's enemies at a cocktail party. How does a government signal that it wants to meet? Where does it acquire the local knowledge needed to identify those adversaries who can act with discretion and speak with authority? How does it anticipate handling the consequences should the talks become public? And very important, how does it determine when conciliation or concessions are not working and that it should revert to deterrence, law enforcement, even war?

The vast resources of the U.S. intelligence community were unable to provide me with satisfying answers to these questions when I was working on the Northern Ireland peace process. The questions have stayed with me ever since. To find the answers I've spent the past three years traveling across Europe, the Middle East, and South Asia talking with hundreds of individuals, including government ministers, military officers, intelligence operatives, and even former terrorists. To uncover the answers is the purpose of this book.

ON JULY 23, 2007, DURING A televised debate of the Democratic Party's presidential candidates, Senator Barack Obama was asked if he would meet—without preconditions—during the first year of his administration with a rogue's gallery of countries hostile to the United States: Iran, Syria, Venezuela, Cuba, and North Korea.

He said he would.

Senator Hillary Clinton immediately challenged him. Criticisms from the Republican presidential candidates were harsher. The resulting furor sparked a debate over the conduct of American diplomacy that continued throughout the primary season and into the 2008 presidential campaign. It has followed President Obama into the Oval Office, as he attempted in his first year to reach out to long-standing American enemies.

Talking to enemies has deep roots. Across cultures, continents, and civilizations, societies have always developed ways for adversaries to settle their differences short of violence. From the Chinese of the Western Zhou dynasty a thousand years before the birth of Christ, to the Bushmen of the Kalahari, to the Abkhazians of the Caucasus Mountains, societies have cultivated elaborate rituals to end fighting and preserve harmony.

The most sacred texts of the world's great religions have all enshrined mediation, conflict resolution, and peacemaking.[1] The Old Testament famously tells the story of King Solomon dividing the baby. In the New Testament, the Lord's Prayer exhorts us to "forgive those who have trespassed against us." The Koran speaks of Muhammad acting as a mediator to successfully avoid open warfare when local clan leaders squabbled over who should have the honor of replacing the sacred black stone when reconstructing the Ka'aba.

In ancient Greece, Aristotle sowed the philosophical roots of resolving differences through negotiation. These ideas were advanced in modern times by diplomatic advisers to French royalty, Cardinal-Duc de Richelieu and François de Callières, and by the Enlightenment thinkers Thomas Hobbes, John Locke, and Jean-Jacques Rousseau.

The history of the United States has numerous examples of leaders engaging with terrorists and rogue regimes. In the early years of the United States, three Founding Fathers—George Washington, John Adams, and Thomas Jefferson—accommodated what today would be viewed as terrorists: They each authorized payment to the Barbary pirates, and the U.S. Senate even ratified a treaty that enshrined the annual provision of naval supplies as "protection."[2] A century later, President Teddy Roosevelt cut a deal with a descendant of the Barbary pirates, a local Berber chief named Raisuli, after he had kidnapped an American resident in Tangier, Ion Perdicaris. "Perdicaris alive or Raisuli dead" was the bombastic battle cry that boosted Roosevelt's reputation, but the less rousing reality was that he secretly worked through the Sultan of Morocco to grant Raisuli's every demand.[3]

Recently, American presidents have negotiated with terrorists and rogue regimes to secure the release of hostages, to arrange temporary ceasefires, and to explore whether a more permanent truce might be possible, although they have sometimes gone to great lengths to disguise their direct involvement. In order to secure the release of the USS *Pueblo*'s eighty-three crewmen, Lyndon Johnson agreed to a confession that the ship had intruded into North Korea's territorial waters for the purpose of spying. Richard Nixon encouraged Israel, Switzerland, West Germany, and Britain to release Palestinian prisoners in their jails so that the Popular Front for the Liberation of Palestine would free hostages on two hijacked airliners. Jimmy Carter spent the last year and a quarter of his presidency negotiating with Iran for the release of American diplomats who had been taken hostage, finally agreeing to return $8 billion in frozen Iranian assets. To rescue seven Americans who had been kidnapped in Beirut, Ronald Reagan agreed to transfer antitank and antiair missiles and spare parts to Iran. Only three of the hostages were freed; one was killed and three more Americans in Lebanon were subsequently kidnapped. The resulting arms-for-hostages scandal, which included diverting funds to support the Nicaraguan Contras and lying to Congress, almost brought down Reagan's presidency.[4]

After Iraq's August 1990 invasion of Kuwait, George H.W. Bush's administration entered into almost constant diplomatic negotiations with Saddam Hussein and his officials before it launched Operation Desert Storm, or what Saddam referred to as the "mother of all battles." Bill Clinton's administration sat down with Hamas in Amman, Jordan, in early 1993 to gain a better understanding of the group and see if it could be persuaded to support the peace process.[5] In the mid-1990s, the Clinton administration engaged North Korea in an attempt to freeze and reverse the country's nuclear weapons programs; I spent the next four years negotiating in Pyongyang and New York City the detailed implementation of this deal. (It ultimately fell apart.) The Clinton administration also held meetings with Taliban representatives in Kandahar, Tashkent, Islamabad, Bonn, New York, and Washington to request the handover of Osama bin Laden and the al Qaeda leadership who were using Afghanistan as a training ground for attacks on the United States.[6] In his January 2002 State of the Union Address, George W. Bush labeled Iraq, Iran, and North Korea as members of an "axis of evil," yet his administration negotiated with Saddam Hussein to get international inspectors into the country, held three rounds of talks with Iran starting in 2007 over securing the border with Iraq, and authorized multiple direct negotiations with North Korea after its October 2006 nuclear test.[7]

These are only a few examples.

Talking to enemies is nothing new, but the track record is mixed. Sometimes talking succeeds and sometimes it doesn't. So when and why do states decide to negotiate? How can they decide whether engagement promotes or harms a country's interests? What can this little-examined, sometimes hidden diplomatic history teach us about lessons learned, mistakes made, and pitfalls to be avoided?

TALKING TO STATE ENEMIES

For centuries, states have often talked to their enemies, even during times of war, for a variety of reasons: power politics, economics, domestic pressures, or even the preferences of idiosyncratic leaders.

A strong state may talk to its enemy if it believes that its relative power position is threatened either by its own decline or by its adversary's rise. A state may try to reach an agreement that locks in its power advantage, slows its decline, or tries to befriend the "new kid on the block." For example, Britain, perched atop its Victorian empire at the end of the nineteenth century, allowed a series of one-sided concessions to the United States in an effort to remove sources of friction between the two countries. This deliberate policy would lead to friendship, then support, and ultimately an alliance during the First World War. After the war, the United States did something similar. It hosted the Washington Naval Conference to preserve America's parity with a still-potent Britain and its advantage over a rising Japan.

A strong state may also talk to an enemy to try to persuade it to change its behavior: to stop doing something objectionable, to start doing something cooperative, or both. Morality has little to do with it. Moral qualms are subordinated in pursuit of a greater good—namely, national self-interest. As former prime minister Yitzhak Rabin famously said with respect to Yasser Arafat and the Palestine Liberation Organization (PLO), "You make peace with your enemies, not with your friends."

During a conflict, it is not possible to reach a peace settlement with an enemy without some form of communication, even if it is to threaten an escalation of hostilities or broker an end to them.[8] In July 1945, the Allied Powers gave Japan the choice of "unconditional surrender" or "prompt and utter destruction." In an attempt to end the Vietnam War and achieve "peace with honor," the United

States met with North Vietnamese officials for five years of on-again, off-again negotiations that ultimately led to the 1973 Paris Peace Accords.

While there is no guarantee that talking to enemy states will promote a country's national interests, there is likewise no guarantee that not talking will do so. Not talking may be simply the stubborn residue of a failed policy. Some states cannot be isolated internationally, defeated militarily, or overthrown by domestic political forces. Keeping diplomatic distance from odious regimes may therefore not achieve a state's foreign policy objectives. For example, America's decades-long embargo against Cuba has done little to reduce Castro's viselike grip on power or increase freedom for the Cuban people.

Holding direct talks with enemies may also send useful signals to other audiences a state wishes to influence. Even a single meeting may allow a state to better mold the diplomatic landscape by winning greater domestic and international support for other options, including military action if the talks fail. The George H.W. Bush administration used this logic when it made a last-ditch diplomatic effort to reverse Iraq's invasion of Kuwait in August 1990 by offering that the president meet with Iraqi foreign minister Tariq Aziz in Washington or that Secretary of State James Baker fly to Baghdad to see Saddam Hussein. "[I]t reassured balky allies such as the Soviets and French that the President was not rushing precipitously into war," Baker later wrote in his memoirs. "And it enabled us to argue that the President should not be undercut by Congress before what I began describing as 'the last, best chance for peace.'"[9]

A weak state may talk to an enemy if it believes that it can best serve its own interests by aligning itself with a stronger power rather than opposing it. In other words, it decides to "bandwagon" with the stronger state rather than "balance" against it.[10] Small states that neighbor much larger ones often make this choice out of necessity and desperation. Thus, after heroically resisting Soviet aggression in two wars over five years, "plucky little Finland" had little choice but to bandwagon with the Soviet Union after the Second World War.

Strong or weak states may also talk to an enemy in the hope of enlisting its help against a powerful third party that potentially threatens them both, on the basis that "the enemy of my enemy is my friend." Winston Churchill once claimed that this maxim guided four hundred years of British foreign policy. Britain, he declared, "always took the harder course, joined with the less strong Powers, made a combination among them, and thus defeated and frustrated the Continental military tyrant, whoever he was, whichever nation he led."[11] Or more piquantly, Churchill explained his justification for aligning British interests with less-than-savory regimes during the Second World War: "If Hitler invaded Hell, I would find it possible to say something benevolent about Satan."

States have sometimes engaged with their enemies in an attempt to save money. For example, a traditional rationale for arms control agreements between the United States and the Soviet Union during the Cold War was that it would result in cost savings that could then be passed on to support social programs at home. In other words, funds would be allocated from guns to butter. The long-term cost savings from implementation of the START I nuclear arms control treaty were estimated to range from $2 billion to more than $17 billion a year over the life of the agreement.[12] (That little of this "peace dividend" was actually realized is disappointing, but beside the point.)

Domestic pressures from time to time have pushed states to talk to other states. The enormous influence of more than 40 million Irish-Americans certainly made itself felt by leveraging the U.S. government to help resolve the Troubles in Northern Ireland. In an extraordinary (if largely benevolent) example of interference in a foreign country's internal affairs, the United States has been the only foreign country to establish a consulate in Belfast and appoint a presidential envoy to the peace process.

Or a desire to talk to enemies may originate from a single visionary individual who wishes to invent a new future for his country, even if this means bucking his own government and domestic opinion. Egyptian president Anwar Sadat broke the cycle of perpetual Arab-Israeli conflict by going "to the end of the world to achieve peace," traveling to Jerusalem in November 1977, speaking before the Knesset, and then signing a peace treaty.[13] Libya's Muammar Qaddafi, once mocked by Ronald Reagan as the "mad dog of the Middle East," in December 2003 announced that his country had agreed to radically alter its allegiances. Tripoli agreed to eliminate its weapons of mass destruction and withdraw its support for terrorism in return for normalizing relations with the United States and ending its international pariah status.

NOT TALKING TO STATE ENEMIES

States have often been willing to test whether negotiations with enemies can achieve national goals, but this is by no means a universal truth. States have rejected engagement for reasons of principle, morality, and pragmatism. Faced with an implacable foe, it may make greater strategic sense for states to balance, contain, marginalize, isolate, or even try to defeat enemies than to engage with them.

The most powerful reason not to engage with certain enemies is the judgment that no amount of concessions will pacify their hostile behavior. Some states may have revolutionary, maximalist, or millenarian aims that discourage any type of compromise except for those undertaken for purely short-term, cynical, or tactical reasons. The ambitions of these states cannot be accommodated, at least not at an acceptable price. Attempts to do so are usually termed "appeasement" and may result in disaster. The historical, oft-used touchstone is Neville Chamberlain's concessions at Munich, which allowed Hitler's Germany to annex the strategically important territory of the Sudetenland. Rather than satisfying Hitler's ambitions, Munich emboldened him to make further demands and seek further concessions.

Appeasement is flawed because it cannot satisfy states that wish to overturn the existing order, not merely negotiate adjustments to it. It strengthens enemies by surrendering strategically important territory, removing military constraints, relinquishing certain defenses, or enhancing the enemy's economic and industrial strength. Further, it weakens future efforts at deterrence because the enemy now has reason to believe that it is stronger than it was before, and the conciliatory state weaker. Appeasement can invite further aggression, as was seen when Hitler attacked Poland less than a year after the Munich Agreement, thereby triggering the Second World War.[14]

Too, democratically elected governments have greater moral authority than repressive regimes and should not squander it. Negotiations between the two may serve to "legitimize" or "validate" a brutal tyrant or dictator who violates human rights. Such meetings not only elevate the status and prestige of undeserving regimes, but they also diminish the reputation and moral authority of democratic states. Then–vice president Dick Cheney vividly captured this sense that engaging with certain states would both stain America's good name and taint its moral superiority when he told a Philadelphia audience in December 2002, "We don't negotiate with evil. We defeat it."[15]

Some argue that oppressive states should therefore be shunned and ostracized, not engaged. Anti-Bolshevik voices in the United States invoked this argument for over a decade, until Washington officially recognized the Soviet Union in

1933; similar arguments were marshaled for three decades against "Red China" until the United States formally established diplomatic relations in 1979. And during the 1960s, 1970s, and 1980s, many countries refused to have diplomatic relations or do business with South Africa as a way of signaling their disapproval of its apartheid system.

A third objection to talking to enemy states is that the very act of sitting down for negotiations confers a benefit that is better withheld. Because tyrants often crave the spotlight of publicity, the risk is that talking may be seen as rewarding bad behavior, blackmail, or threats rather than punishing them. It therefore sends the wrong signal to the regime across the table and to others who may be watching.

If it boosts the morale of enemies, negotiation may also undermine the morale and confidence of a state's friends and allies that may be nervous that deals will be struck without prior consultation or approval. Such talks can cause anxiety and erode the trust on which partnerships and alliances rest. During the Cold War, for example, America's NATO allies worried that Washington might reach a bilateral agreement with Moscow that would shortchange their strategic interests; they feared a deal that would make it more likely for a nuclear war to be limited to Europe and leave the continental United States and Soviet heartland untouched. When I was conducting nuclear negotiations with North Korea in the mid-1990s, a South Korean delegate to the talks worried that I might jeopardize his country's security to accommodate the North. He sarcastically asked me after I had just emerged from a private session with my North Korean counterpart, "What concessions did you make today?"

Important domestic constituencies may object to their government reaching out to states that these groups find objectionable; they often favor instead a policy of condemnation and isolation. The American political system is no stranger to this type of "ethnic politics." Since the abortive Bay of Pigs invasion, for example, Cuban-American groups have lobbied both Democratic and Republican administrations against normalizing relations with Castro's Cuba or even relaxing sanctions against the island. In recent years, human rights groups have objected to the United States holding nuclear negotiations with North Korea until Pyongyang improves its appalling treatment of its own citizens.

Further, negotiating is a poor idea when enemy states have motives other than a genuine desire to reach an agreement. States don't always bargain in good faith. Negotiations may be used by an adversary as a delaying tactic to prepare and strengthen forces for the next battle. This is hardly new. Thucydides noted this type of behavior in his *History of the Peloponnesian Wars*, when the lesser city-states finally decided to challenge the power of Athens but needed to buy time to prepare for the coming war. "This interval was spent in sending embassies to Athens charged with complaints, in order to obtain as good a pretext for war as possible, in the event of her paying no attention to them."[16]

If enemies can't be trusted to negotiate in good faith, then neither can they be trusted to keep any promises they may make. This is a particular risk when democratic states engage with nondemocracies, which tend to lack independent institutional and societal constraints against cheating. Transparency, accountability, constitutional checks and balances on power, scrutiny by local media or nongovernmental experts, and general respect for the rule of law tend to be far more rigorous in democracies than in nondemocracies.[17] And although it is possible that a few dictators and autocrats may care about negative world opinion, the media is significantly handicapped when it tries to ferret out the facts and determine the truth inside authoritarian regimes. Thus, there is always the risk of an asymmetry in compliance with any agreement, with no effective way to enforce adherence to the deal should an adversary backslide, short of threatening to withdraw from the agreement, a step democracies are often reluctant to take. The result is one-sided compliance, where one party is handcuffed but not the other.[18]

A related complaint is aimed not at the negotiation but at the negotiator. A reason not to talk to enemies is doubt over the skill, ability, and toughness of a state's own negotiating team to strike a good deal. Such wariness is understandable, given the stakes involved. In the nuclear talks with North Korea, I represented the views of the United States, South Korea, Japan, and the European Union. Collectively, we were trying to freeze and eventually eliminate North Korea's nuclear weapons programs, but individually, I was the one at the negotiating table entrusted with promoting their views and defending their prerogatives. We sometimes disagreed on tactics, even violently on a few occasions, but they never doubted my deep commitment to our common goal.

If the negotiator does not have the confidence of his host government, however, it is safer not to negotiate at all. The negotiator may fall short in either of two ways. First, he may be guileless and thus outsmarted by more cunning and ruthless adversaries across the table. American conservatives leveled this charge against President Jimmy Carter's chief arms control negotiator, Paul Warnke, claiming that he should not be asked to steward the SALT II talks because he did not believe either that the Soviet Union aimed for nuclear superiority or that it harbored a desire to attack the United States. Second, the negotiator may mistake process for substance. He may be so eager to broker a deal that whenever an impasse is reached, he will make concessions rather than allow the talks to fail. In this case, the negotiation becomes an end in itself, not simply the means to a larger goal. Under both these scenarios, negotiation becomes synonymous with capitulation.

A final reason not to talk with enemies is purely pragmatic: It doesn't work. Talking may be an effective way to clarify differences, but not eliminate or bridge them. These differences may exist not because the two sides don't understand each other, but because they simply cannot agree. In these circumstances, negotiations are a waste of a government's time, energy, and effort. For example, Osama bin Laden has stated that he will end his war against the United States once it removes all U.S. forces from the Middle East, abandons Israel, and withdraws its support for corrupt and oppressive Arab regimes like Saudi Arabia.[19]

In reviewing the arguments on both sides, the decision over whether states should talk to their enemies is far from straightforward. Rationalizations and justifications can be presented for taking either path. History unhelpfully offers ambiguous guidance. Even appeasement, which today connotes craven, cowardly, or unprincipled behavior, has been shown to work successfully at times. (One leading historian, Yale's Paul Kennedy, has remarked favorably upon Britain's "tradition" of foreign policy appeasement starting in the latter half of the nineteenth century and running for over seventy years.[20]) Much depends on the historical and political context, the balance of power between adversaries, the enemy state's motives and intentions, and the preferences of domestic constituencies. One of the greatest challenges for a responsible leader is therefore judging whether it is more prudent to engage with adversaries or oppose them.

TALKING TO TERRORISTS

An even *more* complex challenge for a leader is determining whether to talk to adversaries when they are not states but rather groups that are sometimes collectively, and rather antiseptically, referred to as "nonstate actors"—revolutionaries, insurgents, guerrillas, and terrorists. Often, less is known about these individuals, their organizations, their decision-making, and their ideology than is the case with enemy states. Judging by how rarely governments admit publicly to meeting members of such groups, it also appears more difficult politically for democratic governments to be seen in their company.

It is not immediately clear why this should be so. Historically, a terrorist group presents a far less lethal threat to the state, having far fewer resources at its disposal than a more traditional enemy. Indeed, there are no cases in modern history where terrorist groups not tied to mass political movements have toppled a sitting government and seized political power.[21] Terrorists are rarely successful in even getting a state to change specific policies. One recent study determined that terrorism succeeds only 7 percent of the time in forcing a state to give in to its demands. It concluded that terrorism is "a decidedly unprofitable coercive instrument."[22]

A simple (if grim) body count approach also falls well short of explaining this difference, as the moral balance sheet weighs far more heavily against state enemies. Although terrorist groups have blood on their hands, they are responsible for relatively few deaths; over the last forty years, the number of American victims of international terrorism is roughly the same as the number of people killed by lightning.[23] These numbers pale when compared with the millions who died at the hands of a Stalin, Mao, or Pol Pot, heads of state who for decades were treated with diplomatic trumpets and flourishes by the international community. And during the Cold War, the United States (and the Soviet Union) befriended an array of Third World tyrants and dictators who were massive human rights violators.

One reason terrorist groups are viewed differently from more traditional state enemies may be their different status under international law. Elaborate laws and protocols have been developed over the centuries that accord certain rights and privileges to states and those who act on their behalf, whether government officials, diplomats, or soldiers. These authorize the state to have a monopoly of legitimate violence within its borders and to use force to repel external attacks. These rights and privileges have been denied to anyone else.

A second reason may turn on whether a country has a colonial legacy. Those states that don't, such as the United States, which has not had to wrestle with the practical difficulties of transitioning from subjugating a foreign population to addressing its legitimate aspirations for independence, tend to do less negotiating with terrorists. Those states that do, like Great Britain, are not as wary. As one member of the House of Lords remarked with respect to individuals once labeled as terrorists, "We go from chasing them through the jungle, to sitting across from them at the negotiating table, to knighting them and having them meet the Queen."[24] Absent this type of postcolonial perspective, which tends to view terrorism as a temporary way station to an eventual political accommodation, government officials (and the voting public) may be far less tolerant of talking.

Sometimes a country's political culture may not be conducive to negotiating with nonstate actors. Despite a few self-styled revolutionary movements during the 1960s, the United States has never been home to a significant terrorist movement. Nor has there ever been any groundswell of domestic support for homegrown terrorist groups, whether white supremacist, far-right Christian, or other extremists. Any residual sympathy for foreign "revolutionaries," "insurgents," or "freedom fighters" evaporated on 9/11. President Bush's post-9/11 comments declared a "war on terror" and voiced a moral certainty that eliminated any middle ground when it came to terrorism, its sponsors, or even those who tolerated it: "Every state must make a choice. Either you are with us or against us." In this moral universe of only good and evil, there is not much space for engaging terrorists.[25]

A society's popular culture may also incline against talking to terrorists. In the United States in instances where bank heists have gone bad, negotiating with hostage-takers is seen as justified only to buy time and save lives, but it is expected that the forces of law and order will reassert themselves; in fact, very few perpetrators escape or go free. Not surprisingly, in some of the most popular American movies, such as *Dog Day Afternoon* and *Die Hard,* the negotiations end badly for the criminals. In one of the most culturally important television series of the past decade, *24,* the fictional hero, Jack Bauer, relentlessly pursues, captures, tortures, and kills terrorists, routinely saving the day at the last moment. (Virtually unnoticed is that he often negotiates with terrorists as well, cutting deals to serve a greater good.)

Or it could be that human nature simply reacts differently to acts of terrorism; random, violent shocks occupy a different moral and psychological space. Walter Laqueur, one of the most perceptive analysts of terrorism, may have gotten closer to the truth when he observed, "[T]errorism is blackmail and the victim of blackmail is less likely to forget and to forgive than the victim of almost any other crime; he feels a special sense of outrage because it is not just his life or property that has been affected. He is humiliated, his elementary human rights, his dignity and his self-respect are violated."[26]

Finally, it may be more difficult for democratically elected governments to talk to terrorists because this behavior often contradicts inflammatory public statements that officials have previously made denouncing such groups. When such contacts become known, the public's first reaction is a sense of betrayal and anger at officials who now appear to be either liars or hypocrites. For example, in response to a series of terrorist acts across the Middle East in the mid-1980s, President Reagan boldly claimed, "We are especially not going to tolerate these acts [of terrorism] from outlaw states run by the strangest collection of misfits, Looney Toons, and squalid criminals since the advent of the Third Reich."[27] These expectations came crashing down after the Iran-Contra scandal later revealed that his administration had been cutting deals with some of these same "misfits." Further, because these contacts have occurred in the shadows and have been restricted to a small coterie of trusted advisers, few people outside of the government have been able to comment knowledgeably or place in context what their purpose may have been. Instead, a general sense of outrage tends to be the default option, thereby perpetuating the cycle for future governments.

For all these reasons, states rarely engage with terrorists. But this behavior is not always cost-free. Reticence may come at a price. Engaging these groups may prevent terrorist attacks and thus save lives. They may lead eventually to a ceasefire, the end of hostilities, and peace. Success will depend on many factors, including timing, context, the balance of power between the parties, negotiating skill, the character of the enemy, and domestic politics.

But even failed negotiations can produce dividends. Talks may provide the state with greater insight into the leadership, structure, and ideology of these organizations. They may allow it to recruit agents to work for the state. They may unsettle organizations by provoking internal mistrust and suspicion over possible betrayals.

In short, there may be tangible benefits to talking to terrorists and real penalties for not doing so. But how can a state know which course is advisable? And know this course in advance, before it sits down and "sups with the devil"?

TERRORISM TRENDS

A reflexive, indiscriminate reluctance to talk to terrorists is unfortunate, because trends suggest a growing need for states to understand when and how to talk to terrorist groups in the future.

Traditionally, states have always been faced with the choice of whether to settle their differences with other states through diplomatic or military means. But in the first part of the twenty-first century, states will be confronted more frequently with an even more problematic choice: whether or not to settle their differences with terrorist groups by fighting or talking, or by some mixture of the two. The United States and others urgently need to learn when it may be prudent to talk to terrorists and then how to do so.

The reasons for this urgency are plain: There will be more terrorist groups in the future than in the past. They will have more places to gather and scheme, they will have access to increasingly lethal technology and weapons, and they will direct their hatred at states, the United States perhaps above all. Indeed, in the years since 9/11, al Qaeda has engaged in more terrorist attacks on more continents and with more sophisticated weapons than in its entire history.[28]

Every few years, the CIA's in-house think tank, the National Intelligence Council, issues a report that maps the major trends around the world for the next fifteen years. The past two reports have each highlighted the malaise afflicting the Muslim world and its implications for an increasingly radicalized Muslim population. The 2004 report spoke about a spreading radical Islamic ideology based on "collective feelings of alienation and estrangement" that "are unlikely to dissipate until the Muslim world again appears to be more fully integrated into the world economy."[29] The 2008 report warned, "In the absence of employment opportunities and legal means for political expression, conditions will be ripe for disaffection, growing radicalism and possible recruitment of youths into terrorist groups."[30] A separate CIA threat assessment at this time judged that "the global jihadist movement . . . is spreading and adapting to counterterrorism efforts. . . . Although we cannot measure the extent of the spread with precision, a large body of all-source reporting indicates that activists identifying themselves as jihadists, although a small percentage of Muslims, are increasing in both number and geographic dispersion. If this trend continues, threats to U.S. interests at home and abroad will become more diverse, leading to increasing attacks worldwide."[31]

Most terrorism experts agree with these assessments. One reason is that social and institutional pathologies are combined with a demographic youth bulge in the Middle East in general and the Muslim world in particular. According to the 2009 United Nations Human Development Report, over 60 percent of Middle Eastern societies are under the age of twenty-five.[32] A German sociologist,

Gunnar Heinsohn, has argued that this youth bulge is the best predictor of terror, war and genocide. His key indicator for social unrest is when males between the ages of fifteen and twenty-nine form 30 to 40 percent of the population.[33] By this measure, there will be a deep pool of potential recruits for terrorist groups arising across the Middle East for years to come. Indeed, these young people have already been born.

The forces of globalization will further aid terrorism. Global communications will make it easier to spread extremist ideologies, raise funds, network, buy weapons, indoctrinate recruits, manipulate public opinion, move between countries, and coordinate attacks. Already, mobile phones, websites, instant messaging, Twitter, Facebook, Myspace, electronic bulletin boards, email, blogs, and chat rooms have all been used by terrorist groups for these purposes. The rise of mass media and 24/7 news reporting also means that terrorists will always be able to find a ready audience.

Terrorist groups need space in which to arm, train, and plan. A fairly recent phenomenon has been the growth of safe havens in weak and failing states where the central government is unwilling or unable to exercise its authority. Al Qaeda's use of parts of Afghanistan and the Federally Administered Tribal Areas (FATA) along the border with Pakistan starting in the mid-1990s is the most prominent example. But this is far from an isolated case. Testifying before Congress in February 2004 on the "Worldwide Threat," CIA director George Tenet reported that more than fifty countries have "stateless zones"—these are essentially "no man's land . . . where central governments have no consistent reach and where socioeconomic problems are rife. . . . [I]n half of these, terrorist groups are thriving."[34] The financial hardship caused by the 2008–09 global recession means that many governments will be even harder-pressed to control their own territory and monopolize the use of force. Havens for terrorists will multiply.

Some terrorists may be hiding in plain sight. Over the past few decades, certain terrorist groups have created political "wings" to complement their military operations, as part of a broader strategy to participate in electoral politics and gain legitimacy. The Irish Republican Army (IRA) and its political wing, Sinn Fein, made this move in the early 1980s and by 2005 had emerged as the second strongest political party in Northern Ireland. In the Middle East, Hamas and Hezbollah have waged successful political campaigns. It may be too soon to determine whether this constitutes a future trend among terrorist groups. But in the meantime, it presents a dilemma to the United States and other countries that want to support democracy and fair and free elections, but at the same time do not wish to embrace these representatives for fear of extending recognition to terrorist groups.[35]

Terrorist groups have already demonstrated their ability to increase their killing power by adapting old technologies and developing new ones. Only a few months after the U.S. invasion of Iraq in 2003, insurgents employed off-the-shelf technologies to make roadside bombs more deadly against American troops.[36] During the 2008–9 Gaza war, Hamas developed rockets with an extended range that could strike deep into southern Israel. Numerous terrorist groups have expressed interest in acquiring weapons of mass destruction, and some have actually attempted to do so. The CIA's 2006 National Intelligence Estimate forecast that chemical, biological, radiological, and nuclear capabilities "will continue to be sought by jihadist groups."[37] Terrorism experts believe it is only a matter of time before a terrorist group gets this capability and uses it. Some more pessimistic ones believe that "a nuclear terrorist attack on America in the decade ahead is more likely than not."[38]

Among this growing number of terrorist groups, there are likely to be some with local or limited grievances who may be persuaded to renounce violence in return for political accommodation, economic development, or other benefits that the United States or other countries may be willing to grant. "To say that a movement responds to real grievances," writes Oxford University's Adam Roberts, "is not to say that it is justified in resorting to terror, but it is to say that the terrorist movement reflects larger concerns in society that need to be addressed in some way. . . . To refuse all changes on an issue because a terrorist movement has embraced that issue is actually to allow terrorists to dictate the political agenda."[39] One academic study has maintained that the "vast majority" of terrorist groups currently listed as foreign terrorist organizations by the U.S. State Department have such local or limited grievances.[40] The then-director of the CIA, Michael Hayden, has concurred. "[Y]ou can hive off some of these groups," he asserted in November 2008. "Some are more or less dangerous than others. Some are more or less committed. Some are more or less your friends or more or less enemies."[41]

Evidence over the past few decades confirms that engaging with terrorist groups may pay dividends. All terrorist groups eventually end, but a recent RAND study has shown that between 1968 and 2006, over four out of every ten terrorist groups have ended by renouncing violence and joining a political process. Examples include the PLO, the IRA, and RENAMO, a Mozambique resistance group that later became a political party. Military force has rarely been the main reason for a terrorist group's demise.[42]

Reports from battlefields since the end of the Cold War demonstrate that the military has noted the new wave of threats posed by terrorists and the need to rethink how best to respond. The military understands that the "enemy gets a vote" and he will choose when, where, and how to fight.[43] "We must expect that for the indefinite future," declared the Pentagon's 2010 Quadrennial Defense Review, "violent extremist groups, with or without state sponsorship, will continue to foment instability and challenge U.S. and allied interests. Our enemies are adaptive and will develop systems and tactics that exploit our vulnerabilities."[44]

This means that large-scale wars with divisions maneuvering against each other are increasingly relics of the past. Few adversaries are going to take on the United States in the type of conventional battles that play to American strengths of heavy armor, maneuver, and firepower. Instead, they will seek to exploit the relative weaknesses of U.S. forces by using the asymmetric tools common to terrorists.

The Second Gulf War in Iraq provided the wake-up call. U.S. forces were unprepared for an Iraqi insurgency that started in late summer 2003. The insurgency forced a rewriting of the U.S. Army and Marine Corps *Counterinsurgency Field Manual*, which had not been updated for twenty years. An interim version was published in 2004, a final one two years later. It received 2 million downloads during its first two months online.

Other soldier-scholars have subsequently weighed in. One of the most thoughtful British military officers, General Rupert Smith, has written that modern conflicts will be "wars amongst the people," that military action on a big scale, even if successful, will not eliminate political confrontations that cannot be solved militarily.[45] David Kilcullen, an Australian military officer and anthropologist hired by the United States to advise on counterterrorism strategies in Iraq and Afghanistan, has written in *The Accidental Guerrilla* that the U.S. military needs to reorient its "center of gravity" away from killing or capturing bad guys to protecting the general population. The best way is through a combination of fighting, policing, and reconstruction, which may mean cutting deals with local insurgents and terrorists to win their allegiance.[46]

In response to these trends and developments, in 2006 the Pentagon developed what it called the "Long War" concept, whose premise is that the United States will be battling these types of insurgent and terrorist groups for many years to come. It acknowledged that military force will need to be supplemented by other means. "The enemies we face are not nation-states but rather dispersed non-state networks. . . . [T]his struggle cannot be won by military force alone, or even principally. And it is a struggle that may last for many years to come."[47] The Pentagon viewed diplomacy as an essential counterinsurgency tool for winning the hearts and minds of the local population and enlisting their support in the fight. Importantly, this meant gaining a better understanding of terrorists and insurgents—who they are, where they come from, and what motivates them to fight. It also implied talking to them, which is one reason why Secretary of Defense Robert Gates in late 2007 started publicly calling for an increase in the State Department's budget.[48]

Strategy and Tactics

Clearly, much more work needs to be done. The challenge for states facing a terrorist threat or insurgency is twofold: strategic and tactical.

Strategically, a state must decide whether it makes sense to engage. In deciding when to reach out to a terrorist group, the difficulties and risks for a government cannot be exaggerated. It must first carefully analyze whether a terrorist organization is capable of evolving and eventually abandoning its hostility and violent tactics. It must identify those individuals with whom it can work. Are they discreet, or will they leak word of the meetings to embarrass the government? Are they reliable? Do they have the authority to enter into binding commitments? And most important, do they have the ability to deliver on their promises?

These judgments are among the most difficult that a democratic government will ever face. A miscalculation can destroy the credibility of the sitting government, undermine the confidence of its friends and allies, and diminish its international standing. In the case of Northern Ireland, for example, the British government kept its negotiations with the IRA secret for years. Other governments have employed similar deceptions.

The state must also make a number of crucial tactical decisions. One is determining when the time is ripe to talk. Is the state negotiating from a position of strength or weakness, in its own eyes, in the eyes of its domestic constituents, in the eyes of valued allies, and perhaps most important, in the eyes of the terrorists? A miscalculation could signal weakness, suggesting that the government no longer has the stamina to prolong the fight. This could result in the government losing domestic support and being deserted by its foreign friends. It could also give heart to the terrorists, lead to an upsurge of violence, and extend the terror campaign.

The state needs to determine how much pressure it can bring to bear against the terrorists. The state is always stronger in military terms against a terrorist group, or else there would be no need for a group to resort to terror, but it needs to leverage this advantage at the negotiating table. Bluntly put, how can it punish or reward the terrorists and make these threats and promises credible? Understanding the effective uses and limits of leverage is essential. It requires inventorying one's own leverage, profiling the values and vulnerabilities of the adversary, and understanding how to inflict pain and bestow benefits, directly and indirectly, for national advantage.

At the same time, the state rarely possesses all the leverage; otherwise, it could simply dictate terms. Governments forget at their peril not only that terrorist groups have the ability to punish and reward, but also that they have more leverage than is usually appreciated. As the Irish Republican Army reminded Prime Minister Margaret Thatcher after its failed attempt to assassinate her, the state needs to prevent attacks 100 percent of the time; the terrorist group only needs to get lucky once.

When a decision to go forward is made, the state then faces the further challenge of determining how best to do so. In theory, it does not have to keep the talks secret, but in practice most governments choose to do so, at least initially and often for a long time thereafter. The government has to establish contacts and a regular channel for secure communications. It might use foreign nationals to make the initial contact. Less direct interactions may be more attractive because they offer "plausible deniability"—the ability of a government to deny or walk away from engagement if the contacts become public, if domestic political pressures become too great, if a terrorist event makes even indirect contact politically impossible, or for other reasons. The state can, of course, designate a government official to initiate contact. (Often in these cases, a midlevel official or intelligence officer is tapped.) It can distinguish among mere contacts, extended discussions, and full-blown negotiations—or at least try to do so. (There is an extensive dip-lomatic vocabulary devoted to parsing just these differences and their meanings.) Government officials can meet in jails with imprisoned terrorist leaders, in their home country or outside of it. Other governments or trusted individuals can be asked to provide good offices or serve as mediators or facilitators. A variety of third parties, so-called Track II negotiations, nongovernmental organiza-tions, and international conferences can be used as cover for more meaningful discussions.

If initial contacts reassure the state that it is dealing with reliable people who can deliver on their promises and that there may be room for mutual agreement, then it must gauge when it would be best to move the negotiations out of the shadows and into the light. The transition from the private realm to the public is "the most dangerous phase" for the state, according to Eliza Manningham-Buller, the former head of MI5, Britain's domestic intelligence unit.[49] At this moment, the state is highly vulnerable to an embryonic peace process it cannot fully predict and to other actions it cannot fully control—the anger of domestic constituen-cies like the security forces or the families of victims, the criticism of political opponents, and most worrisome, the behavior of the terrorist group, which may contain its own dissidents who seek to render the talks stillborn by resorting to violence.

Terrorist groups are not monoliths. They are highly political by their very nature. They contain a wide assortment of individuals with often very different motivations for embracing the group's cause, ranging from a high-minded (if misplaced) idealism, to a strong sense of grievance and revenge, to a desire for tight bonds of friendship and camaraderie, to a taste for violence and a socio-pathological personality.[50] States therefore need to understand that the leaders of terrorist groups may also run serious risks if they decide to engage in negotiations; some of their calculations may mirror those of the state. These leaders must first judge that continued violent confrontation will not yield victory and that a peace process may prove more fruitful for realizing at least some of their ultimate aims. They must decide whether to suspend their terror campaign while negotiations continue or whether continuation of the "armed struggle" can enhance their posi-tion at the bargaining table. Moreover, pragmatists may need to persuade more extreme factions in their movement to accept a negotiated settlement—other-wise, hard-liners could discredit and isolate them, or worse. The risks for those who openly advocate compromise and negotiation with the state may be severe, even deadly.

Finally, the state must be willing to walk away from the negotiating table if it decides that talks are no longer productive but are only serving the terrorist group's agenda. Ideally, it needs to develop benchmarks to determine when conciliation or concessions are not working to pacify an opponent and it should revert to its previous policy of deterrence, law enforcement, and counterterrorism. This type of policy reversal poses challenges for any government, because there will be voices inside (and outside) the government for continuing the process, because evidence that the terrorist group is not a serious partner for peace may be contradictory or ambiguous, and because it must admit publicly that it had miscalculated when it first sat down to talk to men with blood on their hands.

Given the importance of the subject, there is regrettably little information currently available to help guide policymakers. Because these types of negotiations have often taken place in the shadows, rarely have these experiences been memorialized, their practitioners interviewed, or their lessons institutionalized. There is no preexisting template or framework for weighing the advantages and disadvantages of either engaging or not engaging. No body of work has been collected. No theories or rules have been developed and tested. Few protocols or studies exist in the open literature or even within most states' intelligence services. Morality offers little guidance and may actually handicap progress toward peace.

Governments, including the United States, have had to make it up as they go along, reinventing the wheel each time.

This history is repeating itself in Afghanistan. The Obama administration seems to grasp some of the new thinking required for dealing with the Taliban, but it has not yet fully thought through all of its implications. In March 2009, President Obama announced that the United States would be talking to the Taliban in an effort to stabilize and secure Afghanistan.[51] The president appeared to recognize that the United States could not kill or capture every Taliban member. Some would have to be co-opted, accommodated, or bargained with in order for Washington to accomplish its mission. Yet only a few days after the president's press conference, his special envoy for Afghanistan and Pakistan, Richard Holbrooke, wondered aloud to reporters in Kabul which Taliban members he should talk to and how he was going to locate them.[52] The United States simply did not understand the internal dynamics and leadership structure of the Taliban.

As this book goes to print, the current "facts on the ground" in Afghanistan complicate enormously any chance for a successful negotiation. The Taliban has regrouped, rearmed, and accelerated its attacks on U.S. and Afghan forces in a bid to reclaim its authority over the country. To reverse some of the Taliban's gains, Obama announced in December 2009 that he would send an additional 30,000 U.S. troops to Afghanistan, but coupled it with a decision to start drawing down American forces after eighteen months, by July 2011.[53] The United States, Afghanistan, Saudi Arabia, Pakistan, and other countries have each made separate and uncoordinated contacts with a variety of Taliban representatives. Still other Taliban representatives have asserted that the organization has no interest in talking to anyone until all foreign fighters—U.S. and Coalition forces—leave the country. The United States military has drafted guidance on how to persuade lower-level Taliban fighters to lay down their arms (which it has termed "reintegration"),[54] while the Afghan government's guidance focuses instead on higher-level political talks with the Taliban leadership (which it calls "reconciliation"). The United States has little faith in President Hamid Karzai, who is viewed as illegitimate, corrupt, and ineffective. Should any talks take place between Kabul and the Taliban, some American officials worry far more that the Afghan government will reconcile with the Taliban than that the Taliban will reconcile with the Afghan government.

CHALLENGES AND CONSTRAINTS

Negotiating with Evil emphatically does not argue that it is always better to talk to terrorist groups. Readers will not find here an automatic green light or blanket approval for a state to talk to any and all terrorist groups. Far from it. Depending on the circumstances, to do so may be a fool's errand. There will always be some groups that are irreconcilable. In these circumstances, a state's choices are reduced to two: waiting until the thinking of the terrorists evolves along more accommodating and pragmatic lines (if it ever does) or capturing or killing all of its members.[55]

At the same time, and just as emphatically, this book argues against those who maintain that a state should never talk to terrorists. The world is a complex place. Under certain circumstances, at certain times, a terrorist group may be willing to renounce violence, limit its objectives, and pursue its goals via peaceful political means. The state has both an ethical duty and a security imperative to test the group's willingness to do so. Sometimes these tests can evolve into a diplomatic process and sometimes even into a peace settlement.

But how can a state know for sure that talking will reap benefits? Alas, it can't. Sometimes states judge the group or the moment incorrectly. Sometimes they are more fortunate and get it right. This book asks what accounts for these different outcomes and what this may mean for future efforts to "negotiate with evil."

Of course, it is not possible to include all possible cases in a single volume. This book examines states that have entered into talks directly with terrorist groups, not with state enemies. It highlights the thinking that *initially* led to these negotiations and guided them as they got started, gained traction, or fell apart. It is a book more about beginnings than endings, because starting a peace process is far more challenging and problematic than continuing one already under way.

That leaves the question of deciding which specific cases should be included. To be candid, some of these have been determined by personal preferences and serendipity. Three of the cases were selected because of my professional experience in Northern Ireland and my policy interest in the Iraq War and the Arab-Israeli conflict when I served at the State Department. With the Basque separatist movement in Spain, I was curious as to why it has survived for more than five decades when the Red Brigades in Italy and the Baader-Meinhof Gang in West Germany have been eliminated. In Sri Lanka, the Tamil Tigers were among the most lethally innovative terrorist groups of the past thirty years.

But this selection process was not entirely random. These cases capture different historical experiences and highlight different outcomes across Europe, the Middle East, and South Asia. In all of these cases, the state initially opposed negotiations, only to reverse course later. They include examples where the state has successfully negotiated an end to terror, where the state has tried but been unable to negotiate an end to terror, where the state has had mixed success, and where the state has refused entirely to enter into negotiations.[56]

I have interviewed hundreds of people, including government officials, intelligence agents, and military and security officers, and *Negotiating with Evil* reflects the strengths and weaknesses of such an approach. The greatest strength was that I could hear from individuals directly involved in grappling with the life-and-death challenges presented by terrorism and how they came to negotiate with people they despised. Often, they could convey a vivid sense of what it was like "being there." They could explain the reasons for and against reaching out to engage with these groups, the patience required, the political and ethical calculations involved, and the failures and victories they experienced. I was also able to interview a number of former terrorists and gain a greater understanding of their perspectives—of their grievances and aspirations, their moral universe, and how they viewed negotiating with a state they despised.

Obviously, this approach has its weaknesses. Personal recollections can be selective or hazy or just plain wrong. Some people are forgetful. Others lie. On more than one occasion, people tried to rewrite history and embellish (or downplay) their personal responsibility for certain events.

I could not always see every individual I wanted to see. Some had died. Some politely declined to meet with me. Others made it clear they resented my contacting them at all and less politely urged me to be on my way.

At a time when the United States and other liberal, democratic societies are under assault from terrorist groups and are debating how best to defeat these threats around the globe, the following chapters yield valuable lessons. We can do better, but only if we learn from the past. At least, that is my hope.

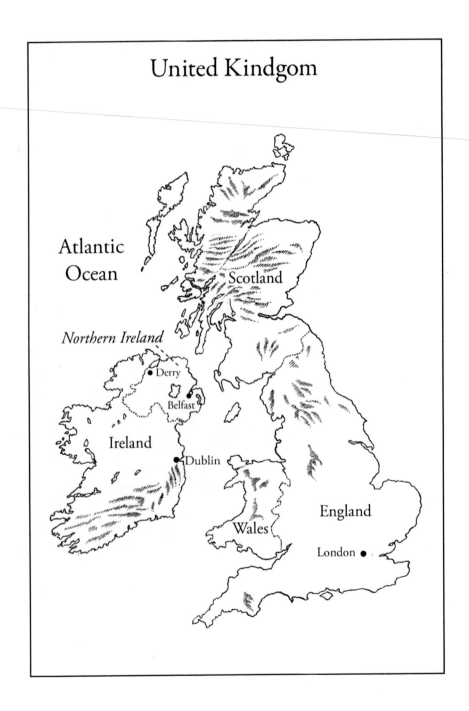

United Kindgom

Atlantic
Ocean

Scotland

Northern Ireland

● Derry

●Belfast

Ireland

●Dublin

England

Wales

London ●

I.

THE IRISH REPUBLICAN ARMY (IRA)

The three senior leaders of the Irish Republican Army (IRA) sat only a few feet across the table from me. The organization had been responsible for much of the violence and heartbreak during the Troubles that had plagued Northern Ireland since the late 1960s. Each man had done his share, but on this day in this room they sat as politicians, representing Sinn Fein, the political wing of the IRA. We were about to have a difficult negotiation. But first, tea and biscuits.

In December 2003, Secretary of State Colin Powell had asked me to become President Bush's special envoy to the Northern Ireland peace process. What Powell either forgot to mention or was too polite to say was that few at the State Department coveted the position, which was viewed as a hopeless waste of time. Different nationalist, political, and religious traditions in Ireland had been fighting for centuries, providing one another with arsenals of injustices, both real and imagined. The prevailing mood was captured by a joke I was told on one of my first trips to Ireland: What is the definition of Irish Alzheimer's?

You forget everything but your grievances.

Our meeting started like many others I had held previously with these men. We first exchanged the normal diplomatic pleasantries. They then politely but firmly explained their views, larded as usual with lessons from Ireland's history, both ancient and modern. When they finished, I prepared to explain the U.S. position. I was about to deliver some very unwelcome news.

I began to recite the script I had memorized beforehand, keeping an even tone. Screaming and pounding the table are the stuff of second-rate melodrama and, in my experience, rarely as effective as they are portrayed on television or in the movies. I also had no illusions that any ranting and raving on my part would make the slightest impression on these hard men.

My key point was that Sinn Fein needed to start publicly encouraging its supporters to cooperate with the police in Northern Ireland. This was a highly emotional issue for the IRA, but I knew that Catholic neighborhoods in Northern Ireland deserved better than the vigilante justice IRA thugs were meting out. I knew that there was no chance the other political parties would ever sign up to a deal and end the Troubles unless Sinn Fein changed its stance.

When I explained that Sinn Fein's leaders would be denied entry visas to the United States if they did not support the police, one of them suddenly burst out of his chair, enraged, and flew across the table to strike me. In a flash, one of his colleagues grabbed him and yanked him back into his seat. I never flinched and, after a beat, resumed making my argument.

Later that day, well after the meeting had ended, I reflected on my composure in the face of this attempted assault and hoped it had underscored the seriousness of my message. But I realized that it had all happened so quickly that I never even had time to react.

Yet the incident made me wonder: Just how short was the distance between the furtive IRA terrorist and the polished Sinn Fein official? Was it possible for them to ever completely shed one skin and assume another? And how could you negotiate with such people under such circumstances, with the threat of violence always hovering over the negotiating table?

A SUREFIRE WAY TO START AN argument in Ireland is to ask what has caused the divisions between the British and the Irish. Most historians trace the roots of the conflict to the late twelfth century, when England invaded the area around what is now Dublin. Other historians cite the English conquest of the country in the late sixteenth and early seventeenth centuries, with the settlement of large "plantations" by English and Scottish Protestant colonists and the resulting dispossession of the native Catholic population. Some look to the Battle of the Boyne in 1690, when the Protestant King William defeated the Catholic King James and ended his claims to the British, Scottish, and Irish thrones, fortifying the Protestant ascendancy. Some believe the great famines of the mid-nineteenth century—when one out of every four people either died or emigrated—cemented Irish enmity toward Britain. Others look to the Easter Rising in April 1916, when a small band of Irish "Volunteers" seized the General Post Office in Dublin and declared an Irish Republic, but were quickly and brutally suppressed, their leaders shot by firing squad. And still others date it to when demands for Home Rule by Irish nationalists gave way during the First World War to demands for outright independence, and the dream of a united Ireland died (at least temporarily) with the partitioning of the island in 1922. The Irish Free State was created in the south; six of the nine Ulster counties in the northeast opted out and remained tied to the United Kingdom as Northern Ireland.[1]

The period of turmoil known as the Troubles started in the late 1960s, when the Catholic minority in Northern Ireland, inspired by Martin Luther King's freedom marches and nonviolent protests, openly opposed discrimination in housing, employment, and voting rights. High unemployment in a weakening economy aggravated tensions on all sides.

In the words of one observer, "Disorder grew out of the conflict between Catholic hopes and Protestant fears,"[2] but sectarian divisions were actually more complex. Politically moderate Catholics sought representation through "Nationalist" parties like the Social Democratic and Labor Party (SDLP), which came to be led by the Derry schoolteacher John Hume. It advocated a reform agenda of equal rights, cross-community tolerance, and power-sharing to improve living conditions for Catholics. Meanwhile, more politically extreme Catholics gravitated to the revolutionary party, Sinn Fein. Far more ideological, it favored the destruction of Northern Ireland and its incorporation into a single Irish Republic (hence the term "Republicans"). The Republican cause also had its military factions, chief among them the Provisional IRA (PIRA, or "Provos," referred to as the IRA), which was Sinn Fein's military arm.

The Protestant side was structured similarly. Politically moderate Protestants supported parties that generally sought to preserve their privileged majority status, resented interference from Dublin, and wanted to remain part of the United Kingdom. They called themselves "Unionists." More radical Protestants shared all these beliefs but had a higher tolerance for the use of violence to defend their positions. Over the years, the radicals coalesced around Ian Paisley, who consolidated his power as leader of the Democratic Unionist Party (DUP). Hard-line religious rhetoric was the defining feature of Paisley's message, although he also appealed to poorer classes within the Unionist community. Protestant paramilitary groups such as the Ulster Defense Association (UDA) and Ulster Volunteer Force (UVF) rose to notorious prominence in the 1960s and 1970s, fueled by sectarianism and a belief that the British state's commitment to Northern Ireland was lacking. These paramilitaries were generally referred to as "Loyalists" because of their "loyalty" to the British Crown.

Starting in 1969, over 3,700 people would eventually lose their lives and 30,000 more would be wounded during the Troubles.[3] The nadir was 1972, when almost 500 people were killed. The number of deaths tapered off after 1976, as both sides gradually dug in for what the IRA termed the "Long War" and the British government called the "Long Haul."

As the war raged, the British and Irish governments periodically tried to establish a legal framework that might one day, it was hoped, allow all the parties to live in peace. In late 1973, the two governments met in the Berkshire countryside to sign the Sunningdale Agreement, which laid the foundation stone for all future political agreements. Sunningdale introduced an "Irish dimension" designed to reassure the Catholic minority that their concerns would be heard, while not unduly panicking the Protestant majority. Under the Agreement, Northern Ireland would remain part of the United Kingdom until a majority of its citizens voted otherwise. It called for a Northern Ireland Assembly at Stormont based on cross-community power-sharing. It also created a Council of Ireland, which would consist of officials from both north and south of the border.

In many ways, Sunningdale was visionary, but as with many visions, it was perceived by some as a nightmare. Although the Council of Ireland was based on unanimity and limited to such secondary matters as tourism, sports, roads, forestry, and animal health, Unionists reacted with alarm, seeing it as the first step on a slippery slope of British concessions that would undermine their community, their identity, and ultimately their way of life. In early 1974, they organized a general strike that toppled the local government. This sequence of British action and Unionist reaction was repeated in 1985 with the signing of the Anglo-Irish Agreement, which progressively deepened the "green hue" of northern politics by giving the Irish government a quasi-formal say in the running of Northern Ireland.

Hunger strikes by Republican prisoners in 1981 resulted in the deaths of ten men, but not before one of these men, Bobby Sands, was elected a member of Parliament. His surprising electoral victory catapulted the IRA's political wing, Sinn Fein, into politics and opened up an alternative to violence for leaders like Gerry Adams. Over the next decade and a half, Adams and a few of his like-minded colleagues engaged in discussions with the Irish and British governments, and eventually the American government, that led to a more formal peace process.

The 1992 election of President Bill Clinton invigorated an American role in the peace process. The United States had been involved earlier, primarily through the efforts of the "Four Horsemen"—Daniel Patrick Moynihan, Tip O'Neill, Hugh Carey, and Ted Kennedy—who drew international attention in the late 1970s to the discrimination against the Catholic community. (Less positively, some Irish-Americans had contributed guns and money over the years to the IRA's war effort.) The Clinton administration energized the peace process by granting Gerry Adams a visa to visit New York and subsequently inviting him to the White House—to the intense displeasure of the British government. It then assigned former senator George Mitchell to help guide the Northern Ireland political parties, and the British and Irish governments, to agree on a framework for peacefully resolving the Troubles.

After months of painstaking negotiations, Mitchell and the parties reached a deal on Good Friday, 1998. The Good Friday Agreement, as it was called, further "copper-fastened" the principle of consent. If majorities in both north and south agreed, Northern Ireland could leave the United Kingdom and join the Republic of Ireland.[4] But the reality was that a Protestant majority in the north made that prospect unlikely for many years to come. In return for accepting this, Sinn Fein was offered a place in a power-sharing government in Northern Ireland.

The Good Friday Agreement fully institutionalized the peace process, which contained more than its share of backsliding, drama, and squalid deal-making. Sadly, it would take another nine years for the IRA to decommission its arms and stand down its Volunteers, for Sinn Fein to endorse the local police service, and for other divisions to be repaired so that a broader political accommodation could be reached that would allow the people of Northern Ireland to manage their own affairs. Prime Minister Tony Blair and Taoiseach Bertie Ahern were instrumental in ushering the parties into the endgame and then finally closing the deal. Almost four decades after the Troubles started, on May 8, 2007, the DUP leader, Ian Paisley, and Sinn Fein's Martin McGuinness, jointly reopened the Stormont Assembly. It made international headlines. Three years later, the two sides seem to be managing, although both parties are facing growing criticism from within their own communities.

In retrospect, there were rhythms to the Troubles, as the conflict ebbed and flowed on the streets and as government officials discussed and debated politics and policies in London, Dublin, and Belfast. Initially, the British had sought outright victory through the IRA's military defeat (although a few officials may have been willing to abandon Northern Ireland altogether). Initially, the IRA had sought to reunite Ireland by forcing the British to withdraw from the north. Eventually, both sides were compelled to adjust their goals, as each realized that force of arms alone could not bring victory. A political accommodation would have to be forged.

Against this decades-long process of violence mixed with halting steps toward conciliation, there were repeated serious attempts to negotiate an end to the bloodletting, along with one set of talks aimed at heading off the deaths of ten men on hunger strikes inside the Maze prison just outside of Belfast. These meetings took place largely between the British government and the leadership of the IRA/Sinn Fein, but they also involved other actors along the way. I joined the peace process in 2003 as the president's special envoy and participated in the last three and a half years of the political endgame, including the final dramatic steps toward reconciliation that culminated in the opening of the Stormont Assembly.

Any full appreciation of this historic moment is not possible without understanding what came before.

GROPING IN THE DARK
THE CHEYNE WALK MEETING, JULY 1972

At the start of 1972, the fortunes of the IRA had been steadily on the upswing. An intensified IRA bombing campaign against military bases, government offices, and police stations the previous year led the British home secretary to declare a state of "open war" with the IRA and detain without trial (i.e., "intern") hundreds of suspected IRA members. The haphazard jailing of Catholics (the IRA had been tipped off days before the planned raids) had created a backlash in the south, which now offered a safe haven for IRA operatives on the run.[5] Recruits flocked to join the Provos. The mouthpiece of the IRA, *Republican News*, declared that 1972 would be "the Year of Victory."[6]

On January 30, a peaceful protest march in the Catholic Bogside area of Derry, sponsored by the Northern Ireland Civil Rights Association, degenerated into a tragic confrontation with the British Army's First Battalion of the Parachute Regiment. Accounts differ as to what initially prompted the violence, but by the end of the day thirteen civilians had died, and a fourteenth died later in the hospital, all Catholics.[7] The events of "Bloody Sunday" aroused sympathy for the Republican cause across Ireland. The Irish government announced a national day of mourning; a crowd used the occasion to torch the British embassy in Dublin. London now shuttered the local Stormont Assembly, which had long symbolized Unionist (and Protestant) domination, temporarily assumed Direct Rule over the six counties, and appointed a secretary of state for Northern Ireland.

With the onset of Direct Rule, the British government now placed itself squarely in the middle of a conflict that few officials in Westminster understood and even fewer cared about. Direct Rule undermined local authorities, especially moderates in the Nationalist and Unionist communities. The British compounded their difficulties by having no strategy for dealing with escalating IRA violence other than more violence. (Ironically, most of the civil rights demands were acceded to; socioeconomic inequalities would take a generation or more to remedy.) Proving the aphorism that nothing is as permanent as a temporary solution, Direct Rule would last uninterrupted for more than twenty-five years.

In mid-March of that year, the IRA announced a brief ceasefire. The Labour Party leader and former prime minister Harold Wilson, and his shadow Northern Ireland minister, Merlyn Rees, traveled to a Phoenix Park estate in central Dublin for a secret meeting with three of the IRA's senior leadership. (Wilson told his aides he would not shake hands with the IRA delegation, a symbolic gesture that elected British officials followed until the Blair years.) The IRA had five demands, the centerpiece of which was the withdrawal of the British from the north. Wilson had no authority to make any deals on behalf of the British government. After four hours, it was clear that the parties were "planets apart."[8] "There was damn all came out of it," recalled one of the IRA participants. "It was just a talking shop, really."[9] The IRA informed their guests that the meeting was over, as was the temporary ceasefire.

Why did Harold Wilson take the risk of meeting with the IRA at this time? As a former prime minister (from 1964 to 1970), he may have felt a latent prerogative to try to fashion a solution to the escalating violence, hoping he could extend the temporary ceasefire as a first step. But it is hard to imagine that Wilson would have been allowed to meet without the approval of the sitting prime minister, Edward Heath. Public records reveal that the British government had been in secret contact with IRA members in the days immediately after Bloody Sunday, and that the IRA had responded positively to the idea of a more formal meeting.[10] Heath could have Wilson assume the political risk if the meeting became public, while he could take the credit if it led to a permanent ceasefire and end to the violence.[11]

Other factors may also have been at work. Labour Party leader Wilson had little sympathy for the Ulster Unionists, who were the natural political allies of his Conservative Party rivals. He harbored doubts that London might ever be able to sort out Northern Ireland. The subsequent release of official papers under the "thirty-year rule" revealed that in 1974, with Wilson by then back again as prime minister, he seriously considered having Britain sever all constitutional ties to Northern Ireland and grant it dominion status, like Canada. This secret plan, code-named "Doomsday," was intended to force Unionists to share power with the Nationalists.[12] (The plan was never publicly unveiled.) Whether Wilson held these views in 1972 is unknown, although there are some hints that he did. These inclinations may have influenced his desire to intervene directly with the IRA at the time.

Wilson would not have been alone in wondering whether it might be best to let the north and the south work out an arrangement as best they could. Senior members of Prime Minister Heath's own Cabinet entertained similar views. "Our own parliamentary history is one long story of trouble with the Irish," grumbled the foreign secretary, Sir Alec Douglas-Home. He told Heath, "I do not believe that they [the people living in Northern Ireland] are like the Scots or the Welsh and doubt if they ever will be. The real British interest would I think be served best by pushing them toward a United Ireland rather than tying them closer to the United Kingdom."[13] The reality was that London was exasperated with all the parties in the North and uncertain over how best to proceed. Compromise by the Ulster Unionists seemed politically impossible, while sterner security measures seemed more likely to roil than calm the situation. Direct Rule was uncharted territory.

With the end of the March ceasefire, the violence quickly resumed. The IRA carried out 1,200 operations in May 1972 and even more the next month.[14] The IRA had developed the car bomb (by accident, as it turned out) and used it, along with land mines and a supply of Armalites (semiautomatic assault rifles) imported from the United States, to deadly effect. But according to the investigative journalist Ed Moloney, who has painstakingly chronicled the history of the IRA, the violence by this time was taking its toll on Catholic communities as well, turning them into war zones. While the fall of Stormont and the onset of Direct Rule were hailed as great Republican victories and the IRA's more militant members wanted to press their advantage, the organization was under increasing pressure from moderate elements of its community to negotiate with the British.[15]

In this atmosphere, the IRA leadership decided to hold a public press conference in mid-June in Derry, where they requested a meeting with the new secretary of state for Northern Ireland, William Whitelaw. They declared that all military operations would be suspended for seven days if Whitelaw accepted the offer within the next 24 hours. Whitelaw refused, saying that he "could not respond to ultimatums from terrorists who are causing suffering to innocent civilians in Northern Ireland and shooting British troops."[16]

But within days of the IRA's offer, Whitelaw had instructed two members of his department, one of whom was an MI6 officer named Frank Steele, to meet with the IRA. Whitelaw never explained the reason for this about-face, but it may have been due to the personal intervention of John Hume, the highly respected civil rights and political leader from Derry.[17] Whatever the reason, this first-ever meeting between the IRA and representatives of a sitting British government took place in a house outside of Derry on June 20. The IRA delegation included a twenty-three-year-old Gerry Adams, who had been let out of Long Kesh prison specifically to help negotiate the arrangements.

The IRA presented three demands as the price for an indefinite ceasefire. One was for a face-to-face meeting between the IRA senior leadership and Whitelaw. The secretary of state had authorized his representatives to accept this offer, but only after the ceasefire was deemed "effective." The two sides eventually agreed on a ten-day testing period.[18] The IRA announced the ceasefire a few days later and told the British who would be on its negotiating team. Ten days after that, the British secretly transported some of the most wanted men in the country from Derry to the home of a junior minister in Cheyne Walk, one of the most fashionable addresses in central London.

Why did Whitelaw agree to meet with the IRA's senior leaders, and what did he hope to achieve? The Heath government simply had few good options. Some

British officials had already concluded that the government would be unable to defeat the IRA militarily; another postcolonial exit might be the best that could be achieved. Seeing if a face-to-face meeting might end the violence thus seemed an idea worth pursuing. Whitelaw acknowledged in his memoirs that there was "a desperate longing on all sides for an end to the senseless violence," including among the Nationalist community and many moderate Unionists in the North. There were also domestic and international political calculations. Wilson had already met with the IRA in Dublin. As Whitelaw recalled in his memoirs, "I knew that I would lose the support of the Opposition parties at Westminster if I turned down a meeting." And the United States, with its politically influential Irish-American community, would not understand why Britain refused to meet with the IRA once the fighting had stopped.[19]

Whitelaw was honest enough to recognize that valid reasons also existed for refusing to meet with the IRA. There were many in his own party and in Northern Ireland who thought "there should be no discussion or negotiation with those engaged in terrorism." Ultimately, he was persuaded by his staff, who had met with the IRA leadership, and by the prospect of the IRA seizing the "political initiative" if he refused its offer. Whitelaw also judged that he would emerge in a stronger position if the talks failed, because he could then win support for stronger security measures from the Catholic community in the North.[20]

After all the maneuvering, the meeting itself proved a great disappointment, a "nonevent" in Whitelaw's words. The IRA presented terms that were more appropriate from a victorious army to its vanquished foe. "The British Government," it stated, "should recognize publicly that it is the right of the whole of the people of Ireland acting as a unit to decide the future of Ireland," a stance that Whitelaw pointed out was contrary to the guarantee Her Majesty's Government had given to Northern Ireland in 1949 that its status within the United Kingdom would only be changed with the consent of the majority. The IRA also demanded that the British withdraw from Northern Ireland by January 1, 1975, and that internment should be ended, with a general amnesty granted to all prisoners, detainees, and wanted persons.[21] All these demands were completely unacceptable to the British.

Given its aggressive negotiating approach, what did the IRA hope to accomplish at the Cheyne Walk meeting?

There is little doubt that the IRA thought it held the upper hand. Within only a few years it had leveraged its violence into a meeting with British leaders, reinforcing the extent of its military threat and emphasizing that no solution to the Troubles would be possible without its participation. As Moloney has pointed out, the IRA felt that "it was on a string of successes when the 1972 cease fire was called."[22]

But the IRA's approach to the talks revealed its inexperience. At the secret June 20 preparatory meeting with the two British representatives, the IRA had insisted that the British carry with them a signed note from Whitelaw that testified to their identities and authority to talk. The IRA had taken the added step of bringing with them a solicitor to examine the note and authenticate it. (Why else would the British officials be at this secret rendezvous?) During the meeting, the IRA delegation requested that the British call the Belfast prison and allow them to speak to one of the hunger strikers to confirm that they had ended their strike, as had been reported. They were told that such a call would "cause an immediate leak" and compromise the secrecy of their meeting. When they later asked that the secretary of state provide them with written answers to their questions, they were informed that this would be "politically wholly impossible," as Whitelaw would then have no control over the letter and how it might be used. The IRA had also not anticipated what a ceasefire declaration might look like, so the British officers dictated some text, which the IRA accepted.[23] And after Cheyne Walk, the IRA issued a public statement revealing that secret talks had taken place, thereby breaking trust with Whitelaw and risking his political career.

Even if the IRA had been tactically more sophisticated, it would not have made much difference. The IRA never expected to reach agreement or win British concessions at this meeting. According to Steele, who talked with the IRA delegation as he accompanied them back to Northern Ireland, the IRA thought all it had to do was continue the war: "The way to get rid of you British," they told him, "as has been proved all over your Empire, is violence. You will get fed up and go away."[24] The thinking at the time was that the IRA needed "one big push" to get the British to withdraw. Over thirty-five years later, Martin McGuinness, who attended the Cheyne Walk meeting as a member of the IRA's delegation, concurred. He recalled that the fall of Stormont had shown that the British could eventually be pressured into making concessions. "We didn't think the Brits would capitulate. But we thought that the Brits could be shown that they would have to withdraw. . . . Our willingness to engage the Brits was part of a political process that would lead to British withdrawal. That was the motive for talking."[25]

In other words, at Cheyne Walk the IRA was laying down markers it intended to collect later.

Perhaps such mistakes on the Republican side should have been expected. It is easy to forget that these meetings were the first time in over fifty years that the IRA had engaged with representatives of the British government. When some of these miscues were replayed to Martin McGuinness in 2009, he plaintively explained, "I was only twenty-two at the time!"[26] Indeed, the entire IRA delegation had no negotiating experience. They were learning on the fly. There was no blueprint to follow other than the 1921 talks between the legendary IRA leader Michael Collins and the British prime minister, David Lloyd George. These talks had led the IRA to compromise its goal of an undivided Ireland and were therefore precisely what the IRA was determined to avoid.

What did the British gain from the Cheyne Walk meeting?

The meeting helped demystify the IRA. The British had the chance to scrutinize and assess their enemy face-to-face. They could make some initial estimates as to which members were more ideological and hard-line and which more flexible and pragmatic.

In contrast to the IRA, however, which at least knew why it wanted to see Whitelaw, the meeting revealed that the British had no strategy other than a vague hope that the IRA could somehow be persuaded to renounce its campaign of violence. The groundwork for the meeting had not been laid properly. The two sides had clearly not agreed on a common agenda for discussion and had very different expectations. The fact that Whitelaw agreed to hold the meeting in the center of London, which required extraordinary operational secrecy and logistics, instead of at any number of remote and isolated locations throughout the United Kingdom, also suggests a lack of serious planning. The primary responsibility has to lie with the British, given their vast experience with similar negotiations during decolonization and their far more extensive resources.

In addition, in the run-up to the meeting, Whitelaw had made a unilateral concession that would have grave repercussions later. As part of his maneuvering to win support from the moderate SDLP, he had agreed to grant "special category" status to four IRA prisoners who had gone on a hunger strike to demand special privileges. This measure allowed the prisoners to wear civilian clothes, avoid prison work, and have more frequent visits, but its true significance was that it validated the Republican narrative that the IRA was engaged in a war of liberation with the British. Its captured members should therefore be treated as prisoners of war, not as criminals or terrorists.[27]

Perhaps, too, it should have been expected that neither party would want the other to think that the desire for talking reflected weakness or lack of resolve. The IRA reacted to these meetings by sending an unmistakable signal that it retained the determination to fight and would increase pressure on the British to withdraw. Only days after Cheyne Walk, the IRA detonated twenty bombs in a seventy-minute period in the middle of downtown Belfast. So many innocent civilians were killed and wounded that it became known as "Bloody Friday." The month following the Cheyne Walk meeting was the deadliest in the history of the Troubles. Talking had led to more bloodshed, not less.[28] Years later, Steele concluded that the ceasefire never stood a chance, as too many people, across all the communities in the North, preferred to go back to war.[29]

Cheyne Walk was not a lost opportunity. It was not an opportunity at all, as the two sides had completely incompatible agendas. They talked past each other. Given their ignorance of each other and lack of trust, neither side had much incentive to appear flexible at these initial meetings. From Whitelaw's account, the meeting was less an exchange of views than an IRA ultimatum to which the British could not agree. It would be two more years before there was another ceasefire.

Thanks to disgust and anger in the Nationalist community over Bloody Friday, and in the absence of any clear political strategy, the British now decided to turn up the military pressure on the IRA. It launched Operation Motorman to clear city blocks under IRA control that had been effectively "no-go areas" for British police and security forces. It placed "military forts" in Republican neighborhoods, improved its intelligence operations, kept the IRA under close surveillance, and started systematically to infiltrate the organization.[30]

Ironically, as these harsher security measures were being implemented, other interested parties viewed the Cheyne Walk talks as a sign of possible British irresolution over its commitment to remaining in Northern Ireland. Britain's engagement with the IRA especially worried the Irish. Dublin ideally preferred a Stormont Assembly with Nationalist representation and some kind of North-South link to counter the Unionist majority. The Irish government calculated that this would best marginalize and isolate the IRA over time.[31] But according to Garret FitzGerald, then a member of the Irish parliament and later prime minster,

"The contacts that had taken place had the effect merely of prolonging the violence by deluding the IRA into believing that a British government would eventually negotiate a settlement with them."[32]

It wasn't just the prospect of prolonged violence that unnerved Irish officials, it was the possibility that the ongoing violence would cause the British to tire and withdraw from the North. The result would be a civil war in the North that Dublin did not have the men, weapons, or training to fight. A senior Irish diplomat at the time remarked that Ireland would have been compelled to intervene. "We would have been drawn into it. It would've been a complete disaster."[33] Years later, FitzGerald still grew agitated at the recollection. "We were vulnerable, extremely vulnerable," maintained Fitzgerald. "The IRA was our enemy more than the British. The IRA could damage Britain. They could destroy us."[34]

The meetings from March through July 1972 did not lead to an institutionalized backchannel where the two parties could meet privately, discuss sensitive matters, navigate through difficult periods like the marching season (when Protestants commemorated historic victories over the Catholics by marching provocatively through Catholic neighborhoods), and perhaps, over time, develop a common vocabulary for a peace process. That would have to wait. A sustainable peace process simply could not exist just then.

But the ice had been broken and the two sides had introduced themselves. These meetings created a precedent that could be useful for the future, when the time was ripe for more serious discussions. None of the parties at Cheyne Walk could know, perhaps could not even imagine, that they would have ample opportunity to continue their discussions in the future, as the war would continue for another thirty-five years.

THE 1974–75 CEASEFIRE

By the end of 1974, peace efforts had failed and the cycle of violence had deepened. Unionist reaction to the December 1973 Sunningdale Agreement, which institutionalized greater cooperation between north and south, led to an illegal general strike that was enforced by Loyalist paramilitary threats and intimidation. Disturbingly, the RUC (the Royal Ulster Constabulary) and British military did little to halt the lawlessness. The strike brought down the Stormont Assembly by forcing the resignation of Unionist politicians who had been willing to share power with Nationalists. Meanwhile, the British had imprisoned hundreds of IRA members, including some of its senior leadership. Another 150 IRA members had died, some at the hands of Loyalist paramilitary groups.

The chief of police in Derry at this time was Frank Lagan, a well-respected Catholic cop in an overwhelmingly Protestant police force. Lagan had solid ties to the Republican and Nationalist communities. He independently concluded that the British needed to create a channel to talk to the IRA, which was under some pressure to halt the violence and was itself searching for a way to reengage with the British. Lagan approached two locals to see if they would act as intermediaries: a businessman, Brendan Duddy, who owned a string of fish-and-chip shops in the Bogside, and Denis Bradley, a Catholic priest who had presided at the marriage of Martin McGuinness and his wife and was well known to the Republican community. They agreed. Over the next twenty years, Duddy served as the key link between the British and the IRA.[35] Whenever Duddy hosted clandestine meetings between the IRA and British officials in his home, Lagan would make sure the local police stayed away.[36]

By the end of 1974, Duddy decided that the two sides needed to talk directly, even though each was reluctant to do so. He arranged for Michael Oatley, the MI6 officer who had replaced Frank Steele, to meet with a senior IRA Army Council officer, who then persuaded his IRA colleagues that British interest was genuine. Duddy's efforts led to the IRA declaring a ten-day Christmas ceasefire, with the suspension of all "offensive military action," on December 22, 1974. A few weeks earlier, some Protestant church leaders had met with the IRA leadership in Feakle, County Clare, in an attempt to halt the bloodshed. The British now used this meeting, which had become public, as the cover story for how the ceasefire had been arranged. It was not prepared at this time to admit to secret contacts with the IRA. During the next few weeks, the ceasefire was extended and renewed as the two sides started meeting regularly in Duddy's home to "tack down" the truce.

What did the British offer to get the IRA to lay down its arms?

The IRA leadership clearly believed that Britain was willing to discuss "structures of disengagement" and "withdrawal" from Ireland if the IRA adopted a sustained cessation of all its violence. In face-to-face meetings with Oatley, they claimed he confirmed that anything could be on the agenda for negotiation, even withdrawal.[37] The British made a number of lesser concessions, including the expedited release of some IRA prisoners, freedom of movement for IRA Volunteers, transferring IRA prisoners in English jails to Northern Ireland, and even the granting of gun permits to two dozen IRA members for self-defense. But by mid-March, the IRA had grown frustrated at what it saw as British stonewalling on any progress toward its key demand. The British pleaded for patience. The IRA asked that, as a gesture of good faith, British troops be removed from nationalist areas of Belfast and Derry, two army bases in West Belfast be removed, and surveillance and screening be ended. The British pleaded for understanding. By the end of summer, the IRA had exhausted both its patience and understanding. The truce was effectively over.[38]

Three different and plausible scenarios can each assign responsibility for the failure of the 1974–75 ceasefire. One is that the British deliberately engaged in an elaborate deception from the beginning, stringing the IRA along, promising, or at least suggesting, that it was willing to discuss a possible British withdrawal from Northern Ireland as the price of getting the IRA into a ceasefire. In this scenario, it was all bait-and-switch, the British betting that the longer the IRA stayed on ceasefire, the more its operational edge would erode. Martin McGuinness had warned his colleagues at the time that the ceasefire was incapacitating the IRA: "We won't last."[39]

Further, Britain could use this time to improve its intelligence-gathering, introduce new security measures, identify IRA members who had relaxed their guard and emerged in public, recruit more informers, and hope to prevent bombs going off in London and on the mainland. Consistent with this approach, the following year saw a new Northern Ireland secretary of state, Roy Mason, a hard-line former coal miner who promised to roll up the IRA "like a tube of toothpaste."[40] For London, the talks then were just a tactic that supported the military effort but did not substitute for it.

A second possibility is that the IRA again fell victim to its own inexperience. It simply heard what it wanted to hear from Oatley and the British. It could not distinguish between the hypothetical possibility of British withdrawal versus the political impossibility of this happening anytime in the foreseeable future.[41] Curiously, when the IRA had the chance to put its demands in writing in early 1975, it did not expressly mention the idea of British withdrawal, a remarkable omission.[42]

The IRA may also have been misled by Unionist fears that Britain's days in the North were numbered. In November 1974, the former Ulster Unionist Party leader Terence O'Neill was quoted in the *Irish Times* as saying, "I do not believe that the British will be willing to put up the men and money for another five years in Northern Ireland."[43] Indeed, these fears were fueling the upsurge in violence against the Catholic community, as Loyalist gangs viciously defended their territory.

There is a variation on this explanation as well. Denis Bradley, who helped Duddy arrange the meetings, blames *all* the parties for their inexperience. "Oatley and the Brits weren't good enough. The Brits should've kept the negotiations going. You make it bigger and make it better and you keep everyone on board. And Brendan and I were kids. . . . Everyone in that room was a novice. We didn't know enough. We were so young. We needed help from others." Bradley thought the Catholic Church had the power, experience, and influence to help the Republicans negotiate with the British, but the Church refused to get involved.[44]

A third possibility is that the communications channel was unreliable. Oatley was new to the game and, by his own admission, "knew absolutely nothing about Northern Ireland" when he arrived.[45] Duddy had him pegged as "a very ambitious MI6 officer." In a March 2008 BBC television program on Brendan Duddy's role in the secret talks, Oatley admitted to his anxiety at hearing that the ceasefire might fall apart in early January 1975. To keep the ceasefire and talks on track, he sought and obtained permission "to say something encouraging about the sorts of talks that could take place." He concedes that he told the IRA he was "prepared to discuss anything you like." When specifically pressed on whether this included British withdrawal from Northern Ireland, Oatley said it did, "whatever that may mean." Duddy independently confirmed that Oatley gave assurances on this point "in very vague terms."[46]

Of course, these explanations for the breakdown in the talks are not mutually exclusive. It is possible that Oatley exceeded his brief, that the IRA swallowed Oatley's promises without adequately testing them, and that higher-ups in the British system consciously maneuvered the IRA into a ceasefire to enhance Britain's security position.

It is easy to blame Oatley for this crucial misunderstanding, and some participants have done so. Denis Bradley believes that "Oatley was seduced by Ireland. He went native. 'I, Michael Oatley, will solve the Irish problem.'"[47] It is clear that Oatley was playing a very risky game, trying to straddle the line between over-promising the IRA and wanting to keep the talks going.

In this, he succeeded, at least temporarily. But the price paid was high.

London has claimed that it never really told the IRA it was willing to withdraw from the North, but that is almost beside the point. The IRA believed that this was a possibility, and British officials cultivated and perpetuated this belief. By never categorically ruling out this option, the British traded short-term benefits in extending the ceasefire and degrading the IRA's operational edge against longer-term consequences that worked against the peace process. (Needless to say, had the ceasefire *really* led to the demise of the IRA, this trade-off unquestionably would have been worthwhile.) By the end of the talks, however, the IRA had concluded it could not trust the British; the negotiations were simply a snare and a delusion. It concluded it could accomplish more during wartime than during peacetime. More precisely, it believed it needed to continue the armed struggle while it was negotiating to maintain pressure on London. This stance would place great strain on British officials in future talks. The IRA concluded also that it needed to test British goodwill in the future by demanding concessions up front. From now on, London needed to always go first. This, too, would place added burdens on future British negotiators.

Thirty-five years later, memories of alleged British duplicity during this time could still stir some of the participants to anger. When I met with Martin McGuinness in Belfast in May 2009, he accused the British of cynically playing the IRA. "The Brits were time-wasting. Not serious at all about peace. There were contacts but no peace process. It was British policy to get people to stop and then do the minimum. Then it would be harder to go back to war."[48]

And yet some important gains for the peace process emerged from these recriminations. Of greatest value was the Derry backchannel that Brendan Duddy had established in his home. This secret channel had already proved its resilience. Oatley had been allowed to meet with Duddy and do business with the IRA at a time when the IRA was wreaking havoc on the British mainland, with bombings at Bradford, Guildford, Woolwich, and Birmingham.

But the Duddy channel would lie unused for many years after the end of the ceasefire, as the IRA tried to regroup in the face of increasing British pressure. Both Adams and Martin McGuinness now assumed greater control of the organization. After Adams was released from prison in 1977, they set out to overthrow those IRA leaders responsible for the ceasefire, accusing them of naïveté and weakness. Adams reorganized the IRA into a more lethal terrorist organization, increased operational secrecy, and developed techniques for IRA members to resist interrogation if they were caught. Under its new leadership, the IRA would oppose any future ceasefires.

The Irish were also displeased by the backchannel talks between the British and the IRA. After an official from the British embassy in Dublin briefed the Irish prime minister, Liam Cosgrave, in January 1975, on the contacts with the IRA, he reported back to London, "In general conversation, he [Cosgrave] laid stress on the traumatic effect it would have throughout Ireland if the impression gained ground that we were prepared to negotiate in any way with the Provisionals."[49] Dublin remained skeptical that any bilateral British-IRA negotiations (even one that brought in the Loyalists) would secure a viable settlement. Rather, it feared that it would trigger a civil war in Ulster that would spill over to the Irish Republic.

But perhaps the largest lesson revealed from the failed ceasefire was that the IRA was still seeking a maximalist agenda. Its preferred outcome remained complete British withdrawal. It would take many more years and many more lives before the IRA adjusted its goals.

THE HUNGER STRIKES

To this day, no single event during the Troubles arouses such strong emotions from Republicans as the 1980–81 hunger strikes. In the course of a few months, ten Republican prisoners starved themselves to death inside the Maze prison, despite the efforts of the British and Irish governments, the Church, and their families to stop them.

The hunger strikes were the product of two related developments. After the failure to extend the 1974–75 ceasefire, new British legislation criminalized Republican violence and elevated the importance of the local police (the Royal Ulster Constabulary or RUC) in enforcing law and order. The regular British armed forces adopted a lower profile. The result was an increasing number of criminal convictions and new prisoners for the jails. The new secretary of state for Northern Ireland, Roy Mason, ruled out any contact with the IRA (or the Loyalist paramilitaries) to give the new security measures time to work.[50] By 1980, over 800 Republicans were in prison.

With so many of its members behind bars, the IRA logically sought to extend its campaign to the penal system and open up a second front.[51] Whitelaw's successor had reversed his impulsive decision in 1972 to grant "special category status" to IRA members. In defiance, IRA members now refused prison clothes; they would wear only blankets. Their protests later included refusing to wash and the smearing of feces on their cell walls. When these gestures failed to move the British government to grant them POW status, they adopted more extreme measures.

THE FIRST STRIKE

In October 1980, seven Republicans refused to take any food until the British satisfied five demands:

1. The right to wear their own clothes (not prison uniforms)
2. The right not to do prison work
3. The right to associate freely with other prisoners
4. The right to a weekly visit, letter, and parcel and the right to organize educational and recreational pursuits
5. Full restoration of remission [time counted for parole] lost through the protest[52]

The goal was to force the British government to grant the IRA prisoners political status. Prime Minister Margaret Thatcher, the "Iron Lady," was typically defiant. "I want this to be utterly clear," she declared. "The Government will never concede political status to the hunger strikers or to any others convicted of criminal offenses in the province."[53] No doubt her determination had been steeled by the IRA's recent actions: the killing of Lord Mountbatten while powerboating off the Irish coast, and the killing of eighteen paratroopers in a single encounter near the Irish border.

In mid-December, as the first of the hunger strikers neared death, the IRA's leadership contacted Brendan Duddy and told him it wanted to settle the protest.[54] Duddy in turn contacted MI6's Michael Oatley. In short order, a document appeared from London and word was passed to the prisoners that the British government had compromised on their five demands. The hunger strike was called off.[55]

However, after the IRA's leadership examined the actual document, which ran to thirty-four pages, they saw it was a rehash of the government's previous positions and maddeningly vague on the particulars. The IRA's "Commanding

Officer" in the Maze, Bobby Sands, said that there "was absolutely nothing concrete in the document . . . it was so wide open, [you] could drive a bus through it."[56] The British said that the question of prisoners' clothing and other issues could be addressed once the strike was over. But before any concessions could be granted, the prisoners had to conform to prison regulations for thirty days, a gesture the prisoners knew would allow Thatcher to claim victory. They refused. Efforts between the prison authorities and Sands failed to bridge the divide and hardened Republican resolve to launch a second hunger strike. No one doubted that this time there would be martyrs.

THE SECOND STRIKE

Bobby Sands started the second hunger strike in late March 1981. This time the hunger strikers staggered their starting dates with a few weeks in between in order to build pressure on London, ensure maximum publicity, and gain wider support for the cause. New volunteers would take their place as they died.

Less than a week after Sands began his fast, the member of Parliament representing Fermanagh and South Tyrone in Northern Ireland died. The Republican leadership was persuaded to allow Sands to stand for the open seat.[57] (Until that time, IRA/Sinn Fein had adopted a policy of "abstentionism," abstaining from democratic politics so as not to legitimize what they viewed as the illegitimate political systems of both Britain and Ireland.) In early April, Sands defeated the Unionist candidate, delivering an enormous propaganda coup to the Republican cause. His electoral victory muddled the British line that these men were mere criminals and backed the inmates' claims to political status. Sands died a few weeks later, on day sixty-six of his strike. Over 100,000 people turned out for his funeral.

Sands was the first hunger striker to starve himself to death inside the Maze prison. By early July, three more men had died. On July 4, the prisoners issued a statement that repeated their demands, but in a more conciliatory fashion. The British government responded, conveying a message through Michael Oatley and Brendan Duddy to Gerry Adams. The British now said that most of the demands could be granted once the hunger strike ended. Reasonable compromises were proposed on prison work and remission as negotiations continued through the month. The only remaining sticking point was free association. Oatley told

Adams that any leak would scuttle the deal; it had to remain secret or else the government would deny that the offer ever took place. The IRA leadership responded by asking for more concessions. Thatcher's government said it could go no further. The hunger strikes continued. More men died.[58]

After the tenth prisoner starved himself to death, the families of the remaining hunger strikers intervened. Once the prisoners lapsed into comas, the families used their legal power to ensure they received proper medical attention. Due to British intransigence and direct family involvement, momentum for further sacrifice withered. The strike formally ended after eight months, in October 1981.

The hunger strikes were to have far-reaching consequences. For Gerry Adams and Sinn Fein, the strikes opened a new phase for the Republican movement—a rejection of abstentionism and the entrance into electoral politics. Sands's election had paved the way. Other opportunities soon presented themselves. The Irish prime minister, Charles Haughey, had called a general election for mid-June 1981. Sinn Fein ran nine prisoners as candidates, including four hunger strikers. Two were elected to the Irish parliament. In August, with the hunger strikes ongoing, Sinn Fein nominated a candidate to fill Bobby Sands's open parliamentary seat. Sinn Fein won again.[59] At Sinn Fein's annual conference later that year, one of the IRA's leaders, Danny Morrison, outlined the strategy for the years ahead: "Who here really believes that we can win the war through the ballot box? But will anyone here object if, with a ballot paper in this hand and an Armalite in the other, we take power in Ireland?"[60]

Decades later, both Adams and McGuinness independently identified this time as a turning point for Sinn Fein.[61] Adams was rewarded by being elected president of Sinn Fein in November 1983. In the general election that year, he won the parliamentary seat for West Belfast. Sinn Fein won 13.4 percent of the popular vote across Northern Ireland, shockingly close to the SDLP's 17.9 percent. It was an impressive start.

For Margaret Thatcher, the hunger strikes solidified her reputation as firm and principled. (To her enemies, she appeared inflexible and coldhearted.) In her memoirs, she proudly recounts how she never compromised. "Above all, I would hold fast to the principle that we would not make concessions of any kind while the hunger strike was continuing. . . . Those who sought a united Ireland must learn that what could not be won by persuasion would not be won by violence."[62]

But was this really true? Not exactly.

As Thatcher herself acknowledged, the British government "was anxious to win the battle for public opinion." She came under pressure to show flexibility from the pope and other prominent Church leaders, Dublin (which greatly feared Sinn Fein's electoral appeal in the south), and the Reagan White House.[63] The record is persuasive: The Iron Lady was intimately involved in the negotiations with the hunger strikers. Along the way, she made concessions—before, during, and especially after the hunger strikes.

As Charles Powell, Thatcher's private secretary, and Douglas Hurd, then foreign minister, told me, the prime minister was "in practice more flexible than she appeared." Her officials in Northern Ireland "would not have made concessions during and after the hunger strikes without her consent." Thatcher "allowed things to happen, reluctantly. There was a struggle in her own mind. She would allow others to do certain things she knew needed to be done. . . . She wasn't happy about it, but she did it when necessary."[64]

This was the pattern with the hunger strikes. Anticipating the start of the first strike, Thatcher authorized that all the prisoners be allowed to wear "civilian type" clothing, albeit not their own clothes. The document the British handed to the IRA in December 1980 promised satisfaction of some of the prisoners' demands on clothing and visits, once the strike was over. During both strikes, IRA leaders were allowed into the Maze prison to talk to the prisoners. In July 1981, the British government again conveyed offers that addressed four of the five demands. Following the end of the hunger strike, the British government largely granted all five demands. The Maze's governor was removed as well.[65]

If these demands could be granted after the hunger strikes, why not before? Did ten men die over a question of timing?

In a sense, yes. Thatcher was willing to make concessions on a quid pro quo basis—that is, London would grant a number of the prisoners' demands once they ended the hunger strike and began to adhere to prison regulations.

But there were limits as to how far Thatcher would go. The timing of the concessions was absolutely critical. She recognized, as did the prisoners, that the hunger strikes were not merely about prison rules. They were a continuation of the IRA's campaign against British authority by other means. She hadn't invited this battle, but once it was joined, she realized that the government had to prevail. Conceding to the demands under the pressure of a hunger strike would hand the

IRA a great moral victory, demonstrate weakness, and invite further demands down the road. This Thatcher would not do.

London's willingness to grant concessions once the hunger strike ended was not simply a case of Thatcher being magnanimous in victory. Although the strike had been broken and the IRA defeated, she knew that publicity from the hunger strike had bolstered Sinn Fein's fortunes. Republicans were on the march politically, at the expense of the more moderate SDLP. The Irish political leaders were especially worried about Sinn Fein making inroads in the south. Thatcher hoped that granting concessions after the fact might dampen Sinn Fein's appeal.[66]

Under different circumstances, could the Thatcher government have engineered a compromise? If the British terms during the first strike had been more detailed and specific, perhaps this would have made it easier for Bobby Sands and Maze prison officials to subsequently reach agreement. When more generous offers were made in July 1981, during the second strike, the prisoners were unwilling to trust Thatcher a second time. By this time, any compromise became more difficult, as the rhetoric and emotions had intensified, certainly after the self-sacrifice of Bobby Sands. Short of outright capitulation by either side, other options became limited, then vanished.

Emotions remained raw in the years following the hunger strikes. The IRA immediately venerated the ten men as martyrs, their faces adorning murals in Republican neighborhoods across Northern Ireland. Thatcher was accused of murder. She characteristically responded that the men chose to die, pointedly adding that this was "a choice they did not give their victims."[67]

THE RUN-UP TO THE DOWNING STREET DECLARATION, AND AFTER

Sinn Fein's electoral successes following the hunger strikes created fears that it would eclipse constitutional Nationalism and the SDLP in the north and spill over to infect the south as well. This frightful prospect caused one British minister to envision living with "a Cuba" next door. To diminish Sinn Fein's appeal and bolster the SDLP, London and Dublin signed the Anglo-Irish Agreement in 1985. It promised an unprecedented degree of cooperation between Britain and Ireland, with a permanent secretariat set up outside of Belfast and staffed by officials from north and south. Thatcher supported the deal against her own instincts, feeling the pressure from Ronald Reagan and hopeful of greater cooperation from Dublin on cross-border security.[68]

The Agreement took Unionists by surprise. They reacted angrily, calling it a "diktat." Where Dublin represented the interests of the Catholic-Nationalist community in the north, Unionists felt betrayed because London did not appear to guarantee their interests. Unionists physically attacked the new secretary of state for Northern Ireland, Tom King, when he visited Belfast City Hall, and over 100,000 people turned out for an "Ulster Says No" rally denouncing the Agreement. Fifteen Unionist MPs resigned their seats at Westminster in protest. Loyalist paramilitary violence also started trending upward, from five murders in 1985 to sixty-two over the following three years.[69]

Shrill emotions seemed misplaced all around. By the time of the Anglo-Irish Agreement, Sinn Fein's electoral momentum had already plateaued; it then gradually declined. In the May 1987 general election, Sinn Fein won only 11.4 percent of the vote. A few years later, Sinn Fein won 10 percent of the vote and Adams lost his West Belfast parliamentary seat. These results suggested that at the heart of Sinn Fein was an irreducible conflict between the armed struggle and support for democratic institutions. In other words, the tension between the ballot and the bullet could not be reconciled into a winning political strategy. A party joined at the hip to a paramilitary group had limited appeal.

Not surprisingly, then, starting in the mid-1980s, the debate within the Republican movement "centered on the ineffectiveness of the armed struggle," a debate that intensified through the end of the decade.[70] The IRA at this time was suffering under a triple assault: the targeting of Republicans by Loyalist paramilitaries, the success of the SAS (Special Air Service) in pressuring the IRA, and the effective penetration of the organization by the security and intelligence branches. By the early 1990s, these branches had put in place excellent coverage of the IRA's activities. Terrorist acts were now increasingly compromised and prevented.[71] The British showed no signs of withdrawing from Northern Ireland.

The evolving politics of the North also placed pressure on the IRA/Sinn Fein. By the early 1990s, both Unionists and Nationalists had started to rethink their strategies. Moderate Unionists had reconciled themselves, at least in principle, to power-sharing and an Irish dimension to political life in the North, while the SDLP and other constitutional Nationalists were favoring local government under the joint authority of Dublin and Belfast rather than insisting on a united Ireland.[72]

For the IRA/Sinn Fein's more astute leaders, these reversals raised questions about whether *either* the ballot *or* the bullet would lead to eventual victory. The IRA did not believe that it had been, or ever could be, defeated, but it was subject to the law of diminishing returns. It could continue with its military campaign, but to what end? A despondent Adams remarked that the British had managed to "reduce the violence to Irish people killing each other."[73] When I interviewed Martin McGuinness in his office at Stormont Assembly in May 2009, he told me, "We saw a military stalemate that could go on not just for years, but for decades."[74]

For the remainder of the 1980s, Adams, relying on what he has termed "a small cadre of leadership activists" that took "a collective approach to problem-solving and developing strategy and tactics," engaged with the British, the Irish, and the SDLP.[75] Adams and the senior IRA leadership kept these talks secret from the rank-and-file Volunteers, from the public, and often from the different parties with whom he engaged.

Adams proceeded cautiously. He first posed a series of questions to Tom King on the nature of Britain's interest in Ireland, its attitude toward self-determination, and a date for British withdrawal. (As with the hunger strike negotiations, Thatcher was aware of this channel and approved its continuing.) The government's response stated that Britain "has no political, military, strategic or economic interest in staying in Ireland" against the wishes of the majority in the north. The "central issue in the conflict" was not the British government's presence in Northern Ireland, the paper stated, but how to bridge the historical, political, religious, and cultural divisions between the Nationalist and Unionist traditions so they could freely determine their own future. This could be achieved only through "the processes of political debate and dialogue." The British government would act as a neutral "facilitator." The process could begin as soon as the IRA went on ceasefire.[76] Some have claimed that this was a novel offer to the Republicans, but it may be closer to the truth that the IRA was now more receptive to this message than before. Either way, it was an open invitation for Republicans to join a peace process.

Adams also needed to convince both Fianna Fail, the leading political party in the south, and the SDLP in the north to join forces with Sinn Fein. Armed with the British response, he approached Fianna Fail's leader, Charles Haughey, who was once again prime minister. Haughey, one of Ireland's most colorful and controversial politicians, rebuffed the overture, fearing that any embrace of Adams could not be kept private for long and would resurrect politically damaging allegations of Haughey's gunrunning to the IRA in 1969–70.[77] Still, he authorized three junior officials to meet with Adams.

Why did Haughey take the political risk and agree to the meeting with Adams, even if he used intermediaries? Partly because Haughey and the Irish government wanted to test whether Adams was serious about halting the war.[78] Haughey also realized that the conflict was damaging Ireland's image and preventing foreign investment and tourism.[79] But perhaps Haughey's private secretary got closest to the truth: ego. Haughey wanted to leave a legacy. As he remarked to Thatcher in 1980, "No one ever left a mark on history by balancing the books."[80]

But Haughey also ensured that he hedged his bets. He confided to one of the three officials, "I don't know if we can trust these fuckers" not to leak news of the meeting. If word got out, "Haughey knew he would not have lasted five minutes." When the official asked Haughey why, then, it was okay for him to meet with Adams, the prime minister replied, "You're dispensable. . . . You're on your own."[81]

In the end, there were only two secret meetings. Nothing came of them. According to Irish officials who attended these meetings, Dublin's priority was to see whether Adams would reinstitute a ceasefire. They felt that Adams was not serious about having the IRA go on ceasefire anytime soon, but instead was interested in joining with Fianna Fail to lessen Sinn Fein's political isolation.[82] With the high political risk and low probability of success, the Irish government broke off the talks.

The meetings were not a total loss, however. Haughey wanted to maintain a backchannel to Adams, which he did via a trusted civil servant, Martin Mansergh. Haughey also suggested that Adams reach out to John Hume, which Adams did in early 1988. This suited Haughey, as he could continue to promote his ideas on the peace process to Adams (and now Hume) via the backchannel. Haughey also insisted that Hume not be told of this arrangement. Adams, despite being disappointed at not being able to talk directly to Haughey, realized that Hume's sterling reputation and moral authority could reduce Sinn Fein's political isolation and refurbish its less-than-pristine image. Adams and Hume met continually during the next five years. These meetings became known as the Hume-Adams process, and they eventually catapulted John Hume to international prominence and the 1998 Nobel Peace Prize.[83]

Some have argued that these overtures constituted the start of the real peace process, and thereby mark Adams as a secret peacemaker from the mid-1980s onward, acting alone against the IRA's "hard men" (a heroic view that Adams has at times encouraged).[84] The weight of evidence does not support this interpretation, which has been carefully dissected by British scholar Martyn Frampton.[85] For one, the pan-nationalist approach did not encompass a repudiation of the armed struggle. The IRA/Sinn Fein was still committed to pursuing its goals by both the Armalite and the ballot box. And neither the Irish government nor British intelligence believed that Adams was sincerely trying to end the armed struggle at this time.

In February 1991, the IRA launched an audacious mortar attack on 10 Downing Street, the British prime minister's official residence. In April 1992, it bombed the Baltic Exchange in the heart of London's financial district, causing £700,000 worth of damage. The following year, it struck the financial center again, this time causing £1 billion in damage. These and other attacks confirmed that the IRA could continue to wreak havoc, and not just in Northern Ireland but on the British mainland as well. As far as the IRA was concerned, its goal remained driving the British out of the north, by force if necessary.

In late 1990, MI6's Michael Oatley had reappeared on the scene, hoping to make a last contribution before he retired. According to Martin McGuinness, Oatley now presented the IRA with a tough message: The British would never withdraw from Northern Ireland. He described a "mile-high wall" that the IRA would never get over.[86] These talks were different in tenor from earlier ones. London felt increasingly confident that it, not the IRA, could set the parameters for settling the conflict.

Oatley's message was part of a more subtle approach at the time to help the IRA/Sinn Fein end the war. British intelligence had learned that the IRA/Sinn Fein was starting to wonder how they could end it. King's successor as secretary of state for Northern Ireland, Peter Brooke, in 1989 tried to signal to Republicans that there was a way out of the cul-de-sac. During an interview marking his first one hundred days in office, Brooke observed that it was difficult to envision the British Army defeating the IRA and it was impossible to envision the IRA defeating the British Army. A few months later he emphasized that Britain was disinterested as to the future fate of Northern Ireland, as long as it was based on majority consent.

Prime Minister John Major continued this channel when he took over in November 1990 after Margaret Thatcher was ousted in an internal Tory Party dispute. Over the next three years, the two sides communicated by exchanging private papers and public statements. The British attempted to nudge the IRA/ Sinn Fein closer to renouncing violence and embracing constitutional politics, alternately offering them a seat at the table and suggesting that a deal might be brokered between the SDLP and the Unionists without them.

It was against this backdrop that the British received a lightning bolt in the form of a note purportedly from the IRA/Sinn Fein's Martin McGuinness in February 1993. The note read, "The conflict is over but we need your advice on how to bring it to a close." Later that year, after the British government–IRA/ Sinn Fein channel was exposed, London tried to use this message as the public justification for talking to terrorists. Adams and Sinn Fein were not amused and accused the British government of fabricating the note. Sinn Fein released a detailed history of its contacts with the British government, starting in October 1990, entitled "Setting the Record Straight."[87] Subsequent maladroit efforts by London to explain its side of the story only made the government look foolish and deceitful.

What was going on here? Denis Bradley has admitted that he actually wrote the note, after he, Brendan Duddy, and Noel Gallagher (a third person involved in the Derry backchannel) had thought it up together. The note was passed along to Oatley's successor, a man named "Fred," who in turn passed it to the government. According to Bradley, the three had taken stock of the peace process and decided it needed a boost. They did not want to repeat their mistake from the short-lived ceasefire in 1974–75, when they maintained their distance and the parties were unable to move the process forward. "At this time [the early 1990s], everyone wanted to do something, but the process was going nowhere," explained Bradley. According to him, Martin McGuinness was telling Bradley and others that Republicans "need to become peacemakers. . . . So we apply the lesson we had learned from the 1974–75 ceasefire and we write the message."[88]

Ironically, the note ended up having a positive impact on the peace process. A senior British intelligence officer years later commented, "Creative ambiguity at certain times might be useful. . . . The message was not necessarily a bad thing. Both sides became more comfortable with the idea of the war being over."[89] The Major government took the "war is over" message very seriously (no doubt because it could gauge IRA sentiment, since the IRA had been extensively penetrated by its security and intelligence services) and immediately convened a special Cabinet committee to discuss it. It then sent a message to Sinn Fein setting out its parameters: The principle of consent would determine the future of Ireland, and Britain would not declare its intent to withdraw.[90]

Aside from these constitutional issues, there remained the question of timing: Would London allow Sinn Fein to join the peace process before the IRA had permanently ceased using violence? Or was an end to the armed struggle a precondition to multiparty talks? London had consistently held that a permanent IRA ceasefire was a necessary precondition. According to two of the most thoughtful scholars of the Troubles, the British government "continued to fear that the IRA might call a halt only temporarily, to facilitate Sinn Fein's entry into talks, before resuming its campaign as before—either during the talks, or in their aftermath if Republicans failed to achieve what they wanted."[91] The British knew that a proper peace process could not tolerate the whiff of cordite and gunpowder in the negotiation room.

Still searching for a deal, London now modified its offer, saying that the ceasefire could be unannounced at first as long as it was coupled with assurances that the violence was well and truly over.[92] Sinn Fein responded with an offer of a two-week ceasefire in May 1993. Major rejected it. One of Major's key advisers stated that the prime minister never wanted to take the risk of publicly talking to Sinn Fein when the IRA was detonating bombs.[93] Sinn Fein was left to complain, "Preconditions represent obstacles to peace."[94]

With the collapse of these backchannel talks, the Anglo-Irish connection was now reenergized. By this time, Albert Reynolds had replaced Haughey as prime minister. A successful businessman who lived twenty-five miles from the border and traveled all over the North ("I didn't care what religion they were, as long as they paid!"), Reynolds actually knew more about Northern Ireland than he was given credit for. He made the peace process his top priority as Taoiseach, believing that only the two governments could deliver the deal because of the need to change domestic legislation. (Britain would have to modify its Government of Ireland Act 1920, which claimed jurisdiction over the territory now belonging to Ireland, and Ireland would have to change Articles 2 and 3 of its 1937 constitution, which laid claim to Northern Ireland.) "Hume and Adams could never complete it themselves because they couldn't deliver the governments," Reynolds explained. Reynolds was also willing to take political risks: "It was the end of my political career. . . . as Taoiseach. Where else could I go?"[95]

In late 1993, the British and Irish governments jointly endorsed the Downing Street Declaration. The Declaration further codified the bedrock British principle of majority consent determining the future of Northern Ireland. It also set a high bar for the IRA/Sinn Fein by calling for a permanent end to paramilitary violence and stating that political parties (i.e., Sinn Fein) needed to "establish a commitment to exclusively peaceful methods" before being allowed to join a dialogue with the two governments and other political parties. The Declaration was miles away from the IRA's official position requiring London to state its intention to withdraw by a date certain. One senior IRA official was quoted as saying, "What we're talking about here is that if we accept this, then we accept that everything we stood for in the past twenty-five years is for nothing."[96]

In the aftermath of the Downing Street Declaration, the IRA now had to meet two preconditions: ending the armed struggle permanently and decommissioning weapons. A changed political environment complicated the political calculations for Adams and Sinn Fein. Public revelation of the Adams-Hume partnership earlier in 1993 had helped launder Sinn Fein's image, but it had come at the price of raised public expectations of an IRA ceasefire leading to a peace process. If Republicans walked away from a fledgling peace process now, Adams and Sinn Fein would lose support.[97] Also, the Downing Street Declaration, coming soon after some of the vilest atrocities of the Troubles perpetrated by both the IRA and the Loyalist paramilitaries, had restored a measure of hope that such a peace process might actually take place.

On August 31, 1994, the IRA announced the "complete cessation of military operations," but the Major government was unclear whether this was permanent. In fact, it wasn't. Adams and the Republican leadership had creatively tried to walk the fine line between mollifying the IRA rank and file and the British government by developing a new approach, which was called the "tactical use of the armed struggle." The IRA would review the ceasefire after four months.[98] But by October, Prime Minister Major had announced that he would make a "working assumption" that the IRA's ceasefire was permanent.

Attention at this time turned to the decommissioning of weapons. For Republicans, decommissioning meant surrender and defeat. The IRA/Sinn Fein leadership repeatedly warned that decommissioning was a nonstarter and that continued insistence on this as a precondition to talks would destroy the peace process. In March 1995, the British softened their stance a bit by suggesting that at least some decommissioning had to have started before Sinn Fein could join a dialogue on Northern Ireland's future with the other political parties. This was not good enough, according to Martin McGuinness, who replied that there was "not a snowball's chance in hell of any weapons being decommissioned this side of a negotiated settlement."[99]

More than a year after the IRA ceasefire (which was still holding), there had been no all-party talks and no decommissioning. To help break this impasse, in November 1995, London and Dublin agreed on a dual-track approach. They would prepare for all-party talks to be started in February 1996 while former senator George Mitchell would chair an international panel to propose a way forward. The Mitchell Commission reported back that decommissioning did not have to take place before Sinn Fein was allowed to participate in all-party talks, effectively eliminating decommissioning as a precondition. But the Mitchell Commission laid out six principles of democracy and nonviolence to which all the political parties would have to pledge "their total and absolute commitment," essentially replacing one precondition with six.[100] Also, the Commission suggested (with Unionist leader David Trimble's endorsment) that elections be held before the parties sat down to talk. The Major government adopted these proposals.

The IRA responded in February 1996, when it ended its ceasefire and detonated a bomb in the Canary Wharf section of London, causing an estimated £1 billion in damage. Sinn Fein had now dealt itself out of the peace process. The stance of the British and Irish governments hardened after the Canary Wharf bombing, as they insisted on an extended period of decontamination after the IRA declared a permanent ceasefire. In June, elections were held for the Northern Ireland Forum, the political body from which negotiating teams would be selected for multiparty talks. Sinn Fein was ineligible to take its seats because of the IRA's resumption of violence. And the IRA was still faced with the same dilemma as before—it didn't want to join the peace process, but a return to the armed struggle would not achieve its goal of driving the British from Northern Ireland.

In spring 1997, Tony Blair and the Labour Party ended eighteen years of Tory dominance by trouncing John Major and the Conservatives. Blair represented "New Labour" and new thinking on the peace process. But he insisted that the IRA commit to a "genuine ceasefire" and that Sinn Fein endorse the Mitchell

Commission principles. He also made clear that the peace process would move forward with the Republicans or without them: "The settlement train is leaving. . . . and I will not allow it to wait for you."[101]

In July 1997, the IRA declared the "unequivocal restoration" of its ceasefire. Sinn Fein signed the Mitchell Commission principles a few weeks later and entered all-party talks in mid-September 1997. All the key stakeholders to the future of Northern Ireland were finally at the same table. Seven months later, Senator Mitchell delivered the Good Friday Agreement. It codified the same principles of "constitutional disinterest" over the North's future, self-determination based on majority consent, and respect for democracy and the rule of law that Britain had been declaring for years. The Good Friday Agreement was ratified in a referendum across the island, with 94 percent of the people in the south and 71 percent of the people in the north voting for it. A diplomatic framework for a future peace process had become institutionalized. A few years later, in 2001, Sinn Fein overtook the SDLP in local and national elections. Republican politics had become more popular than Republican violence.

There was still much work to do. The decommissioning of weapons remained a source of Unionist discontent, plaguing efforts to end the Troubles. The IRA's ongoing violence and reluctance to put its arms verifiably "beyond use" prevented efforts to establish local government at Stormont, undermined the moderate Unionist leadership of David Trimble, and led to growing support for the more sectarian firebrand Ian Paisley.

A turning point came when I invited the partner and sisters of Robert McCartney to the White House for St. Patrick's Day in March 2005. A few weeks earlier, IRA thugs had brutally murdered McCartney outside a Belfast pub, then covered up the crime and intimidated witnesses from cooperating with the police. The McCartney sisters' eloquent, courageous, and determined appeals for justice captivated Irish America.[102] Adams was now shunned by influential politicians and business leaders who had previously rushed to embrace him. At a St. Patrick's Day celebration with Adams sitting in the front row, Senator John McCain denounced the IRA as a bunch of "cowards." His remarks were repeatedly interrupted by spontaneous applause by the overwhelmingly Irish-American audience. The tide had turned. Back in Belfast three weeks later, Adams called for the IRA to completely decommission its weapons and commit itself to a purely peaceful and political way forward. Three months later, the IRA agreed to do so.

Eighteen months after decommissioning, Sinn Fein finally endorsed the police-and-justice system in Northern Ireland, thereby meeting one of the last Unionist demands. In May 2007, Ian Paisley and Martin McGuinness stood side by side, presiding over the reopening of the Stormont Assembly. The Troubles were over.

CONCLUSION

The maneuvers and evasions, the tactics and strategies perpetrated by parties trying to establish a peace process are far easier to discern in retrospect than when they are unfolding. Looking back, there is the temptation to assign greater coherence to the strategies, greater cooperation among government bureaucracies, greater wisdom to the planning, and greater discipline to the execution than they deserve. At least in the case of Northern Ireland and the Troubles, surrendering to that temptation would be almost entirely wrong.

TALKING TO TERRORISTS

Certain threads run through the almost forty years of Northern Ireland's conflict. One was that engagement was not a problem. The British and the IRA/Sinn Fein talked to, and past, each other constantly. The two sides had relatively little trouble establishing a link and maintaining it, certainly when compared with other governments' attempts to start a peace process or end a conflict. Beginning with the tragic events of Bloody Sunday in January 1972, the British government and the IRA maintained a communications channel on and off for the next thirty-five years. These communications were often shrouded from other British agencies and ministers, the Irish government, and Washington. They took place at different levels, ranging from clandestine intelligence operatives to the prime minister. But the channel remained open.

The lines between the British government and the IRA/Sinn Fein also proved remarkably durable. This channel survived some of the most traumatic events of the Troubles, like the hunger strikes, the Enniskillen Remembrance Day bombing, the assassination attempt on Thatcher and her Cabinet at the Grand Hotel in Brighton, and the everyday killing, wounding, and maiming of thousands of innocent people.

As Gerry Adams gradually attempted to disavow any connection to the IRA (which British, Irish, and American officials willingly enabled) and assume a public image as the leader of Sinn Fein, it became easier for British officials to meet with him and other Sinn Fein leaders in public. Once the peace process became institutionalized in the late 1990s, Prime Minister Tony Blair met so regularly with Adams and Martin McGuinness at 10 Downing Street that they seemed more like old friends than the leaders of the IRA.

Ideally, there would have been a single reliable and covert channel between the IRA/Sinn Fein and the British government until the time was ripe for a fully formed peace process. The reality was that there were multiple unreliable and open channels. The IRA/Sinn Fein could get its messages across to the British, both privately and publicly, in a variety of ways that London could not match. Depending on the issue, how much pressure they were under from London, and whether the interests of other actors aligned (or appeared to align) with their own agenda, the IRA/Sinn Fein could use the Irish government, the Americans, the Catholic Church, John Hume, and the media. All of these conduits could echo and reinforce Adams's messages. Until Tony Blair and Bertie Ahern coordinated their policies more closely after 1998, the British had nothing similar with which to pressure the IRA/Sinn Fein.

This multiplicity of actors may have served the IRA/Sinn Fein's needs, but it increased the chances of miscommunication, not to mention deliberate deception. Ideally, the role of intermediaries is threefold: to meet only when authorized to meet, to say only what they are authorized to say, and to transmit back accurately what they've heard to higher political authorities.

In practice, it did not always work this way. During the 1974–75, ceasefire, evidence strongly suggests that Michael Oatley gave the IRA false hope that the British were considering abandoning Northern Ireland. In 1993, the "war is over" memo was a complete fabrication that infuriated the IRA/Sinn Fein. During my time as special envoy to the Northern Ireland peace process, I experienced firsthand Adams's masterful attempts at "spinning" different stories to London, Dublin, and Washington. On one occasion, Adams personally called the British prime minister's office to say that I wanted to grant him a visa to the United States (untrue), but that others in the U.S. government were blocking me from doing so (also untrue). He urged Prime Minister Blair to call President Bush to break the logjam. The ploy failed.

The British and the IRA/Sinn Fein eventually established a diplomatic process that could meet routinely and clandestinely. This took time and effort, and was marked by a number of false starts and setbacks. In retrospect, one Irish government official proposed a benchmark for assessing progress—the ability to move the terrorists away from issuing unilateral demands to drafting joint statements. "Once you get a terrorist group worrying about what language should be in a draft, you're in a good place. . . . It is a sign of success when you're talking to terrorists because that implies there's a political solution to the conflict."[103]

The history of the Troubles suggests that weaning terrorist organizations away from violence to where they feel comfortable jointly drafting public statements is a process, not a single event. Few entities that have not been defeated decisively on the battlefield have been willing to surrender unilaterally. But faced with few or poor options, they may be willing to enter into a series of compromises that cumulatively, over time, shift the terms of the debate and ultimately the nature of the struggle. This proved to be true with Adams and, at a later date, with the IRA. Reflecting back over the long years of the Troubles, Adams remarked, "At some point, we all had to realize that we had to engage in a political process."[104]

TALKING IS NOT A STRATEGY

By itself, talking to terrorists is neither a panacea nor a strategy. The success of an engagement policy will turn on many factors, such as adequate preparation, realistic objectives, timing, credibility, and the balance of power between the parties. Although a diplomatic process provides the parties with a way to confront their differences, it can never bridge divisions. Just talking isn't enough.

The British and the IRA/Sinn Fein met in July 1972 and again in 1974–75. But they quickly realized that simply talking to each other was a fruitless exercise absent a coherent plan or mutual interests. Neither side had very many practical ideas on how to resolve the immediate sources of conflict. In fact, each side had a very poor understanding of the other and no understanding at all on how to build on initial meetings or how to create and then institutionalize a peace process. Instead, each side used these meetings, especially the IRA, to demonstrate its unwillingness to compromise. The IRA set out a maximalist position: total victory. The British refused to sell out the Unionists by vacating Northern Ireland. There was nothing to negotiate except the surrender of the other party.

What is surprising in retrospect is that Britain was not better prepared for the Cheyne Walk meeting, given its colonial and counterterrorism experiences from its days of empire. It surprised people at the time as well. The Irish leader Garret FitzGerald confessed in his memoirs that he had made the mistake of "believing that a British government was actually pursuing any thought-out strategy when its actions in creating uncertainty may in fact have been the product of confusion and muddle."[105] Denis Bradley, who worked closely with Brendan Duddy on the Derry backchannel for the 1975 ceasefire, was far more scathing. Over pints in a Derry pub in May 2009, he told me, "We thought the British had a strategy because they were smart and because we thought that they were better than us. And that was shit!"[106]

In fact, the British did have a military strategy at this time, but one that even some British officials may not have realized. Northern Ireland was not seen as some colonial outpost, to be handed over to the "natives" as the Union Jack was slowly lowered to the strains of "Rule, Britannia." It was an integral part of Britain and would remain so as long as the Unionist majority had a say. Some British politicians spent the first few years of the Troubles waking up to this reality.

Strictly speaking, the military strategy was not to defeat the IRA. Although this would have been welcomed, few thought it likely. And it was not to prevent the IRA from inflicting a military defeat on the British army, which the army did not think was possible in any event. Rather, the strategy was to prevent the IRA from inflicting a *political* defeat on the British government, raising the loss of life and property to such a level that the mandarins and Westminster officials would lose heart and withdraw. In short, the British did not have to prevail. They merely had to ensure that the IRA did not do so. Over time, it was hoped that this military stalemate (and infiltration by the security and intelligence services) would create the political space for a peace process to gain traction and develop. The great contribution of the military and security forces (supplemented in later years by the intelligence services) was that they performed a "holding action" until the two sides could develop a peace process.

The Cheyne Walk meeting, to the extent that it had any larger political purpose, was to probe the IRA and determine whether it could be persuaded to end the violence. Three years later, the British used the 1975 ceasefire to collect intelligence, adopt new counterterrorism legislation, put in place a new array of security measures, and generally degrade the IRA's operational effectiveness. Republicans at the time acknowledged it was a disaster for the armed struggle. Merlyn Rees and Roy Mason used this time to institute a new "Long Haul" strategy that made an IRA victory even less plausible.

For the first few decades of the Troubles, the British military and security forces fought the IRA to at least a standstill. Adams realized in the 1980s that the IRA/Sinn Fein could not drive the Brits out with one "big push," that its military edge was blunted by British tactics and Loyalist violence, that the Sinn Fein political experiment had flagged—*and that conditions were not going to improve anytime soon*—and only then did he devote his considerable talents to fashioning a soft landing for the IRA and Sinn Fein.

THE ROLE OF INTELLIGENCE

The importance of intelligence collection was a second thread running through the Troubles. The ability of tactical intelligence to alert authorities to planned or imminent attacks is essential for maintaining public safety. The ability of strategic intelligence to peer inside a covert organization and understand its personalities, structure, values, and strategy is invaluable to defeating, containing, and especially negotiating with a terrorist group. Each type of intelligence collection demands different approaches and skills. Neither is easy.

Unfortunately for the British, their intelligence system at the start of the Troubles was a disaster, "a complete dog's dinner" in the words of one senior British intelligence officer.[107] The problem was overlapping and competing intelligence responsibilities among the RUC, army intelligence, MI5, MI6, Government Communications Headquarters (GCHQ), and the Metropolitan Police Service. It was not until the Thatcher administration that the problem was finally sorted out, when the Prime Minister dispatched Maurice Oldfield, the retired former head of MI6, to Northern Ireland to rationalize intelligence-collection responsibilities.

If good intelligence is essential, what is it essential for? Here, too, there were competing priorities in Northern Ireland. Because intelligence resources were in short supply, there was always a tension between addressing short-term versus longer-term needs. Here, our current vantage point looking back at these events distorts our understanding. Because we now know that the Troubles lasted for decades, it is easy to assume that everyone "knew" this at the time and acted accordingly. The reality, of course, is that no one knew how long the conflict was going to last, and surely no one ever thought it would last as long as it did. This meant that time, funds, and energies were skewed to the short term, especially at the beginning of the Troubles. When it later appeared that the conflict might last longer, after the 1975 ceasefire, the British then adapted for the "Long Haul." Eventually, the British scored a number of successes, penetrating the IRA, killing or capturing many of its members, and preventing a majority of operations from taking place.

The police and security forces were naturally most concerned about tactical intelligence: stopping the next bomb or sniper attack. The intelligence services, on the other hand, were more interested in strategic intelligence: understanding the organizational structure, personnel, policies, and intentions of the IRA. It especially wanted to infiltrate the Army Council, which made the IRA's key decisions. This was really a clash of two different cultures and missions—reflected in the difference between the police wanting to arrest a criminal and place him in jail, and the intelligence services wanting to recruit a criminal and let him go free to act as an informer. This clash led to allegations, some still unresolved today, that the British government collaborated with IRA members and Loyalist paramilitary who perpetrated vicious crimes, including murder.

But British intelligence played a much larger role in Northern Ireland than just preventing terrorist acts or infiltrating paramilitary groups. The intelligence services were also useful for maintaining contact with key IRA/Sinn Fein leaders all through the Troubles. Northern Ireland, it soon became clear, was not the sort of conflict where one side was going to win a decisive battlefield victory over the other. At some point, the two sides would have to parley. Often, it was preferable to do this in secret. Engaging with terrorists had to be done "in a way that does not contaminate the politicians," according to the former head of MI5.[108] The fact that these meetings took place in the shadows gave the British government the benefit of "plausible deniability," the ability to officially deny contacts with a group it had publicly and repeatedly vilified. This communications channel allowed the British government a way to try to "manage" the conflict by passing messages along to the IRA/Sinn Fein and receiving messages in return.

Using intelligence officers for this type of communication had other benefits as well—they gathered intelligence. At these meetings, the British were able to gain a greater understanding of the IRA's intentions, its goals, its leadership structure, its various factions and internal disagreements. Every meeting or negotiation was an intelligence-gathering opportunity, a type of counterterrorism exercise. The personal impressions of agents could supplement other sources of intelligence—for example, from electronic eavesdropping or informants.

On a number of occasions, British intelligence fed useful information to the government. During the very first period of contact, in June 1972, the IRA unwittingly revealed the growing influence and importance of a young Gerry Adams by insisting that Adams be furloughed from prison to help make the arrangements for the Cheyne Walk meeting with Whitelaw. As early as 1974, the British learned that there was a group within the IRA Army Council that wanted to explore a more political pathway forward. This was reportedly why London agreed to unban Sinn Fein and allow it to register as a legal political party.[109]

Every negotiating team tries to present a united front, and usually designates a single person to talk to preserve that image. But over a period of time or when discussions get particularly heated, other members around the table may be unable to resist voicing their opinions. These interventions may reveal important differences that can be exploited by the other side. Savvy intelligence officers can use the meetings to explore who holds what views, who might be agreeable to compromises, or who could accept less-than-total solutions to the conflict. Savvy terrorists can, too. Gerry Adams conceded that he used his meetings with British officials to act as his own intelligence officer, trying to identify "like minds" among the British who would support his agenda.[110]

Inevitably, there was a darker side to these meetings. Intelligence officers used these opportunities to make judgments as to which IRA/Sinn Fein members might be vulnerable to recruitment, whether because of a sincere change of heart or for more sordid reasons involving sex, drugs, or money. The full list of British informants will probably never be known, but by the 1990s, British security units had effectively penetrated the IRA, including recruitment of the IRA's chief of counterintelligence and its third-ranking official.

THE DANGERS OF TALKING PUBLICLY

While London and the IRA/Sinn Fein met and talked in secret, London consistently denied that these discussions were taking place. Instead, British officials publicly denounced Adams, McGuinness, and other members of the IRA as terrorists, the British government passed counterterrorism legislation, and British security and police forces aggressively pursued the IRA.

At the very least, these denials demonstrated a remarkable degree of official hypocrisy; at worst, successive British governments outright lied to the public. One example came in November 1993, during the prime minister's question time when John Major proclaimed that talking to the IRA "would turn my stomach.... We will not do it."[111] After Major sat down following these remarks, his secretary of state for Northern Ireland, Patrick Mayhew, reportedly leaned over his shoulder and whispered, "But Mr. Prime Minister, we *are* talking to the IRA." To which Major allegedly replied, "I said it would turn *my* stomach. I did not say it would turn *yours*."[112]

How can this behavior be explained?

British leaders may have feared that key constituencies would not understand their engaging with members of a terrorist group they had repeatedly demonized and would therefore punish them in print and at the polls. Certainly, this would have been true of the Unionists (many of whom feared abandonment), the police, and security personnel in Northern Ireland and may have been true of members of the army as well. British leaders may have also been fearful of handing their political opponents a stick with which to beat them, and of the broader reaction from the voting public.

In particular, a mistimed overture or public engagement with the IRA could make the government look foolish and criminally out of touch as to the group's sincerity and motives. The specific danger was that the government would be seen negotiating with terrorists while bombs were going off. This was a far from hypothetical risk. There was evidence that Adams and McGuinness exerted increasingly greater influence over the IRA during the 1980s and 1990s, but the British knew that this influence had its limits and that there were factions within the organization that sometimes went their own way. As Brendan Duddy explained about how the IRA/Sinn Fein works: "One department over here bombs people. The other department over there talks to people. They operate simultaneously. It is very hard for the man in the street to understand this."[113] The politicians understood, which is why they sometimes feared taking a risk they could not control.

When these meetings were revealed, however, the public's reaction was far more supportive and understanding than might have been anticipated. The first senior British official to meet face-to-face with the senior leadership of the

IRA, Harold Wilson, wanted Prime Minister Edward Heath to provide him with political cover by stating that his meeting the IRA had the government's blessing. Heath refused. But when Wilson went ahead anyway and briefed Parliament about his contacts with the IRA leadership, he did not suffer any political damage. Indeed, less than two years later, he was elected a second time as prime minister.

No British prime minister had a more contentious relationship with the IRA/ Sinn Fein than Margaret Thatcher. (Thatcher even imposed a "broadcast ban" on Gerry Adams in October 1988, hoping to "starve the terrorist and the hijacker of the oxygen of publicity on which they depend.") Her government's contacts with the hunger strikers were well known at the time, even if the extent of the concessions to the inmates was not. For these contacts, she faced no criticism. In fact, much of the criticism aimed at her was for not doing more to end the strike.

This record argues for governments being more candid. In other words, politicians should trust the public's judgment and maturity. Thatcher's foreign minister and close adviser, Douglas Hurd, has said that it is really "not that hard" for democratic governments to explain such contacts: "You explain that you're doing this to stop more killing."[114] The public may be more eager for talking than officials realize. Less than ten days after Prime Minister John Major declared that it would turn his stomach to talk to the IRA, an opinion poll showed that a strong majority of British citizens said he should talk to Gerry Adams.

Yet some caution is warranted. It is far from clear that all governments should uniformly admit to the public any and all contacts with terrorist groups. First, not every country has the same history or political culture as Britain. The historical experience of negotiating with leaders of national liberation movements in Britain's colonial outposts produced a sophisticated (or fatalistic) understanding that the world was a messy place and that circumstances may change over time. Lord Palmerston famously expressed this sentiment in the mid-nineteenth century: "We have no eternal allies and we have no perpetual enemies. Our interests are eternal and perpetual, and those interests it is our duty to follow."[115] Should Britain's interests require meeting with the IRA/Sinn Fein, greater public tolerance existed to support this approach. Indeed, talking to people with "blood on their hands" was pursued under both Labour and Conservative prime ministers.

Even so, there were limits. Context mattered. The British government could not be seen talking immediately after an atrocity. A "decent interval" of time must pass, although it is impossible to say how long. More than a few days are needed. The Major government was heavily criticized, for example, after it was revealed that its representatives had met with senior Republicans only two days after bombs placed in trash cans in a shopping center outside of Liverpool killed two children and wounded fifty-six others.

Second, for most of the Troubles, and certainly the first few decades, the mayhem in Northern Ireland was far removed from the British mainland. The conflict was something that most of the British public could read about over morning tea and toast, not something it had to live with—and fear—on a daily basis. Although there were bombings in some of the major British cities, this type of violence was episodic, not continuous, certainly when seen over the course of the conflict. That started to change in the early 1990s, with the bombings in London, and these made it more difficult for the Major government to engage the IRA/Sinn Fein. As a general rule, it is far more difficult for a government to talk to terrorists when a terror campaign hits closer to home and targets civilians.

Perhaps the most important reason Britain could pursue an almost constant conversation with the IRA/Sinn Fein during the Troubles was that senior officials were not seen in the company of the IRA/Sinn Fein. Again, the context mattered. After William Whitelaw's initial foray, no British Cabinet officer met with an IRA/Sinn Fein leader for over twenty-five years. Instead, the go-betweens were confined to intelligence officers and civil servants. Often these meetings were not negotiations but rather conversations, discussions, or an exchange of views. The Irish government adopted the same cautious course. Taoiseach Charles Haughey refused to meet with Gerry Adams. Albert Reynolds only agreed to be seen in public with Adams after he helped deliver the 1994 IRA ceasefire, and then only with John Hume on his flank to provide political cover. A different context made all the difference.

UNANSWERED QUESTIONS

After the Good Friday Agreement was signed, in April 1998, the SDLP leader, Seamus Mallon, famously rendered his verdict, declaring that it was "Sunningdale for slow learners." Mallon meant that the main principles enshrined in the Good Friday Agreement had all been set out twenty-five years earlier in the Sunningdale Agreement.

And yet, sadly, Mallon underestimated the time still needed to close the deal. Even after the Good Friday Agreement, it took another nine years, more violence, and more lost lives for the very slowest learners to catch up and the Troubles to finally end.

So why did it take so long for the parties to reach agreement? Could a negotiated solution have been reached earlier?

One of the great frustrations for negotiators is that they often can see the outline of a deal well before others can. This is due to their greater mastery of the details, understanding of the other side's concerns, and ability to think creatively. This was true in Northern Ireland. Many people involved in the peace process could envision the final outcome, in its general shape if not all of its specifics, years before a settlement was reached. In the mid-1990s, for example, Merlyn Rees, the former secretary of state for Northern Ireland during the mid-1970s, stated that "there is nothing that the IRA can get now that they couldn't have had any time in the last twenty years."[116]

So the question needs to be asked: Could a peace process have been developed sooner? Could all the parties have reached agreement earlier and thus spared the poor people of Northern Ireland so much anguish and pain? If the British, Irish, and even the Americans had been smarter, could the Troubles have ended earlier?

It is tempting to think so, but once the flame of sectarian violence was lit, it would have been very difficult to extinguish short of outright military victory or capitulation by one side or the other.

The IRA thought for a long time that one more "big push" might do the trick in exhausting the patience and political stamina of the British, but they were never able to escalate the violence to such a level, and even if they had, there was no indication that the British would not have matched them and escalated in kind. In short, London did not view Northern Ireland as some faraway colonial outpost, but rather as an integral part of the United Kingdom, at least as long as a majority of the people there wanted it to be.

For most of the Troubles, when the IRA looked to the future, it saw victory, not compromise. The IRA was unwilling to permanently stop the fighting in 1972 when their delegation met with the British or even in 1975 during the extended ceasefire (unless, of course, the British had agreed to withdraw from Northern Ireland). Talking may have brought other benefits, but it could not bridge the political divide at this time.

It is also easy to elide over the larger domestic and international context during the 1970s, 1980s, and 1990s. The times were not always conducive to peace, to put it mildly. Discrimination against Catholics was still prevalent in Northern Ireland for much of this period. Loyalist paramilitaries terrorized neighborhoods. Only after the hunger strikes was Adams able to ease Sinn Fein into electoral politics, and only after the 2001 Westminster and local elections did Sinn Fein eclipse the SDLP as the leading nationalist party. Margaret Thatcher's unrelenting opposition made it more difficult for Republicans to contemplate some type of political accommodation. Dublin's inability (or unwillingness) to prevent the Republic of Ireland from being used as a rear-echelon base camp for IRA raids over the border was another complicating factor. And, of course, the IRA kept on killing and engaging in other violent criminal activities.

Would the conflict have ended sooner if the quality of British intelligence had been better? Better tactical intelligence certainly could have prevented more deaths from bombs and other attacks. Better strategic intelligence would have been nice, but it is unclear how it would have tangibly helped the situation. Even if the British had a better understanding of Adams's agenda in the mid-1980s, when he started reaching out to the British, Irish, and SDLP, would this have made a real difference to the peace process? It is unclear how the British could have helped Adams persuade the IRA/Sinn Fein to renounce the Armalite and armed struggle and embrace a purely peaceful and democratic path, largely because it was unclear whether Adams himself was persuaded at this time.

Whether the peace process could have been accelerated also begs a larger question: Is talking to terrorists worth considering at all unless there is an individual like Gerry Adams sitting across the negotiating table? Is there a person able and willing to adjust his thinking to military and political realities, take risks for peace, and deliver on his promises?

The dilemma for a government is that it may be very difficult to answer this question without first engaging with members of a terrorist group to take their measure and judge whether someone like Adams even exists. The added dilemma for governments is that sometimes individuals moderate their views as they age and mature. The Gerry Adams who opposed all ceasefires and revitalized the IRA in the 1970s and who embraced the bullet and the ballot throughout the 1980s and into the 1990s was not the same Gerry Adams who signed up to the April 1998 Good Friday Agreement. This suggests that governments may sometimes have to engage patiently with terrorist groups for years, even decades, until more pragmatic leadership evolves or emerges.

A former member of the IRA and later a member of Sinn Fein, Danny Morrison, voiced this challenge from a different perspective: "It takes great courage to be pragmatic when you have been fundamentalist for so long."[117] Perhaps, but in Northern Ireland, we can measure in decades the time it took the IRA/Sinn Fein to gain the requisite "courage." The saddest requiem for Northern Ireland is that they could not have done so any sooner.

Spain

Guipúzcoa

San
Sebastián

Bilbao

FRANCE

Biscay

Lapurdi
Behe Nafarroa

Zuberoa

Araba

Navarre

● Madrid

Mediterranean Sea

PORTUGAL

SPAIN

2.

BASQUE HOMELAND AND FREEDOM (ETA)

I suggested we meet in the tea room of the Hotel Angleterre, the fanciest hotel in San Sebastián, a seaside town in the Basque region of Spain. (I preferred very public places, during the daytime, as an added security precaution.) My guest was Eugenio Etxebeste, better known as "Antxon," his nom de guerre from his time as ETA's chief "theorist" and senior negotiator. Now in his early sixties and with little hair, Antxon looked far removed from the young Basque revolutionary who had threatened Spain's interior minister at their first meeting.

Antxon was gracious and pleasant. When I asked about the significance of his lapel pin, he explained that it was in the shape of the historic Basque homeland and then proceeded to take it off and hand it to me. He was intent on explaining the centuries-long struggle of the Basque people for independence. Just as we were about to explore the motives for ETA's negotiations with the Spanish government, I noticed that an elderly man, easily in his seventies, was watching us intently from a nearby table. After a few more minutes, he struggled to his feet and used his cane to limp over to us. He then started speaking in Basque to the former ETA leader. My interpreter whispered that the gentleman apologized for interrupting our conversation, but that he had overheard us talking. She then went silent, her face frozen as she continued listening to what this man had to say. He grew more animated and gestured that something was pulled over his head. After a few minutes, he stopped talking, bowed to me, and then hobbled back to his seat.

By this time, my interpreter had regained her composure and explained that he had recognized Antxon. He was a Basque and had intervened to make sure that Antxon explained to me how the Spanish security forces had tortured him years ago. He said I needed to understand how the Spanish state had behaved toward the Basque people if I was going to write on this subject.

FRANCISCO FRANCO, MILITARY GENERAL, DICTATOR, AND Caudillo de España, por la gracia de Dios, died on November 20, 1975, almost four decades after he had seized power during the Spanish Civil War. His death allowed for a *transición* from his right-wing authoritarian regime to a vibrant constitutional democracy that today has one of the highest per capita incomes in the world. This transition managed to preserve the essential unity of Spain even as it was being tugged by historic assertions of regional and cultural identities. Impressively, Spain accomplished all this while beset by a resilient and relentless terrorist group, Basque Homeland and Freedom (Euskadi ta Askatasuna, or ETA), which has violently asserted its claim for an independent state for the Basque people for the past fifty years. It is the longest-running currently active terrorist group in Europe and one of the oldest in the world.

The ideological father of Basque nationalism is Sabino Arana, who founded the Basque Nationalist Party (Partido Nacionalista Vasco, or PNV) in 1895. Arana imagined a mythical Basque identity based on the distinctive ethnic features of a preindustrial society that stretched over what are today four provinces in northern Spain and three in southwestern France. To preserve a Basque heritage under assault by the twin forces of late-nineteenth-century industrialization and modernization, Arana urged people to choose between Basque and Spanish identities rather than adopt a blend of both.[1] He coined the word *Euskadi* to refer to the Basque nation, designed a national flag, and penned a national anthem.

During the first quarter of the twentieth century, the PNV grew as a political movement in the Basque region. After the Spanish Civil War, political repression under Franco further solidified the Basque identity and the Basque people's opposition to the central government in Madrid. Some of the PNV's younger members, discouraged at the party's prospects for political progress under Franco and inspired by the guerrilla insurgency in Algeria, decided in 1959 to form ETA to bring about an independent Basque state by force of arms. For the next few decades, ETA tried to weave a coherent worldview from three different ideological strands: radical Basque nationalism, anticolonialism, and a Marxist-Leninist class struggle. It never succeeded, though, and the group repeatedly splintered and re-formed, amoeba-like, yet somehow always managed to maintain a core that could inflict terror against the state.

Since Franco's death, this violence has served a two-phased political strategy. The first phase is the demand for amnesty for all ETA members in jail; legalization of all political parties; removal from the Basque country of the state's police and security forces; improvement of conditions for the working class; and Madrid's formal recognition of Basque sovereignty and the right of the Basque people to create their own state. Realization of these objectives would result in a Basque state federally tied to Spain but not yet independent. The second phase is a *programa máximo* that calls for a completely independent and sovereign Basque country. ETA would be willing to renounce the use of violence only at the end of this second phase, after the full implementation of the "maximum program."[2]

Unlike many revolutionary or insurgent movements, ETA never sought to replace a colonial master or depose an unjust ruler. These movements tacitly acknowledge the existing state system; indeed, they want to preserve this order to maximize their influence for the day when they seize power. ETA has attempted something infinitely more ambitious. Its ultimate goal of an independent Basque homeland requires rewriting the boundaries of two sovereign states, Spain and France. In short, ETA has rejected the underlying legal basis for modern Europe dating back to the Treaty of Westphalia in 1648.

While some Spanish governments have been willing to engage ETA to discuss pardons for selected prisoners, the rest of ETA's agenda has been completely unacceptable. Nonetheless, according to the investigative journalist Florencio Dominguez, widely considered the most knowledgeable expert on ETA, "All the Spanish governments, from 1977 to 2007, regardless of their political inclinations, have tried to attain the end of violence through conversations with ETA, but all attempts have failed."[3]

Why did these governments engage with ETA? And why did they fail?

THE PERIOD OF WISHFUL THINKING
1975–82

In the months before Franco slowly expired, many people in Spain feared that his death would trigger turmoil and instability and lead either to a military coup or a descent into factionalized violence and a resumption of the Civil War.[4] Neither outcome materialized. Instead, the transition period, led by the young king Juan Carlos, was characterized by the dismantling of Franco-era institutions and laws, the rapid implementation of parliamentary democracy, the delegation of autonomy to regional authorities, and high hopes for ending ETA's violence. In fact, many believed that the combination of democratization and decentralization would end ETA's terror campaign against the state.

Disappointment was not long in coming. Only days after Franco's state funeral, the Spanish government contacted ETA to explore whether the two sides could meet and negotiate an end to the violence. ETA answered by assassinating the mayor of a Basque town and issuing a communiqué that derided the idea of liberal democracy.[5]

Efforts for greater democratization and decentralization moved ahead anyway. The king acted swiftly to decriminalize forms of political expression that were banned under the Franco regime. The previous law on terrorism was amended, the civil courts assumed jurisdiction over terrorist crimes, and the mandatory death sentence was overturned. During the two years immediately following Franco's death, Spain granted full amnesty to almost 900 ETA members and their supporters and legalized previously forbidden nationalist symbols, like the Basque flag.

Political progress came rapidly. In July 1976, the king appointed Adolfo Suárez as prime minister. The following year, Suárez's conservative political party won the majority of seats in the country's first free general elections to the Cortes, the Spanish parliament. To satisfy Basque nationalism (and other aspirations for regional identity), Madrid transferred authority from the center to the periphery. In 1978, a national referendum approved a new constitution, which enshrined the concept of autonomous communities for "historical nationalities." In May 1980, the three Basque provinces of Alava, Guipúzcoa, and Vizcaya formed the Basque Autonomous Community. The Basque region now had its own parliament, led by the PNV. It could boast of local control over health care, education, taxes, and the police force; the promotion of the Basque language and culture; and a degree of fiscal autonomy that the other regions in Spain could only envy.[6]

However, other trends undercut these encouraging developments, chief among them ETA's ongoing and increasingly lethal campaign of violence. As the country moved toward democracy, the number of terrorist incidents and victims increased, spiking to a high of ninety-six deaths in 1980.[7] A demographic youth bulge in the Basque region in the late 1970s fueled these fires, creating a potential pool of young recruits, many of them unemployed and eager to join ETA.[8]

In addition, some old habits were hard for the inexperienced officials in Madrid to root out. State security institutions that had operated with impunity under the Franco regime still engaged in an overly militarized response to terrorism, including indiscriminate arrests, torture, and extended detentions. Right-wing vigilante groups appeared to enjoy official sanction or at least tolerance. This behavior further incited Basque nationalism and increased sympathy, even support, for ETA's actions against state authorities.

Disorganization did not help. By the start of 1976, "as many as eleven different secret intelligence services were operating in competition with one another, instead of pooling and coordinating their efforts."[9] Eagerness to undo the years of repressive legislation imposed by the Franco regime meant that Spain initially had no permanent antiterrorist legislation, further handicapping efforts to combat ETA.[10]

A critical factor was the sanctuary ETA found just over the Pyrenees Mountains inside France. The French viewed ETA as a national liberation movement justified in using violence against Franco. Sympathy by French politicians, intellectuals, and members of the media meant that ETA could use southwestern France to hide, recruit, raise funds, and plot new attacks. According to Robert Clark, the leading American expert on ETA, "For the 1960s and most of the 1970s, Paris tolerated ETA's presence in France as long as the organization committed no crimes there and refrained from whipping up nationalist sentiment among French Basques. . . . France's chief interest in the whole affair [was] to prevent the insurgency from spilling over onto French territory."[11]

The escalation in ETA's violence at this time also reflected personal rivalries and ideological debates inside the organization. Tensions had existed for some time between the two largest organizations, ETA-Militar (ETA-M) and ETA-Politico/Militar (ETA-PM). They had the same ultimate goal, but ETA-M took primary responsibility for armed attacks and had established contacts with the Irish Republican Army, Germany's Baader-Meinhof Gang, and the Tupamaros in Uruguay.[12] The more political ETA-PM also advocated violence, but emphasized laying the groundwork for a longer-term socialist revolution through organizing workers into labor unions and (after Franco's death) mobilizing voters for elections.

The rivalry between the two branches of ETA led to an increase in violence (with almost 400 deaths between 1976 and 1980), as an "intense competition for ideological hegemony over the entire Basque nationalist movement" played out.[13] Violence was used not just as a means to assert leadership within the organization, but also as a way to signal other important audiences. Under the "spiral" theory of revolutionary struggle, ETA's actions were intended to undermine the path to democracy and provoke state repression, which in turn would radicalize and mobilize the masses to support ETA's goals. ETA thought violence could coerce Madrid into granting concessions and thereby increase the military's mistrust of a civilian government that was perceived as appeasing terrorists. The result would be greater state repression, perhaps even a military coup, which would increase ETA's popularity. The group's assassination of senior army officers and individuals trying to mediate an end to the violence indicated that ETA was unwilling to negotiate seriously with the Spanish government as the 1970s ended.

As Spain transitioned to democracy, a subgroup within ETA-PM was starting to have fundamental doubts about whether the armed struggle was still justified. Some ETA-PM members believed that the need for "patriotic self-defense"—the use of violence against the state—ceased once Franco passed from the scene and the Basque people could express their preferences democratically. A "critical moment" occurred in September 1974, the year before Franco's death, when ETA bombed the Café Rolando, located close to the headquarters of the state security forces in Madrid. Instead of striking a blow against the state, ETA succeeded only in killing twelve innocent civilians. ETA refused to accept responsibility for the attack; internally, it stifled all self-criticism and refused to tolerate any debate between "those who will support revolutionary violence against fascism and those who will support terrorism."[14] This started what became gradually a widening breach between those who did not view the armed struggle as the only way to establish an independent homeland and those who did.

Some of these more moderate (or realistic) members reached out to the government in October 1976 to discuss a possible amnesty and the creation of a new political party. It would take years for these members to split officially from their more radical comrades in ETA-PM and still more time for them to renounce violence altogether (and trust that the government would follow through on its promises). But it appeared that at least some radical Basque nationalists were willing to undertake a personal *transición* to becoming constitutional Basque nationalists. As one member who made this journey during the 1970s summarized his thinking, "We knew that democracy is coming and that the armed struggle would be meaningless when people could express themselves in a democracy. We could have been reactionary, but decided not to take this path.... There was recognition that the armed struggle served no purpose at all and only made things worse for the self-determination process in the Basque country."[15]

Meanwhile, the Spanish government continued its efforts to engage with ETA to try to end the violence. Understanding that it was easier to peel away ETA members than capture or kill them all (and wanting to break with its Francoist past and assert its democratic credentials), Madrid lowered the "exit costs" for any terrorists who wanted to leave ETA by developing generous amnesty and "social reintegration" policies designed to allow them to pursue a normal life. As terrorists were amnestied and pardoned, the government also used some of these men, especially ex–ETA-PM members, to lobby their former comrades to end the armed struggle and promote the idea of Basque nationalism within the constitutional structure, such as the PNV.

As the Suárez government acquired more experience engaging with ETA, it adopted certain informal policies and rules. Issues that might be deemed tactical or nonpolitical in nature—including ceasefires, amnesties, the return of prisoners to the Basque country, and bargaining over the release of hostages—could be addressed.[16] But more strategic issues that implicated the integrity of the Spanish state—including the integration of Navarre into the Basque Autonomous Community, the withdrawal of all Spanish security forces from the Basque country, and the Basque people's right of self-determination and sovereignty—were completely off-limits. Law-and-order issues could be discussed. Political issues could not.

At the same time, how the government described its interactions with ETA assumed outsized political significance. The word "negotiation" was highly charged and grew to have special meaning within the context of Spain's domestic politics. This term connoted that the government was discussing strategic issues dealing with the unity of the state, the third rail of Spanish politics. The word "dialogue" was slightly less incendiary, while "conversation" was the most neutral and inoffensive. "Talks" were used to describe a type of preliminary testing phase to see if more substantive discussions could follow.[17] These informal practices would be followed by Spanish governments for the next thirty years.

By the start of the 1980s, ETA members could see that democratic institutions had taken hold, that political dissent was tolerated, and that Basque political parties could successfully elect deputies to the national and Basque parliaments. Yet ETA's continued violence handicapped those less radical Basque nationalists who wanted to advance the cause through the political process. In late 1980, ETA-PM announced that it would cease all attacks and called upon ETA-M to do the same. ETA-M rejected the appeal and underlined its opposition by detonating a bomb the following day that wounded three policemen.

In September 1982, ETA-PM formally disbanded. The leadership announced at a press conference that "we will continue struggling with non-violent methods. . . . Armed struggle and ETA have now fulfilled their role."[18] The negotiations had accomplished far less than the group had originally sought. The amnesty and social reintegration of ETA members took place, but it was selectively and slowly implemented. The Spanish government had refused to address the group's other demands.[19] The more radical members of ETA-PM migrated to ETA-M.

TALKING TO ETA: LOST OPPORTUNITIES?

The immediate post-Franco years were clearly a time of great hope. Political and social freedoms that had not been possible, even conceivable, under Franco, were discussed openly, legislated, and then implemented. People could envision the end of ETA.

After Franco's death, ETA greeted the new Spanish government with an escalation of violence, but also presented repeated opportunities to engage in discussions. In fact, during the transition, the Spanish government and ETA were in regular contact. Despite the bloodshed, the government seized these opportunities, often using a number of intermediaries to meet with ETA's different factions in prisons, in the Basque country, and outside of Spain. Like the majority of Spanish society at this time, government officials believed that greater autonomy for the Basques, and greater liberalization across Spanish society more broadly, would persuade ETA to abandon the armed struggle.

Could the Spanish government have negotiated the end of ETA at this time? Was ETA's demise ever a realistic possibility or mere wishful thinking? Were there missed opportunities for ending the violence?

The Suárez government and its successor decided to test ETA's intentions and explore the types of agreements and compromises that different elements in the terrorist group might be willing to accept. These tests revolved around three related questions: First, could ETA's members be persuaded to abandon the armed struggle and participate in democratic politics? Second, did they have a leader who was capable of adjusting the group's thinking to the new political environment, and who also controlled the men with guns? And third, was the price ETA demanded for abandoning the armed struggle one the Spanish government could afford to pay?

Over a period of six years, from 1976 to 1982, ETA answered the government with a resounding no, with one limited exception. Only members of ETA-PM, and of that faction only a minority, would lay down their weapons and be socially reintegrated into Spanish society. More radical Basque nationalists made clear through their ongoing violence against the state (as well as through threats and attacks against their more moderate comrades) that they had little interest in surrendering their dream of a sovereign Basque state. Ironically, as the Spanish state deepened its engagement with ETA, the number and lethality of ETA's attacks increased.

Some observers think that Spain missed an opportunity to negotiate an end to the violence when a young Basque leader named Argala controlled ETA-M and was willing to talk to government officials. After initial contacts in 1977 and preliminary talks through 1978, Argala died in France from a car bomb. Did his death really end "the last and best hope for a peaceful settlement of the conflict," as one American academic expert phrased it?[20]

This seems an overly romanticized view of the ETA leader and the thinking inside the organization at the time. The military faction dominated the political faction; in short, violence trumped talking. Within ETA, Argala led the most militant faction, and there is no evidence to suggest that he was willing to even consider abandoning the idea of a Basque nation. At most, he was willing to engage with Madrid only over the process by which ETA could reach this goal. Also, more radical rivals within the organization preferred killing to talking, which accounted for the rising death toll in the Basque country.

If ETA-M was unwilling to participate in a political process that did not guarantee in advance the Basque people's historic rights, evidence also suggests it was
unable to do so either. It did not have the competence or experience to initiate a
peace process, never mind sustain it over time. José Maria Benegas, a leader of the
Basque Socialist Party and one of the go-betweens used by the Spanish interior
minister, Rodolfo Martin Villa, to arrange a meeting with ETA's leaders in Geneva in 1977, recalls that "it was very difficult to finalize the meeting." In preliminary talks, "they didn't have anything prepared except unfeasible ideas over venue,
timing, the proposed agenda, and other details, so we couldn't make any progress,"
he told me over coffee in his downtown Madrid office. ETA-M "devoted more
time to 'methodologies' [a rehashing of Spanish history and Basque grievances]
than to the substance of the issues . . . the preparations were very complicated."[21]
Eventually, Martin Villa rejected talking to ETA-M after the group demanded
that journalists be invited and that the meeting be billed as between "equals"—in
other words, between Spanish officials and representatives of a sovereign Basque
country.[22]

No Spanish government could acquiesce to ETA's nonnegotiable demands
on self-determination and independence and hope to remain in power. Indeed,
making too many accommodations or concessions to ETA risked a right-wing
backlash that could undermine the fledgling experiment in Spanish democracy. A
parliamentary exchange between Prime Minister Suárez and Socialist Party opposition leader Felipe González in May 1980 partially lifted the veil on this political
reality. After a Basque deputy accused Suárez of authorizing negotiations with
ETA two years earlier, the prime minister replied, "I have never been in agreement
with any negotiation of the government with ETA. At no time." González rose
to rebut the prime minister, claiming that "he and I have talked personally about
the subject of negotiation with ETA." Suárez stood firm, insisting, "The government at no time has been ready to negotiate with ETA. . . . ETA has tried on
many occasions to negotiate . . . with the government. The government has always
said that it does not negotiate with ETA, and I repeat what I have said before.
That is all."[23]

Of course, the Suárez government had been in constant communication
with ETA during this time. While other politicians (including González) and
the media knew about these contacts, the military and security forces did not.
A "conspiracy of silence" ruled because of a shared fear of a possible relapse to

Franco-style authoritarianism.[24] These fears appeared to be realized on February 23, 1981, when 200 members of the Civil Guard, led by Lieutenant Colonel Antonio Tejero, stormed the Cortes and attempted a military coup. Due to King Juan Carlos's steadfast support for democracy, the coup collapsed within hours. But even the failure highlighted the domestic constraints within which the Suárez government and its successors had to operate.

Evidence also suggests that ETA leaders had a difficult time in controlling those who were opposed to talks; there has reportedly never been unanimous commitment within ETA to negotiations. These internal disagreements caused ETA's positions to shift and harden during talks. ETA's representatives either toughened their positions or risked being labeled as traitors by their colleagues. (Any breach of the truce or ceasefire by more militant ETA members during these talks posed serious domestic problems for the Spanish government.) Commenting on Geneva and subsequent interactions with ETA, Benegas said, "There has never been a serious preparation before the meetings." His postmortem on the 1977–78 period was that this "was not a lost opportunity because ETA not only did not cooperate, but the violence also got worse during this period. They were using France as a base for planning attacks, developing strategy, collecting a revolutionary tax, and other things. They had no intention of ending the war except on their own terms."[25]

THE END OF ETA-PM: HOW MUCH OF A PRECEDENT?

The Spanish government had greater success in winding down ETA-PM. The basic bargain was "peace for prisoners," where ETA members who left the group and renounced violence would be amnestied or pardoned and then socially reintegrated. This type of negotiation reduced the dispute from more abstract and intangible issues involving identity, historical interpretation, and the nature of the Spanish state to more pragmatic and tangible ones, such as jail terms and family visits. For Madrid, this approach seemed a useful precedent to use with ETA-PM's more militant comrades.

But was it? Could the state craft a similar set of inducements to lead ETA-M away from violence?

The government's working assumption was that ETA understood that Spain was too strong to be defeated militarily and too democratic to be destabilized.

The most that ETA could aspire to was better treatment of prisoners and more beneficial terms for social reintegration. To the surprise and disappointment of future Spanish governments, the assumption turned out to be wishful thinking. When Spain tried the same tactics with ETA-M, offers on prisoners were taken for granted. ETA-M believed the government should make this concession as a matter of right, without ETA-M having to make concessions in return.[26] Additionally, ETA-M wanted to avoid the stigma of negotiating the return of prisoners, which is what defeated armies do. It implied that it was on the losing side of a war.

Another reason for this failure was ideological. ETA-PM represented the more political faction inside ETA, and so its members could more easily envision changing the status quo by promoting the cause of Basque nationalism within a constitutional system. If their "narrative of victory" did not end in complete triumph, they could argue (or at least rationalize) that they were working within a democratic process that theoretically, one day, perhaps, would allow them the possibility of reaching their goal. ETA-M, on the other hand, represented the group's Marxist-Leninist faction and viewed victory in more violent and absolutist terms—the capitulation of the Spanish state to its demands. Entertaining any solutions short of this goal was seen as heresy.

A third reason grew from the personalities and rivalries within the group. According to a number of experts, ETA-M could never follow the path of ETA-PM unless it could claim credit for originating the plan. According to Florencio Dominguez, "M saw what PM did and used it as an example of what not to do. M took an antivirus to prevent them from being infected by the same disease."[27] Teo Uriarte, a former ETA-PM member, agreed: "ETA has now been inoculated against accepting a similar arrangement, along with the idea of creating an autonomous political party. . . . I am tired of telling the government that history never repeats itself."[28]

By the early 1980s, ETA had set its course. A negotiated end short of its maximalist demands was out of the question. An insightful Basque observer of ETA summarized the situation: "Rather than acknowledge the realities and the limits of what could be achieved during the *transición*—and seek to strengthen the path of reform—radical Basque nationalism instead opted for all-out confrontation with the Spanish state."[29] The state was about to readjust its course in response.

THE PERIOD OF HIDDEN AGENDAS
1982–96

In 1982, Felipe González was elected as Spain's prime minister. Any notion that his new Socialist administration would be more sympathetic to ETA and its aims than its conservative predecessors was quickly disabused.

Right-wing vigilante groups that targeted ETA members and Basque nationalists had existed in the years immediately following Franco's death. What occurred during the González administration was different. To eliminate the safe havens ETA members found over the border in France, senior officials in the González government secretly assembled the Grupos Antiterroristas Liberación (or GAL) to track down and kill ETA members. Over the next few years, until it stopped operations in 1986, the GAL was responsible for killing twenty-nine people (twenty-seven in France) and wounding more than thirty others.[30]

The GAL's higher purpose was not eliminating ETA members; it was to persuade the French government to stop turning a blind eye to ETA's presence. Madrid wanted Paris to crack down on ETA's operations and extradite ETA members to Spain. The González government had initially tried to convince Paris that Spanish democracy was genuine, that the Basques had no reason to resort to violence, and that any returned ETA members would receive fair trials. When that approach stalled, the GAL was created.

The GAL's targeting of ETA and its assault on Spain's democratic values have been termed "the dirty war." The González administration's support for death squads badly tarnished its reputation and resulted in the conviction and imprisonment of some of its most senior officials. Most people believed the scandal reached the prime minister's office. It undermined the domestic political consensus needed to adopt new counterterrorism measures. And it provided ETA's supporters with a new argument to support the group's ongoing use of violence. The Spanish state and ETA now appeared to share a type of moral equivalency.

But the evidence also clearly indicates that the GAL's activities shifted French policy and severely degraded ETA's effectiveness. Over the course of just a few years, France dramatically enhanced its counterterrorism cooperation with Spain. (A spike in attacks inside France at this time by Middle Eastern terrorist groups also accelerated a new get-tough approach.) Pressure on ETA increased, especially after the French authorities arrested Josu Ternera, one of ETA's most senior members. According to Rafael Vera, Spain's director of state security at the time, "It reached the point where ETA leaders started having bodyguards."[31]

Like its predecessors, the González administration also reached out more directly to ETA. In the mid-1980s, it initiated talks with an ETA leader, Txomin Iturbe, in Andorra. This started a series of contacts between Spanish officials and Iturbe over the next few months. But ETA soon broke off these preliminary talks and the violence resumed.[32] By this time, the political and security environment in which the group operated had changed; ETA was now being actively pursued on both sides of the border. Suffering from a series of reverses, in late 1986 ETA sent word that it wanted to talk with the Spanish authorities.[33] Madrid responded by sending an official to meet with Iturbe in Algeria, where he now resided after being expelled from France. For the next three years, the González administration and ETA engaged in their most intense and sustained attempt to end the war.

THE ALGIERS "TALKS"

The González government was under no illusions that the Algerian channel would lead to ETA's demise. The group had given no indication that it was willing to abandon its maximalist demands or even support anything other than a temporary ceasefire. According to Juan Manuel Eguiagaray, a Basque Socialist politician and one of the lead negotiators in Algeria, "None of us, including Felipe González, was optimistic about the talks. I was pessimistic."[34] Rafael Vera, who also participated in the talks, was blunter: "Felipe González didn't want the negotiations to take place. He thought these meetings were a waste of time. They were meaningless. So why go? Why bother?"[35]

However, meeting with Iturbe in Algiers served several hidden Spanish agendas simultaneously. Domestically, it played quite well. "The Spanish government wanted to convince the public that it had explored every option to end ETA's armed struggle," Eguiagaray told me during our meeting in Madrid. "If the government failed in the talks, it wouldn't be for a lack of courage. Even though the government was skeptical, we thought why not try? This was a risk we could take."[36] One reason it could afford to be so bold was that two earlier agreements had provided political cover for González against partisan criticism for engaging with ETA. In December 1987 the main political parties in Spain had signed the "Madrid Pact" that rejected all *political* negotiations with ETA. The following month the Basque nationalist and nonnationalist parties had endorsed the government's policy toward ETA by declaring that the aspirations of the Basque people had already been set by the Spanish constitution and Statute of Autonomy. ETA had no right to negotiate on behalf of the Basque people.[37]

The Algiers talks were also aimed at influencing French policy. In fact, after publicly and repeatedly vowing that it would not negotiate with ETA until the group first suspended violence for six months, González waived his promise because he was pressed by France's president François Mitterrand. Rafael Vera explained the high-level posturing to me over afternoon drinks at his elegant mountaintop home outside Madrid. "When we started talking to France about getting greater security cooperation over the border, Mitterrand proposed to González that the only way he could increase pressure on ETA was if Spain gave ETA a chance to end the struggle peacefully in a public negotiation. If this negotiation did not work, it would be easier for Paris to help with rounding up ETA."[38] In other words, Mitterrand said he needed a public offer of negotiations in order to persuade his own administration to help Spain eliminate a terrorist group. This was why the González administration decided to restart talks with ETA only two months after the group had perpetrated its most deadly terrorist attack, in June 1987, when it bombed the garage of a crowded Barcelona supermarket, killing twenty-one people and injuring hundreds more.

(France reportedly tried to leverage the situation to promote its economy as well. A few years earlier, the Spanish interior minister visited Paris to press the French to cooperate more fully on suppressing ETA. He was told that Paris might have greater enthusiasm if Spain would buy French products, such as its high-speed rail lines. On a different occasion, at a time when both Spain and France were bidding to host the summer Olympics, a senior French security official told his Spanish counterpart that "France would deliver all of ETA's members to Spain" if it withdrew from the competition.[39])

France was not the only foreign government Spain was trying to influence. Algeria at this time played host to a number of different terrorist groups. Again, Vera: "We wanted the government of Algeria to cut its links with the "friends" of ETA. . . . ETA used Algeria as a training ground. We tried to convince the Algerian government to expel all the ETA members. [Algeria was home to over thirty at the time.] The Algerians said they would do so, but first Spain had to negotiate with ETA."[40]

But this was only part of the story. Vera, the director of state security, viewed the Algiers talks as a ripe counterterrorism opportunity. During the earlier period following Franco's death, the government had been unable to gather much intelligence on ETA, its different factions, and its internal disputes. It had been unaware of the split between ETA-PM and ETA-M, for example. "Most of what we learned came from when we released prisoners" for social reintegration, recalled Vera.[41]

Vera believed that he could be more effective in preventing terror attacks if he had multiple lines into the organization. "In my time [in the government], I always had several channels open to ETA. I could use these channels to gauge their temperature. . . . For me, political information was police information." Thinking that the talks with ETA were doomed to fail, Vera had prearranged with the Algerian government to have it expel all of the ETA members to certain Latin American countries. Vera had also prearranged with these countries to have the ETA members placed under house arrest, where they would be secretly watched. Their phones and fax machines were all tapped; their moves and meetings recorded and relayed to Spanish intelligence. "What I really wanted were ETA members in third countries where they could be monitored. . . . We had microphones everywhere. We were able to arrest a lot of command cells [in Spain] because of this surveillance. This was my goal. . . . I used it to roll up ETA. . . . I could learn more when they were in foreign countries than when they were in Spanish prisons."[42]

For Vera and others in the Spanish government, the talks in Algeria were beside the point. "The government was convinced these talks would fail," asserted Vera. "But what we were interested in was what the French and Algerian governments would do after the failure. . . . The goal was to influence the behavior of France and Algeria, not to negotiate with ETA."[43]

In fact, the government broke off talks with ETA only once during these three years, after ETA bombed the Guardia Civil barracks at Saragossa, killing eleven people, including five young girls. The June 1987 bombing of the garage at the Barcelona supermarket had been more deadly, but this time circumstances were different. "There was still a threat of a military coup," recalled Vera. "There was discontent in the army. The Saragossa bombing was seen as a direct attack on the military. Some military still didn't understand how a democratic system worked." A few years earlier, disgruntled military colonels had tried to assassinate both

González and King Juan Carlos. "We stopped it and played it down so as not to alarm the public and give publicity to the plotters."[44]

However, Vera did think there could be a slight chance that ETA's leader, Txomin Iturbe, was different from his predecessors, because he had suggested at times that ETA's use of violence was a dead end. Iturbe was willing to meet with Spanish officials, and also appeared to exert control over the men with guns. But when he met with Spanish officials in January 1987, he rejected any deal like the one offered to ETA-PM and repeated ETA's maximalist demands. All that was negotiable was the process for realizing these demands.

Before the two sides could meet again, Iturbe died in a car crash in Algeria. (Eguiagaray: "We were suspicious, but it turned out that it was a real car crash."[45]) Eugenio "Antxon" Etxebeste, viewed as a hard-liner, took over.

For the next two years, Etxebeste and Spanish officials engaged in intermittent "pre-talks" while ETA continued to wage war and the Spanish state (with greater assistance from France) increased its pressure on the group. In late 1988, ETA told Madrid that it would announce a two-month ceasefire the following month. After ETA released its statement (indicating a much shorter, two-week ceasefire), Spain sent a senior-level delegation to Algiers, led by Rafael Vera, now the interior minister, and Juan Manuel Eguiagaray.

Thus started the most serious round of talks between ETA and the Spanish government since the social reintegration of the ETA-PM members years before. Etxebeste did almost all the talking. The rest of his delegation consisted of two members of ETA's Madrid cell. (French security had caught them in France and then sent them to Algiers without informing the Spanish government.)

Etxebeste, a member of ETA for thirty-four years, and I discussed the Algiers talks when we met in the Basque country in July 2009. "ETA wanted to show its willingness to overcome the 'war situation' by having a negotiation where both sides could solve the issue and establish a democratic framework so that the Basque people could decide their own future." His goal was to persuade Madrid that the Basque people had a special history that deserved a special political solution. "We tried to clarify to the government the political situation from the time of Franco's dictatorship through the transition to the so-called democracy. We argued that there hadn't been real democracy in the Basque country. The Basque country could not accept democracy as it was in the rest of the country. . . . The will of the Basque people and the historical reality of the Basque country were not considered. We wanted to explain that the type of democracy the Basque people demanded was still pending." Once the Spanish government acknowledged this historical interpretation, then the two parties could work together to solve the armed conflict.[46]

The memories of the Spanish delegation differ slightly. When Etxebeste and Vera first met, Etxebeste sized up Vera and told him, "You're on our list," meaning marked for death. Vera shrugged it off, replying that the risk was all part of his job. Eguiagaray admitted that meeting the ETA members "was very tough. I had spent all of my life in the Basque country. My friends and colleagues had been killed by ETA. It was not very easy for me to meet with them, especially the two activists [from the Madrid cell] who had committed 'blood crimes.'"

Nonetheless, the Spanish succeeded in getting ETA to extend the two-week ceasefire to three months; Spain promised not to arrest ETA members during this time. Interestingly, Madrid hoped that an extended discussion might socialize the terrorists. "We were trying to get them accustomed to talking to government representatives. Then perhaps we could get them involved in a diplomatic process, then maybe they would see that they can talk to the government so that it would be harder for them to withdraw from the talks and return to violence."[47] Yet Etxebeste was hardly fooled. He knew that the Spanish were dragging their feet. "The government denied us legitimacy," he complained years later. "It wanted us to surrender. The government wanted to introduce dialogue to weaken the liberation movement, to create contradictions within the movement and to get us to surrender."[48]

Spain held about 600 ETA prisoners at this time, but the dilemma for Madrid was that ETA only wanted to talk about history and politics. Spain could not control the agenda. As Eguiagaray recalls, "They never wanted to talk about prisoners. They always deferred the topic whenever we put it on the table. We thought that they thought it was symbolic of ETA already being defeated. . . . The main point was for us to arrive at a moment when they would . . . discuss their members in prison. Unless we could talk with them about prisoners, there was no other basis for possible agreement. We could not talk about autonomy for the Basque country."[49]

Meanwhile, back home the Algiers talks led to increasing violence. As Etxebeste told me years later over tea in San Sebastián, each side wanted to demonstrate that it was "negotiating from strength." ETA increased street confrontations with the local authorities in the Basque country to show that it could always summon up forces to oppose the state. Did talking cause an escalation of the violence, then? Etxebeste: "Perhaps. But perhaps it also showed both parties that more effort was needed to overcome violence, since violence wasn't taking us anywhere."[50]

Eventually, the contradictions between ETA and the Spanish position proved untenable. After months of preliminary sparring, Etxebeste thought that the parties would shift to a second phase. "But when we moved to the details of how the political negotiations would proceed, they balked. As long as they had ETA in a truce and were not making any substantive concessions, they were happy to talk. But at the possibility of discussing Basque self-determination, the government pulled back."[51] This is essentially correct. ETA had proposed a joint statement in which it would agree to continue with the truce if the government admitted it was willing to negotiate political issues related to the Basque country. The Spanish government could never agree to this. Stymied in Algiers, the ETA leadership decided to break off the talks over Etxebeste's protest, announcing in April 1989 that "all fronts are open." Algeria expelled Etxebeste to the Dominican Republic, where he was placed under house arrest and monitored closely by Vera.

Again, some observers have argued that these negotiations and especially Iturbe's untimely death marked another missed opportunity for peace. Yet the parties directly involved in the talks disagree. When asked if a negotiated solution would have been possible if Iturbe had not died in a car crash, Etxebeste replied, "No. I can explain this very easily. . . . What I did afterward was continue what he would have done."[52]

Spanish officials also deny it was a missed opportunity, largely because the Algiers talks played out exactly as they expected. For Vera, it was primarily a means to influence French and Algerian policy and have the ETA members placed under close surveillance in friendly Latin American countries. The added benefit for the González administration was that when the talks failed, ETA got the blame.

After Algiers

Even after the failure of Algiers, the two sides did not lose complete contact. In 1992, Spain was scheduled to host the summer Olympics in Barcelona and the International Expo in Seville. Both events would provide a global stage for ETA's violence.

ETA was well aware of these opportunities and the negotiating leverage they presented. Etxebeste: "We knew we had this leverage. We offered a period of 'goodwill' as long as the government agreed to return to the agenda [i.e., political negotiations] in Algeria."[53] Vera and his colleagues were likewise aware of their potential vulnerability. They made sure not to signal to ETA that the situation conferred any advantage. They also asked the George H.W. Bush administration for security and counterterrorism assistance. And they secretly reengaged with ETA in the Spanish province of Navarre.

These talks were known only to a very tight circle of officials around González. José Maria Benegas, who participated in these covert talks, engaged in a bit of subterfuge to advance the government's agenda. Working through a Basque pacifist organization, he drafted a memo that outlined ETA's conditions for the talks—conditions that of course the Spanish government had already endorsed. These included those ETA members who should serve on the negotiating team, that the negotiating team ought to remain unchanged for the duration of the talks, that ETA would promise not to engage in any killings or bombings, and that there should be no public statement announcing that the two sides were talking. The document was sent to Etxebeste in the Dominican Republic without any evidence of the government's hand. Etxebeste adopted the advice as ETA's own.[54]

The two sides secretly met in Navarre. As the talks progressed, the González government promised to bring Etxebeste from the Dominican Republic to the United States for further talks. Spanish officials were dispatched to Santo Domingo, but to their surprise were told by the Dominican Republic that they would not be allowed to meet the prized houseguest. A new Spanish interior minister had undermined the plan. Opposed to the government meeting at all with ETA, he secretly told the Dominican Republic to block the meeting. Benegas uncovered the truth a few days later and briefed González, who was furious and pledged to try again in two weeks' time. Benegas explained the situation to ETA, but ETA decided to break off the talks anyway.[55]

Would Etxebeste's presence in the United States have made any difference? Again, it was highly unlikely that these talks would have produced any serious breakthroughs. ETA had still not fundamentally shifted its ultimate objective of Basque independence.

But Madrid had accomplished what it had set out to do. ETA did not spoil either the Barcelona or Seville spectacle. The group had successfully managed to plant a bomb in one of the Olympic buildings, but it was found and defused; Spanish authorities never acknowledged it publicly so as not to credit ETA.[56] Spanish security also dealt a severe blow to the group by arresting its three-man "Supreme Council" in the French town of Bidart only weeks before the start of the Olympics. In fact, Spanish security officers had been tailing the "Bidart-3" for six months before they moved in. According to Vera, "We wanted to arrest them as close to the opening of the Olympics as possible so that ETA would not have time to regroup."[57]

THE PERIOD OF LAW AND ORDER
1996–2004

Amid high unemployment and corruption scandals, Felipe González's 1996 re-election bid was defeated by José Maria Aznar, the leader of the conservative Popular Party (PP). Aznar and his team now adopted a new policy that rejected engagement and instead emphasized a tough law-and-order approach to dealing with ETA.

As Aznar described it to me over coffee at a Georgetown hotel, "When I took over, the general thinking was that it was impossible to have a police or military victory over ETA, that you needed to have intermediaries to conduct negotiations with terrorists, but under the table, it was possible to talk to terrorists." Aznar clearly rejected this approach. "I decided to put on the table a total battle against ETA, without exception."[58] This "total battle" also meant banning newspapers, youth groups, social clubs, and political parties that had connections with ETA.

An anecdote from this period highlights the sea change from the González to the Aznar administration. Aznar's national security adviser, Rafael Bardaji, recalled in amazement that the González administration had set up a hotline with ETA. "On my first day in office, I received a call from an ETA representative in France, offering to play the same role for my government as with the Socialists."[59] Bardaji terminated the hotline.

González's counterterrorism approach, where talks were seen primarily to collect intelligence and shape domestic and international perceptions, would clearly no longer do. The Aznar administration broke off all contacts with ETA. Aznar's perception was that "González never thought it was possible to defeat terrorism. I like to put terrorists in jail."

Indeed, Aznar was skeptical of negotiations, under almost any circumstances. "My personal approach is that any policy is appeasement if it means negotiating." The government should enter negotiations "only if a terrorist group is in failure, only if a terrorist group accepts the decommissioning of weapons and states that it renounces violence."[60] In other words, ETA would need to surrender before the Aznar government would be willing to talk.

According to former national security adviser Bardaji, "Aznar always thought we could solve ETA by force."[61] Yet despite their tough language and policies, within a few years after taking office, Aznar's team found itself in negotiations with ETA.

What accounted for this reversal?

THE BLANCO MURDER AND AFTERMATH

On July 10, 1997, ten days after Spanish authorities freed a prison official who had been seized by ETA and held captive for 572 days, ETA kidnapped a young Popular Party official, Miguel Angel Blanco, and threatened to kill him within 48 hours unless all of ETA's prisoners were transferred to jails closer to the Basque region. The countdown to the deadline mesmerized the public. Hundreds of thousands of people all across Spain protested ETA's action. The Aznar government refused to bend. Blanco's corpse was discovered after the deadline expired.

The Aznar government capitalized on the harsh anti-ETA backlash in the Basque country to support a new get-tough approach. (It also cleverly managed to condemn ETA while not disparaging legitimate expressions of Basque nationalism.) As a first step, the interior minister, Jaime Mayor, now reversed Vera's policy and requested the extradition to Spain of ETA members living overseas, like Eugenio Etxebeste. Etxebeste no longer needed to be kept available for negotiations if the government had no intention of talking.[62]

ETA responded to Aznar's policies by assassinating five Popular Party officials in the Basque country and other regions of Spain. But violence did little to increase ETA's support in the Basque country or bring independence any closer, so it adjusted its political strategy. Instead of trying to engage the central government, ETA now used its political wing, Herri Batasuna, to reach out to the leading Basque political party, the PNV, in the hopes of building a pan-Basque alliance. ETA's motivation at this time is still debated, but it appears that the group wanted to strengthen its negotiating position for future talks with the government by aligning itself with the Basque nationalist parties.[63]

Regardless of ETA's intent, the PNV welcomed these overtures for its own reasons. The PNV rejected Aznar's hard-line stance of no dialogue. No matter how illegitimate ETA's violence, the PNV believed that ETA was a radical manifestation of an underlying, unresolved political conflict that could be ended only through negotiation. It also never believed that ETA could be defeated militarily by the police and security forces because of the reservoir of unshakable social support ETA enjoyed (roughly 10 percent of the people) in the Basque country.[64] And since ETA had been created as an offshoot of the PNV, the PNV always believed it understood the terrorist group better than anyone else and might be able to wean them away from violence. "I was always in favor of talking," Xavier Arzallus, the *éminence grise* of the PNV, asserted to me in his Bilbao office. "ETA-PM gave up the armed struggle and we thought we could do the same with ETA-M."[65]

Other motives, both local and cynical, moved the PNV. Aznar's military defeat of ETA would harm the cause of Basque nationalism and diminish the PNV's political influence. Also, the PNV had entered into a coalition with Aznar's conservative Popular Party after the 1996 election, and worried about alienating its supporters on the left.[66] Working with ETA would solve that problem. Further, the "dirty secret" was that the PNV had used the specter of ETA's violence to wring political, financial, and other concessions from Madrid. (For example, the amount of per capita resources obtained from the Spanish state for the Basque region is almost two-thirds higher than the average resources obtained by other regions across Spain.[67]) For all these reasons, the interaction between PNV and ETA has been characterized as a combination of "conflict *and* collusion"[68]

Thus began a series of secret talks between the PNV and ETA. (The Aznar government was completely in the dark. It only learned of these talks after they were over, from a mid-level official in Catalonia.[69]) Initially, the PNV resisted talking directly with ETA members, instead opting to speak only with officials from Herri Batasuna. But Herri Batasuna did not have the authority to speak for ETA in these negotiations, and the PNV gradually found itself dealing directly with ETA.[70] According to José Luis Zubizarreta, a Basque nationalist politician involved in the talks, "It was like a seduction. . . . The PNV did not realize what was happening at the time. We thought that the police action and other steps by the Aznar administration had weakened ETA so much that the PNV could persuade ETA to end the struggle and join the PNV. But ETA thought that the PNV had been weakened because it had a terrible relationship with Aznar and the Popular Party."[71]

In this the PNV had badly miscalculated. Instead of bringing ETA in from the cold, ETA was intent on elbowing aside the PNV and placing Basque nationalism in service to ETA's agenda.

These secret talks produced two results. The Basque nationalist parties, including those associated with ETA, drafted the Estella Agreement, which was announced in September 1998. This Agreement was modeled on a Basque nationalist (mis)interpretation of Northern Ireland's Good Friday Agreement. It called for all the parties involved in the conflict to come together, with no preconditions, on the basis of mutual respect, to seek a negotiated political solution.[72] No Spanish government could agree to this.

The second result was ETA's public announcement, three days after the Estella Agreement, of a "general and indefinite" ceasefire. The announcement now publicly revealed ETA's strategic shift. Instead of addressing its demands to the central government, ETA now emphasized nationalist unity among all the Basque nationalist parties.

Yet the secret talks leading to ETA's September 1998 announcement should have raised red flags within the PNV about the wisdom of joining forces with ETA. ETA members had come armed to the meetings with the PNV and placed their revolvers on the table during discussions. At one of these meetings, ETA handed the PNV delegation a document and told them that they could review it but not make any changes. The document called for a "general and indefinite" ceasefire, the formation of a coalition including all the Basque nationalist parties, and the establishment of a new constitutional process where the PNV would leave the Basque legislative assembly and join a new "virtual" assembly representing the historic Basque nation.[73] ETA was demanding that the PNV abandon its substantial political power and official responsibilities and join instead a parallel parliament with neither political power nor responsibilities. The senior PNV official looked at the document and told ETA that it was "not living in reality." The proposal was unacceptable, "because it would be political suicide for the PNV."[74] ETA remained undeterred.

ETA's "General and Indefinite" Ceasefire

If the PNV had been fooled, it was now the Aznar government's turn to miscalculate. Perhaps because of the country's exhaustion and exasperation with ETA's violence, the group's declaration of a "general and indefinite" ceasefire raised public expectations that the conflict might finally be ending. After the arrest of the Bidart-3 and the tougher approach by the Aznar government, many believed that ETA was now looking for a way to end the violence and join the ranks of constitutional Basque nationalists.

Even some members of the Aznar government were not immune to these hopes. One of Aznar's closest confidants, Javier Zarzalejos, recalled, "We thought this was the beginning of the end. It triggered a sea change in public opinion."[75]

"ETA released a statement calling for a 'general and indefinite' ceasefire," Aznar later recalled. "Personally, I never believed them. But my problem was public opinion. The government had to be responsible. The government had to test ETA."[76] Zarzalejos concurs: "Aznar had to respond to the changed mood that had gripped the country and the extraordinary public expectations that ETA's statement had aroused. The government had to do something. The government could not simply appear adamant in its position not to talk."[77] Even the hard-line interior minister, Jaime Mayor, appreciated the domestic political realities, although he remained skeptical about what he termed ETA's "trap truce." "No one [in Spain] would understand if the Popular Party did not take this opportunity to see if ETA really was willing to end the armed struggle."[78]

Assessments by the government's intelligence services (the Guardia Civil, the Policía Nacional, and the Secret Service) also contributed to Aznar's about-face. Despite being ignorant of the ETA-PNV talks that led to the ceasefire announcement, the intelligence services "were certain that this was the end of ETA," according to Mayor. "The Guardia Civil and the Policía Nacional both thought that the combination of ETA's weakness and the social reaction to Blanco meant that this was the end."[79]

In fact, the intelligence assessment was considerably more complicated. The different intelligence units did not agree on ETA's intentions. One judged that ETA was weak and wanted to do a deal. As one senior official summarized this assessment, "Their arguments were very academic and logical but without any hard evidence." A competing judgment came from the intelligence unit of the

Guardia Civil, which argued that ETA was rearming and reorganizing itself. The contradictory assessments could not be reconciled.[80]

Had a crucial piece of information been known at the time, Aznar and his team may have decided not to engage with ETA at all. ETA's September 1998 announcement had used the word "indefinite." It was unprecedented, and was immediately seized upon by those who believed (and who dearly wanted to believe) that this time ETA was sincere about ending its armed struggle. It created the political pressure to which Aznar ultimately succumbed.

But "indefinite" had a very different meaning for ETA. "Indefinite" did not mean "forever" or "perpetual." It meant an uncertain amount of time, perhaps lasting as long as a few months.

The PNV, which had been in talks with ETA for months, knew at the time that ETA only intended to extend the ceasefire for up to four months and that the government and public at large had grossly misinterpreted ETA's announcement.[81] Yet for their own reasons, they remained silent. Though a coalition partner with Aznar's Popular Party, they did not inform anyone in the Aznar administration. Aznar and his senior officials only learned of this betrayal years later, when I told them during the fall of 2009. Needless to say, they reacted with shock, anger, and disappointment.[82]

Recalling the government's approach at this time, former interior minister Mayor told me, "We agreed to have 'testing negotiations' to see if the ceasefire was really indefinite. We had not negotiated the truce, so we needed to see for ourselves if it could be extended indefinitely. If this was the first time that ETA was saying that it was willing to stop the killing, then we had to test if this was possible."[83] Former national security adviser Rafael Bardaji stated, "We wanted just to test their willingness and sincerity. Just a first stage. No demands, very exploratory. No preconditions, no demands, no timetable." Aznar himself was crystal clear on their instructions: "I established one public condition: ETA had to give a total renunciation of violence, indefinitely. I never authorized a negotiation. Never, never."[84]

In late 1998, the government's three-man delegation met twice in the Basque region with representatives of Herri Batasuna. Nothing came of these meetings, except perhaps to convince the government that it needed to meet directly with ETA if it wanted an answer to Aznar's condition. In any event, Herri Batasuna officials refused to meet anymore with the government.

It took five months to set up another meeting. In the meantime, to keep prospects for talks alive and show Spanish society that his government was doing as much for peace as was democratically allowable, Aznar did something out of character: He appeared to surrender to one of ETA's long-standing demands. For years, ETA and the families of imprisoned ETA members had demanded that the prisoners be moved to jails closer to the Basque country to make it easier (and less expensive) for family visits. Aznar now agreed to move over a hundred ETA prisoners to jails closer to the Basque country, even though ETA was violating the ceasefire by repeatedly engaging in street violence. Aznar admitted, "There was some domestic political pressure. So I would move them from one jail to another, but not closer to the Basque region. It was a shell game."[85] Javier Zarzalejos is closer to the mark: "Basically, this was a public relations management exercise."[86]

On May 19, 1999, ETA and the Spanish delegation finally met in secret outside Geneva. Inevitably, the talks failed. ETA would not agree to any prearranged agenda. It had no sense of what Madrid could or could not discuss. According to Zarzalejos, who was a member of the Spanish delegation, "It was very difficult to talk to these people. They were out of touch with reality, living clandestinely, living in a world of their own." ETA made dramatic and wild claims, asking whether Madrid would revise its relationship to the Basque country, whether the central government was willing to accept the democratic will of the Basque people, and whether Navarre would be allowed to join with the Basque region.[87] All of these issues had either been decided or dismissed years earlier.

After the Geneva meeting, the Aznar administration issued a press release acknowledging the secret talks with ETA. This was due to Aznar's desire to demonstrate that he was in firm control of these talks and was not conceding to ETA's demands. The administration also wanted to differentiate itself from the lack of transparency and the "dirty war" of the González years.[88]

On November 28, 1999, ETA announced its return to the armed struggle. More than just a fourteen-month ceasefire had ended. "This period marked the end of an old hope that there was some room for ETA to evolve if the government of Spain could be generous and give ETA a way out," regretted Zarzalejos. "It was a lesson for the whole society."[89]

But the government was able to salvage some important counterterrorism benefits from this experience. Once the ceasefire had been announced, ETA members had relaxed their guard, which made them easier to identify and track.

With less day-to-day concern over bombs going off, the intelligence services were able to shift gears and focus more on understanding ETA's structure and organization. Spain improved its counterterrorism cooperation with France during and after the ceasefire; France now provided more information on ETA's movements. The Spanish government also received help from the Clinton administration in decoding ETA's encrypted messages.[90]

All this would prove useful, as ETA now recommitted itself to violence. Twenty-three people were killed in 2000, the highest total since 1992, and six hundred Basque policemen and security personnel were dispatched across Spain to guard a wide array of people thought to be under threat from ETA.[91]

AZNAR'S REELECTION AND THE POLITICAL PARTIES ACT

In March 2000, José Maria Aznar won a second term as prime minister, this time with an outright majority of seats in the Cortes. With ETA's rejection of further talks to end the conflict, with its surge in violence before the election, and with the opposition Socialist Party now proposing a new law that would unite all the political parties against terrorism, Aznar had the domestic political support to adopt even stronger measures against the group. The reaction to the 9/11 attacks on the Twin Towers also shifted the political landscape within Spain, across Europe, and globally.

The Aznar administration now decided to change its emphasis from strict security and policing measures to more rigorous legislation aimed at "drying up the social and financial sea in which ETA swims."[92] A few years earlier, Giovanni Falcone, an Italian magistrate who prosecuted the Sicilian Cosa Nostra, had introduced an innovative investigative technique based on tracking "the money trail" among the Mafia's many businesses. Now a Spanish judge, Baltazar Garzon, decided to adopt this approach and shut down and seize all the media, social, political, and financial assets of the ETA support network.[93]

Acting through the Cortes, Aznar expanded the legal reach of Garzon and the Spanish courts by passing the Political Parties Act in June 2002.[94] Garzon ordered the political wing of ETA (now called Batasuna) to cease all its activities and ordered the Basque parliament not to seat its members. When Basque parliamentarians refused, Garzon had them arrested.[95] In March 2003, the Supreme Court upheld the law banning Batasuna. This immediately shut down a significant source of ETA's funding, as Batasuna was channeling 8 to 10 million euros annually to ETA from public funds intended to support political parties.[96] Later that year, the Cortes toughened its penal code against those convicted of terrorism, extending sentences and requiring as a condition of parole that prisoners pay reparations to the victims of their crimes and cooperate with authorities in counterterrorism efforts.[97] According to the former national security adviser Rafael Bardaji, "By 2004, we were very close to putting an end to ETA."[98] More objective observers concurred: ETA "was socially and politically defeated by the beginning of the new century, even if its remaining leaders and members maintained the will and capacity to kill."[99]

THE PERIOD OF LOST ILLUSIONS 2004 TO THE PRESENT

On March 11, 2004, radical Islamists detonated ten bombs that killed 191 people and injured more than 1,700 others as the morning trains pulled into Madrid's central station. Aznar blamed ETA even as evidence suggested that responsibility lay elsewhere. Amid the resulting political uproar, four days later Spain elected as prime minister the Socialist leader José Luis Rodriguez Zapatero. He seemed determined to repeat the mistakes made by his predecessors and to ignore their lessons.

In November 2004, the Spanish media published a letter from six ETA prisoners that had been intercepted by the security forces. The prisoners rejected calls to launch a hunger strike and instead recommended that ETA should lay down its arms and adopt a political effort to engage in "the institutional and mass struggle." ETA's leadership formally dismissed their request and expelled the members from the organization.[100]

But a few days later, Batasuna, banned just the year before, was allowed to hold a political rally in the Basque town of San Sebastián. Its leader was Arnaldo Otegi, a former member of ETA-PM and then ETA-M after the split. He had spent eight years in prison before being elected a member of the Basque parliament. Otegi used the moment to announce a new political strategy. The so-called Anoeta Declaration proposed a peace process that would consist of two tracks: a political and legal track that would lead to a referendum in the Basque country on a new constitutional framework and a technical track that would have Spain and

France engage with ETA in talks covering "demilitarization, prisoners, refugees and victims."[101]

A few months later, Batasuna sent a letter to the prime minister claiming that it was not seeking a negotiation that would lead to independence for the Basque country. In May 2005, Zapatero publicly signaled that he was interested in starting a new dialogue. He intended to replace Aznar's tough law-and-order approach with a policy designed to end ETA through negotiations.

During the remainder of the year, Zapatero authorized the head of the Basque branch of the Socialist Party to meet with one of the most notorious of the ETA leaders, Josu Ternera, in Geneva and then in Norway. These talks resulted in ETA's declaration of a "permanent ceasefire" in March 2006. As part of the deal, the Spanish government would verify the ceasefire for six months and then begin a formal dialogue with ETA. Zapatero declared that this ceasefire statement was different from previous ones, largely because of the word *permanent* (this was similar to how hopes had been raised by the word *indefinite* in 1998).[102] In late June, the prime minister announced (well short of the six-month testing period) that he was ready to start a direct dialogue with ETA.

The talks ran into difficulties almost immediately. Despite the ceasefire, ETA continued its violence. The Spanish security forces continued to arrest ETA members; Otegi was briefly jailed. In the talks, ETA refused to discuss technical matters such as weapons decommissioning and prisoners until the political and legal track had started. By August, the incipient peace process had stalled and ETA had started to issue public threats.

The government and ETA met again in mid-December 2006. The two sides agreed to hold another meeting the following month. To encourage ETA to commit to a peace process, Zapatero decided to move ETA prisoners closer to the Basque country. (A prison at Santander was being refurbished to house another two hundred prisoners in anticipation of this move.[103]) On December 29, Zapatero felt confident enough to ask rhetorically at a news conference, "Are we better off now with a permanent ceasefire, or when we had bombs, car bombs and explosions? This time next year, we will be better off than we are today."[104] The very next day, ETA detonated a massive car bomb in the parking lot at Madrid's brand new Barajas airport, killing two Ecuadorian immigrants and causing tens of millions of dollars in damages. ETA assumed responsibility for the attack, then asserted that the ceasefire continued in effect, perhaps reflecting a confused leadership or divided lines of authority.[105]

Whatever ETA's motives, Zapatero had clearly misjudged the moment. He compounded his political difficulties by not immediately terminating the talks with ETA, saying only that they had been suspended, and by referring to the attack as a "tragic accident," not as the terrorist event it so obviously was. The leader of the opposition Popular Party ridiculed the prime minister: "What is your word worth after all this? You have been fooled by a pack of murderers."[106] The peace process formally collapsed in June 2007, when ETA announced the end of its ceasefire and vowed to "take action on all fronts to defend the Basque Country." The prime minister pledged to take all steps to defend the public's safety.[107]

Whether out of arrogance or ignorance or some combination of the two, Zapatero had clearly believed he could end the conflict. (Upon becoming prime minister, he had reportedly bragged to his aides, "I am the General now and ETA will surrender to me.") José Luis Zubizarreta remarked that the prime minister "had an information deficit and too much optimism. He was overconfident that he could solve the ETA problem. He thought he had a special gift, the golden touch."[108]

More charitably, the desire to bring an end to the national nightmare had caused the Zapatero administration (and many others in Spain) to ignore some of the hard lessons learned from the country's previous dealings with ETA. This was the triumph of hope over experience. The process he created was not transparent. He used Herri Batasuna representatives as intermediaries instead of dealing with ETA directly. He agreed to a dialogue along two tracks, with the political track suggesting that Madrid was willing to contemplate the transfer of sovereignty to the Basque country. He also used international mediators, especially veterans of the Northern Ireland peace process, who understood few of the realities of the Basque country. The talks would most probably have failed anyway, but the process raised the public's hopes and lowered chances for success.

Perhaps most of all, there was a sense that Zapatero's overtures had revitalized ETA at a time when the group was reeling after the Aznar years and the impact of the Political Parties Act. The former ETA-PM member and current Basque Socialist Teo Uriarte passed harsh judgment on the Zapatero experiment: "Zapatero restored ETA when they were down."[109]

Ironically, ETA's actions had undermined the most sympathetic prime minister the group had ever had. When I raised this point in the context of the Barajas airport bombing with Batasuna leader Arnaldo Otegi, he sighed and then admitted, "We've made many mistakes."[110]

CONCLUSION: CONFLICT REGULATION
VERSUS CONFLICT RESOLUTION

As this book goes to print, ETA's quarrel with the Spanish state enters its sixth decade. The terrorist group has been responsible for the deaths of more than 825 people. It counts around a hundred members today, scattered mostly across Spain's border with southwestern France. In recent years, Spanish authorities have routinely arrested ETA's senior leaders. Spain's prisons hold more than 450 ETA members; France holds another 160.

ETA's future prospects look bleak. Demographic trends across the Basque country indicate declining numbers of native Basque children. ETA can grow only by diluting the ethnic component of its ideology in the hope of attracting new members or by focusing on smaller and smaller cohorts who prize their Basque identity to the exclusion of all other allegiances. This inability to attract recruits has resulted in ETA's drafting new members from disaffected youth gangs with inadequate education; in other words, teenage thugs.

When combined with increasingly sophisticated, coordinated, and effective counterterror operations by Spanish and French authorities, this trend has meant that ETA has no mature political leadership capable of reformulating its ideology or reconsidering its mission. It is instead dominated by a younger and more violent leadership that gives little thought to longer-term strategy.[111] Although ETA has had several leaders capable of new thinking, the only political conversions in ETA's history have occurred while ETA members were serving long jail sentences.

Despite its organizational challenges, ETA still exacts a high price. The Basque government spends 225 million euros per year fighting ETA and protecting its officials and citizens—more than it spends on public housing. Not surprisingly, a 2008 survey in the Basque country showed that 98 percent of respondents favored ETA's dismantlement.[112]

Arguably, the moment of maximum danger for the Spanish state was the period of *transición*, when the state's new democratic institutions were still fragile. But this was also the time when ETA was racked by internal defections (ETA-

PM/ETA-M) and Madrid moved smartly to create greater opportunities in the Basque country for alternative, nonviolent expressions of Basque nationalism, culture, and identity, as well as to provide generous funding for greater economic and social well-being. Widespread government repression or the popular uprising predicted by ETA's spiral theory of action/authoritarianism/action never materialized. The question ETA has presented—whether terror would ever force Spain to cede sovereignty to the Basque country—has been answered. It won't. No Spanish government would do so, under any circumstances.

ETA's Strengths and Weaknesses

Any country afflicted by a terrorist or violent separatist group is to be pitied. But it is Spain's particular misfortune to have been saddled with a terror group that has been both exceptionally resilient and an extraordinarily poor negotiating partner.

Along with its propensity for violence, ETA's resilience may be its most distinguishing feature. It has refused to accept that Spain is too strong to be defeated militarily and too democratic to be destabilized. ETA has remained an active force despite the increasing sophistication and effectiveness of the Spanish security forces in hunting down its members, despite unprecedented and broadly shared prosperity across the Basque region, and despite the Spanish state's delegation of authorities to the Basque region to honor virtually all of the Basque people's claims to culture and identity. Its survival as Europe's longest-running terrorist group has been a wretched but impressive "accomplishment."

This accomplishment has been abetted by ETA's proximity to the French border. Although there is today greater cooperation from French authorities, aggressive enforcement against ETA members has been uneven. For example, Aznar complained that during his time as prime minister every arrest of an ETA member in France was provided by information collected by Spain and then presented to the French authorities.[113] Observed a knowledgeable Basque commentator in 2009, "[I]t is striking that more than twenty years after the French altered their asylum policy and the two governments began to cooperate more closely in the suppression of ETA, all of the group's senior structures and personnel continue to be located in France."[114]

Although ETA has survived, it has been a complete failure as a nationalist/ separatist movement. It has failed to wrest concessions over self-determination and independence from the Spanish government. It has failed to rally more than a marginalized minority of Basque society to its banner. In modern Spain, ETA's age-old dispute with constitutional Basque nationalists over autonomy versus sovereignty is increasingly devoid of real meaning for the average Basque. ETA's ideological rigidity—its all-or-nothing mentality—has rendered it irrelevant to the daily lives of the overwhelming majority of the Basque people, except for when it engages in periodic spasms of violence.

ETA has proved no more competent as a negotiating partner, suffering from inexperience, poor leadership, and inflexibility.

ETA has had repeated difficulties in even starting talks with Madrid, according to numerous Spanish and Basque officials from across the political spectrum. It has insisted on elaborate (and politically unacceptable) preparatory arrangements before meetings. It has resisted reaching a common agenda to frame the talks in advance. Its negotiators have not always been very sophisticated. It has suffered from a lack of institutional memory; this was especially apparent when it replaced negotiators during ongoing talks with the Zapatero administration, in December 2006. All the members of the organization have not always supported talking; some have advocated violence as the only pathway to success. The leadership has at times been unable to prevent these dissident members from subverting talks by resorting to violence. The leadership itself has had heavy turnover, hindering sustained and rigorous thinking about the group's goals. And ETA has not always been patient. It has sometimes ended its ceasefires and returned to violence before talks could fully play out.

It is important that there has been no political wing that could influence the men with guns. Within ETA, the political has always been subordinate to the military. ETA has always manipulated Batasuna and its predecessors. This has inhibited any evolution in ETA's thinking. According to Florencio Dominguez, "There has been no real ideological debate inside ETA for the past thirty years."[115]

But a deeper malaise troubles ETA: No one has the authority to determine that the pursuit of an independent and sovereign Basque nation should be altered or even abandoned. According to the Basque PNV politician Joseba Egibar, "They feel frightened. They get vertigo when they confront the history of the last fifty years. Who makes the decision to stop this historic mission? Who has the authority to take this decision?"[116] Again, Dominguez: "ETA doesn't have anyone like Gerry Adams, no one who is capable of thinking politically and flexibly and who also controls the military."[117] José Maria Benegas also noted the absence of an Adams-like figure: "We haven't been as lucky here as in Northern Ireland because we do not have someone like Gerry Adams who, with his authority, could tell the military wing to stop, that this has to end."[118] Without such a figure, it is unlikely that the disparate elements of the ETA enterprise—the military, Batasuna, prisoners and the association of prisoner families, and youth and other groups—can congeal behind some pragmatic modification of the group's traditional mission.

ETA thus finds itself unable to write a narrative of victory that can allow it to place in storage the ultimate dream of a Basque homeland. It cannot write an alternative to the *programa máximo*, or even summon the rationale for a pause to await a more propitious historical moment to reassert the quest for a Basque homeland. Until that moment, ETA is condemned to repeating the past, and repeating its past failures.

This accounts, at least partially, for why ETA continues to insist on nothing less than self-determination and full sovereignty for the Basque people. "We must still ask why ETA insists on defining their struggle in the most uncompromising and intransigent terms possible," wrote America's foremost expert on ETA, Robert Clark, over twenty-five years ago. "Why does ETA choose to struggle for goals that many people think are clearly impossible?"[119] For ETA, little has changed since then. It has consistently sought maximalist goals and refused to deviate from them, except for tactical time-outs in 1989, 1999, and 2005–6. As it plainly stated in an April 2000 communiqué, ETA does not aspire to a "peace process" but to a "process of nation-building."[120]

Hard Lessons Learned

Spanish governments have adopted a variety of approaches to try to eradicate ETA, involving at different times the use of extralegal force, enhanced security and policing, creative legislation, and direct engagement. Each has had its limited successes. But none has ultimately prevailed, at least not yet. The past fifty years thus provide some hard lessons.

First, talking to ETA has not worked. With the single exception of talks with ETA-PM in the late 1970s and early 1980s, engaging with ETA has not persuaded the group to modify or abandon its demands. Aside from tactical ceasefires, ETA has not reduced its violence. Each offer by Madrid to parley may even have reinforced ETA's view that violence works in bringing the government to the negotiating table. In the early years after Franco, ETA's terrorist violence in the middle of talks risked provoking a military backlash against the newly elected government and the new democratic institutions. In later years, it merely exposed and embarrassed Zapatero for badly overestimating ETA's willingness to compromise.

But talking produced some ancillary benefits. During the González years, engaging with ETA helped persuade Paris to extend greater cooperation in hunting down ETA cells inside France. It also allowed Rafael Vera to implement his plan with the Algerian government to ship ETA members to friendly Latin American countries, where Madrid could keep close tabs on them. For every Spanish government, talking to ETA allowed it to show the public that it was peacefully trying to resolve the conflict. The government could use the talks to shape public opinion by portraying ETA as the obstinate partner resisting a negotiated solution.

Not talking to ETA has not worked either, at least not yet. A purely military solution to the conflict is nowhere in sight. In recent years, ETA's leaders have been rounded up almost as soon as they ascend to the top spot. Despite these repeated blows, ETA persists. When leaders are arrested, they are replaced.[121] Calls by prisoners for disbanding the group are ignored.[122] The attempt to use the Political Parties Act to change the culture in the Basque region by rolling up ETA's supporting infrastructure has damaged the group but not eliminated it.

As one looks back over the history of talks with ETA, the depressing conclusion is that genuine opportunities to end ETA's violence have *never* existed. As long as ETA has clung to its *programa máximo* and Madrid has refused to entertain even the possibility of actual Basque independence from Spain (even indirectly through a local referendum), there has never been a chance for an end to the armed struggle. At most, there were opportunities to split off some elements of ETA from its most intransigent members. Opportunities also existed for Spanish authorities to learn more about ETA and its internal workings, sow mistrust among its members, infiltrate the group, and arrest and imprison its members. This was part of a larger counterterrorism approach. It was not reconciliation. This was conflict regulation, not conflict resolution.

The verdict of José Maria Benegas, who has spent an entire career trying to end ETA's existence, is sobering: "After the Franco years, we thought violence would be meaningless in a democracy. The government thought it could help ETA end the armed struggle. But we were mistaken. The more democratic Spain becomes, the more ETA kills."[123]

How Does ETA End?

I asked each person whom I interviewed how he thought Spain's decades-long struggle with ETA would end. Unsurprisingly, there was little consensus.

Former ETA members emphasized the need to continue talking. Arnaldo Otegi: "At the start, the problem is to understand our differences. First, there must be a level, a degree of trust. The other side must come to the negotiating table with goodwill. . . . We are at the end of a cycle and violence now has no use."[124] Eugenio Etxebeste, the chief ETA negotiator in Algiers: "Inevitably, sooner or later, we have to sit and talk with open minds and end this in a negotiated solution. It will take both sides."[125]

Former prime minister Aznar, on the other hand, believed that ETA could be eliminated through a tough and sustained law-and-order approach, citing Spain's success at eliminating other homegrown terrorist groups. The security and intelligence agencies must have the resources needed to perform their jobs, he maintained.[126]

But most politicians, officials, and counterterrorism experts favored a blended policy approach. They argued that Spain needs to continue weakening ETA, infiltrating its ranks, breaking the cycle of recruitment of young people, eroding ETA's social support in the Basque country, drying up its sources of finance, trying to identify and influence more moderate leaders (like Arnaldo Otegi), cooperating with Paris to eliminate sanctuaries inside France, and welcoming those ETA members willing to renounce violence and be socially reintegrated.

A negotiated solution will only be possible when ETA understands that it cannot win. The agenda should be limited to ETA renouncing the armed struggle and pledging itself exclusively to peaceful expressions of its political preferences. In return, the government could be magnanimous on the treatment of prisoners, with prisoner relocations, visitation rights, and paroles, pardons, and amnesties all being on the table. In time, Batasuna and perhaps some other social groups could be unbanned.

None of this is likely to happen anytime soon. ETA is today more distant than ever before from realizing its goal of an independent Basque homeland, even if it is still capable of violence. Its war has been lost but the battle continues. For the Spanish people, it means that the terror may be limited, it may be reduced, but tragically, it is unlikely to be eliminated anytime soon.

Reflecting on the past fifty years of ETA's struggle in July 2009, former ETA member Otegi admitted to me, "This is a structural problem. We don't know if there is a solution."

Sri Lanka

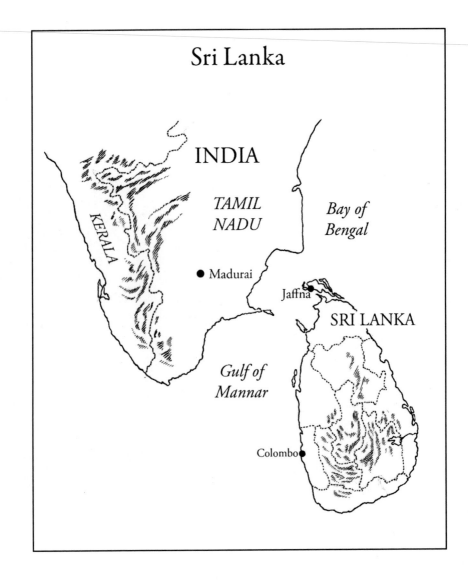

INDIA

KERALA

TAMIL
NADU

● Madurai

Jaffna

Bay of
Bengal

SRI LANKA

Gulf of
Mannar

Colombo●

3.

THE LIBERATION TIGERS OF TAMIL EELAM (LTTE)

For a country no longer at war, the security was impressive. Soldiers with automatic weapons stood at the entrance to the military compound in downtown Colombo, with others behind concertina-wired barriers and fortifications. After a credentials check and a brief phone call, my car was escorted by a military jeep to a ramshackle villa guarded by more soldiers. I got out of the car and entered a waiting room on the ground floor. A houseboy started up an overhead fan that did little to ease the oppressive afternoon heat and humidity.

The object of all this security was Karuna Amman, an ethnic Tamil and the former senior military commander for the Liberation Tigers of Tamil Eelam (LTTE), a terrorist and separatist group formed in the 1970s by Velupillai Prabhakaran. For more than twenty-five years, Prabhakaran's goal had been to carve from Sri Lanka an independent Tamil state in the northern and eastern provinces.

Karuna had joined the LTTE as a teenager soldier. Over the years, he has been accused of multiple war crimes and human rights abuses, including the slaughter of policemen, the ethnic cleansing of Muslims, the creation of death squads, and the recruitment of child soldiers. In March 2004, he left the LTTE with almost 6,000 fighters, forming a competing liberation group and dealing a heavy blow to Prabhakaran's claim that the LTTE was the sole representative of the Tamil people. Fighting between the two factions degraded the LTTE's ability to wage war on the Sri Lankan government. Eventually, battlefield setbacks caused Karuna to subse-

quently cast his lot with the government. After the LTTE's defeat in May 2009, Sri Lanka gratefully made Karuna the minister of national integration and reconciliation. For his betrayal of the LTTE and the cause of a Tamil homeland, a score of "Black Tiger" suicide bombers were reportedly still attempting to assassinate him.

After ten minutes, the houseboy guided me upstairs to Karuna's private "study." No books could be seen, only framed pictures of him posing with Sri Lankan politicians and a drinks trolley lined with bottles of Johnny Walker and Bailey's Irish Cream. He greeted me at the door, dressed in flip-flops and wearing a loose shirt opened to mid-chest. He shook my hand like an embarrassed teenager, his eyes cast downward, his grip weak and slightly damp. The luxuries of civilian life had drained his charisma and command presence.

We talked for an hour and a half, about why he first joined the Tamil Tigers and his life with them. Like many Tamils, he had left school and joined the insurgency after the anti-Tamil pogroms of July 1983. I asked whether the human rights charges against him were true. Unsurprisingly, he denied them all.

Then I asked why he had decided to leave the LTTE. He explained that he had become tired of all the fighting and thought that the government's offer for greater autonomy for the northern and eastern provinces was reasonable. He believed the LTTE should accept the compromise and end the war. But Prabhakaran was steadfast in demanding nothing less than an independent Tamil state. This led to a tense confrontation between the two leaders at a meeting of the LTTE's senior military, political, and intelligence officers at the group's secret jungle base camp. Prabhakaran called Karuna a traitor to the cause and compared him to Mahattaya, a former senior LTTE official who had also been labeled a traitor, then tortured for months and later executed.

When the meeting ended, Karuna had retreated to his assigned residence at the base. Fearing for his life, though, he sneaked out and hid in a different barracks. He used his cell phone to contact the international monitors who were supervising the ceasefire agreement then in place and asked them to send a helicopter as soon as possible. They told him one would not be available until the morning. After a sleepless night, he choppered out before Prabhakaran knew what had happened.

Karuna's portrayal of himself as a man of peace willing to risk his life by speaking truth to power was compelling. It was also a lie. According to numerous Sri Lankan officials, the government's offer of greater provincial autonomy came in 2002; Karuna didn't leave the LTTE until March 2004. Prabhakaran had accused *him of treachery not because of his support for a peace settlement, but because he thought Karuna had been stealing the group's funds. Karuna didn't leave because of his disgust at all the blood, violence, and human misery accumulated over more than two decades. Nor because he supported a compromise short of an independent Tamil state. He left because he feared for his own life.*

Our interview ended and I took my leave. Making my way downstairs, I noticed that his laundry had been hung out to dry on the wooden banister. My last impression was avoiding placing my hand on any of his damp, ready-to-wear dress shirts as I negotiated my way down the darkened stairway.

IN THE SPRING OF 2009, the Sri Lankan military offensive steadily moved north, tightening the noose around Velupillai Prabhakaran, his twenty-four-year old son and heir, Charles Anthony, their bodyguards, the LTTE's senior military leadership, and its depleted army, along with tens of thousands of civilian "human shields." By May, Prabhakaran was in desperate straits, down to a handful of dedicated and fanatical followers. Intercepted communications showed a series of frantic calls from Prabhakaran to his supporters all over the world, including those in Canada, Britain, Malaysia, Singapore, India, and the United States. That month a Sri Lankan Special Forces army unit tracked Prabhakaran down in a lagoon, where a single shot to his head—whether by soldiers or by his own hand is unknown—killed him. His dead body was carried on a litter, his low-riding camouflage military fatigues revealing plum-colored underwear. Karuna had accompanied the army unit to the front expressly for this moment—to identify Prabhakaran's body. Karuna had no doubt. The soldiers gathered around and took pictures with their cell phone cameras of the man responsible for inflicting so much pain and suffering on the country. They handed Prabhakaran over to Karuna's men, who stripped and desecrated his body, dragging it through the mud. The body was then burned and the ashes scattered.[1]

Few predicted that the LTTE, one of the most feared and innovative terrorist organizations in the world, would end like this, or even that it would end at all short of its declared goal of an independent Tamil homeland. Founded by Prabhakaran in May 1976 with a handful of men and weapons, it evolved into a ruthless, disciplined, and relentless armed movement, responsible for the deaths of tens of thousands of Sri Lankans, the ethnic cleansing of over 50,000 Muslims and Sinhalese, and the displacement of over one million people. The FBI has stated that its tactics "inspired terrorist networks worldwide, including Al Qaeda in Iraq."[2] Its cadres carried around their necks a vial of cyanide to be used in case any of them were about to be captured alive. Prabhakaran didn't invent the suicide bomber, but he pioneered its use, employing both male and female suicide bombers ("Black Tigers") and child soldiers ("Child Tigers"). The LTTE is the only terrorist group that has managed to assassinate two world leaders, India's Rajiv Gandhi and Sri Lanka's president Ranasinghe Premadasa, along with a host of other senior Sri Lankan political and military officials. It had its own navy and air force. At its height, it replicated the functions of a state, with its own courts, police force, tax system, motor vehicle registry, and health clinics over the island's northern and eastern provinces.

How had Sri Lanka reached this point?

For hundreds of years, the Tamils and Sinhalese (and Muslims and Christians) had largely managed to coexist peacefully on the island. When the British consolidated power over the island in 1815, the minority Tamils became the privileged class, and their higher levels of education gave them greater status and access to much-coveted government positions. Ethnic conflict was largely unknown until after Sri Lanka achieved its independence from the British in 1948.[3] In the following decades, the majority Sinhalese used the democratic system to correct the perceived historic injustices they suffered under colonial rule. The new legislation had the effect of discriminating against the Tamil community, especially with respect to education, land reform, and government jobs (for decades, no Tamil youths were recruited into the military and few into the police service).

With political and legal options blocked for any redress of the Tamils' legitimate grievances, by the early 1970s more and more Tamil nationalists had taken to militancy to express their demands for a separate state.[4] Periodic eruptions of mass rioting by Sinhalese against the Tamils caused further alienation and sparked calls for retribution. In May 1976, Tamil politicians called for the nonviolent creation of a separate Tamil state, but flirted with the use of extraconstitutional violence to attain it. Sinhalese nationalists balked at even small concessions of greater regional autonomy, fearful that they might eventually lead to the breakup of the state and the creation of a single Tamil nation that would include the 60 million ethnic Tamils living in the southern Indian state of Tamil Nadu just a few miles across the water. (For this reason, the Sinhalese have been called "a majority with a minority complex.")

Yet the conflict was always more complex than a simple ethnic antagonism. Divisions of caste, social class, and regional origin existed within the Tamil community; there were also the distinctive "Hill Country" Tamils who worked the tea plantations. If these Hill Country Tamils are included, then more Tamils lived outside of the northern and eastern provinces claimed as the group's historic "homelands" than lived inside them. In the eastern province, Sinhalese and Muslims significantly outnumbered Tamils.[5]

The Sinhalese and Tamils may have worked out their differences over time through peaceful means. But the "Black July" 1983 riots against the Tamil community ended that possibility, irretrievably radicalizing a generation of angry and desperate Tamil youths. The immediate trigger was the Tamil Tigers' ambush and killing of thirteen Sinhalese soldiers in the northern city of Jaffna, the traditional capital of the Tamils. The army brought the soldiers' mutilated bodies back to Colombo for a public funeral, which unhinged the crowd that had gathered at the cemetery. Amid the ensuing rioting, looting, and general mayhem in Colombo and other cities, it was clear that elements in the government had prepared for this moment to terrorize the Tamil community and destroy their homes and businesses. In other words, it was less spontaneous riot than organized pogrom. Police and security forces either colluded in the violence or stood by and did nothing; famously, fifty-three suspected Tamil terrorists were murdered while in a maximum-security prison. The president did not declare a curfew until the worst of the rioting was over. When he finally addressed the country four days later, he did not condemn the anti-Tamil violence or express sympathy for the victims. Estimates of those killed ranged from 200 to 2,000, with about 100,000 made homeless.[6]

In the wake of Black July, the Sri Lankan government declared emergency rule and banned the main Tamil opposition party from parliament. It amended the constitution to outlaw any party from advocating succession or separatism from Sri Lanka. Tamils were now disenfranchised; political discourse evaporated. The exodus of Tamils from the southern provinces to the north in the wake of the riots reinforced Tamil identity and intensified the desire for an independent homeland.

The impact of the riots was also felt beyond Sri Lanka's shores. Regionally, the emigration of 150,000 refugees from Sri Lanka to Tamil Nadu forged tighter links between the two communities. India's prime minister, Indira Gandhi, seeking to win the votes of the Indian Tamils, decided to champion the Tamil cause by providing not only humanitarian assistance to the refugees, but also arms and training to the Tamil militants through Delhi's foreign intelligence agency, RAW (Research and Analysis Wing). India also calculated that Sri Lankan leaders would never negotiate seriously with the Tamils unless the Tamils were to pose a threat to the government. Empowering the militants was one way of providing that leverage.[7] The LTTE could now use Tamil Nadu as a rear-echelon training-and-staging area for its cadres, and for raising funds and procuring weapons.

With the influx of southern Tamils and the promise of arms and training, the LTTE transformed itself over the next few years from a local gang with less than 600 cadres to a potent terrorist organization with over 10,000 members.[8] Prabhakaran used this growing strength to methodically intimidate and elimi-nate his rivals in a violent frenzy of "revolutionary consolidation," reducing an alphabet soup of forty-two different Tamil separatist movements to a single orga-nization: the LTTE. Inside Sri Lanka, hit-and-run attacks and random roadside bombings now gave way to well-organized massacres of Sinhalese Buddhists and sophisticated attacks on Colombo's international airport and Central Telegraph Office. Prabhakaran's unrestricted use of terror escalated tensions between the Sinhalese and Tamil communities, hardening Sinhalese attitudes and enraging the Sri Lankan military, which started viewing every Tamil as a terrorist.

In this spiral of violence, an increasing number of Tamils, especially the tens of thousands of ethnic Tamils who had fled Sri Lanka, saw the LTTE as their champion and protector, and believed that true security could only be achieved through the creation of a separate state of Eelam. This Tamil diaspora—in India, Southeast Asia, Australia, Europe, Canada, and the United States—would become an influential source of political and financial support for Prabhakaran during the following decades.

Yet as the LTTE's bloodletting escalated, India started to rethink its earlier pursuit of electoral votes. An independent Tamil state carved out of Sri Lanka would create an uncomfortable precedent and would pose grave risks to India's national unity. Delhi was already battling its own secessionist movements, most notably in the strategically crucial states of Jammu and Kashmir. A Tamil state would boost Tamil pride and identity and would encourage Tamil Nadu to merge with Sri Lanka's northern and eastern provinces to form a "greater Eelam." The Tamil militants were also gradually wearing out their welcome in Tamil Nadu, engaging in a variety of violent and criminal behavior. For its own narrow purposes, India decided it needed to rein in the militants and shore up the fragile unity of the Sri Lankan state.[9]

In July 1985, India ordered the parties to come to Thimpu, the capital of Bhutan. The Tamil side proposed what became known as the four "Thimpu principles"—recognition of the Tamil nation, of the existence of an identified Tamil homeland, of the right of Tamil self-determination, and of the right to citizenship for all Tamils. The Sri Lankan delegation declared the first three demands "wholly unacceptable," as they would mean Colombo's official capitulation to the creation of an independent Tamil state.[10] As a counteroffer, it insisted as preconditions to any agreement that the militants renounce violence and decommission their weapons. A few weeks later, the Tamil side walked out of the talks, blaming the Sri Lankans and angering their Indian hosts.[11]

Although short-lived and unsuccessful, the Thimpu summit exposed a number of themes that would play out in later talks between the Sri Lankan government and the LTTE. At Thimpu, a third party tried to extract concessions from the Sri Lankan government and then tried to sell them to the Tamil parties. The unbridgeable dilemma was that the most Colombo could offer was insufficient to satisfy even the LTTE's minimum demands. The Colombo government could not accept an independent Eelam.

Thimpu also revealed that the Tamil militants were just as inflexible and impervious to external pressure as the Sri Lankan government. India had armed, financed, trained, and protected the Tamil rebels for the past two years. Further, Delhi had ordered Colombo to restrict its forces to their barracks during the ceasefire. (The LTTE used this opportunity to mine all the roads leading in and out of the military camps.[12]) But despite their massive debt to India, the Tamil militants refused to compromise their core goal of a separate Tamil state. Their refusal exposed the contradiction at the heart of India's policy of supporting an armed separatist group without supporting the creation of a separate Tamil state.[13]

After Thimpu, the conflict resumed with greater intensity, carnage, and civilian atrocities by both the LTTE and government forces. In late May 1987, the government launched a coordinated land, air, and navy assault code-named Operation Liberation to rid the north of the LTTE once and for all. As Sri Lankan forces routed the LTTE and laid siege to the northern city of Jaffna. India became alarmed at the unfolding humanitarian crisis and the potential for domestic unrest in Tamil Nadu. In early June, the Sri Lankan navy stopped a flotilla of Indian fishing boats from reaching Jaffna with 38 tons of food and other relief items. The next day, Prime Minister Rajiv Gandhi authorized an airdrop of supplies, disregarding Sri Lanka's sovereignty.[14]

Over the next few weeks, Rajiv Gandhi and his Sri Lankan counterpart, President J. R. Jayewardene, engaged in secret negotiations to settle the conflict. (Many of the terms and conditions had in fact been discussed the year before, when the two parties tried to reach an agreement but failed.) Jayewardene knew he had little negotiating leverage. India had already threatened to invade his country if Sri Lanka had tried to intercept India's airdrop of food supplies. India could also rearm the LTTE anytime it chose. (In fact, RAW had already started doing so.)

On July 29, the two leaders announced the signing of the Indo–Sri Lankan Accord. The Accord provoked a strong reaction among Sinhalese nationalists, who rioted in Colombo and its suburbs at the infringement of the country's sovereignty.[15] The prime minister and other officials refused to attend the welcoming ceremonies for Rajiv Gandhi, who was attacked by a Sinhalese soldier while reviewing a Sri Lankan honor guard.

Although the Accord acknowledged the "unity, sovereignty and territorial integrity" of the Sri Lankan state, the key concession was Colombo's agreement to merge the northern and eastern provinces, which the text described as "areas of historical habitation" of the Tamils. Further, this arrangement would be made permanent, subject to a referendum a year later. Less controversially, the Tamil language was granted official status. The Accord also stipulated that hostilities would cease within 48 hours; 72 hours after that, the LTTE cadres would disarm and the Sri Lankan military would withdraw to its barracks. India would end its support for the LTTE and repatriate all militants from Tamil Nadu. A joint Indo–Sri Lankan observer group would monitor the end of hostilities, and an Indian peacekeeping force (IPKF) would help enforce the ceasefire.[16] From Jayewardene's perspective, the real prize was getting Delhi's help in disarming the Tamil militants.

The Indo–Sri Lankan Accord was a failure in almost every way.[17]

Curiously, the LTTE had not been a party to the agreement. Before the Accord was signed, India had flown Prabhakaran to Delhi to meet personally with Gandhi to win his support. At the meeting, the Indian prime minister promised Prabhakaran that the LTTE would receive 5 million rupees

($300,000) per month, that it would dominate the merged northeast legislative council, and that no one from competing Tamil groups would be represented on the council.[18]

Apparently, Prabhakaran acquiesced to the agreement, or agreed to it on a temporary basis, or accepted it as the price he had to pay to leave Delhi and be returned to Jaffna; subsequent accounts differ. Gandhi may have had his doubts about Prabhakaran's commitment, as he felt the need to reassure Jayewardene afterward that the Indian army would disarm the LTTE if Prabhakaran reneged on his word.[19] Sure enough, within days Prabhakaran had denounced the Accord, calling it an "act of betrayal" and claiming that he could never accept anything less than a separate state of Tamil Eelam.[20]

In early October, Prabhakaran underscored his opposition when the LTTE ambushed an Indian patrol and "necklaced" five Indian commandos by placing burning tires over their heads. This brutal event announced the start of a guerrilla war. For the next three years, the Indian presence grew from a few thousand peacekeepers to a military force of over 100,000 at its peak. Local resistance grew as the IPKF struggled to wage a counterinsurgency war with an ill-defined mission, inadequate training, and poor knowledge of the language and local terrain. The IPKF faced the same challenge as the Sri Lankan military in distinguishing between civilians and LTTE guerrillas. Instead of protecting the Tamils, its forces ended up killing many of them.

The IPKF failed to either disarm the LTTE or destroy it. But it came close. The IPKF's overwhelming numbers, as well as its creation of a proxy Tamil National Army, threatened to squeeze and eliminate the LTTE. A desperate Prabhakaran turned for help to the new Sri Lankan president, Ranasinghe Premadasa, whose election campaign had called for the IPKF to leave Sri Lanka and for the government and the LTTE to forge a purely national solution to the conflict. In April 1989, Premadasa declared a ceasefire against the LTTE. In May, a senior LTTE delegation was invited to Colombo and housed in the Hilton Hotel. The talks resulted in Premadasa releasing LTTE prisoners, including convicted terrorists, and closing army camps in the northern province. More important, Premadasa agreed to covertly supply Prabhakaran with funding, arms, ammunition, and equipment for the LTTE to use against the Indian-backed Tamil National Army.[21] The secret deal soon leaked out, infuriating the Indians and hastening their withdrawal.

After losing more than 1,200 soldiers, the IPKF finally left Sri Lanka in March 1990. For India, the final tragedy came the following year, when a young female suicide bomber sent by Prabhakaran placed a sandalwood garland around the neck of Rajiv Gandhi at a campaign rally outside Madras. She then detonated her explosive vest, killing herself, Gandhi, and sixteen others.

Prabhakaran emerged as the uncontested winner from India's intervention. He had outwitted and outmaneuvered his adversaries; he had manipulated and betrayed his erstwhile allies. He could now claim to have defended the Tamils against the Indian invaders and defeated "the fourth largest army in the world."[22] After the IPKF left, "with almost no effort the LTTE improved its position by taking possession of large stockpiles of sophisticated weapons and supplies" while Sri Lanka's troops were confined to barracks.[23] Prabhakaran now controlled the northern and eastern provinces, roughly one-third of the country. In addition, the government's moral authority to fight the LTTE had been severely compromised by Premadasa's sordid arms deal. Within a few months, the LTTE broke off talks with the government and resumed the war. It continued its "killing of Tamil dissidents and drove out and killed Sinhalese and Muslim civilians in the north and east in its quest to create a mono-ethnic Tamil separate state."[24] Over the next few years, LTTE suicide bombers assassinated the defense minister, the navy chief, the national security adviser, and President Premadasa himself.

By the early 1990s, the lessons from the Thimpu talks, the Indo–Sri Lankan Accord, and Premadasa's backchannel dealings with the LTTE were plain for all to see. These failed policies had foundered on a number of erroneous assumptions, but none more central than the gross misjudgment of Prabhakaran's character, his messianic obsession with an independent Eelam, and his brutal authoritarianism. He had refused to play the role of Gandhi's client or Premadasa's partner. He could not be co-opted, marginalized, or sidelined. He stamped out dissent and murdered political and military rivals. He was a serial human rights violator who employed human bombs to terrorize. No one could be under any illusion that he was a partner for peace.

And yet negotiating an end to the conflict remained politically popular with an electorate bludgeoned and exhausted by the war and seemingly out of other options. If defeating the LTTE militarily appeared impossible, and surrendering to Prabhakaran's idea of a separate Eelam was unimaginable to the Sinhalese majority, then voters would rally behind the party that could promise to

ism industry. The following year, the LTTE used another truck bomb to try to topple the twin-towered World Trade Center in downtown Colombo. All the while, the LTTE continued to assassinate political opponents and murder ordinary Tamils, Sinhalese, and Muslims.

Despite some battlefield victories, the Sri Lankan military performed poorly. It had no coherent military strategy or doctrine. According to an American military analyst, "leadership was generally indifferent, morale often poor, equipment inadequate and overall numbers insufficient for the task. . . . The Tigers smuggled in arms with relative ease (and captured significant quantities from the government), while expanding their forces and inflicting several severe—and severely embarrassing—catastrophes on their opponents," such as when they overran the army base at Mullativu on the northeastern coast and killed over 1,400 soldiers.[30]

Infighting and corruption among the generals also played a role. Lucrative arms deals lined the pockets of the senior military, while shortchanging frontline soldiers. In 2000, an estimated $80 to $120 million out of an annual defense budget of $800 million was reportedly diverted as kickbacks to politicians and military officers.[31] Kumaratunga was alleged to have complained, "Give me ten honest generals and then I'll win the war!" She spoke with special knowledge, as her own uncle was chief of the army. She once called him "the most corrupt man in my government."[32] Meanwhile, over 20,000 soldiers deserted.

During late 1999 and in 2000, government forces suffered a number of setbacks to a resurgent LTTE, especially in two battles that came to be known as the "Vanni Debacle," where the Tigers recovered over 1,000 square kilometers of territory, and the "Elephant Pass Debacle," which isolated over 40,000 soldiers from a land route to the mainland.[33] The military's attempt to clear the main supply route to Jaffna in Operation Victory Is Assured had failed miserably, with Karuna chasing its forces back toward Colombo. The LTTE's attack in July 2001 on the air force base adjoining Colombo's international airport (destroying both military and commercial planes) showed once more its ability to bring the fight to the south and weaken the country's already fragile economy. For the first time since independence, in 2001 Sri Lanka experienced negative economic growth of −1.4 percent.

Even with the Sri Lanka military's shortcomings, the LTTE was not strong enough to prevail. The two sides descended into a bloody war of attrition and stalemate. By the end of the 1990s, the international goodwill that had initially greeted President Kumaratunga in 1994 had evaporated. Colombo now had to be concerned that foreign aid donors would condition developmental assistance on the government's willingness to reengage the LTTE diplomatically. Sri Lanka contacted the Norwegians to reach out to the LTTE and help end the conflict.[34] Norway was selected because there was a domestic political consensus that it was already familiar with Sri Lanka as it had engaged in development projects in the south, it was not a large or powerful state with significant geopolitical interests of its own, and it had experience in peace processes in different parts of the world.

Despite Norway's shuttle diplomacy, the government and the Tigers quickly reached an impasse. Prabhakaran immediately requested a deescalation of hostilities leading to a ceasefire, probably trying to husband his group's strength and lock in the existing "military balance" that favored the LTTE.[35] The government preferred to start talks without stopping the war, wanting to recover territory and strengthen its bargaining position. In July 2001, Kumaratunga appealed to her political opponents to form an all-party government to address the national crisis. They refused. The following month, she announced that the government was willing to enter into a ceasefire. This time the LTTE refused. In early December, the opposition party won a comfortable majority in parliamentary elections by campaigning on a promise to bring peace to a weary country after six long years of war. Ranil Wickremasinghe became prime minister.[36] Prabhakaran and Wickremasinghe each declared a unilateral ceasefire before the month was out.[37] With the full backing of the Norwegians and support of the international community, Colombo now began its most serious and sustained diplomatic effort to bring an end to the conflict.

With Norway's assistance, the two parties drafted and agreed to a formal Cease Fire Agreement (CFA) in February 2002.[38] The CFA was no doubt a good-faith attempt to bring an end to hostilities so the two parties could work out a more permanent political solution. But both the process and the substance raised serious concerns.

Procedurally, the government and the LTTE were not on equal footing when it came to drafting text. The Norwegians first presented drafts to the LTTE and worked out agreed language. The Sri Lankans then had to react to this text. The Sri Lankan officials complained about the undue haste with which the agreement went forward.[39] This process would be repeated during the next few years, with the Norwegians faxing documents to the LTTE first for its approval and only afterward sending them on to Colombo. In practice, this may not have posed much of a problem. Sri Lanka's intelligence service had the ability to intercept Norway's faxes to the LTTE.[40]

A more serious procedural shortcoming was Norway's decision to lead the Sri Lanka Monitoring Mission (SLMM), which would oversee implementation—and catalogue violations—of the CFA's provisions. This created an inherent conflict of interest with Norway's other role: to advance the peace process. It would open Norway to charges that it was overlooking or minimizing ceasefire violations so the parties could remain at the negotiating table. Sri Lanka, the LTTE, and India had all pushed for Norway to wear both hats. Norway initially resisted, but finally relented. It should have resisted more strongly.[41]

Substantively, the CFA contained provisions that inclined toward the LTTE. Sri Lanka's armed forces would disarm all non-LTTE paramilitary groups, leaving these communities to Prabhakaran's mercy. LTTE members would be allowed to perform "political work" freely across the northern and eastern provinces, but government troops and officials were not accorded the same right in LTTE-controlled territory. There was no language preventing the LTTE from importing weapons to rearm its cadres. The CFA was silent on the issue of child recruitment.

Sri Lanka's peculiar constitutional arrangements further complicated the government's ability to manage the peace process. Under the Sri Lankan system, Prime Minister Wickremasinghe had the authority to conduct the negotiations. But President Kumaratunga was commander in chief of the armed forces. Moreover, one year after the December 2001 parliamentary elections, Kumaratunga had the constitutional authority to dissolve the parliament at any time, effectively sacking Wickremasinghe, and call for new elections.

What made this "cohabitation" arrangement poisonous, however, was that these two politicians were long-standing and bitter personal rivals from opposing political parties. Consequently, the prime minister refused to allow the Defense Ministry or Service Chiefs to scrub the draft CFA for fear that they would provide the information to Kumaratunga, who would then criticize the prime minister and subvert the peace effort. The lack of Defense Ministry expertise in the process was one reason for the CFA's unrealistic time frames for deconflicting forces, which led to difficulties later. This segregation of information would continue throughout the peace process, with ministers not sharing information or conferring with each other between rounds. The mistrust and dysfunction from this "ferocious cohabitation war" would plague the government's peace efforts with the LTTE.[42]

More significant than the government's internal problems, the LTTE had given no indication that it had modified its ultimate objective; quite the contrary. At an international media event on April 2, 2002, Prabhakaran reemphasized his commitment to a separate Eelam and reconfirmed his instructions for his cadres to shoot him if he ever surrendered his demand for an independent Tamil homeland.[43]

Nonetheless, Norway was able to initiate a peace process that would allow the CFA to take hold and the two sides to address their substantive differences. Starting in September 2002, the parties met six times over the next year, in Thailand, Norway, Germany, and Japan.[44] At the first round, held at a Thai naval base, the LTTE's head of delegation, Anton Balasingham, sounded encouraging notes by suggesting that the Tigers would be agreeable to a federal model and to entering "the democratic, political mainstream."[45] In his annual Heroes Day speech on November 27, honoring LTTE members who had died for the cause, Prabhakaran endorsed the concept of power-sharing within a single state.[46]

A few months later, at the December 2002 meeting in Oslo, the talks reached their high-water mark. Both parties formally agreed "to explore a solution founded on the principle of internal self-determination founded in areas of historical habitation of the Tamil-speaking peoples, based on a federal structure within a united Sri Lanka." At last, here was the elusive formula that would grant the Tamils substantial autonomy, but within a single country.

It was not to be. Almost immediately reports circulated that Prabhakaran was furious with Balasingham for agreeing to the communiqué. Government negotiators noticed that Balasingham was under great pressure; at one point in the talks, he drew a line across his neck, indicating that his throat would be cut if he discussed some of the core issues on the government's agenda. His role subsequently appeared to be diminished in developing the LTTE's negotiating strategy.[47] The LTTE spent the next year attempting to reverse the implications of the communiqué.

The parties convened for three more rounds of talks during the first quarter of 2003. Yet a review of these negotiations reveals more movement than progress. Perhaps fearing the imminent demise of the talks, the Norwegians energetically tried to construct an interlocking web of committees, subcommittees, and working groups, replete with outside experts and confidence-building measures, in the hope that procedural dynamism could somehow compensate for the LTTE's aversion to discuss substance. Or in the hope that with enough time, the Tamil Tigers might grow to appreciate the political and economic advantages of a genuine peace process.

The approach didn't work. In April 2003, the LTTE unilaterally withdrew from the peace talks "for the time being," ostensibly because its officials were not invited to a meeting later that month in Washington that would prepare the parties for a Donors Conference in Tokyo in June. (The LTTE knew that the United States would deny entry to Balasingham and others on the delegation because they belonged to a U.S.-deemed Foreign Terrorist Organization.)

Whatever the true reason, Balasingham explained that the delegation withdrew because the LTTE was facing the "excessive involvement of the 'international custodians of peace' in the negotiating process," and that their "interlinking political pressure with economic assistance" was creating an imbalance in the talks in Colombo's favor.[48] In other words, the LTTE feared what it termed a "peace trap"— that it would be pressured by the United States, Japan, and others into making political concessions.

The timing of the walkout revealed that the LTTE would not adjust its behavior even to gain access to the billions of dollars in reconstruction and rehabilitation funds that would be pledged by the Donors Group.[49] The donor countries conditioned release of any funds on the LTTE's renouncing terror and a final settlement that enshrined human rights, the rule of law, and democratic principles. And the government, not the LTTE, would decide where the funds would be allocated and which projects would be funded. These preconditions the LTTE could not accept. Better that the Tamils in the northern and eastern provinces not receive any funds at all than Prabhakaran have to modify the LTTE's behavior and relax his iron grip over the two provinces.

Although formal talks were suspended, the two parties remained in touch via the Norwegians. During the next few months, the Sri Lankan government passed a number of proposals to the LTTE for the economic reconstruction and development of the northern and eastern provinces. The LTTE rejected them all.[50] But in late October, the LTTE responded with its own plan, which it termed an Interim Self-Governing Authority (ISGA). The two provinces would be merged, the LTTE would exert complete control over administration, and an election formula would allow the two provinces the right to declare independence after five years.

The ISGA was a blueprint for a separate sovereign state in the north and east of the country, not a formula for power-sharing within a single state.[51] It was a transparent attempt to rectify Balasingham's "error" in agreeing to the Oslo communiqué and to roll back the LTTE's commitment to a Tamil homeland within a unitary state.

For President Chandrika Kumaratunga, Wickremasinghe's bitter political rival, this was too much. She had long believed that the prime minister had been too conciliatory in the peace talks, which had allowed the LTTE time to regroup and rearm.[52] She saw the ISGA as the first step toward an independent state. While the prime minister was visiting the United States in early November 2003, she launched a "constitutional coup," removing three cabinet ministers, including the minister of defense, and replacing them with officials from her own party. Ten days later Norway suspended its facilitating role, citing the disagreement between president and prime minister. The peace process was over.

What had gone wrong?

In retrospect, it is hard to unravel all the motivations and assumptions that lay behind Prime Minister Ranil Wickremasinghe's policy toward the LTTE. But it appears he had three broad goals: to arrange a ceasefire and initiate a peace process that would lead to the negotiated end of the conflict, to launch an ambitious economic reform program that would create jobs nationwide, but perhaps especially for unemployed youth in the northern and eastern provinces, and to enlist international political and financial support for both of these policies.

Wickremasinghe's approach was based on a few assumptions. The first assumption—widely shared among the country's other politicians, the military, and the people—was that the decades-long war against the LTTE was militarily unwinnable. Just before he became prime minister, the armed forces had suffered severe reversals at Elephant Pass and the Vanni, while the country's main air force base had been heavily damaged. The LTTE were skilled, highly motivated, battle-hardened, and tenacious fighters. They were an adaptable force that could wage conventional war in the north, guerrilla war in the east, and a terrorist campaign in the south, and were funded by criminal activities and a passionate diaspora. Government forces, on the other hand, were often poorly led and equipped. They were tactically incompetent and strategically inept. Moreover, history did not favor the government: Few insurgencies had ever been defeated militarily. Influential members of the international community—including the United States, India, Norway, and Japan—subscribed to this same assumption.[53]

Wickremasinghe's second assumption was that the peace process and economic development were mutually reinforcing—progress in one would positively impact the other. As the government's chief negotiator in the peace process, G. L. Peiris, explained, "The negotiation process was going to engender an atmosphere of peace, which would energize the economy and encourage investment . . . economic development and the peace process couldn't be disentangled—they're two sides of the same coin."[54] With a liberal economic plan entitled "Regaining Sri Lanka" that aimed for 10 percent annual growth, Wickremasinghe hoped that more jobs would alleviate youth resentment and temper their susceptibility to Tamil extremism. Even a short period of relative peace would be a welcome respite for a battle-fatigued country and allow the economy to recover.

The prime minister's third assumption was that the involvement of foreign powers would increase the chances for success in the CFA and peace talks. By inviting first the Norwegians as facilitators and monitors, and then the Donors Group, led by Japan, the United States, Norway, and the EU, he wove what he termed "an international safety net." Their involvement would pressure the LTTE to honor the ceasefire and show more flexibility in the peace talks. An international audience could also offer financial inducements to encourage progress, while threatening to withhold benefits for bad behavior. Should the peace talks fail and the parties go back to war, Colombo would have powerful witnesses to its commitment to peace as a counter to the LTTE's propaganda.

All three of these strands came together in the prime minister's strategy. Since the prevailing view was that the LTTE could not be defeated militarily, Wickremasinghe had only two options: surrender or negotiation. Under no circumstances could any Sri Lankan government contemplate the breakup of the state, so the prime minister engineered a framework that promised a potential pathway to peace. The hope was that as long as the CFA held and the peace talks continued, economic development could take place. With new jobs, fewer young Tamils would want to join the LTTE. The international safety net of states would pledge funds and backstop the Colombo government. Some also held out hope that the LTTE, or at least some of its delegation members, might moderate their views as they left the jungle and were exposed to new ways of thinking.

Under the grim military, political, and economic circumstances in which Wickremasinghe found himself, this may not have been an ideal strategy, but it was the best one available.

The peace process did produce some positive results. For all its shortcomings, the CFA fashioned a degree of stability the country had not seen in decades. There were no suicide attacks. Only one soldier died during the CFA's first two years, when he strayed into an LTTE forward defense zone.[55] International donors pledged billions of dollars in reconstruction aid. The LTTE appeared to consider a federal solution for the first time ever, and the two parties conducted the talks in a positive and constructive atmosphere.[56] Wickremasinghe had engaged with the LTTE just well enough, and had held off Kumaratunga just long enough, to win a short period of relative peace and stimulate a recovering economy.

Ultimately, however, Wickremasinghe's approach was unsustainable. It failed, doomed by a combination of personal, political, and international factors.

The most obvious constraint was the venomous rivalry between him and President Kumaratunga. For the negotiations to have any chance of success, the government's side of the table had to be unified; the major Sinhalese parties needed to support the peace process. That did not happen. According to the lead negotiator, G. L. Peiris, "the President had one objective. . . . She wanted to get rid of that government at the earliest opportunity and install a government headed by her, no matter who constituted that government, whether that government could run at all, whether it could function even at the basic level."[57] Their rivalry distorted the government's conduct in the negotiations, making it difficult to take decisions and impossible to implement any.[58] At the same time, Wickremasinghe neither bargained a way forward with the president nor confronted her. His chief negotiator believed that he "didn't have the courage to make a decision on what to do."[59]

The president may have been jealous of her prime minister's stealing the banner of peace that she had been carrying since 1994, but many of her criticisms rang true. At the top of the list was the prime minister's apparent eagerness for a peace agreement at almost any price.

Wickremasinghe believed that if only Prabhakaran could be enticed into a peace process that could then be sustained, the LTTE would eventually abandon violence and adopt a more moderate and democratic approach, respectful of human rights and political pluralism. Government officials cited examples, like the Mau Mau rebellion in Kenya and the ANC in South Africa, where insurgent movements over time had evolved into mainstream political parties. Consequently, the prime minister was eager to satisfy the Tigers and keep on satisfying them, whether they initially reciprocated or not. According to Peiris, Wickremasinghe "was willing to appease Prabhakaran. . . . There was the feeling that we cannot let him walk away from the talks. Whenever he transgressed the ceasefire, we never confronted him head on."[60] Another senior government official also involved in the talks stated that Wickremasinghe "thought that if we can keep the LTTE in the political mainstream long enough, then we can wean them away from militancy and terrorism."[61]

The weak CFA became one of the battlegrounds where the government's policy and patience were tested. Implementation of agreed-upon measures was uneven at best. Between taking a principled stand on LTTE violations and risk bringing down the peace talks or letting things ride and hoping for the best, the government's goal became keeping the peace process going at all costs. Preserving the CFA became an end in itself. Peiris explained how the LTTE exploited the government's position: "It was a progression. They tried something trivial and the government acquiesced. So they then went a little further the next time. The LTTE kept going." Under the circumstances, Colombo had little choice but to try to cover up the LTTE's violations. Again, Peiris: "Some of it was hidden from the public. Some of it was played down. There was an effort to stop public opinion from being inflamed."[62] Still, the media was full of leaks of the LTTE's ceasefire violations, many coming from Kumaratunga's office.

Even more telling than these anecdotes are the statistics from the Sri Lankan Monitoring Mission (SLMM). Although some violations were far more serious than others, the relative numbers are still instructive: From the CFA's inception to April 2007, the LTTE was responsible for 3,830 violations, the government 351.[63] According to one of the government's negotiators, "the administration in Colombo was so keen to preserve the CFA that it would have no qualms bending backwards to appease the Tigers."[64] A member of the government's own Peace Secretariat has written, "The LTTE has made a joke and a mockery of the prohibitions contained in the CFA."[65] The real problem was that the SLMM had no enforcement mechanism. All it could do was "name and shame," an approach that was clearly ineffective.

If the Sri Lankan government was unwilling to help itself, the international community could not help it either. Wickremasinghe's assumption over the role the Donors Group would, or could, play was misplaced. Commented Peiris, "Ranil had great faith in the role of the international community to control events in this country. . . . There was an abiding faith in the power of those four governments to control events."

But the United States, already mired in Afghanistan and, after the spring of 2003, in Iraq, was never going to send Marines storming ashore to battle the Tamil Tigers. And the Donors Group was never going to underwrite the peace process with a blank check. The $4.5 billion pledged in June 2003 in Tokyo was heavily conditioned on an end to the conflict and a commitment by Prabhakaran to engage in civilized behavior. When pressed, Peiris admitted that the whole concept of the international safety net "was a bit woolly. It didn't really stand up to much scrutiny. . . . It was not thought through very well analytically."[66]

The whole edifice of assumptions, wishful thinking, appeasement, and maneuverings may still have worked out if they did not all rest on the character of the LTTE leader. The success of the prime minister's approach depended on Prabhakaran's willingness to compromise, to settle for an end to the conflict on something less than a separate state of Eelam. Aside from a fleeting moment in the first few rounds of the peace talks, which he soon disavowed, nothing in his history suggested that he would be willing to agree to greater autonomy for the Tamils but within a unitary Sri Lankan state.

Subsequent accounts reveal that Prabhakaran was *never* sincere about the peace process. As Wickremasinghe's critics had charged, Prabhakaran wanted the CFA and the peace talks to demarcate, validate, and legitimize the borders of an independent Tamil state. General Kapila Hendawitharana, the head of national intelligence, told me in Colombo that Prabhakaran had summoned all his military leaders to meet with him in the Vanni in 2001, before the Cease Fire Agreement. "I will give you five years. I will give you whatever you want to fight. Any arms. You train your cadres," he told them. "The peace talks are a farce. In five years we will go back to war. You need to train your cadres to be the equal of the army." Karuna also confirmed to me that Prabhakaran wanted the talks to drag on "for at least five years while the LTTE built up its arms."[67]

No one invested more time and effort in the peace process than G. L. Peiris. So perhaps it is not surprising that he is both the most thoughtful and bitter in his judgment: "In a sense, [the peace process] was a misreading of the character of Prabhakaran. . . . Everything that happened in Oslo was perhaps a sham. . . . Serious discussion was never on their agenda."[68]

There was another party at these talks: the Norwegians. How should their contribution be judged?

Like any third party, Norway was an easy target to blame. From the start, some Sinhalese wondered why *any* third party was needed to help them with the LTTE. After the talks failed, it was often easier to criticize Norway than the Sri Lankan government (who had, many forget, invited the Norwegians in the first place). This comes with the territory. Still, during my conversations in Colombo in March 2010 about lessons from the failed peace process, it was a little surprising to hear firsthand the angry recriminations leveled by many Sri Lankan officials toward the Norwegians. Much of this anger and disappointment seemed "displaced." These officials were really upset with the actions and behavior of their own political leaders and armed forces.

No one should criticize the commitment and courage of the Norwegian facilitators or the members of the SLMM. Many of them repeatedly risked their lives in an effort to end the conflict. Indeed, Norwegian officials receive high marks from many of the Sri Lankan (and American) officials involved.

But others have questioned their judgment. Some of these criticisms hit home. Others fail to appreciate the role Norway was asked to play, first by President Kumaratunga and later by Prime Minister Wickremasinghe.

First, critics state that the Norwegians never insisted that the two sides agree upon a set of shared values or a common framework for resolving their differences. The LTTE never renounced terror. It never committed to democratic principles, political pluralism, and international standards of human rights. Former Sri Lankan officials complained that the Norwegians exerted heavy pressure on the government not to suggest anything along these lines that would sabotage the peace process. "Norway, knowing the roadblocks, resisted."[69]

This criticism conveniently forgets that the Norwegians were not dealing with friendly Scandinavian countries like Sweden or Finland but with Prabhakaran and the LTTE. Indeed, Sri Lanka's own delegation adopted this same approach during the talks, intentionally omitting or deferring some of the most sensitive issues it knew the LTTE would not accept. One of the negotiators later characterized this approach as "let's start in the baby pool and work toward the deep end."[70]

The gradual approach may not have worked, but it is hardly unique to these types of thorny negotiations.

A more pertinent criticism was the perpetual manpower shortage in the SLMM. With only seventy personnel at its height, it "was too small and unprepared to monitor the LTTE's deliberate and methodical violations of the CFA."[71]

A larger criticism was that Norway did not have any metrics for measuring failure (repeated CFA violations apparently did not count) or even any internal circuit breakers where they could take stock. A cold-eyed assessment became progressively harder, not easier, over time as the peace process gathered momentum, as more effort was invested, and as public expectations grew. (A March 2003 public opinion poll showed that 84 percent of all Sri Lankans believed that peace could be achieved through dialogue, including more than 95 percent of Tamils.[72])

If the Norwegians ever harbored any reservations about the CFA and the peace process, they did not voice them. But no one should have expected them to. As Wickremasinghe, Kumaratunga, and the Norwegians appreciated, even an inadequate CFA was far better than a full-scale return to war. And the Norwegians, after all, had been hired to facilitate the peace process, not walk away from it.

Finally, the most politically loaded criticism was that some Norwegians were biased toward the LTTE. Norway's special adviser to the peace talks, Erik Solheim, is most often singled out in this regard. Some errors in judgment may have occurred, and these likely eroded the Sri Lankan government's confidence in Solheim and some of his colleagues. (In June 2001, his role in the peace process was downgraded after the Kumaratunga government reportedly objected to his facilitation efforts.[73]) This, too, may be inevitable in any peace process.

In my personal conversations and correspondence with a wide range of current and former Sri Lankan officials, much of this debate, and residual anger, centers on the elusive concept of "parity of status." This phrase occurs nowhere in the CFA or in any of the official documents that Norway or either of the two parties produced, but the concept crucially informed Norway's approach to the entire peace process. It meant that Norway would treat the LTTE, an internationally designated terrorist organization, as equal with the Sri Lankan government. This approach would best guarantee, Norway reasoned, that the LTTE would join a peace process and provide the best chance to reach a negotiated settlement.

In practice, how Norway interpreted parity of status ranged from the trivial to the significant. For example, Anton Balasingham and G. L. Peiris would each be introduced officially as "His Excellency," and the LTTE delegation would be entitled to the exact same number of hotel rooms as the government's delegation. It meant that neither the LTTE's nor the Sri Lankan delegation's bags would be checked by customs, since they were covered by "diplomatic immunity."[74] At its most extreme, it meant that Norway would attempt to formally designate the LTTE's "Sea Tigers" as a "de facto naval unit," with demarcated training and live-fire zones, similar to the Sri Lankan navy.[75]

The suggestion of parity between a terrorist group and a sovereign state, with its implication of moral equivalence, would understandably infuriate any government official or professional diplomat. But Sri Lanka's officials had an added reason to object: Sharing a similar status with the LTTE accurately reflected the inconvenient facts on the ground. At this time, Prabhakaran was the de facto leader of what was essentially a ministate within Sri Lanka. His forces occupied 10,000 square kilometers, and had repeatedly humiliated the military and embarrassed the government. Recall that the LTTE had not sued for peace. Kumaratunga has asked the Norwegians to facilitate a peace effort after the Jaffna talks and her disastrous "war for peace" initiative. Further, Wickremasinghe had been overwhelmingly elected on a platform that promised to bring peace to the country. He had accepted, eagerly, the LTTE's offer to stop the fighting. He also immediately endorsed the CFA draft, warts and all. In short, Colombo had little leverage at this time. Prabhakaran did, and pressed it home.

Norway's decision to adopt a parity-of-status approach to the peace talks is still controversial in Sri Lanka. This is understandable, given the passions aroused by a long-standing and brutal civil war. But blaming Norway, rather than the factors that led to Wickremasinghe's poor strategic options, is unfair to the Norwegians. On the whole, Norway did not favor the Tamils. It did favor an evenhanded approach that it judged stood the best chance of success.

The 2002–03 peace talks failed to end the conflict. They failed a second time: as a cautionary tale. Undeterred by the LTTE's walkout and its serial violations of the CFA, President Kumaratunga made no changes to the CFA—not a word—after her party won a parliamentary majority in the April 2004 elections. Even after the Tigers had assassinated yet another senior government official, this time the country's foreign minister, an ethnic Tamil, in August 2005, her government merely condemned the LTTE. One of her own officials dismissed the effect of such criticism as "water off a duck's back."[76] Now firmly back in charge, she even tried to revive the peace process.

Mother Nature provided the two sides with a new opportunity in December 2004 in the form of a massive tsunami that rocked the island and killed an estimated 35,000 Sri Lankans living along the southern and eastern coasts. The Kumaratunga government entered into secret talks with the LTTE and in June 2005 signed the Post-Tsunami Operational Management Structure (P-TOMS), which was designed to rebuild damaged homes and businesses and channel aid to victims and their families. Although the LTTE was only in charge of 15 percent of the affected area, the P-TOM would have given the Tigers operational access to two-thirds of the country's coastline, the adjacent sea, and up to two kilometers inland. International funds would be distributed through a regional committee the LTTE would dominate. (This was precisely the type of plan that Kumaratunga would have heatedly objected to had Wickremasinghe been its author.) But before the P-TOMS could be implemented, a Sinhalese nationalist party challenged the constitutionality of the arrangement, and the Supreme Court issued a stay order the following month.

By this time, both the LTTE and the government were coming under internal pressure. In March 2004, the senior LTTE commander in the eastern province, Colonel Karuna Amman, formally broke with the LTTE, along with almost 6,000 cadres, and formed a separate Tamil political movement. "In defecting from the LTTE, Karuna invoked the deeply held resentment of eastern Tamils toward the northern Tamils [like Prabhakaran] who had long dominated over them and spoken for them."[77] When I talked with him in March 2010 at his "villa" on a Sri Lankan military base, Karuna characterized the source of his dissatisfaction much more pithily: "The east provided the troops and the north provided the terror."[78] After Karuna's defection, Sri Lankan intelligence officers immediately contacted him. Karuna requested that he and his men join the Sri Lankan army. He was told it was impossible. But the intelligence service realized that here was a golden opportunity to weaken Prabhakaran militarily, enhance Colombo's knowledge of the LTTE, and score a propaganda coup all at the same time. Karuna and his senior officers were brought to Colombo to meet the media.[79]

In the November 2005 presidential elections, Chandrika Kumaratunga was constitutionally barred from seeking a third term. But the favorite, Ranil Wickremasinghe, was upset by Mahinda Rajapaksa, who won with 50.3 percent of the vote. (Rajapaksa's slim margin of victory was secured after Prabhakaran had instructed the Tamils not to vote for Wickremasinghe.[80]) Prabhakaran greeted the new president in his Heroes Day speech with "an urgent final appeal" for peace, warning that the LTTE "next year [would] intensify the struggle for self-determination." Apparently Prabhakaran could not wait until "next year," as his cadres started attacking government forces and civilians, including children and Buddhist monks, within weeks of Rajapaksa's inauguration.

Mahinda Rajapaksa was a different type of politician with a different plan for resolving the ethnic conflict. But like Sri Lankan leaders before him, he initially preserved the CFA and tried to engage the LTTE in renewed peace talks. The two parties met in February 2006 in Geneva; the talks went nowhere. A few months later, the Norwegians ferried the parties to Oslo, but this time the LTTE refused even to enter the same room as the government negotiators.[81]

With the diplomatic process exhausted, and surrender out of the question, starting in 2006 Rajapaksa methodically created a viable military option.

Rajapaksa and his senior advisers had studied the country's previous failed attempts to defeat the LTTE and had drawn certain lessons. In order to avoid the infighting that had so debilitated the Wickremasinghe administration, Rajapaksa broadened his coalition by forming a government with members from both leading Sinhalese political parties. He needed to prevent the demoralization of the troops that had afflicted previous campaigns, so he promoted competent commanders and made his brother defense secretary; they then ensured that the armed forces were properly sized, equipped, and provisioned. Because Rajapaksa wanted to decrease India's suspicions over Sri Lanka's treatment of its ethnic Tamils, Colombo enhanced its joint intelligence cooperation with Delhi. Further, to reassure India that foreign powers would not encroach on India's sphere of influence, Rajapaksa agreed to ask Delhi for military training and equipment first. Only if India decided not to help would Sri Lanka then turn to foreign suppliers, such as China and Pakistan, who would be less willing than Western arms suppliers to halt arms sales over human rights concerns. And most important, Rajapaksa learned that Colombo had to be willing to prosecute the war to its conclusion and not pull back because of international pressure.[82]

In July 2006, the LTTE gave the government the excuse it needed when the Tigers closed the sluice gates of an eastern reservoir, cutting off water to more than 60,000 people. In response, the government launched a major offensive to crush the LTTE. A year later, the government had ousted the rebels from the east. In January 2008, Sri Lanka formally withdrew from the CFA, and the peace monitors left the country. The government pressed its military advantage.

By late 2008, the Norwegian ambassador in Colombo, Tore Hattrem, assessed it likely that the LTTE was going to be defeated militarily. As he explained to me over lunch at his official residence in March 2010, he now focused on trying to save as many civilian lives as possible. After being contacted by members of the Tamil diaspora, in early 2009 Hattrem traveled to Thailand to meet with Kumaran Pathmanathan (aka "KP"), the LTTE's senior leader outside the country, to see if he could persuade Prabhakaran to hand over civilians to the International Committee of the Red Cross.[83] In response to international pressure, in February and April 2009, the Sri Lankan government allowed a "humanitarian pause" to facilitate a civilian transfer. But Prabhakaran refused on either occasion to release any of his "human shields," even shooting those who tried to escape. By May 19, 2009, Prabhakaran was dead. Sri Lanka's long national nightmare was finally over.

As of mid-2010, there has been "no sign of renewed LTTE militancy." The deaths of Prabhakaran and his senior military leadership, and the subsequent arrest of his likely successor and the LTTE's international leader, "has crippled the organization."[84]

CONCLUSION

Sri Lanka's great tragedy was having to face a terrorist/separatist campaign led by a fanatical, murderous psychopath who would stop at nothing short of an independent Tamil homeland. But Sri Lanka's greater tragedy was having a succession of leaders at first unwilling to address the legitimate grievances of the Tamil people, and who were later blind to the ruthless nature of Prabhakaran, a man who championed these grievances, but for his own maximalist ends.

Given the almost unspeakable evil that Sri Lanka had to confront, one can understand, even empathize with, the series of political leaders who over thirty years tried to make peace with the LTTE. Whether out of desperation or just out of other options, time and again they explored a negotiated solution to the challenge presented by Prabhakaran and his dream of an independent Tamil homeland. Perhaps at times they even prayed for some miracle—India's intervention? the international safety net? a coup against Prabhakaran?—that would deliver them from the seemingly endless bloodshed that had overwhelmed their country.

It is far more difficult, however, to understand the behavior of the country's leadership on two related points: its treatment of those Sri Lankan citizens who would live under the LTTE's authority in any devolved arrangement and the quality of statesmanship during a time when the country faced a grave threat to its survival.

A staple of every government negotiation since at least the 1987 Indo–Sri Lankan Accord was the willingness to devolve power and authority from the center, Colombo, to the periphery, the northern and eastern provinces. The details varied, but each devolutionary plan tried to address in some measure the grievances, concerns, and aspirations of the Tamil people.

What appeared reasonable in theory would have been nightmarish in practice. Each government proposal would have given the LTTE dominion in the northern and eastern provinces, with enhanced legitimacy, influence, and power. Each government proposal risked placing a large percentage of the population—Tamil, Sinhalese, and Muslim—under a fascist dictatorship. They would have been the collateral damage of any peace agreement.

Nor could Sri Lanka's leaders plead ignorance. Over a period of decades, Prabhakaran had amply demonstrated just what life was like for those poor souls under his rule. He was one of the world's greatest human rights violators, compared by some to Cambodia's Pol Pot. Any dissent was quashed; any opposition was eliminated. It is doubtful that any government negotiator (or, for that matter, many members of the Tamil diaspora) would have voluntarily welcomed a similar opportunity to live under the LTTE's authority. In all these schemes, Colombo was not simply proposing to modify the social contract under which the government was responsible for safeguarding the well-being of its people. It was pretending that one did not even exist in the first place. This was an abdication of its own commitment to democratic principles.

That Sri Lanka did not suffer this type of "solution" was not due to the government's lack of effort. Rather, it was due to Prabhakaran's lack of sophistication. A more cynical leader would have eagerly agreed to a merged northern and eastern province, grabbed as much territory and as many benefits as possible, consolidated his position and power, then reneged and pressed for an independent Eelam.

Apparently, Prabhakaran could never bring himself to lie in such a fashion. It may have been his only virtue.

The record of government engagement with the LTTE also raises serious questions about the quality of statesmanship. For every Sri Lankan political leader from J. R. Jayewardene until Mahinda Rajapaksa, the primary goal was getting elected and staying in power. The secondary goal was dealing with the LTTE. Personal political interests consistently superseded the nation's interests.

As Milinda Moragoda, a veteran politician and Cabinet minister in the Rajapaksa administration, explained about Sri Lanka's politics: "It's a tribal system. You belong to one tribe or the other. . . . Southern politicians always sought to use the conflict for the advantage of one party or the other. . . . Getting the credit or outflanking the opposition seems to me to be the more important point than dealing with the LTTE."[85] In this type of political culture, the LTTE was simply a means to an end—not peace (although that would have been nice should Prabhakaran ever have compromised), but more important, political power. Engaging the LTTE when in power, or opposing engagement when out of power, was a game that each Sinhalese party tried to exploit for partisan advantage. The main enemy was one another, not the LTTE. Partisan politics trumped any shared concept of national interest.

For example, many of the same people who incessantly criticized the 2002 Cease Fire Agreement when they were out of government had supported the quite similar 1995 Declaration of Cessation of Hostilities when they were in government.[86] In addition, Kumaratunga's criticism of Wickremasinghe, the CFA, and his handling of the peace process caused her to oust him. Yet after her party secured a majority in parliament, she kept the CFA intact, tried to revive the peace talks, and signed an agreement for humanitarian assistance in the tsunami-affected areas that ceded so much authority to the LTTE that the Supreme Court invalidated major sections of it as unconstitutional. It is hard to see any shared concept of the national interest and the country's greater good in this behavior.

Engaging the LTTE was placed in service to the political ambitions of one Sinhalese party or the other. Whichever one could get the credit for ending the war, or get credit for ending the killing even temporarily, would be rewarded at the polls. "The great prize was peace," observed Bradman Weerakoon, adviser to nine presidents and prime ministers and the grey *éminence grise* of the Sri Lankan civil service. "Cessation of the suffering of the Sinhalese people would give them [the political leadership] political mileage that would make them unbeatable."[87] If necessary, the country's political leaders were willing to sacrifice democratic principles and jeopardize the nation's security to gain partisan advantage or deny it to their political enemies.

No doubt Prabhakaran tried to manipulate the two leading Sinhalese parties against each other. He may even have been successful from time to time. But to attribute the selfish behavior of the Sri Lankan leaders to his maneuvering is giving the LTTE leader far too much credit. He was hardly a Metternich in the jungle, as evidenced by a raft of missteps and miscalculations, including his opposing the Indo–Sri Lankan Accord; his assassination of Rajiv Gandhi; his alienation of the LTTE's best military commander, Karuna; and his tilting the election from Ranil Wickremasinghe to Mahinda Rajapaksa. In this case at least, Prabhakaran was not the source of the problem.

Reviewing Sri Lanka's sad history over more than three decades, one cannot escape the conclusion that the Sri Lankan people were badly let down by their political leaders. Not because these leaders were venal or corrupt, although many of them may have been. But rather because they placed their selfish and narrow-minded interests ahead of the country's interests. Partisan, short-term political advantage was all.

"Country first" apparently did not translate into Sinhalese.

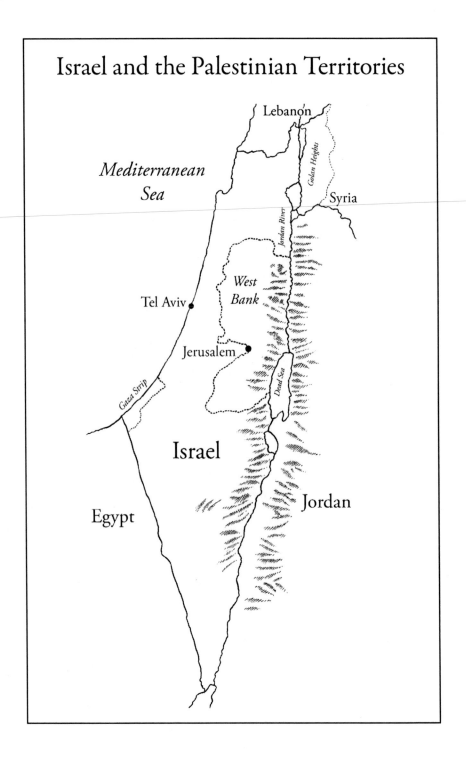

Israel and the Palestinian Territories

Lebanon

Mediterranean
Sea

Golan Heights

Syria

Jordan River

West
Bank

Tel Aviv

Jerusalem

Gaza Strip

Dead Sea

Israel

Egypt

Jordan

4.

THE ISLAMIC RESISTANCE MOVEMENT (HAMAS)

I had asked the American embassy in Amman to bring together some university students to discuss Middle East politics and U.S. foreign policy. I had found these discussions among the most interesting when I traveled, as students were much more willing to share their unvarnished thoughts, fears, and criticisms than older and more diplomatic government officials. It also provided me with a window into what the next generation of leaders in the region were thinking.

Two dozen of us gathered in the living room of the cultural affairs officer. The students were a mix of Jordanians and Palestinians, roughly reflecting the demographic makeup of Jordan. The young men were dressed in jeans and casual shirts, the women more modestly. I was introduced, and if my background impressed any of them, they didn't show it. To break the ice and get the conversation started, I asked if we could go around the room and they could tell me their names, what they were studying at university, and what they wanted to do in life.

Their responses would not have been out of place on any American college or university campus. A few wanted to continue their studies in graduate school, some wanted to get a job and make money, others weren't sure.

Until we came to an attractive young woman wearing a headscarf. In flawless English, she explained that she was a Palestinian and was studying computer science. She wanted to get married after university and have lots of children. And she wanted them all to grow up and become suicide bombers who would kill lots of Jews.

I was speechless. I looked around to see if the reaction among her colleagues was as horrified as mine. They, too, sat there silently. After a few seconds, another student spoke up. "You don't mean that," he said. I exhaled and thought to myself, "Good. Better if one of her friends sets her straight than me."

"You don't mean Jews," he continued. "You mean Israelis." Murmurs of agreement were heard around the room, as the students nodded their heads approvingly at the clarification.

TO ITS MANY CRITICS, THE "ISLAMIC Resistance Movement" (Harakat al-Muqāwama al-Islāmiya), or Hamas, is an Islamic terrorist group that has employed "martyrdom operations" responsible for the deaths of hundreds of Israelis over the past twenty-five years, has launched thousands of rockets indiscriminately against civilians, and is dedicated to the destruction of the Jewish state. While it also engages in well-publicized charitable activities, they mask the "financial and logistical support network for its terrorist operations. . . . There is no meaningful distinction between the group's political, social and terrorist leadership."[1]

For Hamas's supporters and sympathizers, however, it is an authentic political movement that resists an illegal occupation. It engages in a wide array of social, educational, medical, governance, and charitable activities that benefit Palestinians in the Occupied Territories.[2]

Not in dispute is that Hamas, whose name is an acronym that means "zeal," or "enthusiasm," transformed a branch of the Muslim Brotherhood into a far more active and militant organization. The rise of Hamas since its founding in 1986 has benefited from two broad trends across the Middle East: the greater fusion of religion with politics (what has been termed the "Islamization of politics") and the retreat of the Palestinian cause from Arab priorities.[3]

The 1979 revolution in Iran that deposed the shah and introduced an Islamic Republic was the most important marker of the growing influence of Islam in regional politics. It also acted as a model for other fundamentalist movements to emulate—most notably, in Algeria, Sudan, Egypt, and southern Lebanon. The assassination of Anwar Sadat, the bombing of the U.S. Marine barracks in Beirut that caused the United States to withdraw its forces from Lebanon, the mujahideen resistance to the Soviet Union's invasion and occupation of Afghanistan, the Algerian civil war (where over 160,000 people died), and the rise of Hezbollah (with inspiration, training. and funding from Iran) testified to the ability of fundamentalist Islamists to affect the destinies of their countries. This wave of Islamic fervor spread to the Occupied Territories and primed a new generation of "mosque youth" more susceptible to armed resistance and Hamas's agenda.[4]

During this same period, the cause of Palestine receded from a top-of-the-agenda item for the Arab states. Sadat's historic trip to Jerusalem and the resulting Israel-Egypt peace treaty, combined with the humiliating 1982 evacuation of the Palestine Liberation Organization (PLO) from Lebanon to Tunis, effectively eliminated the military option from the conflict with Israel. Israel's security was strengthened further with the signing of the U.S.-Israel Strategic Cooperation Agreement in 1981 and the destruction of Saddam Hussein's Osirak nuclear reactor the same year. Meanwhile, the Iran-Iraq War drained time and attention in the Arab world from the plight of the Palestinians. If the Palestinian people wished to resist Israel, they would have to do it themselves. The locus of resistance to Israeli occupation moved from outside the territories to inside them.

Within the occupied territories, Hamas gained from comparison with the increasingly unpopular Fatah, the political party that dominated and controlled the PLO under the leadership of Yasser Arafat. Hamas, led by a pious, quadriplegic, middle-aged schoolteacher named Ahmad Yassin, delivered much-needed social services that the PLO should have been providing. According to two Israeli scholars, "Hamas's grassroots leadership projected credibility, dedication, and integrity compared with the PLO's outdated and notoriously corrupt leadership, unscrupulous bureaucracy, and abandonment of the armed struggle in favor of a luxurious lifestyle."[5]

An additional reason for Hamas's popularity was its willingness to inflict pain and suffering on Israelis in revenge for the pain and suffering Israel was inflicting on them. Hamas's founding charter, drawing inspiration from the rabidly anti-Semitic *Protocols of the Elders of Zion*, called for an Islamic jihad against "the unlawful seizure of Palestine by the Jews." The destruction of Israel and the recovery of all of Palestine, from the Mediterranean Sea to the Jordan River, is the organization's historic goal, and jihad was the only way to attain this goal. (Hamas subsequently clarified its charter to explain that it was not opposed to all Jews per se, just Zionists.) Over the years Hamas has engaged in various forms of resistance, including strikes, demonstrations, popular uprisings, military attacks, and suicide bombings.

But Hamas has also demonstrated a willingness to suspend violence. Periodically, Hamas has unilaterally initiated "ceasefires," "calms," or "cooling-off periods." From 1993 to 2002, for example, Hamas unilaterally announced nine separate ceasefires.[6] From March 2005 to June 2006, Hamas participated in another ceasefire that coincided with its participation in municipal and legislative elections. Hamas has also offered to negotiate humanitarian issues indirectly, through third parties like Egypt or the Red Cross.

At different times, Hamas has sought diplomatic solutions to the conflict that fall short of its ultimate desires by offering Israel a *hudna*, or time-bound ceasefire. The concept of *hudna* has ample precedent within Muslim history, dating back to the Prophet's agreements with his adversaries in Mecca and the Jews in Medina and with Saladin's arrangements with the Crusaders. In recent times, it has also been invoked by Anwar Sadat and Yasser Arafat to provide religious justification for reaching peace agreements with Israel.

In 1993, Sheikh Yassin first proposed the idea of a *hudna* with Israel that would last ten to twenty years. For Hamas, this would have been an interim arrangement, a way station on the road toward the full realization of its historic mission. Yassin conditioned this offer by requiring that Israel first withdraw to the pre-1967 lines, remove all settlers from Occupied Territories, and release all Palestinian prisoners.[7] Hamas could accept a more limited state in Gaza and the West Bank as long as this was a temporary measure, it could accept international monitors in the territories for a limited period of time after Israeli withdrawal, and it could enter into talks with Israel after Israel withdrew from the Occupied Territories.[8] For Hamas, this offer was part of its "liberation in phases" strategy to recover all of the Holy Land. Israel rejected it out of hand.

Hamas repeated its offers of a *hudna* later in the 1990s, after Israel's severe military response to Hamas suicide bombings resulted in the imprisonment of Hamas members and the collective punishment of Palestinians. An additional element at this time was the call for a general referendum by all Palestinians, both inside and outside the Occupied Territories, on the question of electing the leadership and ratifying any political agreements with Israel.[9] The idea of Hamas submitting to the freely expressed will of the Palestinian people for a two-state solution would be repeated in subsequent years.[10]

Israel was not the only adversary Hamas faced. Virtually from its inception, Hamas was opposed also by the Tunis-based PLO leadership, who worried about a movement that it could not control, that was overtly Islamic (as compared with the secular Fatah), and that would siphon off recruits and financial support, especially as it was seen leading the resistance against Israel in the Occupied Territories. The PLO's challenge became more complex after December 1988. In the wake of the First Intifada, the largest revolt in Palestine since the mid-1930s, Arafat and the Palestinian National Council desperately tried to reassert the PLO's primacy in the Arab-Israeli conflict over Hamas and other Muslim fundamentalist groups violently resisting the occupation. It did so by accepting the existence of Israel, pledging to give up terrorism, and endorsing "all relevant UN resolutions" (meaning the acceptance of a two-state solution, but with no reciprocal Israeli guarantee for a freeze on settlements or the establishment of a Palestinian state). In return, the Reagan administration opened a dialogue with the PLO as the "sole legitimate representative of the Palestinian people." Hamas thus became the party of choice for all those opposed to the peace process.[11]

The slow but steady advance of the peace process during the 1990s tightened the constraints on Hamas. With the Madrid peace conference, the Oslo Accords, and additional confidence-building agreements with Israel, the PLO (and after June 1994 the Palestinian Authority) gradually assumed responsibility for preventing violence and terror attacks from Hamas and other groups in the West Bank and Gaza. Hamas now had to battle not only Israel, but also the Palestinian Authority (PA), whose prisons during the 1990s held more Hamas members than did Israel's. As the PA became a "partner for peace," it assumed greater responsibility for maintaining security in the Occupied Territories. In short, the PA became "Israel's policeman," with far more (and better-armed) police and security forces than Hamas's military wing, the Martyr 'Izzidin al-Qassam Brigades. In response, Yassin declared a "merciless war" against Arafat, labeled the PA a tool of Israeli intelligence, and declared that peace with Israel would be a "crime against Islam."[12]

Hamas's dilemma was that it risked losing popular support whether it opposed *or* supported the peace process. If it remained in opposition, it risked alienating Palestinians who supported the PA and the two-state solution. Its attacks could be used as excuses by Israel to halt the peace process, remain in the Occupied Territories, and maintain security measures and economic restrictions that inconvenienced and humiliated the Palestinians. Although resistance to Israel might increase Hamas's popularity temporarily, it would also bring reprisals by the PA and Israel, erode Hamas's ability to deliver social services to its community, and risk turning the people against the movement. But if it supported the peace process and cooperated with the PA, it would reduce the movement to a marginalized opposition party, eliminate its distinctive Islamic identity, and signal the abandonment of its historic mission.[13]

Like many relationships in the Middle East, however, the one between Hamas and the PA was more complex than it appeared on the surface. The PA was also caught in a bind. Arafat had to satisfy Israeli and U.S. demands to crack down on Hamas and other terror groups resisting Israeli occupation in order to continue the peace process and to avoid being labeled a terrorist himself. Yet if he did so, he would lose credibility among the people, especially if the peace process lagged and daily life for the Palestinians did not improve.

The PLO and Hamas thus engaged in an uneasy and wary coexistence; neither side had the will or ability to destroy the other. Khalid Mesh'al, who assumed the leadership of Hamas in 2004 after the assassination of Sheikh Yassin, characterized how the relationship evolved over time: "The PLO met Hamas in the beginning with total disregard, then it tried to cast doubt on its authenticity, then it endeavored to belittle it and refused to recognize it, then it went into a stage of open confrontation followed by an attempt to contain it."[14]

The PA's intermittent efforts to "contain" Hamas did not prevent the movement from engaging in terror attacks against Israel. The Qassam Brigades had been formed in 1992. Its members received training and financial support from Iran, to the tune of $15 million per month.[15] Yet over the years Hamas has maintained that it is not a terrorist group, but is engaging in legitimate and lawful resistance. Thus, it denounced the 9/11 attacks, the Madrid train bombings, and the London subway bombings. It has not attacked Israeli interests outside the Occupied Territories (which it defined as including Israel proper).[16]

Until 1994, Hamas refrained from targeting civilians. In February of that year, Baruch Goldstein, an Army reservist and member of an extreme right-wing settler movement, killed twenty-nine Palestinians and wounded over one hundred and fifty more at the al Ibrahimi Mosque in Hebron. Hamas responded with suicide bombings inside Israel. Hamas repeated, or attempted to repeat, these suicide attacks in subsequent years. Hamas explained and defended these tactics as a means to bring the Palestinian struggle home to the Israeli people by striking population centers and to deter new immigrants from coming to Israel. Hamas also timed some of its attacks to undermine the ongoing peace process.

With the eruption of the Second Intifada (the al-Aqsa Intifada) in September 2000, the collective rage and frustration of the Palestinians at their meager inheritance from the Oslo peace process ramped up the violence and lethality against Israel. Prime Minister Ariel Sharon responded to these attacks by launching military operations into Gaza, establishing a security barrier by greatly expanding a network of fences and trenches partly along the 1949 Armistice line, or "Green Line," demarcating the West Bank, and unilaterally withdrawing all Israeli settlers and troops from Gaza. Suicide bombings declined, but Hamas countered by escalating rocket and mortar attacks. Since 2001, Hamas has made a habit of targeting civilians, launching multiple indiscriminate rocket and mortar attacks from the Gaza Strip. In 2008, over 3,200 attacks took place, exposing approximately 1 million people, or 15 percent of Israel's population, to the threat.[17]

For most of the first two decades of its existence, Hamas concentrated on delivering social services, performing charitable activities, and actively resisting Israeli occupation. However, it refrained from participating in Palestinian national politics for fear of legitimizing the Oslo process, although it had run candidates for student, professional association, and municipal elections. In late 2004, however, it decided to contest seats for the Palestinian Legislative Council election scheduled for January 2006. Because of its increased popularity, Hamas calculated that it would do well, fueled by the PA's woeful underperformance in providing security (especially in Gaza), by its mismanagement of the economy, by its flagrant corruption and nepotism, by its not ending the occupation, or even by preventing the proliferation of new Israeli settlement growth. Disunity inside Fatah after the November 2004 death of Yasser Arafat also increased Hamas's comparative advantage.

On January 25, 2006, Hamas won seventy-four seats, a majority; Fatah won only forty-five. The Quartet (consisting of the United States, Russia, the European Union, and the United Nations) immediately stated that there would be no recognition of, no dialogue with, and no financial assistance to a Hamas-led PA until Hamas complied with three conditions: It must recognize Israel, renounce violence, and accept all previous Israeli-Palestinian agreements. After Hamas formed a government without Fatah in March, the United States and the EU announced that they were halting all assistance to the government, but that humanitarian aid would continue through international relief organizations and NGOs. Israel also declared that it would start withholding approximately $50 million per month in tax and customs receipts it collected for the PA. In addition, a number of foreign banks refused to lend services to the Hamas-led PA for fear of violating U.S. antiterrorism legislation.

Hamas's leaders refused to meet any of the three conditions. But over the coming weeks and months, the Islamic movement sent signals that it wanted to engage. In February 2006, the Israeli newspaper *Yediot Ahronot* reported that Hamas had sent Israel a secret letter requesting a new channel of dialogue with Israel and the United States.[18] In editorials in American and European newspapers, Hamas's leaders requested that the United States honor "fair and free elections" and engage in a dialogue; to Israel, it offered again the possibility of a *hudna*.[19] Israel and the United States rejected the overtures, and repeated their opposition to direct talks until Hamas renounced violence, recognized Israel, and accepted all previous agreements between Israel and the Palestinians.

In addition to its international isolation, Hamas faced numerous domestic obstacles to governing. It enjoyed far less popular support than the election suggested; for one, it didn't win a majority of the vote. The results were more an indictment of Fatah and the PA than an endorsement of the Hamas agenda. Almost three out of four Palestinians did not expect the overwhelming Hamas victory. When asked why they chose Hamas, 43 percent of Palestinians who voted for Hamas said they did so with the hope of ending the PA's corruption, while 19 percent voted for Hamas for religious reasons. Less than 12 percent voted for Hamas because of its political agenda.[20]

The mistrust, enmity, and factional warfare between Hamas and Fatah brewed for another year, further diminishing the quality of life for more than 3.5 million Palestinians. (More than eighty Palestinians were killed in the first two months of 2007 alone.) In February 2007, Saudi Arabia tried to broker a deal and rescue the Palestinians from full-scale civil war. It appeared to succeed when Hamas and Fatah formed a unity government the following month.[21] The new government's platform fell short of endorsing the three conditions, however. The Mecca Agreement stated that the Palestinians had the right to "resistance in all its forms" and to "defend themselves against any ongoing Israeli aggression." It committed only to "honor" or "respect" (not "accept") previous agreements signed by the PA and PLO. It did not renounce violence or recognize Israel.

In the end, the civil war was delayed by only three months. After Mecca, the

PA tried to reassert its authority in Gaza by confronting Hamas and destroying its military and security forces. In June, tensions between the PA and Hamas forces quickly escalated. Amid vicious fratricidal conflict that saw Fatah members thrown from rooftops and patients executed in hospitals, the PA was routed in less than a week. According to Efraim Halevy, the former head of Mossad, Israel's external security service, "To the astonishment of Hamas, the PA forces dissolved and disintegrated."[22] The PA leader, President Mahmoud Abbas, denounced Hamas's action as a "military coup" and dissolved the unity government.[23] Hamas now completely controlled Gaza, while the PA controlled the West Bank. Israel placed an economic blockade on Gaza in an attempt to isolate Hamas and undermine its appeal by showing Gaza residents that they would suffer under a Hamas government.[24] Hamas responded with more rocket and mortar attacks. A year later, in June 2008, the two sides verbally agreed to a six-month ceasefire (*tahdi'ah*) negotiated with Egypt's good offices. Hamas pledged to halt all rocket attacks, while Israel promised to relax the blockade.

By December 2008, the ceasefire had broken down, with each side accusing the other of bad faith. (General Dani Arditi, the head of Israel's National Security Council at the time, admitted to me over lunch in Tel Aviv that both sides shared responsibility for the breakdown.[25]) On December 27, Israel launched Operation Cast Lead, an air attack that was followed by a ground assault into Gaza on January 3. Israel's goals were to degrade Hamas's ability to threaten Israeli villages and cities with rocket fire, cripple Hamas's ability to reconstitute and rearm its forces, and, they hoped, delegitimize the movement in the eyes of the Palestinians. By displaying overwhelming force and relentlessly punishing Hamas, Israel also intended to recover a measure of "strategic deterrence," its ability to intimidate and deter its enemies that was thought to have suffered badly from Israel's performance in its war against Hezbollah in southern Lebanon during the summer of 2006.

On January 18, a day after Israel had announced a unilateral ceasefire, Hamas and other militant groups agreed to a one-week ceasefire to give diplomats a chance to work out a more permanent truce. By January 21, Israel had pulled all of its forces out of Gaza. The war had resulted in the deaths of thirteen Israelis and approximately 1,300 Palestinians, two-thirds of whom, according to Israel, were Hamas fighters or militants. Israel also destroyed large arms caches and smuggling tunnels between Egypt and southern Gaza. An estimated 46,000 Gaza residents were displaced.[26] By early 2010, unemployment exceeded 80 percent and Gaza's civilian population remained dependent on international relief organizations for basic necessities. Israel continued to restrict the flow of goods and people into and out of Gaza.

Clearly, the Gaza war and its aftermath badly battered Hamas. Hamas's viability both as an Islamic resistance movement capable of punishing Israel and as a government capable of performing its civic responsibilities had been severely eroded.

Despite it all, though, the movement exhibited a remarkable resilience. It refused to surrender political power to Fatah in the cause of unifying the Palestinian people. It also refused to officially sacrifice its ideological goal of an Islamic Palestine stretching "from the river to the sea" to pursue a two-state solution. It preserved an irreducible core of support and retained a loyal audience that would continue to back its use of violence against the Jewish state.[27] Hamas had survived and continued to provide both military and diplomatic challenges for Israel.

ISRAEL'S ENGAGEMENT WITH HAMAS

Six of us sat around the conference table in the Israeli Foreign Ministry, three from the State Department's Office of Policy Planning and three of our Israeli counterparts. These talks were part of routine, informal discussions of the strategic landscape, with the two sides assessing regional developments and trends and sharing their concerns.

A few months earlier, in June 2004, Prime Minister Ariel Sharon had declared that Israel would unilaterally withdraw by the end of the following summer all Israeli settlers from the Gaza Strip and four settlements in the northern West Bank. Those who refused to leave voluntarily would be evicted by Israeli security forces. Sharon's announcement had surprised Israel, the Palestinians, and the United States. I had a number of questions that needed answers.

"I am a little uncertain about how you're thinking about 'the day after' in Gaza," I remarked to my Israeli colleague. "Gaza isn't like a summer rental, where you lock the door when the rental term is up, put the keys through the mail slot, and then walk away." Israel had a stake in making sure that Gaza was an economic and political success story. This wasn't charity. It was national self-interest. The last thing Israel needed was a failed state on its border.

"What plans do you have for helping the Palestinian Authority succeed?" I asked. "What's your strategy?"

My Israeli counterpart smiled and shrugged his shoulders, his body language suggesting that he wished his side had good answers as well. "You don't understand," he replied. "We don't do strategy. We do tactics. We'll see what happens and then we'll respond."

Israel and Hamas were not always mortal enemies. Israel's initial forbearance for Hamas's charitable work in the 1970s and 1980s gave way to hostility mixed with periodic engagement in the early 1990s and then to a hardening of its position against all forms of direct or indirect engagement, with only a few exceptions on humanitarian grounds.

The precursor to Hamas, the Muslim Brotherhood in Palestine, was formed in 1967 and tolerated by Israeli authorities for many years. For the next two decades, the number of mosques in Gaza doubled, with Israel's consent; the Muslim Brotherhood's social and charitable services operated openly under Israeli license. Palestinian nationalists were deported or imprisoned, but the Muslim Brotherhood was allowed to organize with little interference.[28]

After Hamas emerged during the First Intifada as a political and military force, some observers alleged that Israel had quietly promoted the movement as an alternative to weaken and discredit the PLO (a line spread at the time by the PLO and since confirmed by senior Israeli security officials). Israel was more concerned in the 1970s and 1980s with terrorist threats from militant Palestinian groups and had misjudged Hamas's political and military potential. According to Ami Ayalon, the former head of Shin Bet, Israel's internal security service, "In a way, we created or at least helped the Muslim movements in the 1970s and 1980s. We decided that the best way to fight the Palestinian national movement was to try to empower a movement that did not have nationalist aspirations. The Muslim Brotherhood had a pan-Arab agenda. We didn't understand at the time the threat that Hamas could pose."[29] The former head of Mossad's Research and Analysis Unit, Uri Ne'eman, concurred: "We supported the Muslim Brotherhood because their agenda was basically helping the poor and educating the masses. Their approach to Israel was not important enough at that time to think of them as a future enemy. We thought it was good to use them against the PLO. . . . It was divide and rule"[30]

Eighteen months after the start of the First Intifada, Israel declared Hamas a terrorist group once the movement's role in supporting the uprising became clearer to its intelligence units. Israel now targeted its religious charities and institutions, interdicted its sources of funding, arrested Sheikh Yassin in May 1989 and sentenced him to fifteens years in jail, imprisoned members of its military wing, and even deported over 400 Hamas (and Palestinian Islamic Jihad) members to Lebanon.

Israel's shifting relationship with Arafat and the PLO also played a part in this policy reversal. The possibility of a peace settlement had grown with the Madrid peace conference in October 1991 and the start of the Oslo peace process. Expelling militants to Lebanon and cracking down on Hamas lessened the dangers not only to Israel, but also to those in the Palestinian movement with whom Israel was talking. As Ne'eman has explained, in the early 1980s "we thought we should support these people [Hamas] because they are the enemies of our enemies [the PLO]. But by the early 1990s, we thought we should fight these people because they are the enemies of our partners."[31] Hamas was now seen as a "total spoiler" of the developing peace process and no longer as a useful weapon against the PLO.[32] In response to these moves, Hamas moved much of its leadership abroad to serve in conjunction with the movement's more vulnerable internal leadership in Gaza and the West Bank.

Yet Hamas's animosity did not prevent Israel (and the United States) from talking directly with it after the Arab-Israeli peace process gained momentum in the early 1990s. Israeli officials attempted to engage Hamas in an effort to halt the armed resistance, establish a routine communications channel, and bring the movement formally into the peace process.[33] In 1992, then–foreign minister Shimon Peres declared that Israel was "ready to negotiate with extremists from Hamas if they were freely elected in the Occupied Territories." In early 1994, then–prime minister Yitzhak Rabin also publicly expressed interest in talking with Hamas.[34] During this time, Israel worked to publicize Hamas's demands for renouncing violence by offering to release jailed Hamas leaders so they could travel abroad and discuss these demands with their colleagues and supporters.[35] Hamas rejected all overtures, declaring that "the language between us and the occupying enemy forever shall remain a language of resistance and struggle and not one of negotiations, concessions, or capitulations."[36]

Nonetheless, Hamas repeated and enlarged its offer of a *hudna* to Israel in September 1997. King Hussein of Jordan conveyed Sheikh Yassin's proposal for a thirty-year *hudna* and "discussion of all matters" to Israeli Prime Minister

Benjamin "Bibi" Netanyahu; the king would act as mediator. Three days later, Israel delivered its response. The Israeli secret service, Mossad, badly botched an assassination attempt against the head of Hamas's Political Bureau, Khalid Mesh'al, in Amman, Jordan, embarrassing King Hussein and imperiling the Middle East peace process. King Hussein not only forced Israel to provide the antidote that saved Mesh'al's life. (Thereafter, Mesh'al became known in Hamas as "the martyr who would not die.") But also, as the price for releasing two captured Israeli agents, the king demanded that Israel free Sheikh Yassin from prison, where he was serving a life sentence plus fifteen years for complicity in the kidnapping and killing of two Israeli soldiers.[37]

In reality, Israel was not interested in a ceasefire. Hamas was a sideshow. The main event at this time was the PLO and the peace process. Also, Israeli decision-makers viewed Hamas as an implacable enemy sustained by the belief that God was on its side. Unlike Arafat and the secular PLO, Hamas's religious identity meant that it could not be "bought." Any conciliatory gesture from them must therefore be a trap.

Ongoing violence by Hamas during this period seemed to justify Israel's refusal to entertain any offers for a temporary pause in the conflict. Not unreasonably, Israel believed that Hamas would only use a pause to rearm and regain operational strength for the next round of violent resistance. From Israel's perspective, Hamas's "liberation in phases" looked like a plan for the "destruction in phases" of the Jewish state.

Since the mid-1990s, Israel's official policy has been not to engage with Hamas either directly or indirectly, despite no shortage of issues to discuss, periodic hints of realism and flexibility from the Hamas leadership, and additional offers of *hudnas*. Israel has chosen not to explore whether Hamas's use of violence is religiously mandated or shaped by grubbier political factors. It has decided not to discuss directly with Hamas leaders whether the movement's inconsistent statements and tactical flexibility might reflect an underlying willingness to rethink its stance on the existence of the Jewish state or whether new leadership within Hamas might be identified and encouraged. It has chosen not to learn firsthand whether an Islamic movement is capable of evolving politically.

Instead, Israel has adopted a variety of military, financial, and diplomatic sanctions to marginalize, discredit, and suppress Hamas, and has lobbied other countries to do the same.

WHY NO NEGOTIATIONS?

Although the Israeli government has officially rejected both direct and indirect talks with Hamas on strategic issues that deal with the peace process, it is an open secret that Israeli officials have often violated that policy to engage in *indirect* talks with Hamas on tactical issues. From time to time, the Israeli media have even published the dates for the meetings and the names of Israel's negotiators.

INDIRECT ENGAGEMENT ON TACTICAL ISSUES

Israeli officials are in broad agreement that Hamas has shown no interest in meeting the Quartet's three conditions and having two states living side-by-side in peace.[38] During the past twenty years, however, necessity has required that Israel talk indirectly with Hamas on a variety of issues that may be broadly categorized as tactical or humanitarian. Typically on these occasions, Israel has communicated its preferences to Hamas through third parties—primarily Egypt, but also the United Nations and Germany.

Since Israel's unilateral withdrawal from Gaza in September 2005, indirect engagement has increased as Israel and Hamas have tried to work out issues relating to the day-to-day management of activities in Gaza, such as the flow of goods and people at border crossings from Egypt and Israel. There have been discussions relating to health issues, such as joint measures for the early warning and prevention of infectious diseases like the avian and swine influenzas. The two sides also managed to agree indirectly on a June 2008 ceasefire.

For the past few years, Israel and Hamas have engaged in indirect negotiations over the return of Corporal Gilad Shalit, who was abducted by Palestinian militants in June 2006. Israel used the good offices of Egypt's security services and then, after this effort failed, turned to Germany's Federal Intelligence Service, or BND. In October 2009, the BND had some limited success by getting Hamas to release a video of Shalit, proving he was still alive, in return for the release from jail of twenty female Palestinian prisoners.[39]

There has been no controversy in Israel over its indirectly engaging Hamas to secure Shalit's safe return. Indeed, the case has seized the country's imagination, because of the relentless public relations efforts of the Shalit family and, perhaps most important, the ability of the Israeli public to empathize with the distraught family over their missing son in a country where virtually every citizen serves in the military.[40]

But controversy has surrounded the reported price tag to obtain Shalit's return. Some Israelis have objected to the prospect of releasing hundreds of unrepentant and still-dangerous terrorists with much Israeli blood on their hands. Others have quietly noted that the "exchange rate" of these prisoner swaps clearly benefits Hamas and raises the value of taking Israelis hostage. There are worries, too, that any exchange would increase the stature of Hamas among Palestinians while undermining the position of the PA.

If there is little objection in principle to discussions of issues of humanitarian necessity, why doesn't Israel admit publicly to these indirect talks with Hamas? Some senior Israeli officials believe that Israel should admit to them when it comes to negotiating the release of captured soldiers. Shaul Mofaz—as the former minister of defense, former chief of the General Staff of the Israel Defense Forces, and currently a member of the Knesset—has been at the center of the debate. He understands the reasons for the country's official policy, but believes the state needs to do more to keep faith with the soldiers who risk their lives for Israel. "We need to convince the Israeli people and the soldiers that the state of Israel will do its very best to gain the return of the soldiers in the hands of enemies, even terror organizations calling for the destruction of the State of Israel. . . . It is a balancing approach."[41]

For now, Israel comes down on the other side of this balance. The lack of acknowledgment of even indirect talks with Hamas brings some benefits and few risks. It allows the government to maintain "plausible deniability." Israel's ability to deny that it is engaging with Hamas gives it greater control over how the issues are reported and perceived domestically, which helps the government manage and shape public expectations. In Israel's fractious political system, where governments often depend on coalitions of parties from the far ends of the political spectrum, official admission of even indirect talks with any terrorist group would at best create problems for the prime minister and at worst bring down the government.

Israel also fears that were it to engage with Hamas, the door would then be opened wide for others to do so. The concern is that engagement would lead to a gradual erosion of sanctions against Hamas and a weakening of its isolation. Over time, this could lead to its eventual legitimization without requiring any fundamental change in the movement's philosophy toward Israel in exchange. Hamas would be strengthened economically, diplomatically, and militarily. Further, there would be no way for Israel to control the agenda. Though Israel may wish to talk to Hamas about sewage treatment in Gaza, others may have loftier and more strategic issues in mind.

Finally, there is little risk for Israel in its current arrangement with Hamas. The past few years have proven that the two can do business. While the current methods are probably less efficient than direct talks, Israel can satisfy its immediate needs and limited tactical objectives without either triggering a domestic backlash or creating an unhelpful international precedent. This arrangement appears to satisfy Hamas as well. Every indication suggests it only wants to engage for the similar set of very practical reasons Israel shares, such as ensuring the flow of goods and services into Gaza or seeking the release of their prisoners from Israeli jails.

DIRECT ENGAGEMENT ON STRATEGIC ISSUES

Traditionally, the risks for Israel talking directly to Hamas about strategic issues like the peace process and a possible two-state solution have significantly outweighed any potential gains.

Interestingly, Israel does not refuse to talk to Hamas simply because it is a terrorist organization.[42] It has talked with those it has considered terrorists and terrorist organizations in the past, such as Yasser Arafat and the PLO. But Hamas has been placed in a different category because it aims at the ultimate extinction of the Jewish state. It is not merely Hamas's terror that troubles. It is the agenda: the creation of an Islamic state and the end of Israel.

Consensus prevails across the political spectrum in Israel on this point. There is nothing to negotiate with Hamas other than the terms of its own destruction. According to Dan Meridor, the deputy prime minister, "Hamas doesn't want to talk to us about Israel on this land, which they view as a holy Muslim land. So what is there to talk about? Their view is that we're just a passing accident of history."[43]

Prime Minister Netanyahu said in a January 2010 press conference, "You make peace with an enemy who wants to stop being an enemy and move to peace. But an enemy that just wants to cut you to pieces and has no intention of seeing you walk this earth and wants to obliterate you is not a partner for peace. That distinction is crucial. . . . I mean, the late Anwar Sadat and the late King Hussein didn't say, "Well, our goal is to obliterate Israel—now let's enter peace negotiations for the sake of this obliteration."[44]

Complicating matters is the question of who speaks for Hamas and controls the movement. Its internal and external leadership have different priorities. The inside leaders, based in the Occupied Territories, are more conciliatory to the PA and express a greater willingness to be viewed as a legitimate opposition party. But the outside leaders, based in Syria and elsewhere in the region, are more hostile and willing to consider violence. More troubling for Israel is the prospect that neither leadership group really directs the movement, but rather both are subject to the desires of Hamas's sponsors—Syria and especially Iran—which provide funding, military training, and weapons. Iranian president Mahmoud Ahmadinejad's serial denials of the Holocaust, his repeated statements that Israel should not exist, and, most important, Iran's relentless push for a nuclear weapons capability have made him and his regime Israel's number-one enemy. The country would therefore not want to make any concessions to Hamas that might suggest weakness and embolden the Islamic movement's most generous patron.[45]

Two additional reasons reinforce Israel's position against engagement. First, unlike the secular Fatah, Hamas is viewed as a religious organization and therefore less likely to settle for anything less than recapturing all of historic Palestine. Again, Meridor: "When you get God into the discussions, God never compromises."[46]

Second, even if Hamas explicitly modified its desire to reclaim all of historic Palestine, Israel would still hesitate to engage, because of the implications for the PA and the peace process. Since December 1988, when Yasser Arafat and the PLO accepted Israel's existence and a possible two-state solution to the conflict, Israel has viewed the PLO as a potential partner for peace. While the peace process has had its ups and downs over the years, no Israeli government has been able to deny the reality that the Fatah-led PLO, and now the PA, provides the best chance for managing, and perhaps one day even ending, the conflict.

If Israel ever were to negotiate with Hamas on the larger issues that divide the two communities, it would deal a death blow to the Fatah-led PA on both pragmatic and ideological levels. Israel's negotiating with Hamas would undermine the PA's legitimacy and credibility as the sole representative of the Palestinian people. It would destroy any chance of Israel's ever reaching a peace agreement with Mahmoud Abbas and the PA. While having lunch at a seaside Tel Aviv restaurant in February 2010, the former head of Mossad's Global Operations, Intelligence, and Foreign Relations, Yoram Hessel, told me, "The worst effect you have is the impact on President Abbas. You stab him in the back, you stab him in the belly. You undermine Abbas while everyone else is trying to support him." Abbas and the PA understand this, which is why, surprisingly to some, they are as adamant as Israel that third parties stay away from Hamas.[47]

More broadly, engagement between Israel and Hamas would alarm many of Israel's moderate Arab neighbors—Jordan and Egypt among them—who would worry not only about undermining secular Palestinian nationalism, perhaps irrevocably, but also at the strengthening and legitimizing of religious Palestinian nationalism. Giving Hamas a place at the table would encourage other Islamic movements throughout the region that directly threaten the stability of many Arab states. In response, Israel's relations with these states would suffer, halting and even reversing a recent trend toward a measure of diplomatic recognition and greater economic and security cooperation from moderate Arab states.

Not only does Israel have no desire to talk to Hamas, it also doesn't need to. Few voices inside or outside of Israel have called for engagement with Hamas.

In the past, Israel has shown that it is willing to run risks for peace. After Hamas's victory in the 2007 elections, some Israelis thought that Hamas was now a new "fact on the ground" that called for a reassessment of the country's "no-talks" policy. But these calls—and any illusions that Hamas might be a new partner for peace—vanished after Israelis witnessed the ferocious violence of Hamas's June 2007 coup in Gaza, the constant barrage of rockets and mortars, and the "tunnel industry" that relentlessly smuggled explosives and weapons into Gaza.[48]

The desire to continue the isolation of Hamas has been reinforced by the perception that by almost any measure, Israel has been winning the war. The costs to the country of Hamas's resistance have been tolerable or at least manageable, especially after construction of the separation barrier reduced suicide attacks. According to Shin Bet, 2009 marked the first year in a decade when there were no suicide attacks inside Israel.[49] Also, Operation Cast Lead sent a strong message to the Hamas leadership that Israel could inflict enormous damage on their ability to operate as a resistance movement and, moreover, that it could do so whenever it chose.

There has also been no external pressure from the United States, Europe, or the other Quartet members for Israel to negotiate or even meet with Hamas until

Hamas recognizes Israel, renounces violence, and accepts all previous Israeli-Palestinian agreements. Some fraying around the edges of the international embargo against talking to Hamas has occurred, with the most prominent outlier being former president Jimmy Carter, who traveled to Damascus in April 2008 to meet with Hamas's leadership-in-exile.[50] None of this has had any impact on Israel's policy toward Hamas.

CONCLUSION

During the past two decades, Hamas has sent mixed and confusing messages. Its founding charter is an anti-Jewish, anti-Zionist rant, yet Khalid Mesh'al and other Hamas leaders have claimed that it is outdated and that its extreme language should be ignored; they have even suggested it may be rewritten. Hamas has engineered suicide attacks and launched rockets and mortars that have killed and wounded hundreds of Israelis, but it has also renounced violence for long stretches and offered *hudnas*. It has refused to accept the validity of previous agreements between the Palestinians and Israel, but has agreed to respect them. It has repeatedly stated that it will not recognize Israel's right to exist, but it has also accepted the fact of Israel's existence. It claims it is on a mission from God to reclaim all of historic Palestine, yet it has said it will abide by the will of the Palestinian people if they choose to accept a two-state solution and coexistence with Israel.

These mixed messages have caused a few observers to argue that Hamas has in fact been moderating its views and to propose that Israel should explore whether there is any common ground. The verdict of a leading Israeli scholar who has studied Hamas for years is that the Islamic movement's statements "certainly signify a process of political maturation and a willingness to consider a two-state political solution. This process is reminiscent of the path pursued by the PLO under Yasser Arafat."[51]

Proponents of engagement argue that Israel should talk with Hamas directly on the issue of a *hudna*. The former director of Shin Bet, Ami Ayalon, has contended that Sheikh Yassin's offers suggested an important course correction for the Islamic movement—that the date for recapturing all of Palestine could be delayed or postponed, perhaps indefinitely. Yassin's precise motivation remains uncertain, Ayalon asserts, but it is likely that he was responding to "facts on the ground" during the 1990s. After Oslo, he realized that the peace process, not resistance, enjoyed the broad support of the Palestinian people. A *hudna* lasting decades was sending two messages to Yassin's followers: that they could afford to be patient because time was on their side, and more important from Israel's perspective, that recapturing all of Palestine would not happen in their lifetimes. Yassin was modifying the movement's tactical goals, but this was all he could do because the strategic goal of restoring all of Palestine to the Muslims was divinely directed and therefore could never be modified. Yassin was now unilaterally defying Hamas's founding charter, which had placed no time restriction for Islam's ultimate victory.[52]

The former Mossad chief Efraim Halevy has also proposed that Israel meet with Hamas and explore the parameters of a long-term ceasefire. On ideological grounds, Halevy asserts, Hamas cannot bring itself to officially admit that it cannot destroy Israel, but the movement is realistic. "What is changing before our eyes is a clear process of recognition by the Hamas leaders that their ideological aspirations are unattainable and will not be attainable in the foreseeable future." Hamas's leaders have stated that "they are willing or want the establishment of a Palestinian state within the provisional 1967 borders. Provisional until when? They do not say and they do not know."[53] Halevy has argued that this presents Israel with more opportunity than risk, dismissing the idea that Hamas would use the *hudna* to prepare the movement for the next round of violence: "If Hamas uses the next thirty years to rearm and mass capabilities, so what? We can use the next thirty years to do the same thing. We can intervene if we don't like what we see. We're not going to be sitting ducks. . . . Besides, I know of no terrorist who can be recruited now for a mission he'll be told about in thirty years' time. He'd be middle-aged, with children and grandchildren."[54]

These voices calling for a fundamental rethinking of Israel's relationship with Hamas are strictly in the minority, at least for now. It is not just that the Israeli government assesses that its national security is stronger without a *hudna*, it is that the incentives all run in the opposite direction.

The Islamic movement's violence in Gaza has been reduced dramatically. It remains weak, isolated, and increasingly unpopular there. Israel's friends and partners have followed a policy of not talking as long as Hamas maintains its maximalist position toward the Jewish state. Israel only faces domestic pressure to engage Hamas on humanitarian issues, like trying to secure the return of Gilad Shalit. These it can satisfy through indirect negotiations.

In addition, the dynamics of the peace process strongly reinforce Israel's preference not to talk to Hamas. Its primary partner in the peace process, the Fatah-led PA, has been firmly opposed to any engagement by Israel with Hamas as long as Hamas is not part of a unity government. Despite real misery and hardship in Gaza, there is little evidence that any significant opposition has arisen, or is even capable of arising, against Hamas, given its almost total control after its June 2007 coup. And the PA remains too weak either to compel Hamas to form another unity government and support the peace process, or to move forward without the backing of the Islamic movement.

As long as the Palestinian national movement is divided between the PA and Hamas, Israel is absolved from having to make the difficult decisions necessary for a final peace settlement and a two-state solution, such as the status of Jerusalem and settlements throughout the West Bank. There has *never* been any domestic consensus on these issues. Making these decisions would involve bruising and highly personal battles among competing political parties, pragmatists willing to cut a deal, those opposed to the peace process, and the self-righteous who claim to have a direct line to the Almighty. No Israeli government has been eager to have this debate. In this sense, Hamas has been a kind of solution. Its militancy has allowed Israel to avoid the tough decisions.[55]

Israel has no long-term plan or strategy for dealing with the Islamic movement and appears uncertain as to how, or whether, its relationship with Hamas might change. For the time being, Israel prefers to keep its distance and watch closely to see if Hamas indicates a willingness to adjust fundamentally its stance toward the Jewish state. As a former senior Mossad official explains, "The most important task for any intelligence agency is to provide early warning of intentions. Most of the time and attention is devoted to doing this to detect the possible outbreak of conflict. But this works the same way for peace as it does for war. So there is no need for direct talks with Hamas, because we are always looking to see if they have had a change of heart."[56]

Iraq

TURKEY

SYRIA

IRAN

Tigris River

Ramadi
Fallujah

Baghdad

ANBAR
PROVINCE

IRAQ

Euphrates River

SAUDI ARABIA

KUWAIT

5.

THE ANBAR AWAKENING (SAH'WA AL-ANBAR)

As the former Coalition Provisional Authority (CPA) official revisited the decisions emanating from the CPA's Baghdad compound, the two dozen men in the room stiffened their posture and narrowed their eyes. I had invited them to this conference room at a tony hotel in Tampa, Florida. The purpose was academic in nature: to discuss and debate events that had taken place years earlier and half a world away in Iraq. The military called this type of exercise an "After Action Review."

But as the former CPA official continued to explain, justify, and rationalize U.S. policy, these men were transported far from Tampa and back to Iraq. To the dusty villages, the lush palm groves, and the unsmiling Iraqi faces that had stared back at them from bleak cinderblock homes. To the violence, the instant terror, the adrenaline rush, and the perpetual anxiety of living in an alien and frequently hostile environment. Memories of the men they had left behind—their men—flooded back. The words of the former CPA official did not relieve their pain. They made it worse.

As I looked around the room at the captains, majors, colonels, and generals, their hands were shaking. They were doing all they could to control their rage at this former civilian official who now personified all that had gone wrong in Iraq.

I decided it was a good time to take a coffee break. A few minutes outside the conference room calmed tempers. We then reconvened and the discussions continued throughout the day.

The military officers now took turns giving their perspective on events in Iraq. I asked why they had not reached out earlier to the Sunnis who were being savaged by al Qaeda—tortured, raped, and beheaded. They explained that the mission in Iraq was underresourced from day one and that Anbar in particular was seen as a backwater, with far too few troops to cover an expanse of territory as large as North Carolina. They explained that their casualties in Anbar Province from 2003 to 2006 were greater than anywhere else in Iraq. They explained how difficult it was to understand Iraqi culture and society. The "human terrain"—the interlocking networks of family and personal relationships, the hierarchy of tribal status and the distinction between those who held real power and those who merely claimed to have it—was largely a mystery.

An Iraqi participant spoke up. He had been a former Ba'athist, a general in Saddam's army, and later, with the support of the Americans, the mayor of a town on the Euphrates River. "What didn't you understand?" he testily asked in a thick accent. "How could you not see what was happening to us in 2004, 2005? Al Qaeda was killing our people. We were conducting funeral processions past your posts and burying our dead every day."

The anger and grief in his voice were unmistakable. Then I noticed: His hands were shaking, too.

FEW DEVELOPMENTS FROM THE AMERICAN WAR in Iraq have been as celebrated as the tribal movement referred to as the "Anbar Awakening," the switch in allegiance by tribes in Anbar Province from supporting al Qaeda in Iraq (AQI) and the insurgents to the U.S. forces. Until the Awakening, Anbar had been the epicenter of resistance to the American occupation and disproportionately responsible for U.S. casualties. This tribal movement rescued a politically and militarily "lost" province.[1] It helped prevent a humiliating American retreat that would have plunged the country into greater chaos.

The obstacles to success were imposing, the combat environment relentlessly violent. Anbar was home to forty-eight major tribes and was overwhelmingly Sunni, the ethnic group most closely aligned with Saddam Hussein's murderous regime. It bordered six other Iraqi provinces and three countries, none of which had secure borders. Temperatures during the summer months usually exceeded 115 degrees; inside most American military vehicles, the temperatures averaged 20 to 30 degrees higher. The Pentagon had decided that Anbar would be an "economy-of-force" effort, which meant that there would never be enough troops to patrol and secure the province properly. Soldiers joked that Anbar contained one-third of Iraq's territory and two-thirds of Iraq's problems.

Perhaps because of the Anbar Awakening's success, its causes and consequences have been widely mischaracterized and misunderstood. The conventional wisdom is that the Awakening started in the summer of 2006. It was led by a powerful and charismatic sheikh in the provincial capital city of Ramadi. It was nurtured and encouraged as part of a masterful counterinsurgency (COIN) strategy that had been fundamentally rethought and reengineered by the U.S. Army and Marines. It was largely "nonkinetic," involving not the use of force but only reconstruction funds, information operations, and "three cups of tea." It succeeded because President George W. Bush decided to "surge" the troops in January 2007. It succeeded because of dumb luck. It eliminated al Qaeda. It was then duplicated across Iraq in later initiatives, such as the Concerned Local Citizens (CLC) and Sons of Iraq (SOI) programs.

None of these claims is true.

So how did the Anbar Awakening really happen?

The Awakening cannot be reduced to a discrete moment, a solitary sheikh, or a single Anbar tribe. Rather, it was a series of disjointed tribal uprisings throughout Anbar Province that started fitfully as early as 2003, were suppressed, and then gathered new life and momentum in 2006 and 2007. In retrospect, it is easy to see a linear progression of events that led to its ultimate success. In reality, it was far more complex, even convoluted. The path to the Awakening was full of missed opportunities, bureaucratic infighting, sectarian hatreds, world-class incompetence, medieval brutality, personal rivalries, arrogance, and ignorance.

Many factors led to the Awakening; without any one, it would not have occurred. Abu Musab al-Zarqawi, AQI's leader, and his followers had to miscalculate the impact their extreme religious beliefs, casual violence, encroachment on traditional tribal business, and random terror would have on the tribes. The Sunni Arabs had to conquer their fear, anger, mistrust, and injured pride before they could imagine themselves allying with the United States. The American military had to overcome the misguided policies imposed by civilian officials in Washington and Baghdad, as well as its own analytical and operational shortcomings.

SETTING THE STAGE FOR FAILURE

Occupying and administering Iraq was always going to present problems, but the decisions the United States made in early 2003 rendered a tough challenge even tougher. The United States was grossly unprepared to assume responsibility for Iraq. According to the official U.S. Army history, "Phase IV" plans for how to secure a political victory in Iraq after the end of major combat operations were "poorly conceived and poorly coordinated."[2]

In January 2003, two months before the war started, the Pentagon created the Office of Reconstruction and Humanitarian Assistance (ORHA), headed by retired Lieutenant General Jay Garner. ORHA was inserted in Iraq in late April. During its short life, the understaffed ORHA proved incapable of restoring basic services, distributing humanitarian assistance, or establishing law and order. U.S. military forces, with no orders or training to deal with the situation, watched passively the escalating looting, crime, and rioting in the first few weeks of the American occupation.

Confusion over ORHA's mission—was it humanitarian relief, transitional authority to an Iraqi government, or countrywide administration with military authority?—was never resolved. Rather, the issue became moot with the arrival in early May of L. Paul "Jerry" Bremer III as the head of the CPA. The CPA's mission was clear: to exercise supreme executive, legislative, and judicial functions while rebuilding the state's infrastructure.

Only days after arriving in Baghdad in mid-May, Bremer issued four decrees that created an ideal environment for the insurgency to take root and grow. First, he eliminated from the government payroll anyone who belonged to the top four tiers of the Ba'ath Party. This immediately purged tens of thousands of managers, technicians, and professionals who had only joined the party to get a government job. Second, Bremer dissolved the Iraqi army, police, Ministry of Interior, and presidential security units. Third, he decided that there would not be an interim Iraqi government in the short term. And fourth, he started shutting down state-run industries.[3]

The first two orders placed hundreds of thousands of men out of work; the impact on their extended families and other dependents was great.[4] The third order, not to quickly transition to an Iraqi government, made the U.S. and Coalition forces seem more like occupiers than liberators, which further alienated the

Iraqis. As Jay Garner recalls, he woke up on May 17 and found "three or four hundred thousand enemies and no Iraqi face on the government."[5] Expressed differently, CPA had instantly joined together the men with guns with the men with brains and energized all of them to hate the United States. The fourth order closed inefficient businesses in the hope that a free-market economy would flourish. In the meantime, tens of thousands more Iraqis were now without jobs.

The basis for these decisions lay not just with wildly unrealistic notions of how easily the United States could mold a new Iraq into a modern, pro-Western democratic society. It was also based on wildly unrealistic notions over how peacefully and rapidly the three leading ethnic/sectarian groups—the Shi'a, Kurds, and Sunnis—could themselves reach consensus on power-sharing.

Bremer's orders, more than the war itself, overturned the existing order in which the Sunnis had dominated the Shi'a and the Kurds. CPA's orders disproportionately affected the Sunnis, as they had served as the core support for Saddam and the regime despite being less than 20 percent of the population. The Shi'a would now be the dominant ethnic group inside Iraq.

For the Sunnis, Bremer's order removing them from positions of power and authority all over the country made de-Ba'athification look a lot like de-Sunnification. As a former Ba'athist leader protested, "We were on top of the system. We had dreams. Now we are the losers. We lost our positions, our status, the security of our families, stability. Curse the Americans. Curse them."[6]

For the first time in modern memory, "the Sunni Arabs were forced to confront the loss of their ascendant power *as a community*."[7] As Colonel Derek Harvey, a senior military intelligence officer with extensive experience in Iraq, commented, "The United States upset the apple cart. We took from those who had and gave to those who had not. In that society, when you lose, you lose for generations."[8]

Sunni fears of marginalization appeared to be further confirmed when the CPA unveiled in mid-July the Interim Governing Council (IGC), an advisory body of Iraqi nationals. The IGC seemed to have been handpicked along sectarian lines, which elevated Shi'a and Kurdish representation at the expense of the Sunnis. Many of the Shi'a on the IGC were rumored to have close connections with Iran, which the Sunnis believed was infiltrating the country and undermining its sovereignty. Those few Sunnis selected for the Council were exiles and largely unknown inside the country. With the demise of the Ba'athist Party, the artificial creation of a pro-Shi'a IGC, and the emergence of an all-powerful CPA now managing Iraq's affairs, the Sunnis saw no political way forward to express their grievances and seek relief.

But they could take up arms in opposition. Before the war, the CIA had warned that the Iraqis could respond to a conventional military defeat by launching an insurgency.[9] The three key elements were all present: motive, means, and opportunity. The American occupation and Bremer's orders provided ample motive. The means were easily available: The entire country was an arms depot, with an estimated 250,000 tons of unsafeguarded weapons located in over 10,000 caches.[10] The disorder and chaos in the wake of Washington's failure to plan adequately for Phase IV provided the opportunity.[11]

The resistance started slowly and gained momentum during the spring and summer of 2003. It was largely a Sunni Arab phenomenon.[12] Motives varied. Part of the resistance was a nationalist backlash against a foreign military presence, fanned by calls from the mosques for the Sunnis to fight as a religious duty. Former military officers and Ba'athist members of the regime fought to restore Saddam, to restore the old order without Saddam, or simply to restore a measure of their lost dignity and self-respect. Some participated to avenge deaths of friends and family or from a deep sense of tribal or personal honor after suffering humiliating treatment by U.S. soldiers. With unemployment at well over 50 percent, many Sunnis also saw the insurgency as a way to make money.[13] (The bounty for attacking U.S. and Coalition forces was $100, and $500 if a Bradley or Abrams armored vehicle was disabled.[14]) Although Saddam had welcomed foreign jihadi fighters to Iraq prior to the war, many were more enthusiastic than effective. They formed only a fraction of the insurgents.[15]

Most of the violence was in the form of small roadside bombs or sporadic mortar fire; the military initially judged the attacks as "anemic and uncoordinated."[16] Throughout the spring of 2003, the Bush administration dismissed the insurgents as "dead enders," "noncompliant forces," or "former regime elements." But by mid-July, the new commander of Central Command, General John Abizaid, admitted that the United States was facing "a classical guerrilla-type campaign." The resistance "is getting more organized and it is learning. It is adapting, it is adapting to our tactics, techniques and procedures."[17]

Abizaid was reacting to the number of attacks on Coalition forces, which continued to climb, doubling from June to July. The death of Saddam's sons, Uday and Qusay, in a firefight with U.S. forces that summer had no impact on the insurgency. The violence intensified dramatically in August, with deadly attacks on the Jordanian embassy and UN headquarters.[18] A few months later, the insurgents narrowly missed killing Deputy Defense Secretary Paul Wolfowitz in his hotel room in Baghdad's fortified Green Zone. The following day, the headquarters of the International Committee of the Red Cross was bombed. In November, a top-secret CIA report endorsed by Bremer stated that the insurgency was gaining support among the people.[19] U.S. casualties reached a new record that month, with up to 1,000 attacks on Coalition forces. American troops did not have an updated doctrine or the training for dealing with this type of enemy.

If Abizaid was quick to recognize the nature of the conflict, he was far slower in grasping the source of the violence. The United States did not understand whom it was fighting. The insurgency's decentralized and fragmentary nature made it even more difficult for the U.S. military to counter. According to former-Marine-turned-author Bing West, "our military was facing an enemy that had no head, no central nervous system, no hierarchical command and control that could be destroyed. There was no structure to the Sunni insurgency. It was like swatting bees."[20] The only political agenda appeared to be inflicting pain on U.S. forces and running the United States out of Iraq.

The lack of tactical and strategic intelligence on the insurgency severely handicapped the military. Immediately after the end of major combat operations, Washington had assigned the intelligence community a higher priority: to find the weapons of mass destruction (WMD) that had been the main justification for going to war. The Iraq Survey Group (ISG) tasked with this mission had close to 1,400 intelligence officers and support staff combing Iraq for WMD.

If the military did not have the ISG's resources and manpower, it did have the CIA. But the Agency started in Baghdad with less than one hundred officers and cycled through three station chiefs in the first nine months. The violence and insecurity hindered case officers from traveling alone out of the Green Zone, and their lack of language ability and cultural understanding further hampered their effectiveness.[21] The military suffered from an overwhelming shortage of human intelligence (HUMINT) from Iraqi sources who could offer strategic insights into the insurgency. According to Ben Connable, a Marine intelligence officer, "We never had enough skilled linguists, we never had enough interpreters. We only had 25 to 30 percent of what we needed as a bare minimum."[22] As more soldiers died, Rumsfeld complained in December 2003 about the need for better intelligence and wondered whether U.S. forces were defeating the insurgents faster than they were regenerating.[23]

Meanwhile, in mid-December 2003, Saddam Hussein was seized from a "spider hole" not far from his home town of Tikrit; his "delousing" by an American military doctor was watched by tens of millions in Iraq and around the world. Despite the Bush administration's high hopes that his capture would break the back of the insurgency, it had no impact.

The insurgency in Anbar Province had gathered deadly force by this time, but it had not always been so. The CIA had long-standing relationships with many of the Anbar tribes and had been communicating with them before the start of the war. As U.S. forces had converged on Baghdad in April 2003, tribal representatives actually escorted the senior Iraqi military commander to the highway leading into Anbar. The Iraqi commander promised that he would discharge his fighters if the Americans promised not to use force in Anbar; the sheikhs would escort U.S. troops into the cities.[24] Many of the tribes had opposed Saddam and thought that the United States would now use them to help govern the province, as the British had done years before.

The Sunnis were soon disappointed. The CPA's decisions in spring and summer 2003 slowly turned many of them against the American presence. All of the shortcomings of the U.S. occupation were magnified among the Sunnis in Anbar. Complicating stability and security operations was the fact that Anbar was still seen as sideshow. In early September, there were fewer than 10,000 soldiers operating across the province.[25] It had two police trainers, which worked out to one police adviser for every one million Iraqis, and only one CPA representative.[26]

It is difficult to generalize on the nature of the U.S. engagement with the people of Anbar during 2003 and early 2004. The province was too large, the troops spread too thinly, the security environment too hostile, and the experience of individual soldiers too varied. But many troops talked to the locals, as much as the language barrier allowed. Engagement ran the spectrum, ranging from parleys over tea between senior U.S. military commanders and eminent sheikhs to units patrolling the streets to soldiers forcibly entering homes at night and interrogating (and humiliating) military-age men in front of their families. Some of these latter encounters likely produced new recruits for the insurgency.

Making a complex situation worse was the absence of any overall guidance on how U.S. forces should engage with the locals.[27] There was no central plan.

Again, Connable: "We had no idea what to do when the fighting stopped. No clue. We made it up as we went along."[28] The military reached out to the locals according to how commanders perceived the threats in their area of operations. "Engagement was personality driven. Some guys got it and were good at it. Other guys didn't get it or didn't want to get it. They were more comfortable with kinetic operations."[29]

Others argued for a less kinetic approach. Even as the violence gradually escalated throughout 2003, some U.S. intelligence officers believed that the majority of the Iraqi army and Ba'ath Party members were waiting and watching, thinking the Americans would rescind Bremer's orders and call them back to military service.[30] According to an Iraqi leader, at this time "many of the tribal elite continued trying to convince the now unemployed and de-Ba'athified Sunnis to wait and see the next U.S. move. . . . The tribal elite and Sunni moderate majority still expected the U.S. would give a reasonable share of power to the Sunnis in the next government, even though the Bremer laws were confusing them."[31]

Yet the CPA resisted anything that would empower the Sunni tribes. Ideological members of the Bush administration likened the Ba'ath Party and its support for Saddam to the Nazis. Washington's concept was that the urban, professional class would build a modern Iraq. Antiquated tribes who profited from smuggling, banditry, and hostage-taking had no place in the new state. The CPA also argued that the center needed to be empowered before the periphery; Iraq needed a strong central government. Delegating authority to the provinces would undermine that goal.

The result, according to John McCary, an Army human intelligence collector then serving in Anbar, was that "civilian and political leadership in Baghdad and Washington consistently undermined initiatives that showed early promise by adhering to ideologically strict policies with little relevance to what was happening on the ground."[32]

In response to requests to engage in cooperation with the tribes, U.S. military officers complained, "The standard answer we got from Bremer's people was that the tribes are a vestige of the past, that they have no place in a democratic Iraq."[33] In his memoirs, George Tenet, the former CIA director, recounts how he and others lobbied Bremer to allow the agency to reach out to the Sunni tribes. They were always rebuffed, told that they were "dancing with CIA's old pals."[34] For McCary, the message was clear: "The CPA wanted to bolster the power and legitimacy of the fledgling government in Baghdad, and viewed any local initiatives not under its control as undermining the authority of the federal government."[35]

Less well known until now is that CPA killed an initiative that had originated at the highest levels of the National Security Council. In the fall of 2003, the NSC decided that the United States needed to reach out to the Sunnis. A senior CIA case officer in Baghdad who had had dealings with the Sunni military leaders before the war was tapped to contact them. The Sunnis were initially reluctant, complaining that the United States had betrayed them before by telling them to remain in their barracks, lay down their arms, and await the call back to service. The case officer countered by telling them that they didn't have a better offer. They should meet with U.S. officials and discuss how they could best be reintegrated into society. After they eventually agreed, he reported back to his contact in the CPA. The CPA official said that Bremer did not want to do this and that the CIA should just keep them talking. The case officer replied that this was not a clandestine operation. It had to be handled publicly by CPA. He was told again that Bremer did not want to do this. The NSC initiative went no further.[36]

The CPA was no more deferential to the senior military commander in Iraq, General Ricardo Sanchez. "[General] Abizaid and I repeatedly met with Paul Bremer and urged him to work with us in the process of tribal engagement and reconciliation," Sanchez complained. "But he adamantly refused to do so."[37] In late 2003, Sanchez proposed creating a directorate to coordinate outreach efforts to the tribes. Bremer argued that it was a civilian, not military, function and belonged under CPA's control. According to two senior military intelligence officers who supported Sanchez's idea, CPA took it over, then starved it of staff, budget, and support.[38] It would take more than three years for Sanchez's idea to be properly institutionalized, in 2007, by General David Petraeus.

Faced with an out-of-touch CPA that they believed placed their men at greater risk, some military officers simply ignored or disobeyed orders and took the initiative. Starting in the autumn of 2003, U.S. military units operating in Anbar attempted to work with tribal leaders to secure their areas. According to McCary, "Despite higher-level directives to avoid engaging with tribal leaders, several units led proactive campaigns to engage and support tribal initiatives. Commanders . . . had to modify their approaches to fly under the radar of inappropriate higher-level policies, preventing them from becoming public or widespread."[39] Military officers also did end-arounds to get public works contracts into the hands of friendly sheikhs who were willing to help them. The standard approach of awarding contracts to the lowest bidder would have resulted in local sheikhs demolishing anything that outsiders had constructed. "I blew a lot of that off," said one lieutenant colonel. "They were trying to work it like a U.S. thing, like a U.S. contract. I helped the Iraqis work the system. I told them what the low bid was and helped them determine what the price they had to come in under was."[40] A British general in Iraq approvingly characterized these efforts as "consent and evade."

Despite all the setbacks, by the start of 2004 the U.S. military had reason to be cautiously optimistic. Saddam had been captured. Iraqi politics was beginning to reassert itself after the CPA announced it would wind down and have the Iraqis take ownership of their country by June 30.

Army Major General Charles Swannack, Commander of the 82nd Airborne Division in Anbar, thought the province in pretty good shape as he prepared to hand it over to the Marines in March. He claimed that his forces had been "Phase IV oriented from Day One," meaning that they were actively engaging in efforts to win the hearts and minds of the locals. In a press conference on January 6, 2004, he declared that the United States had "turned the corner" in dealing with the insurgency and that they were "on a glide path toward success."[41]

But in late March, four American contractors working for the Blackwater security company drove into the wrong part of Fallujah, a city of about 200,000 in Anbar. They were surrounded and killed and their bodies were burned. The charred remains of two of the men were suspended from a bridge. More chilling than the horrific killings were the pictures of Iraqi children smiling and celebrating their deaths.

President Bush personally decided that the murders were to be avenged by invading Fallujah, contrary to the advice of his senior military officers, who saw the lynchings as a clever trap to draw U.S. forces into the type of urban combat where their advantages of maneuver and firepower would be diminished.[42] The decision was not discussed ahead of time with members of the Iraqi Governing Council.[43] On April 5, the Marines launched Operation Vigilant Resolve and encountered stiff resistance. As they methodically cleared the city block by block, accounts of the battle were transmitted across Iraq and the Middle East by al Jazeera and other Arab media. Televised pictures of the city's devastation and human suffering alienated the Iraqi population and inflamed public opinion.

Less than a week into the battle, the Marines were ordered to halt. The senior Marine general, James Mattis, argued that they were only a few days from victory. But leaders on the Iraqi Governing Council had threatened to resign just a few months before the United States was going to transfer authority. CPA feared that it would not have any Iraqi leaders to assume power at the end of June.[44]

The uneasy standoff in Fallujah had both prompt and longer-term consequences. In the short term, the Sunni insurgents celebrated a great victory over the Americans. The insurgency metastasized across Iraq, as new recruits flocked to join. (CPA's vacillation at this time over how to handle the challenge presented by Moqtada al-Sadr, a Shi'a firebrand, and his Mahdi Army, further suggested that the United States would blink first and back down from a fight.) Just as important, the Sunni tribes who were cooperating or thinking about siding with the United States now refused to have any contact with the Americans. After Fallujah, a Marine intelligence officer later told me, "We knew this was going to mean the end of our efforts to engage with the tribes for some time."[45] The handling of the battle, both the initial decision to start and the decision to stop, also revealed the fault lines in the Iraqi political system and the poor judgment of CPA and Bush administration officials.

To try to make the best of a bad situation, an arrangement was cobbled together by the Marines and CIA to provide cover for the U.S. retreat from the city.[46] A former Ba'athist general was placed in charge of the "Fallujah Brigade," which consisted of 2,000 local residents, many of whom were known to be insurgents. Any semblance of security quickly evaporated. "Large insurgent units organized, trained, and staged within the city. Incident levels actually *increased* as insurgents gained control of the city and then clashed with coalition forces."[47] Vehicles and weapons that had been provided by the United States were used against American troops. "By the end of June, Fallujah had once again become an insurgent stronghold, with leaders of the 'Fallujah Brigade' openly aligning with the insurgency and calling for Islamic government in the city."[48] The mishandling of Fallujah highlighted the poor coordination between U.S. military and civilian leaders, the danger of having indigenous forces "stand up while U.S. forces stand down," and a sense of foreboding that the insurgents might be winning.

Some military officers thought that tribal leaders who could be trusted might be found elsewhere, outside the country, in Amman, Jordan. This led to one of the oddest episodes of the Iraq war—the outreach to tribal sheikhs who had decamped to Amman after the U.S. invasion. Some sheikhs may have left Anbar because they were deemed too important by the tribes to risk remaining in a chaotic environment. Others may have left out of cowardice. Some had real power and influence. Others had none and were "living at home in their mother's basement," in the words of an American military officer working in Amman at the time.[49]

Regardless of their true status, all the sheikhs used the same line with the Americans: "You're talking to the wrong people. I can turn the insurgency on and off like a faucet." After the aborted Fallujah campaign and the sorry performance of the Fallujah Brigade, some Marine officers were especially eager to find a way to suppress the insurgency. Said one former Marine intelligence officer highly skeptical of these efforts, "It was tantalizing that this might be possible. And to be the guy who met the guy who ended the insurgency was intoxicating."[50]

The episode in question, as recounted in a splashy *Vanity Fair* piece in May 2009, took place in Amman in July and August 2004. A Sunni sheikh named Talal al-Gaoud met with senior U.S. officials and military commanders. He explained that the Americans had made many errors since occupying Iraq, but that he could help. He introduced the Americans to other Sunnis who claimed they had links to an insurgent group called the Iraq National Resistance Council. The Americans were told that the insurgents would form an Auxiliary Security Force that would be commanded by former officers from Saddam's army. The Americans would supply the weapons and $108 million to start. The offer was relayed to Washington, where it was shut down. According to *Vanity Fair*, all American lives lost after the summer of 2004—over 2,000—were due to this "fatal error," this "lost opportunity."[51]

The charge was a stunning indictment of the Bush administration, but it was untrue. Talal al-Gaoud had been meeting with U.S. officials since February 2003. Through his personal network, he had ample channels to the Americans and Iraqi officials in Baghdad if he genuinely wanted to help. No one had ever heard of the insurgent group the Iraq National Resistance Council. Its demands were very different from those of other resistance groups like the 1920 Revolution Brigades, Ansar al-Sunna, and especially Zarqawi's Monotheism and Jihad. The offer rested on two flawed assumptions: that the insurgency was a cohesive unit and that it could be turned off by puppetmasters pulling the strings back in Jordan. As further confirmation that the Americans were being played, none of al-Gaoud's partners returned to Anbar in 2006 and 2007 to compete for funds and political status after the Americans began supporting the Awakening movement.[52] An intelligence analyst summed up the encounter: "On our part, it was a combination of naïveté, wishful thinking, and ignorance." The best that could be said was that this misguided adventure advertised to the tribes that the United States was in the market for any deal that might curb the insurgency.

The security environment in Iraq continued to deteriorate for the remainder of 2004. The transfer of power in June to the Iraqis did nothing to quell the insurgency. Violence rose dramatically during the summer and fall. The number of Americans killed in the three months following the June handover was the highest of the war.[53] Fallujah was being used as a base of insurgent operations throughout Anbar Province. In Ramadi, insurgents had eliminated Iraqi government control over the city. Posters in mosques warned members of the National Guard and police, "Quit or we'll kill you." Anbar's governor resigned after his three sons were kidnapped. The deputy governor was kidnapped and killed.[54]

Self-inflicted wounds had further damaged the U.S. mission. In January 2004, the Iraq Survey Group had stated that Saddam had destroyed all of his WMD stockpiles in the 1990s. In April, the Abu Ghraib prison scandal had broken. Pictures of Iraqi men being tortured and sexually humiliated by female soldiers did incalculable damage. (One consequence was that many insurgents would now fight to the death rather than surrender and be taken prisoner by U.S. forces.) And in June, the 9/11 Commission Report concluded that there were no contacts or operational ties between Saddam and al Qaeda. Two of the rationales for invading Iraq—WMD and links to terrorism—had melted away, while the third, democracy promotion, had been badly tarnished.

During this period, Zarqawi made his move to own the insurgency. He was already notorious for his videotaped beheadings of foreign hostages, in which he was alleged to participate personally. In 2003, he moved south from his base in Kurdistan and spent the next year recruiting disgruntled members of Saddam's regime and foreign fighters. A letter to bin Laden, released by the CPA in February 2004, has Zarqawi explaining that he planned to work with the Sunni tribes to wage war on the heretical Shi'a, which would trigger a Shi'a backlash and sectarian civil war. In the ensuing chaos, the Americans would leave Iraq and radicalized Sunnis would rally around his leadership.[55] By the fall of 2004, he had formally pledged allegiance to Osama bin Laden and placed his organization in service to al Qaeda central. In return, Zarqawi gained access to al Qaeda's global network of financial and technical resources, personnel, and propaganda support.[56]

At this time, Zarqawi had several hundred foreign fighters under his control, a very small part of the insurgency, and a larger number of Iraqis.[57] Despite the relatively small size of his forces, he had a disproportionate impact, because the types of attacks his organization conducted—vehicle bombs and suicide attacks— caused mass casualties, intimidated fence-sitting Sunnis into supporting AQI, and instilled fear throughout the populace.[58] Zarqawi and AQI further complicated the Coalition's mission: Should it be waging a counterterrorism campaign against AQI or a counterinsurgency campaign against the bewildering array of ex-Ba'athists, secular Sunni nationalists, traditional Sunni Muslims, ultraradical Salafis, and Wahhabi Islamists that opposed the U.S. presence?[59]

Washington was still in denial, not understanding the war it was in, whom it was fighting, and what it needed to do to prevail. In December 2004, Colonel Harvey flew back to Washington to brief Rumsfeld and the Joint Chiefs of Staff. His message was clear: the United States was losing to the insurgency, which was getting stronger. Rumsfeld did not want to hear the message, pushing back aggressively and challenging Harvey's conclusions. But he recommended that Harvey brief the National Security Council and the president. The Defense Department sent over Harvey's PowerPoint brief ahead of time, with a caveat by the Joint Chiefs saying that these were Harvey's personal views and did not represent those of the JCS. A few days later, Harvey briefed the president and his senior advisers. After the Army intelligence officer left the Oval Office, Bush turned to his aides and asked skeptically: "Is that guy a Democrat?"[60]

With Iraq's national elections scheduled for January 2005, the U.S. military command decided that Fallujah could not remain under the control of the insurgents. In early November, the Marines launched Operation Phantom Fury. By this time, the city was home to thousands of insurgents; the fighting was often house-to-house. By the end of December, the Marines had cleared the city and set up polling centers for the citizens to vote. Not many would (only 2 percent of the Sunnis in Anbar ended up voting). The Sunnis, embittered at their reduced role in a Shi'a-dominated Iraq and hoping to render the elections illegitimate, had decided to boycott. The Shi'a won in a landslide and then proceeded to write a new Iraqi constitution that favored its agenda and that of the Kurds.

From here on out, the Shi'a could use the power of the state to seek revenge against the Sunnis.[61]

The level of sectarian violence and American casualties continued to mount in 2005. The Iraqi Security Forces had proven incapable of taking the lead in combatting the insurgents.[62] Nothing provided the hoped-for "tipping point" that would stabilize and pacify the country—not Saddam's capture, not the transfer of authority from CPA to the Iraqis, not the retaking of Fallujah, and not the January 2005 national elections. No signature event, or even the accumulated blood and treasure expended by the United States and its Coalition partners since May 2003, had slowed the insurgency's momentum.

One reason was that amid the inadequate force levels, battlefield confusion, and poor intelligence, senior military leadership had developed a fundamentally flawed understanding of the conflict. General Abizaid thought the presence of U.S. forces stimulated resistance. In a frequently repeated phrase, U.S. troops were the "virus" and the insurgency was the "antibody." The obvious remedy was to remove U.S. forces (a policy Rumsfeld favored) and the insurgency would die down. The problem was that wherever U.S. forces pulled back (or where they were posted in insufficient numbers), the insurgency grew, since there was no effective Iraqi government presence to counter it, and local police more often than not supported or sympathized with the insurgents.

In the meantime, as the United States was trying to bolster the new Iraqi government during 2005, Zarqawi and AQI were growing their influence in Anbar by aligning with the tribes. Their message was simple: "We are Sunni. You are Sunni. The Americans and Iranians are helping the Shi'a—let's fight them together."[63] Zarqawi brought charismatic leadership, along with money, weapons, organization, and a support network, to conduct strikes against U.S. and Iraqi forces. AQI also brought highly motivated foreign fighters willing to carry out devastating suicide attacks.

Some tribes willingly joined forces with AQI, thinking that a tactical alliance would allow them to leverage AQI's assets for their own ends. Other, more reluctant tribes, were co-opted or coerced by AQI to unite behind its banner.

But the tribal leaders soon realized they could not control Zarqawi and AQI. Intimidation and violence were no strangers to Anbar, but the level of AQI's grotesque and indiscriminate brutality was excessive, even for the tribes. "Out in the wild Western desert, things often tend to play out like *The Sopranos* . . . except that AQI changed the rules of the game by adding roadside bombings, murder of children, and death by torture."[64] AQI killed anyone suspected of collaborating with the Iraqi government or volunteering to join the local police. AQI also tortured and murdered tribal sheikhs, mullahs, doctors, professors, and other leaders. Some were drowned, others beheaded. In one notorious example, four family members were decapitated, with each head placed on the body and left in the August sun for a week. After the relatives were finally granted permission to collect the bodies for burial, AQI detonated TNT that had been hidden on the corpses. Another eight people died, with more wounded.[65] Sometimes entire families were slaughtered, from the little children to the elderly. As one Anbar woman later recounted, "I cannot describe the horror we lived in. Those were very bitter days. Those days we lived in hell. We looked like ghosts out of a cemetery."[66]

In addition to the wholesale violence, AQI offended religious norms by enforcing an extremist version of Islam. Fingers were sliced off for smoking cigarettes. AQI trampled tribal honor and customs by forcing the sheikhs to marry off their daughters to AQI fighters from outside the tribe or by using local women for sex by "marrying" them for a few days. AQI also infringed on the tribes' black-market activities, shutting down businesses, assuming control, or creating such an unstable environment that the tribes could not conduct normal activities.

The more astute tribal sheikhs also suspected that they shared different strategic goals from Zarqawi and AQI. The tribes were, at heart, fighting to restore a lost order where they had been privileged or at least left alone to pursue their own interests. Over time it became increasingly apparent that Zarqawi had a far more ideological and revolutionary agenda. He intended to use the war to expel the Western "crusaders" along with all other non-Sunni groups, thereby destroying Iraq's multiethnic, multiconfessional diversity. In short, Zarqawi was planning to lead the tribes back to the Dark Ages. He would establish an independent Islamic state that would then expand its writ across the Middle East.[67]

It is impossible to generalize about how Anbar's tribes, subtribes, and clans viewed AQI. Tribal leaders responded differently to Zarqawi's campaign of murder and intimidation; certain tribes even had divided allegiances. Some tribes were more offended by certain types of AQI behavior, such as taking over lucrative black-market businesses, than by other types. Views evolved over time, as AQI's offenses multiplied. Each tribe had a different threshold before it could summon the courage to rise up and break free from AQI's embrace.[68]

MITCHELL B. REISS

At this time, the Sunni-led insurgency not affiliated with AQI was being squeezed from two sides—by U.S. troops and increasingly by a predatory and malevolent AQI. Tribal leaders were uncertain whether they could survive the pressure from both. The tribes faced a choice: They could explore an accommodation with the Americans or take on AQI by themselves.

Various U.S. agencies and individuals had continued to talk to the insurgents since the end of major combat operations in the spring of 2003. By 2005, these talks centered on whether the insurgents would lay down their weapons and support the new Iraqi government.[69] Fearing that their cities would suffer the same fate as Fallujah (where over 18,000 buildings were destroyed or damaged), some tribal leaders wanted to cut a deal. In return for U.S. arms, ammunition, and vehicles, the tribes would help root out AQI and the other insurgents. But their men would not join the Iraqi security forces (for fear of being posted outside the province) and would not serve alongside American troops (for fear of inciting their own people who sympathized with the insurgency). The United States was unwilling to accept these terms. At this time, U.S. policy was to transition all responsibility to the Iraqi government. This meant channeling all Sunnis through Baghdad as a way to shore up the fledgling central government. The last thing the Americans wanted was to create additional, localized armed militias. Any deal was stillborn.[70]

If aligning with the Americans was not possible, then some tribes tried to resist AQI and avenge its atrocities by themselves. Such efforts rarely ended well for them.

The first prominent example was the Albu Mahal tribe located in and around the town of al-Qaim, in the northwestern part of Anbar, near the Syrian border.[71] The Marines had been there in 2004 but withdrew that summer to fight in Fallujah. At that time, it appears, the Albu Mahal redirected its attacks against AQI, angry at its "treatment of civilians, importation of foreign fighters, and encroachment on their control of the black market."[72] The turning point was the assassination of the chief of police, a member of the tribe.[73] In response, the tribe formed a militia named the "Hamza Battalion" to defend it against AQI. But the Albu Mahal was numerically the smallest of the three tribes around al-Qaim. AQI was able to win over the two larger tribes by intimidating some people and buying off others. According to the principal sheikh of the Albu Mahal tribe, "The first path was by scaring people, and the other path was financial. The families were in financial difficulties. None of them had any finances left on them. [AQI] was spending huge amounts of money, giving it to people. So in this way, they gathered supporters around them."[74]

Armed with greater numbers, and superior intelligence on the location of the Hamza Battalion members, AQI now seized the initiative and routed the Albu Mahal, which fled the area.[75] It was not until November 2005, when the Marines launched Operation Steel Curtain with the remnants of the Hamza Battalion, that most AQI would be cleared from al-Qaim. This time the Marines maintained an aggressive presence in the city, supported by the Albu Mahal. They also made sure to incorporate all three tribes into the new security forces. Three months after Operation Steel Curtain, 400 locals had joined the police. By the summer of 2006, the number was up to roughly 850 men, largely from the Albu Mahal tribe.[76]

A potentially more significant uprising emerged in Ramadi, with the formation of the Al Anbar People's Committee in late 2005. The Committee's intention was to resist both AQI and Coalition forces. Its leaders were the head of an influential tribe centered in Ramadi and a senior member of the 1920 Revolution Brigades, a nationalist insurgent group, but the Committee was more rooted in religious affinities than the tribes. Some Sunnis had come to understand that their earlier boycott of the January 2005 elections had only served to empower the Shi'a and that continued violence along the lines Zarqawi proposed would further marginalize their influence.[77] They created a nine-man Al Anbar People's Committee to secure the city so people could participate in the National Assembly elections in mid-December.

AQI recognized the threat the Committee posed to its position and took immediate steps to destroy its new rival. When the Committee called for young men to enlist at a police recruiting station outside an abandoned glass factory in early January, a suicide bomber killed himself and about seventy tribesmen.[78] The tribal sheikhs then told AQI that it was no longer welcome. AQI responded by murdering seven of the nine committee members within the next two weeks. According to a Marine intelligence officer deployed to Ramadi at the time, AQI "absolutely eviscerated" the Committee: "public beheadings, assassinations, IEDs, night letters, the whole gamut of al Qaeda in Iraq's arsenal."[79] In the face of AQI's savage onslaught, the Committee did not have the broad grassroots support to sustain its opposition. The resistance fell apart.

There were also isolated rebellions by bands of Sunnis who sought revenge against AQI. A well-known vigilante group was the Anbar Revolutionaries, which some tribal members formed in late 2004 or early 2005 in response to AQI's terrorizing their leadership. According to a U.S. intelligence officer, the group was real but the Americans had made up the name as part of an information operation to unsettle AQI. The name caught on among the Sunni vigilantes, who adopted it as their own.[80]

The significance of the Anbar Revolutionaries probably lies less with the actual damage they inflicted on AQI than with the honor they bestowed on the Sunni tribes. They signaled that the tribes would not roll over passively for AQI, that they would not all be intimidated by Zarqawi. Rather, they had the ability and the will to strike back with a vengeance.[81] The rise of the Anbar Revolutionaries—along with earlier attempts by the Albu Mahal, the Al Anbar People's Committee, and other sheikhs—also raised the idea among some close observers that the tribes might one day be agreeable to teaming up with the Americans against AQI.[82]

However, none of these initial tribal efforts, what John McCary has termed the "sparks before the fire," managed to gather the necessary combustion to push back AQI much beyond its localized area, and then only temporarily. None spread elsewhere in the province to trigger an Anbar-wide tribal uprising.

Why not? If the Anbar tribes were not strong enough to defeat AQI, why didn't U.S. forces step in, support these "mini-awakenings," and help turn the sparks into flames? Why did the United States miss this opportunity to jump-start the awakening a year earlier?

I posed these questions to the participants at the January 2010 conference.

Some participants questioned whether these initial tribal efforts at retaliation truly were missed opportunities. Some military officers had very good working relationships with the sheikhs. They argued that the tribes could have approached U.S. commanders directly but chose not to for their own reasons. One intelligence officer thought maybe the Sunnis had to fail on their own first before they would consider turning to the Americans.

Other participants argued that the American side should shoulder some of the blame. Some military units simply didn't understand what was happening. There were never enough troops. Because commanders were stretched thin, it was difficult to recognize what was happening in their area of responsibility. Constant troop rotations also meant that commanders left their area just as they were learning the local personalities, tribal politics, and societal dynamics. There were never enough skilled linguists or interpreters. "How do you know you're talking to the right people? Who do you trust?" The Americans simply did not understand the human terrain. According to a former Marine intelligence officer, "We didn't recognize at this time that [empowering the local tribes] was the way for us to solve the insurgency."[83]

Other units knew, or at least sensed, that some tribes were in a fight with AQI, but did not seize the moment. Supporting the Sunni militias was not consistent with U.S. policy or endorsed by senior commanders.[84] The conventional wisdom was that the Sunnis could not be trusted. The gamble with the Fallujah Brigade had, after all, failed badly. The Sunnis in Anbar were believed to be thugs, bandits, and smugglers. They could well have been shooting at U.S. troops the day before.

Some U.S. officers were also more comfortable focusing on kinetics than engaging in tribal outreach. "A hearts and minds approach did not scratch the immediate itch," commented one Army officer. The former mayor of Tal'Afar agreed. "If all you have is a hammer. . . . A great many U.S. soldiers and officers had no idea what to do, how to respond, except for using violence."

The main reason, most participants agreed, was plain: The United States had the wrong strategy. Senior military leadership saw the U.S. force presence as provoking the insurgency. There was no appreciation at this time at the highest levels that the "center of gravity" was the Sunnis—the people were the prize. Killing insurgents was the mission, but it would have little impact as long as the people did not have security.

Consistent with this flawed concept, General George Casey, the commander of the Multi-National Force in Iraq (MNF-I), had disengaged U.S. forces from the population, positioning them on large, isolated forward operating bases (termed FOBs) outside of the major cities. U.S. force levels would be downsized as the numbers of Coalition-trained Iraqi security and police forces increased. (In this, Casey was aligned with the White House, which in November 2005 had issued the "National Security Strategy for Victory in Iraq." The document was designed to reassure the American people that U.S. forces would be standing down as Iraqi forces stood up.[85]) This approach did nothing for enhancing security in Anbar, since most Iraqi security forces were deployed in the south, not where the insurgency was raging. And most of these forces could not operate effectively without partnering with the Americans. By late 2005, the plan was for 108 FOBs to be consolidated in 50 bases; 15 combat brigades would be reduced to 8.[86] It seemed as if the United States military already had one foot out the door.

After the December 2005 election success and the creation of the Al Anbar People's Committee, Casey decided to draw down U.S. forces. His decision to send home the two battalions that had been brought over to Iraq to help with election security sent a very clear signal that "we've won and we're done."[87] Fairly or not, the judgment of the men at the conference in Tampa was that he was trying to please his political masters. He understood the politics back in Washington better than he did the situation in Anbar. (Rumsfeld and all of Casey's top generals agreed with his assessment that American troops on the streets were the problem.) Whenever there was some progress, Casey took this as a reason to reduce troop levels. "We should have doubled down, but instead we folded," commented one conference participant. His plan for winning the war—by transitioning to the Iraqis, whether they were ready or not—looked a lot like losing, slowly.

In early 2006, it looked like the United States might lose not slowly but suddenly. On February 22, 2006, al Qaeda in Iraq blew up the Golden Dome Mosque in Samarra, one of the holiest Shi'a sites in the world. None of Zarqawi's depredations had managed to unify Shi'a outrage and galvanize them into taking reprisals against the Sunni.[88] Until now.

The Samarra bombing transformed a low-level clash between the Sunni and Shi'a into a full-scale sectarian war. The conflict had a crude, self-perpetuating logic. Shi'a fears now rationalized the growth of militias to defend the community. The Shi'a could also leverage the instruments of government power they controlled, especially the Ministry of Interior, to seek revenge. This fed Sunni fears, which led to increased support for the insurgency, which in turn allowed openings for AQI to prey on the Shi'a and restart the cycle of fear, violence, and insecurity all over again.

Detailed maps of Baghdad developed at this time by the U.S. embassy, with different colors representing concentrations of Sunni and Shi'a, turned from a blending of colors to monochrome as Sunnis were methodically killed or driven out of their homes and neighborhoods. The carnage was extraordinary, even for Iraq. During the spring of 2006, each morning U.S. forces would find over a hundred bodies in the streets, some with drill bits still in their skulls and bearing other signs of torture. Zarqawi's strategy appeared to be working perfectly.

In late spring, a few senior intelligence officers drafted an analysis on the status of the U.S. war effort for Major General Michael Maples, the director of the Defense Intelligence Agency. It was nicknamed the "Doomsday Paper" by its authors, and its circulation was tightly controlled. Said one of its authors, "It was never disseminated because it was too volatile." The report concluded that absent fundamental changes in U.S. strategy and the direction the country was heading, intervention by Iraq's neighbors was likely, with American forces leaving the country. Maples shared it with only a few key people, including General Casey.[89]

Nonetheless, in mid-June, Casey announced further troop cuts. Over the next sixteen months, the military would downsize from fourteen to six brigades.[90] Neither the ethnic cleansing after the Samarra bombing nor the warnings of his intelligence officers would deter the senior military commander in Iraq from transitioning to the Iraqis and bringing U.S. forces home.

The Marine Corps intelligence officers in Iraq shared the same concerns as their Army counterparts. It was during this period that Marine Colonel Peter Devlin prepared a PowerPoint presentation on the "State of the Insurgency in al-Anbar." It confirmed AQI's ascendency. "AQI is the dominant organization of influence in al-Anbar, surpassing nationalist insurgents, the Iraqi Government, and MNF [the Multinational Force] in its ability to control the day-to-day life of the average Sunni." Like the Doomsday Paper, it concluded that the United States could not win if it maintained its current course. "The social and political situation has deteriorated to a point that MNF and ISF [the Iraqi Security Forces] are no longer capable of militarily defeating the insurgency in al-Anbar."[91]

Devlin asked Major Ben Connable to turn the PowerPoint slides into a written brief, which was then circulated to a broader group of senior officials. The brief was leaked to Thomas Ricks, the well-regarded war correspondent for the *Washington Post*. When he published the story, in September 2006, it caused a sensation, especially as it appeared only a few months before the midterm elections. It seemed to many as if the Marines were throwing in the towel.

That was not the memo's intention. It was written not to support calls for an American withdrawal or to influence the elections but to send a message to Casey on the need for *more* U.S. combat troops. "Understand the context," said a former U.S. military officer with excellent knowledge of these events. At the time, attack levels across Anbar were rising steadily. The two U.S. battalions operating in Ramadi were in daily gun battles with insurgents and were firing heavy artillery and guided missiles into the heart of the city. Further, during the August troop rotation, the Marines had not received all the troops and equipment they had requested. "The memo was a 'Fuck you, George Casey.' You think you've won the war. Well, you haven't."

As Baghdad turned into a charnel house, as violence spiked in Anbar, and as the war played out politically back in Washington, U.S. troops were caught in a civil war they still did not fully understand and were burdened with a strategy they knew had failed. The Army and Marines had neglected counterinsurgency training for thirty years after Vietnam, and the new *Counterinsurgency Field Manual* had not yet been published.[92] But many of the units in Anbar were on their second or third tours of duty in Iraq. By this time, the troops had become more sophisticated in their dealings with the tribes.

And they still had a job to do. The Ready First Combat Brigade's commander, Colonel Sean MacFarland, was told to "take back Ramadi, but not to make it another Fallujah." The problem was that the city was essentially in enemy hands. AQI had declared Ramadi the future capital of the "new Islamic caliphate." In terms of the number of attacks on Coalition forces, Ramadi was three times more dangerous than any other Iraqi city on a per capita basis. The provincial government did not function. Anbar's governor, who had survived dozens of assassination attempts, was holed up in the city center and protected by a Marine rifle company that was attacked almost daily. Fewer than 100 Iraqi police reported to duty each day; those who did were too intimidated to go out on patrols. [93]

Since wiping out the Al Anbar People's Committee in January, AQI had kept up its campaign of violence and intimidation. It had formed a Shura Council with the other Iraqi insurgent groups and authorized the murder of anyone working with the Americans or joining the police. One local sheikh refused to cooperate with AQI in placing IEDs along Route Michigan, one of the main roads into the city for U.S. convoys. AQI abducted the sheikh's children and placed their severed heads in a cooler that was delivered to the steps of Ramadi General Hospital.

Drawing from a detailed plan developed by the Marines, MacFarland's approach was based on both kinetic and nonkinetic elements, what the military call "full-spectrum operations." He did not have enough firepower to secure such a large city with only the limited number of U.S. forces under his command, and Iraqi army units were not always reliable. Based on his previous experience in securing Tal'Afar, MacFarland knew that he needed to have the support of the local leaders and people. They constituted his center of gravity.

The kinetic element involved attacking AQI's safe havens and then moving into the neighborhoods one at a time to "directly challenge the insurgents' dominance of the city." He had a tank or infantry company establish combat outposts, or COPs, in defensible local structures in disputed areas. These outposts acted as "lily pads" to launch quick-reaction strikes and serve as safe houses for special-operations forces. They also acted as "fly paper" to attract AQI fighters who could not match the skill and training of American forces. Daily battles turned these combat outposts into "miniature Stalingrads" as the U.S. side repulsed AQI's attacks.[94] As MacFarland recounted afterward, "With new outposts established in an ever-tightening circle around the inner city, we wrested control of areas away from the insurgents."[95]

Implementing the plan was bloody and time-consuming. MacFarland said it was "like a knife fight in the dark." But there never was any question that the Americans would establish these combat outposts. After all, the United States had not lost a single engagement with insurgent forces in the three-plus years of occupation. Whether they could hold these outposts and establish security in the city, however, was another story. That depended on the nonkinetic element—winning the support of the local tribes.

There is a military saying that insurgencies are blunted by conventional forces but they are defeated by police. The only way U.S. forces could secure the local population was by standing up an effective local police force. But police recruiting languished after the failed Al Anbar People's Committee. That would change only if the sheikhs defied the threats and intimidation from AQI and supported the American effort.

Knowing which sheikhs to reach out to as potential allies was handicapped by ignorance of the human terrain. "I was trying to make sense of what was happening. I was in the middle of a scrum," MacFarland admitted. "We had a 20 percent understanding level when we went into Ramadi at the start."[96] Remarked Lieutenant Colonel Tony Deane, the commander of Task Force Conqueror in Ramadi, "Everyone knew who the bad guys were except for us." Even if U.S. commanders could identify possible partners, it was unclear whether any would talk to them. In Ramadi at this time, just being seen with an American often brought a death sentence.

But the Americans did not need to know which sheikhs were the most powerful, because they devised a simple, pragmatic test: Could the sheikhs deliver tribesmen for the police? MacFarland had calculated, "We're not going to figure out how the politics of the tribes work. I'll leave that to the tribes. It was like Americans trying to understand a cricket match." But if the sheikh had the influence (*wasta*) to persuade the tribe's sons to join the police, the Americans would support him. The goal was to ramp up the number of police so that police stations could be established throughout Ramadi to secure the people.

In early June, Deane had been introduced to a relatively minor sheikh, Sheikh Ahmed Bezia Albu Risha. During the previous three years, AQI had killed his father and two brothers, yet he was still willing to openly support the Americans. "To me, it was clear that this guy was on the team, but we weren't giving him enough game-time. Ahmed always said he wanted to arm the tribes, which we were not going to do. They were willing to fight; it was just a matter of figuring out how to harness them."[97]

A few days later, Deane was ordered to secure a police recruiting site, but a shortage of soldiers meant that he would have to pull out of the town of Ta'meem in western Ramadi, where his unit was stationed. Instead, he went to Ahmed Bezia. "I told him that we could hold the recruiting in the tribal area and that if he got 500 recruits, we would build a police station in his area. I had zero authority to make such a promise, but I knew that I could build it if I had to." Organizing the recruitment on the sheikh's home turf would reduce Deane's security overhead. The tribe would vet the recruits and reduce the chances of any suicide bombers infiltrating the site. Plus, given the low number of police in Ramadi at the time, Deane thought it worth taking the risk to see if the sheikh could deliver 500 new Iraqi policemen.[98]

Ahmed Bezia delivered around eighty police recruits, not as many as originally promised but enough to almost double the size of the entire Ramadi police force in a single morning. Deane was also impressed by how the sheikh and his younger brother, Abdul Sattar Albu Risha, reacted when their home was mortared by AQI that morning. They did not flinch but continued with the recruiting drive, even though their wives and children were in danger. "Pretty hoo-ah, actually," commented Deane.

In the weeks and months ahead, Abdul Sattar would publicly play an influential role in organizing the tribes and leading what came to be called the Anbar

Awakening. But for Deane in those first few meetings, no lightbulb went on. There was no "Eureka!" moment. Sattar appeared to be "more prodigal son than tribal leader. Ahmed was the sheikh. Sattar was his brother." For now, all that mattered was that the two men could supply candidates for the police force. "We didn't know Sattar was *the* guy," reflected Deane. "He was just another guy with a goatee."[99]

The Albu Rishas represented a minor and somewhat disreputable tribe. Deane would learn later that Abdul Sattar was best known around Ramadi for being a "road gangster." The religious leaders initially "all disliked" him "because he was not a religious person."[100] The more established sheikhs, too, thought it preferable that a figure like Abdul Sattar deal with AQI, rather than men of higher status and position. Said a major tribal leader, it was "the right job for the right man, and bad will be accountable to the bad . . . we chose the bad one, which was Sattar, because he was a troublemaker, and he had a bad record."[101] Harder for them to admit was that Abdul Sattar was willing, even eager, to walk point while the other sheikhs remained in the shadows.

Deane struck up a friendship with Abdul Sattar, and started spending three to four hours a night, three to four nights a week with him, between his command responsibilities. The investment paid valuable dividends. Abdul Sattar continued to deliver new police recruits and use his tribal connections to persuade other sheikhs to send their sons as well.[102]

By early September 2006, Abdul Sattar had convinced some sheikhs to stand together, openly with the Americans, against al Qaeda in Iraq. On September 14, forty-one sheikhs met at Abdul Sattar's residence, with Deane's unit and the Ready First providing perimeter security. The sheikhs signed a proclamation establishing the Emergency Council for the Rescue of Al Anbar and pledging to drive AQI from Anbar province. (Within the month, they changed the name to *Sah'wa al-Anbar*, or the Anbar Awakening.) Abdul Sattar was elected the Council's leader.

The hard work was far from done. The Anbar Awakening Council controlled only a small area. The city was still violent and insecure. Just nine of Ramadi's twenty-one tribes supported the Awakening Council; the others were either aligned with AQI or still on the fence. Weapons were in short supply. Neither the Anbar government, which saw the Council as political rivals, nor the Nouri al-Maliki government in Baghdad, which was dominated by Shi'a and focused on its own troubles, was willing to provide arms and ammunition.

Further, senior U.S. military leaders were not all convinced that the Awakening Council's members could be trusted. They feared that the police would sell or give their weapons to AQI. The Iraqi National Intelligence Service (INIS) in Baghdad was reporting to the Americans that the Awakening Council consisted of former Ba'athists and closet supporters of the insurgency. Recalled Derek Harvey, the Army intelligence officer, "There was lots of dissension in MNF-West about whether you could work with these guys."[103] Even Abdul Sattar was not above suspicion. A few weeks after the Awakening was announced in Abdul Sattar's living room, Brigadier General David Reist, the deputy commander of the Marine Expeditionary Force, directed Lieutenant Colonel Deane to arrest the Council's leader. Deane refused.[104]

Questions also arose over the Awakening Council's cohesion and effectiveness. Each sheikh could agree on eliminating AQI, but after that his interests diverged into narrower concerns over his own power base and what was best for his tribe. There was a lot of internal squabbling and jockeying for power and status. Council members bickered over acquiring and allocating weapons, which sheikhs would represent the group at meetings with U.S. officials, and how they could win reconstruction contracts.

Meanwhile, AQI had not gone away. On October 15, 2006, it proclaimed the Islamic State of Iraq, removing any doubt about its ultimate intentions. The public announcement of the Awakening Council now identified which sheikhs AQI would target for assassination. Violence in Ramadi and across Anbar escalated throughout the fall. The Awakening appeared to have no impact in degrading AQI. The director of the CIA, Michael Hayden, testified in mid-November that "Iraq's endemic violence is eating away at the state's ability to govern. . . . Despite Zarqawi's death [in June 2006], al Qaida continues to foment sectarian violence and seeks to expel Coalition forces."[105] At this time, "the tribes were just getting hammered, trying to survive."[106]

There were nonetheless a few encouraging signs. Over the next few months, the Awakening tribes, especially the large al-Thiyabi tribe, placed their sons in the police. By the end of December 2006, five more tribes had swung over to join the Awakening. They brought with them over 4,000 police recruits. The Iraqi government paid their salaries, thereby making them accountable to a central authority and giving a bump to the local economy.

For those tribesmen who could not join the police (the elderly, the illiterate, and youngsters), but still wanted to protect their tribal areas, MacFarland's junior officers made up from whole cloth the "Provincial Auxiliary Iraqi Police," a glorified form of neighborhood watch groups. The Ready First gave them uniforms and training, and paid them from Commander's Emergency Response Program (CERP) funds.[107]

Just having young Sunni men join the local police or auxiliary forces was a net plus to MacFarland's mission because it meant they were no longer trying to kill American soldiers. When requested, U.S. units provided tactical assistance (such as air support) and would conduct joint patrols and operations with the Iraqi police. They treated Iraqi wounded at their base hospitals. U.S. commanders also looked the other way when former insurgents with "American blood on their hands" joined the police or auxiliary forces.[108]

The Awakening Council conducted its own information operations to "shape" the battlefield. Through the media, the Council would announce that entire tribes had abandoned AQI and supported the Awakening, when only a few members of the tribes had switched allegiances. Said one sheikh, "if we had a 10 percent success, we said it's 90 percent . . . when the terrorist heard it, it's grand, it's big. So they started to flee the area by themselves."[109] In addition, some Council members went to the mosques and told the clerics to use their weekly sermons to oppose al Qaeda and support the Awakening or else they would be killed.[110]

None of these developments were understood or even noticed back on the home front. Just as some commanders in Anbar were seeing small but tangible signs of progress, domestic political pressure intensified to withdraw all U.S. forces, and soon. That fall in the midterm congressional elections, Democrats campaigned to end the war. Republicans took a beating, losing their majority in the House. President Bush fired Defense Secretary Rumsfeld a few days later. In early December, the bipartisan Iraq Study Group, cochaired by former secretary of state James Baker and former congressman Lee Hamilton, issued its report. It concluded, "Despite a massive effort, stability in Iraq remains elusive and the situation is deteriorating. The Iraqi government cannot now govern, sustain and defend itself without the support of the United States." The report recommended that the United States immediately start a "responsible transition" to Iraqi control.[111] The following month, an estimate by the National Intelligence Council added to the gloom. It judged that "the overall security situation will continue to deteriorate" and outlined three possible scenarios: deepening chaos leading to partition, the emergence of a Shi'a strongman, or anarchy.[112] The Awakening was not mentioned in either document.

Despite the prevailing pessimism, a small group of people in Washington had believed for some time that the war could be won, but only if the United States changed its military strategy to defeat the insurgency and increased, not withdrew, American combat forces.[113] By January 2007, they had persuaded the president to announce a "surge" of American troops and replace General Casey with General David Petraeus as the new commanding general of MNF-I. On January 10, the president announced "A New Way Forward" on national television. He ordered six more Army brigades and two more Marine battalions to Iraq, a total of 21,500 soldiers. (In the end, a helicopter brigade and additional troops raised the number to almost 30,000.) Critics thought the president was simply "reinforcing failure."[114]

Petraeus arrived in Baghdad in early February. Although the odds of succeeding were stacked against him, the general had a few advantages. A few months earlier, Raymond Odierno had arrived in Iraq for his second tour, this time as commanding general of III Corps. Before his new posting, Odierno had ordered his staff to rethink and plan a more effective counterinsurgency strategy. Moving the troops off the FOBs and securing the population would be emphasized, precisely the approach Petraeus would take when he assumed command. For the first time since the United States invaded Iraq, its two senior officers had a common understanding of the nature of the war they were fighting *and* a plan for defeating the insurgency.

Even before the surge brigades arrived throughout the first half of 2007, the announcement had helped shape the battle space, signaling to the tribes (and AQI) that the United States would stay in the fight instead of cutting and running. But Petraeus's greatest asset may have been a sense of desperation among the military and political leadership back in Washington. The military was out of reserve forces. President Bush was out of options. If Petraeus failed, the United States would lose in Iraq. As a senior military officer at the January 2010 Tampa conference on the Anbar Awakening described the thinking at this time, "Let's just see what works, because we're desperate. No idea is a bad idea."

When Petraeus got to Iraq, AQI was still hammering the Awakening tribes. The slow and stupid insurgents had been killed by now; those who had survived were battle-tested and resilient. According to Major General John Allen, the first three months of 2007 were the "darkest hour of the violence in Anbar."[115] AQI's many acts of ferocious fighting against the Awakening Council and its supporters included a coordinated suicide attack and assault on Abdul Sattar's home; three suicide chlorine gas attacks in Amiriya, Fallujah, and Ramadi; and the destruction of a mosque in Habbaniyah to punish an imam who had condemned AQI.[116] AQI was still on the offensive. The Awakening tribes still could not stand up as U.S. forces stood down. They were simply not strong enough to resist by themselves.

Almost imperceptibly, little victories started to emerge. Ramadi remained a problem, despite the efforts of Colonel MacFarland and the Awakening Council. In April 2007, Lieutenant General Odierno had to send a Marine surge battalion there to finally clear the city of AQI. Tribal sons who had joined the Iraqi police now started returning from the training centers in significant numbers and patrolling the streets. Their value was less in taking down AQI than it was in providing intelligence to U.S. forces. To take advantage of this new trove of local knowledge, Petraeus had also surged intelligence capability. Petraeus had more ISR (intelligence, surveillance, and reconnaissance) assets at his disposal than any previous commander. He created fusion centers that brought together intelligence analysts with special-operations forces to provide commanders in the field with quick-reaction targeting of insurgents. He also set up a Force Strategic Engagement Cell (F-SEC) to institutionalize outreach to the insurgents and promote reconciliation.[117]

Petraeus also decided to effectively remove the Sunni insurgency by placing it on the U.S. payroll. Unlike the Anbar Awakening, which was initiated by the tribal sheikhs, this effort was designed by the Americans. The Sunnis were being invited to abandon what they had termed the "honorable resistance" against the occupying Americans and side with U.S. forces against AQI. Petraeus did not ask permission in advance from President Bush.[118] As for the Iraqi prime minister, "Maliki could have cared less about Anbar. If they all killed each other, that was fine by him."[119]

The Americans and the Sunnis at this time forged an alliance of self-interested convenience, what Thomas Ricks has called a "second marriage for both sides." Petraeus needed to do something dramatic to quickly halt and then reverse the death spiral. Reconciliation with the insurgents promised the biggest immediate payoff. The Sunnis were under assault from three sides: the Iraqi security forces, the American troops, and a new competitor, the Shi'a militias that had ethnically cleansed Baghdad and other ethnically mixed cities after Zarqawi's bombing of the Samarra mosque in February 2006. As Sunni refugees fled Baghdad for Anbar, their stories of atrocities at the hands of Shi'a gangs increased fears among the tribes that they would be next. The sheikhs assumed (rightly) that this extra-legal, vigilante violence was being either facilitated or tolerated by elements of the Maliki government. It was clear that AQI could not protect them.

The U.S. military sought to capitalize on this Sunni dilemma. A Marine intelligence officer in Anbar at this time recalled the cold-blooded message he delivered to the insurgents. "[I]f you stop shooting at us and you stop blowing us up, we will stop wrecking your house, we will stop killing your kids. We will stop doing all the things you say we do wrong, and you can get rid of al Qaeda in Iraq, which you don't like anyway, because you don't want to grow your beard a certain length and you want to have pickles and ice and all the stuff that they won't let you have. And when the Shi'a come to slaughter you, you'll be ready to fight them."[120] Working with the Americans appealed to many of these Sunni men, since "their main goal was to get a paycheck, ammunition, permission to use their weapons, not be targeted by the ISF or U.S. forces, secure their areas, and obtain reconstruction contracts."[121]

The insurgents were initially designated "Concerned Local Citizens," which soon morphed into the "Sons of Iraq" (SOI). The cost of the SOI program was about $30 million a month, but money wasn't the most controversial aspect of the program. It was the people the Americans were now partnering with. Lieutenant General Odierno addressed this issue head-on in guidance to his forces: "We are going to be striking deals with people who have killed American soldiers. That may turn your stomach, but that is the way forward."[122] A senior commander intimately involved in the SOI program recalled the confusion and complexity in reaching out to the insurgency in Anbar at that time: "There was chaos on our side, chaos on their side as well. We didn't know what we were doing. But you take risks." He quickly added that "these are qualified risks, because you are basing your actions on your experience and judgment." He was under no illusions that some very bad people were joining the SOI program. As for these men having belonged to the insurgency in the past, he was coldly pragmatic: "Why would you want to talk to anyone who *doesn't* have blood on their hands?"[123]

During these first few months of 2007, Petraeus and Odierno had gone "all-in," surging across the board—working with the tribal sheikhs, connecting them to the civilian leadership, enhancing intelligence collection, paying the insurgents to change sides, and ramping up the numbers of Iraqi security forces. These bets, however, were slow to pay off in Anbar.

Instead, the most tangible evidence of the surge was casualties. The new strategy required that American soldiers live among the Iraqi people, which meant that they were more exposed to AQI and the insurgents. As the number of Americans killed and wounded multiplied, patience ran thin back in Washington. In mid-April, Senate majority leader Harry Reid declared that "this war is lost and the surge is not accomplishing anything."[124] (Officers attending the Tampa conference who were in Iraq at the time recalled that some of their soldiers came to them weeping when they heard Reid's news clip.) 2007 would turn out to be the most lethal year of the war.

The good news was that Petraeus and Odierno had identified the right operational concept for success. They had enough forces, with 155,000 troops in Iraq by midsummer. The Sunnis and their extended tribal networks could map the human terrain for U.S. forces. The Americans could operate "within" the Anbar tribes, rather than outside and against them. This priceless local knowledge allowed U.S. forces to more clearly "see" the battlefield.

But time was their enemy. In April, the Democratic-led Congress had placed conditions on U.S. funding for the war. The administration would need to show that it had met eighteen benchmarks of success by September. When the time came, Petraeus and Ambassador Ryan Crocker, who arrived in Baghdad a few weeks after Petraeus, would have to make that case as best they could.

During the early summer, the violence continued, hitting new highs for casualties in June and July. But it fell dramatically in August, when large numbers of Sunnis joined the Awakening and especially the SOI. It also did not hurt that the Iraqi government offered to reinstate 46,000 former members of Saddam's army at their former rank or provide full pensions during this time. As people felt safer, they were more willing to provide information to the military, which could then uncover weapons caches, raid safe houses, and kill and capture AQI members.

On September 10, Petraeus appeared before Congress. Political passions were high. That day, the antiwar group MoveOn.org had taken out a full-page ad in the *New York Times* questioning the general's integrity and patriotism.

Before a national television audience, Petraeus explained that there had been a marked decrease in violence in August, and it looked as though this trend might hold and deepen throughout the fall. "The most significant development in the past six months has been the increasing emergence of tribes and local citizens rejecting Al Qaeda and other extremists. This has, of course, been most visible in Anbar Province. A year ago, the province was assessed as 'lost' politically. Today, it is a model of what happens when local leaders and citizens decide to oppose Al Qaeda and reject its Taliban-like ideology."[125] He recommended the drawdown of the first Army brigade in December 2007, with four more brigades and two Marine battalions rotating out by July 2008. It was a bravura performance. Skeptics of the war remained, but much of the political venom had been drained.

As the war entered its fifth year, it was clear that the surge had accomplished its tactical objectives. Violence in 2008 was down markedly and U.S. troops were still on schedule to come home. There was "bottom-up" success, but this had not been matched by "top-down" political reconciliation. The surge had not resulted in the Iraqi political parties using this time of greater calm to resolve their fundamental disagreements over sharing power. Political reconciliation had gone agonizingly slowly. Iraqis engaging each other proved more difficult than Iraqis engaging Americans.

In November 2008, Barack Obama defeated John McCain to become the forty-fourth president of the United States. In late February 2009, speaking to the Marines at Camp Lejeune, North Carolina, the new president announced his strategy for Iraq. He declared that all U.S. combat brigades would be removed by August 31, 2010. The remaining forces would train, equip, and advise Iraqi Security Forces, conduct targeted counterterrorism operations, and protect civilian reconstruction projects. He said he intended to withdraw all American forces from Iraq by the end of 2011.[126]

As President Obama acknowledged in his Camp Lejeune remarks, Iraq was not yet secure and the war was not yet won. But the United States had not lost. The Anbar Awakening was one of the reasons why.

CONCLUSION

The Anbar Awakening was the first move in what became a province-wide movement against AQI. By the end of 2008, the Anbar tribes had joined with the United States against al Qaeda in Iraq.

What accounts for this?

Sorting out the jumble of reasons behind the Awakening and assigning to each its proper weight is challenging. Some stories remain vague or obscure. (For example, the role the CIA played is hidden, and it may never be publicly revealed.) Too, American attempts to recapture the history of the Awakening always underplay the Iraqi side, because of language barriers and the difficulty of interviewing the key players, some of whom have died.

Other stories are biased. There is the natural human temptation to inflate one's own role while diminishing or even dismissing the work of others. Personal jealousies and institutional rivalries, between the Army and Marines, for example, color both American and Iraqi narratives.

And then there is the normal fog of war. Many of the American participants in Ramadi and Anbar during 2006 and 2007, even general officers, still do not fully understand all the reasons the Awakening was successful. Junior officers were expert in their areas of responsibility but less certain of events that occurred outside these areas. Senior officers could see the larger picture but often did not have the granularity of detail that affected men and decisions on the ground.

But some reasons are clear.

For engagement to work, the United States had to make a number of dangerous, demanding, and intellectually difficult changes, ranging from Tony Deane's initial willingness to invest time night after night in the home of Abdul Sattar to Generals Odierno and Petraeus developing a fresh operating concept for the war and then expertly orchestrating its implementation. A new focus on stabilization and victory, not transitioning to the Iraqis or to a hasty U.S. exit from the country, signaled to the Sunni resistance that the United States was "in it to win it." Colonel Sean MacFarland refused to stay hunkered down on his FOB and conduct "drive-by COIN" in and out of Ramadi. In the summer of 2006, he insisted instead that the Ready First live among the people, which was the first large-scale demonstration that U.S. forces could "clear, hold, and build" in conjunction with local Iraqis. It meant putting steel on targets, and slugging it out with AQI and the insurgents through the fall and winter of 2006 and then through the spring and summer of 2007. As Petraeus matter-of-factly recalled when we met in his CENTCOM office in Tampa in April 2010, "Sectarian violence didn't burn itself out. We defeated it."[127] It meant operating "inside the tribes," which would provide U.S. forces with the local knowledge needed to understand the human terrain. And it meant having the additional surge forces to accomplish all these tasks.

If there was one constant, it was the willingness from day one of many outstanding American officers, from the platoon to division level, to engage, negotiate, cajole, threaten, befriend, and empower local leaders and reconcile with the tribes. For most of the war, there was no comprehensive engagement plan. It was all ad hoc, a process of trial and mostly error until the Anbar Awakening Council in September 2006. Sean MacFarland could have spoken for many of these officers when he candidly admitted at the Tampa conference, "A certain amount of luck was involved in turning Ramadi because we were really flying by the seat of our pants."

It meant taking risks. It meant continuing to engage the local sheikhs even when success was far from assured. By 2006, it meant ignoring or disobeying orders—what the Army sometimes euphemistically calls "leaning forward in the foxhole"—after lower-level commanders decided that their local knowledge was superior to anything back at headquarters. (Risk-taking was a little easier in Anbar, since it was seen as peripheral to the heavyweight fight taking place in Baghdad.) It meant refusing to go home in humiliation and defeat after sacrificing so much, even if engagement with the tribes (and insurgents) at times skirted the boundaries of insubordination. In other words, the Awakening's success depended on the intelligence, initiative, uncommon determination, and everyday courage of the American soldiers in the battalions, brigades, companies, and platoons responsible for rescuing Ramadi and the rest of Anbar Province.

At the same time, some civilian and senior military leaders also refused to quit, especially when the situation looked dire in 2005, 2006, and the first seven months of 2007. They kept working the problem, despite the backbiting, finger-pointing, second-guessing, and defeatism emanating from Washington and the think-tank community. The military demonstrated that it is an extraordinary learning organization, constantly reexamining, reassessing, and rethinking its concepts, doctrine, and operations. In Iraq, and especially in Anbar, it learned just in time.

The United States could not have prevailed without the unwitting cooperation of Abu Musab al-Zarqawi, AQI's leader. Zarqawi had an ideal opportunity to inflict a historic defeat on the United States: a chaotic environment, a weak central government, large ungoverned spaces, a sympathetic Sunni population, foreign fighters willing to martyr themselves, and after late 2004, an external support structure in al Qaeda that could provide weapons, money, and strategic guidance.

And yet he failed. His demise was hardly inevitable. Indeed, for a long period of time, it looked like Zarqawi might prevail. Although his excessive brutality had repulsed the Anbar tribes, it had also intimidated them. AQI's vicious repression and religious extremism offended many Sunnis, but was not sufficient to trigger a backlash, with a few isolated and short-lived exceptions. But then the United States caught a break. "Samarra took place and the Shi'a rebelled and unhinged the Sunni strategy. The Sunni insurgency was winning up to that point," said Derek Harvey, the senior military intelligence officer.[128] The attack on the Golden Dome Mosque, holy to the Shi'a, unleashed a sectarian war, precisely as Zarqawi had intended. The Shi'a militia now ravaged Sunni neighborhoods in Baghdad and other ethnically mixed villages, towns, and cities.

When this onslaught was added to the existing threats to the Sunni community from both Iraqi security and American forces, the Anbar tribes were forced to rethink their alliance with AQI. The aftermath of the Samarra bombing sharpened the contradictions between Zarqawi's sweeping Islamist agenda and the insurgents' largely nationalist and local concerns.

AQI helped the Sunni tribes see that it posed a greater danger than the Americans. Zarqawi miscalculated by underestimating the Sunnis. (Sean MacFarland has observed, "It's good when your enemy is dumber than you are and the locals can see the difference."[129]) Zarqawi was unwilling to exercise some restraint, curb his organization's excesses, support a more nationalist agenda, and attend to the economic, educational, and other basic needs of the community. "Had al Qaeda been more like Hezbollah in Lebanon," General John Allen stated in his keynote address at the January 2010 Tampa conference on the Anbar Awakening, "we'd still be fighting in Ramadi right this second." Ironically, it was the *insecurity* of the Anbar tribes caused by Zarqawi's overzealousness that made the subsequent American offers of security through partnership so attractive.

Unlike the U.S. military and the Anbar tribes, AQI was not a learning organization. "Thank God for Zarqawi," reflected Derek Harvey. "I wake up every morning grateful for him."[130]

Even so, the Anbar Awakening Council, as defiant and heroic as its founding sheikhs undoubtedly were, would probably have been defeated had it not been for its alliance with U.S. forces. And even this alliance would probably not have saved the Awakening tribes, had it not been for the surge of additional U.S. forces in the first half of 2007. The extra U.S. forces, along with the signal they represented that the United States would stay as long as needed to defeat the insurgency, were essential for success. According to Petraeus, "The Anbar tribes did not really flip until there was a U.S. presence. The U.S. surge was crucial to getting the tribes to flip, but we needed U.S. force density first. Then the tribes were flipping up the Euphrates, one after another. And then, later, we would pile in with CERP dollars and reconstruction contracts."[131]

Ambassador Crocker, who worked hand-in-glove with Petraeus during this period, emphasized that the surge forces gradually created a "virtuous cycle." The surge gave the Anbar tribes the confidence that the United States troops had their backs against AQI and that the tribes would not wind up the way their compatriots in western Anbar had in 2005. As the Awakening spread into Baghdad, the Shi'a began to see that the Sunnis were standing against a common enemy, AQI, rather than fighting the Shi'a. This launched a reassessment among the Shi'a of the extremist Shi'a militias that many had previously viewed as perhaps a necessary evil in the sectarian conflict. Now they were seen as more evil than necessary. By early 2008, this had created a political climate in which Prime Minister Maliki could move against the Shi'a militias in the southern city of Basra with the support of the Shi'a population, something that would have been politically impossible a year before. The Sunnis, in turn, saw Maliki acting like a national rather than a sectarian leader, which made it easier for the Sunni coalition to rejoin the government in mid-2008.[132]

Could the Anbar Awakening have happened sooner? Could the Sunni resistance have joined up with U.S. forces and eventually the Iraqi government before 2006 and 2007?

Like everything else about Iraq, the answer is complicated. Keith Mines, the lone CPA official in Anbar Province in 2003, believes that in the first year of the occupation "there was a golden opportunity to achieve a measure of stability and we failed to seize that opportunity."[133] The official Army history also sees this period as "a window of opportunity that could have been exploited to produce the conditions for the quick creation of a new Iraq."[134]

Perhaps most persuasively, General Petraeus believes that engaging the tribes was possible much earlier. "We did it the first summer. Sure." Reaching out to disenfranchised Sunnis was the key. "A blind man on a dark night could see that you couldn't throw tens of thousands of individuals out of work and out of society and expect them to support the new Iraq," the general told me in April 2010.[135]

Petraeus's confidence was based on his earlier experience in Iraq. In the summer of 2003, CPA supremo Jerry Bremer had personally agreed to allow Petraeus, then commanding the 101st Air Assault Division occupying Mosul, a town northwest of Baghdad, to start a reconciliation process by evaluating the Ba'athist faculty members at Mosul University. But Bremer assigned responsibility for the vetting to Ahmed Chalabi, a Shi'a member of the Iraqi Governing Council who fiercely opposed all Ba'athists and former regime supporters. "He slow-rolled it," said Petraeus.

Reconciliation never happened on Petraeus's watch in Mosul, but he was adamant that "the opportunity was always there. H. R. McMaster in Tal'Afar did reconciliation by another name," referring to the classic counterinsurgency campaign waged by Colonel McMaster and the 3rd Armored Cavalry Regiment in 2005 and 2006.[136] He also cited MacFarland, who took risks to replicate this reconciliation effort in Ramadi. It was no accident that the Awakening Council started there. And Petraeus as MNF-I commander then committed the entire organization to supporting reconciliation in 2007. It is easy to forget just how controversial these decisions were at the time.

Others disagree with Petraeus. Crocker does not think the Anbar Awakening could have happened any sooner. The Sunni tribes had not yet suffered enough to make the leap to ask for U.S. assistance. Before the Awakening, "they were not sure we could protect them or even if we would. And they weren't sure that they wanted us to protect them," said Crocker.[137] Graeme Lamb, the British general Petraeus had entrusted with the FSEC engagement unit, concurred: "What we did in Iraq in mid-2006—had we tried to do it in mid-2004, it would have crashed and burned. Because at the end of the day, people hadn't exercised their revenge. They hadn't stood at the edge of the abyss and looked into it."[138] Derek Harvey agrees with them both. "Sattar would not have been successful a year earlier because the Sunnis didn't think they were losing yet. Without us, Sattar was going to die."[139]

So who is right?

If reconciliation efforts had come earlier, would the Sunnis have been receptive, as Petraeus maintains? Or did they have to suffer, lose, and grieve before they could see the American occupiers not as enemies but as potential allies, as Crocker, Lamb, and Harvey argue? Likewise, did the Americans have to suffer, lose, and grieve before they could see the Anbar tribes, the insurgents, the ex-Ba'athists and former regime elements as potential allies and not as enemies? Did both parties have to go through the meat grinder before they could accommodate each other?

General Petraeus has famously and repeatedly said that "the big idea is that you can't kill your way out of an industrial-strength insurgency." The policy implication is that military and civilian officials will sometimes need to reach out and engage with enemies to test whether mutual interests can trump violent differences and end the bloodshed.

But Petraeus also has distinguished between those groups who are reconcilable and those who are not. Reconciliation cannot be forced. Some individuals and groups will be more amenable than others; calculations may change over time. Reconciliation will depend on a host of factors: the correlation of forces, looming threats, economic distress, honor, humiliation, and many others.

Whatever the motivation, reconciliation often requires a profound psychological adjustment. In Anbar, many Sunnis initially harbored feelings of humiliation and rage at the American invasion and occupation. These grew with the marginalization and disenfranchisement of the Sunnis under Bremer and the CPA. No doubt a few Sunnis were willing to adjust and reconcile themselves rather quickly to a new order that privileged the Shi'a community, if only because they pragmatically concluded they needed a job with a salary to meet basic needs. An aggressive tribal and religious outreach strategy along the lines Petraeus proposed in the summer of 2003 could have enticed many of these Sunnis and prevented at least some of them from joining or tacitly supporting the "honorable resistance."

But as Chalabi's opposition to reconciliation demonstrated, the Shi'a majority at this time were suspicious to the point of paranoia at the prospect of a Ba'athist resurgence. The Shi'a, who controlled the government after June 2004, would have opposed any dedicated effort at rehabilitating substantial numbers of Ba'ath Party members and former regime elements and placing them back on the public payroll.

Some opportunity was lost here, but it is difficult to quantify. Harvey thinks that "we could have made real gains in Anbar and Babil provinces in 2003, but Salah Din, Diyala and the upper Tigris River Valley would have been more difficult given the Chalabi approach and Bremer's actions."[140] He does not think that hard-line nationalists and Ba'athists would have flipped at this time.

For many Sunnis, this window for reconciliation remained open for the rest of 2003 and the first quarter of 2004, until the barbaric murder of the four

Blackwater contractors in late March 2004. The resulting U.S. battle for Fallujah inflamed Sunni (and Shi'a) passions. Combined with the uprising by Moqtada al-Sadr's Mahdi Army in Baghdad that same month, U.S. and Coalition forces now responded with much more aggressive, kinetic approaches to conflict resolution. The character of the U.S. occupation, and the scope and intensity of the resistance, changed. Interest in reconciliation efforts disappeared on both sides.

Reconciliation largely remained dormant throughout the next few years, when Zarqawi and AQI increased their attacks against U.S. soldiers, attempted to provoke a sectarian war, and gradually asserted their dominance over the Sunni insurgency. A few tribal leaders tried to break free from AQI, only to be pitilessly brutalized for their disloyalty. Still, with a few exceptions (such as Tal'Afar), the tribes were psychologically unable to approach U.S. forces in 2004 and 2005 and team up against AQI. They preferred to resist AQI on their own or submit passively to its yoke. It is hard to see how any large-scale reconciliation was possible at this time.

In the aftermath of the February 2006 Samarra bombing and the ferocious Shi'a backlash, some of the Anbar tribes were ready to make common cause with U.S. forces. Whatever harsh feelings they had for the Americans were now eclipsed by a desire to avenge the havoc and human suffering AQI had triggered. Even so, just a minority of Ramadi's twenty-one tribes initially joined the Awakening Council. Reconciliation was still a work in progress. Only when the United States surged forces into battle space in 2007 and started to rout AQI was a broader reconciliation possible. Tribal fears of AQI retribution needed first to be alleviated. Tribal confidence that it was joining the winning side needed first to be boosted.

U.S. attitudes also changed during this period, affecting Sunni perceptions. According to the former mayor of the Anbar city of Tal'Afar, Najim Abed al-Jabouri, the Sunnis noticed in 2006 and 2007 a changed American approach. U.S. officials had by this time admitted that many of the early CPA decisions had been shortsighted, poorly implemented, or just wrong. American commanders on their second and third tours now resisted orders from the Iraqi Ministries of Interior and Defense to retire or eliminate former Ba'athists from the Iraqi police and security forces. And the Sunnis noticed that the United States increasingly criticized Iran's nuclear weapons program and warned against Tehran's support for Shi'a militias. Iranian opposition to the United States was a "red flag" to the

Sunni resistance groups and suggested that they might be able to make common cause against rising Persian interference in Iraq.[141]

Throughout 2007 and 2008, opportunities for reconciliation improved in tandem with an improved security situation. As innovative and daring as General Petraeus's SOI program was, it would have withered and died had it been adopted a year or two earlier. By leveraging all of America's military, economic, and diplomatic assets in early 2007, he created the conditions for the Anbar Awakening to survive and prosper and for the SOI to expand beyond anyone's imagination, to 103,000 men by the end of 2007. In war as in peace, timing is everything. Petraeus's great contribution was that he made his own timing.

One lesson is that opportunities to engage and reconcile may be fleeting. Leaders may have only moments to exploit the opening or risk having it close, perhaps for years. In Iraq, the ideological opposition of the Bush administration, the CPA, and the Iraqi Governing Council to rehabilitating and reintegrating Ba'ath Party members came at a high price, paid for with the lives of U.S. soldiers and Iraqi civilians. There was an opportunity during the first year or so of occupation, until the first battle for Fallujah. Once closed, it did not reopen for over two more years.

The Anbar Awakening suggests also that the U.S. military and civilian officials need to be more receptive to indicators that insurgents may want to engage. The United States repeatedly failed to spot signals that certain Anbar tribes were willing to join forces with the Americans to battle AQI. These "sparks," or mini-awakenings, were missed in 2004 and 2005. This was part of a larger intelligence shortfall that handicapped the first few years of the U.S. mission in Iraq.

Even when signals were not missed, the United States did not have the force presence to support those Sunnis who were willing to partner. Political engagement, like counterinsurgency operations, requires a certain critical mass of forces for it to be effective. Until the surge, there were never enough U.S. soldiers to convince many of the Anbar tribes to switch allegiances. The minority of tribes who joined the Awakening in September 2006 did not have sufficient strength to defeat AQI, even with the Ready First's assistance. For the next six months, AQI relentlessly attacked them. In February 2007, attacks on U.S. forces in and around Ramadi still averaged between thirty and thirty-five a day. The Awakening would have struggled and ultimately failed without the added influx of surge troops. As more U.S. forces became available, more tribes were willing to join up.

And what lesson does the remarkable career of Abdul Sattar reveal? If he had not existed, or if Lieutenant Colonel Deane and then Colonel MacFarland had not found him—almost by happenstance—and nurtured him, it is possible that another Anbar sheikh would have eventually emerged, perhaps one from a tribe with greater standing. But given AQI's ongoing campaign of intimidation, there were not a lot of volunteers about.

The Americans quickly realized that Abdul Sattar was special. Whatever he lacked in status and prestige, they could provide with additional *wasta* through CERP funds and reconstruction contracts. They were astute enough to realize that Abdul Sattar was precisely the type of partner they needed to get closer to the people and operate from inside the tribes.

Another lesson from the Awakening is personally uncomfortable to discuss, given my admiration for the courage and sacrifice of the outstanding young officers who served in Anbar and whom I have personally gotten to know over the past few years. Bluntly put, some officers ignored or disobeyed orders. In 2006, the U.S. mission was to focus on transitioning to the Iraqi security forces, to remain on the FOBs, and to not reach out to the tribes and certainly not the insurgents. Instead, some officers engaged the Anbar tribes and lived among the people, anticipating the shift in strategy that Odierno and Petraeus would introduce a few months later. It turned out to be the right move. It worked out this time. But for these men, there is a very good chance that the United States would have been chased out of Iraq, leaving the country and the region in chaos. There is even an argument, a persuasive one, that the soldiers deserved better commanders.

Regardless, this aspect of the Anbar Awakening is worrisome for the precedent it may create. If a lesson from the Awakening is that junior officers can disobey or ignore senior officers' intent, directives, and orders, then the risk to the military and the country is that a generation of soldiers will move up through the ranks who are used to operating at the outer edges of the command structure, and beyond. It is not a model that the U.S. military or its civilian masters would want to see replicated anywhere else in the future.

The success of the Anbar Awakening presented the United States with an opportunity it did not have before—to withdraw from the country in victory, not defeat. In August 2010, the United States downsized its presence to roughly 50,000 military personnel, largely in supporting roles. The U.S. goal for Iraq is "sustainable security." As this book goes to press, this goal has not been fully met and the war in Iraq is not over, but the country is more stable and its future prospects are brighter than at any point since 2003.

For Iraq, the success of the Anbar Awakening could not guarantee reconciliation among the three major ethnic/sectarian groups: the Sunnis, the Shi'a, and the Kurds. But it has provided the parties with more time and political space— really, more opportunity—than before to reconcile.

Some accommodation has occurred, but true reconciliation has been elusive. Prime Minister Nouri al-Maliki created a reconciliation commission in June 2007.[142] One of its prime responsibilities was to vet any Iraqi who wanted a job in the public sector, especially those from the SOI. The goal was to offer many of these men positions in the Iraqi security forces, while retraining some and offering public-works jobs to others. As of mid-2010, though, only a small percentage has been allowed to join the Iraqi police or security forces. The risk is that former insurgents will revert to their previous habits and take up arms against U.S. and Iraqi forces in the future. Most experts predict that low-level sectarian violence is likely to continue for some time.

Nonetheless, the Anbar Awakening offers the Iraqi people a useful lesson as they struggle to forge a new country. It represents an extraordinary example of reconciliation: how the Anbar tribes journeyed from conspiring and attacking American soldiers to eventually embracing their former enemies. The willingness to engage, to understand, and to show mutual respect was essential. Iraq will need a good deal of these qualities in the years to come.

CONCLUSION

LESSONS EARNED

NINE DAYS AFTER 9/11, PRESIDENT George W. Bush spoke before a joint session of Congress and a national television audience. "Every nation, in every region, now has a decision to make," the president warned. "Either you are with us, or you are with the terrorists."[1]

Less than a decade later, the world has not changed fundamentally. Terrorist threats have not abated and may actually have increased. The ideological clarity of the American people in condemning terrorism remains undimmed. The United States and others still face mortal threats from terrorist and insurgent groups. Osama bin Laden is still alive. Al Qaeda is still a deadly and dedicated enemy, and has inspired the creation of other terrorist groups. The detention facility at Guantánamo is still in business. Every morning, senior U.S. officials still receive the Terrorist Threat Matrix, a summary of threats against the United States collected during the previous 24 hours. Once a week, President Obama meets with his senior counterterrorism and intelligence experts for "Terror Tuesdays," the chance to discuss recent terrorist developments and trends.[2]

But America's responses to terrorism have evolved in subtle and sophisticated ways over the years. Gone is much of the bravado in official statements, most notably when President Bush taunted our adversaries in the Middle East to "bring 'em on."[3] The special CIA unit dedicated to hunting down bin Laden was disbanded years ago, a function of the difficulty in locating him and an appreciation of the fact that the United States has had other, more urgent priorities.[4] The new *Counterinsurgency Field Manual* developed by the Army and Marines has placed more emphasis on protecting civilian populations than on killing bad guys; it has privileged peace and stability over justice. Debates over how to prosecute two still-unfinished wars, in Iraq and Afghanistan, have set the limits of blood and treasure that the American people and political system will support.

The United States has purchased, at a high cost, a measure of wisdom this past decade. It has gained a new sense of pragmatism. America has learned that victories will be neither quick nor painless. It has learned that judging is easy, but understanding is hard, and so has started to invest time and money to better understand its enemies and their languages and cultures. The American people have learned that killing or capturing every terrorist is not operationally possible, politically feasible, or financially affordable. And that the attempt to do so may even be counterproductive, spawning more terrorists than it removes from the battlefield.

Which means that talking to some of them may sometimes be a good option.

And yet the very idea grates. It smacks of rewarding not just bad behavior but depravity. There is an unresolved tension between the head, which understands the practical reasons for parleying, and the heart, which is sickened by those who slaughter innocents. For the United States, this dilemma has a long tradition: the contest over whether "realism" or "idealism" should guide American foreign policy. How should presidents decide between protecting America's interests and promoting its values? Or is it possible, somehow, to strike the proper balance between the two?

In truth, determining when to talk to terrorists is not always difficult. Broadly speaking, terrorist groups fall into one of three categories: the irreconcilables, the reconcilables, and those who lie somewhere in between.

For the irreconcilables, no solution short of agreeing to their entire agenda will satisfy them. This was the judgment of U.S. forces in Anbar with respect to Abu Musab al-Zarqawi and al Qaeda in Iraq (AQI). It is Israel's assessment of Hamas, as long as the Islamic movement cannot bring itself to recognize Israel, renounce violence, and accept all previous Israeli-Palestinian agreements. And as long as ETA insists on an independent Basque homeland, this will also be Spain's assessment of ETA. In these cases, governments have no choice but to kill or capture these groups, choke off their funding, and diminish their appeal to potential recruits and supporters by an aggressive information campaign.⁵ This is not a hard call.

The reconcilables are those groups that have signaled a willingness to talk, that are open to some compromise short of their ultimate goals and victory. Their demands—if not their methods—may be reasonable, seeking to right historic injustices in political representation, housing, education, and access to jobs and land. They may also insist on pardons for past crimes, help in reintegrating their people into society, and a promise that the state security forces and local police will not seek retribution. Led by Abdul Sattar Albu Risha, many of the Anbar tribes reconciled with U.S. forces in 2006 and 2007, along with over 100,000 Sunni members of the "honorable resistance" who were willing to join the Sons of Iraq program. In these cases, governments need to proceed with caution, but an end to the violence is in sight. This is not a hard call either.

And then there is the third category—those groups that fall somewhere between the other two. The statements and actions of these groups are ambiguous, vague, or contradictory, suggesting at times that they may be willing to compromise and at other times that they would never do so. Or some of their members may declare a desire for a more political and peaceful approach, but their actions (or the actions of other individuals or factions within the group) may demonstrate a preference to continue fighting. One day they may claim they want a negotiated solution. The next, they may detonate a bomb or assassinate a government official.

For democratic governments, this third category is the one most fraught with political risk. The government is operating in a netherworld of secrecy and uncertainty, with a partner of unproven reliability and veracity, and where factions in the terrorist group may eagerly try to spoil any efforts to abandon the cause short of total victory. A senior CIA officer who worked in Iraq in 2003 and 2004 had developed his own back-of-the-envelope classification system. He told me, "For a few, someone like Zarqawi, you just have to kill him. Him and the people around him. But the others? Maybe they can be turned. You have to do it on a case-by-case basis. Some are reconcilable, some aren't. You have to be careful, but you can make judgments over time."⁶

Even so, such judgments are tricky. Not all engagements end as well as London's with the IRA/Sinn Fein. At a certain point during the Troubles (the precise date is vague), the British government decided that the IRA/Sinn Fein was worth engaging because it might genuinely renounce violence and pursue its agenda solely through peaceful political means. This judgment call was vindicated years later, when Sinn Fein signed up to the 1998 Good Friday Agreement, and was finally validated in 2007, when Sinn Fein agreed to reopen the Stormont Assembly as the junior partner to Ian Paisley's DUP.

It is also possible that such talks will end in failure. For example, many Sri Lankan political leaders believed (really, hoped) that Prabhakaran was sincerely committed to a peace process. Regrettably, they miscalculated. The LTTE was incapable of modifying its maximalist agenda. For Prabhakaran, ceasefires and negotiations were merely tactics to give the LTTE time to rest, rearm, and prepare for the next round of war until it achieved an independent Eelam.

Here is where democratic principles of openness, transparency, and accountability may be compromised, subverted, and even violated. How does a government explain to its public its judgment to sit down with a ruthless and unscrupulous terrorist group? How can the government go forward if bombs may still go off, if security forces are still under attack, and if innocent lives are still being threatened?

Over the years, some countries, including the United States, have either sidelined these questions by engaging covertly with terrorists or ignored them and proceeded to "negotiate with evil" anyway. This book has looked at four examples of governments that have decided to talk to terrorists and one example where the government officially has denied it does so but has carved out exceptions in certain circumstances. These talks have presented a series of hurdles the government must surmount, like a steeplechase, with dangers lurking around every turn.

These dangers are not trivial. They can gravely weaken the state and strengthen terrorist groups. They can bring down a government. They can harm relations with key friends and allies. They can cost the lives of security forces, police, and everyday citizens.

But these case studies also provide a wealth of lessons, rules, and guidelines that can shape the future behavior of governments when they contemplate talking to terrorists.

War by Other Means I

Any negotiation with a terrorist group is the continuation of war by other means. So the first rule is that no government can hope to win at the negotiating table what it can't defend on the ground. There is little point in even attempting to start a peace process with terrorists if the state has not already generated significant negotiating leverage on the battlefield. Appealing to the "spirit" of the talks, to abstract notions of fairness, to their better angels, or to some undefined and intangible greater good won't get you very far.

Ideally, the government should demonstrate its superiority through a combination of security measures, police work, and social and economic programs that address as many of the terrorists' grievances as possible. At a minimum, the government needs to have battled the terrorists to a standstill so that neither side can fully impose its will on the other. Only in this manner can the government convey to the terrorists that they will pay a price—a battering from the security and police forces—if they refuse to talk or if they abandon talks already begun.

The government also must demonstrate it has the stamina to slog it out for a very long time. If the terrorist movement believes that the government's commitment is wavering, fleeting, or time-bound, it will simply try to wait it out. It would believe, rightly, that time is on its side and it will prevail. For any government caught up in this type of fight, therefore, endurance is a tactical necessity.

The clearest example is Britain's battle with the IRA. For decades, members of the IRA believed that they could drive the British out of Northern Ireland. One more "big push"—whether by inflicting sufficient casualties in the North or by setting off enough bombs on the mainland—would demoralize the British and cause them to withdraw. But the British proved tougher and more resilient than the IRA anticipated. Only after the British security forces fought the IRA to a standstill and showed no sign of withdrawing from Northern Ireland, after the intelligence services infiltrated the IRA's leadership, after the targeting of Republicans by Loyalist paramilitaries, and after it was clear that continuation of the armed struggle was a millstone around Sinn Fein's political fortunes did Gerry Adams and the IRA/Sinn Fein decide to seek an end to the violence. As Martin McGuinness confessed to me in May 2009, "We saw a military stalemate that could go on not just for years, but for decades."[7] Gerry Adams put it even more emphatically to me: "Dialogue is essential. The alternative is war forever. We were not prepared to do that."[8] This was the necessary condition the British had to establish—and sustain—before any peace settlement was possible.

Spain, also, had to establish its dominance before ETA would agree to come to the table. By the mid-1980s, ETA was being squeezed, first by government-backed assassinations conducted by the *GAL* ("the dirty war") and later by greater security cooperation between Madrid and Paris. In late 1986, ETA indicated it wanted to talk, which led to the three-year negotiation in Algiers. Fifteen years later, the government of José Maria Aznar requested the extradition of ETA members living overseas and adopted a tough law-and-order approach to ETA and its social and financial support network. ETA responded by declaring a "general and indefinite" ceasefire, which led to another round of talks with the government.

The Sri Lankan government could not get the LTTE to the negotiating table as long as Prabhakaran held the upper hand. But when the military balance shifted, as it did in 1989 when the Indian peacekeeping force threatened to destroy the LTTE, Prabhakaran reached out and cut a secret deal with President Premadasa to have Colombo provide funding, arms, ammunition, and equipment to the Tigers. This rule can work the other way as well. In 2001, with the LTTE exhausted by a military stalemate, Prabhakaran agreed to a ceasefire that would lock in the LTTE's recent battlefield advantages and entered into a peace process with Colombo.

The same type of dynamic played out in Anbar Province. In this case, the United States had to prove to the Sunni tribes that it could match AQI's strength and sustain its combat presence—in other words, that the Americans were the strongest tribe. Before the summer of 2006, only a few isolated Anbar tribes tried to partner with U.S. forces; this usually ended badly for them as there were not enough troops to sustain the initial cooperation and counter AQI. Even the Anbar Awakening Council had the allegiance of only a minority of the tribes around Ramadi. Abdul Sattar, the Council's leader, was the exception in his willingness to ally publicly with U.S. forces at this time. Only after the surge was announced in January 2007, and only after the surge forces moved into battle space in Anbar, did the tribes start "flipping up the Euphrates, one after another," according to Petraeus.

Even an organization as uncompromising as Hamas is not immune to the balance of political and military power. Sheikh Yassin first proposed the idea of a *hudna* with Israel as a way to counter the PLO's appeal among Palestinians after the Oslo Accords. Hamas repeated its offers of a *hudna* later in the 1990s, after Israel's severe military response to Hamas suicide bombings resulted in the imprisonment of Hamas members and the collective punishment of Palestinians.

Diplomacy has its time and place, but power rules.

WAR BY OTHER MEANS II

What if the intelligence community assesses that the terrorist group is not serious about peace, even though it still says it wants to talk to the government? Terrorists may say they want to talk for a variety of reasons: Because they want a tactical pause to relieve the pressure from the security forces, because they want time to rearm and reorganize their forces for battles yet to come, because they want to appeal to a domestic audience that yearns for peace, or because they want to signal to foreign constituents who provide moral and financial support that the government, and not the terrorist group, represents the true obstacle to resolving the conflict.

Under these circumstances, is it still worth talking, even if there is no real prospect of a successful negotiation?

The answer is yes, sometimes.

In these cases, the government needs to be crystal clear that this is not a genuine negotiation but a very different exercise entirely—a counterterrorism operation. The purpose is not to strike a deal with the terrorist group but to use the talks to undermine it.

A number of techniques can be employed. At the tactical level, skilled intelligence professionals can gather intelligence and create files on individual terrorists—their personal histories, relationships and rivalries, ambitions, foibles, and vulnerabilities. This information can be used to pit members of the group against one another. According to a senior MI6 officer, talking to these types of groups "unsettles them tremendously. Their egos are stroked by your interest in talking to them, but it causes suspicion and mistrust inside the organization."[9] Information can be used to blackmail or recruit terrorists to inform on their colleagues. Informants can tip off the police and security services to prevent criminal activities and acts of terror. For example, by the early 1990s, the British security and intelligence branches had so effectively infiltrated the IRA that many of the IRA's terrorist plans were stillborn, either compromised or prevented before they could inflict harm.

Betrayal can take another form. In the case of insurgencies and terrorist groups, governments may be facing more than one threat simultaneously. "Since different movements battling for similar causes often draw from similar constituents, former fighters are ideally positioned to give government counter-insurgency forces the information they need. If part of a movement begins to cooperate with the government, it can help identify fellow fighters, reveal lines of supply, explain communication methods, or otherwise reveal a range of vital tactical information."[10] Witness the U.S. military's success in reaching out to the Sunni tribal sheikhs in Anbar Province.

Former members can also help shift allegiances. In the immediate post-Franco years, the Spanish government used former ETA-PM members to lobby their former comrades to end the armed struggle and promote the idea of Basque nationalism within the constitutional structure, in organizations such as the PNV.

Skilled intelligence professionals can also use talks to gain strategic insights into the group's thinking, plans, organizational structure, personnel, and leadership. They can identify who holds the reins of power and detect fissures in the group that can be exploited. They can talent-spot younger members who have the potential to rise to leadership positions, which the British claimed they did with a very young Gerry Adams in 1972. Or talks can simply keep open lines of communication for the future, when new thinking may emerge within the group, when new government leaders may adopt a more flexible approach to the talks, or when the situation on the battlefield may force the two sides to recalculate their prospects for military victory and decide that a ceasefire or peace agreement may be the better option. Again, this was the game MI6 played with Michael Oatley and others who maintained contact with the IRA during the Thatcher years.

The Spanish government's negotiations with ETA in Algiers represent the best example of negotiations as an elaborate counterterrorism scheme. Rafael Vera, the director of state security, viewed the Algiers talks as an opportunity to gather intelligence on ETA, its different factions, and its internal disputes. Anticipating that the talks would fail, Vera had prearranged with the Algerian government to have it expel all of the ETA members to certain Latin American countries, where they would be placed under house arrest and secretly watched. Their phones and fax machines were tapped. "We were able to arrest a lot of command cells [in Spain] because of this surveillance," Vera told me in July 2009. "This was my goal. . . . I used it to roll up ETA. . . . I could learn more when they were in foreign countries than when they were in Spanish prisons." The Algiers talks were a "performance . . . an example of a political negotiation with a police objective."[11]

Complicating an already murky picture is that many negotiations are both genuine and not quite what they seem. They can be legitimate attempts to peacefully resolve the conflict and also vehicles for intelligence-gathering. They can combine elements of both.

Any counterterrorism effort should be open to signals that the terrorist group might consider resolving the conflict peacefully. Similarly, the intensity of some peace negotiations may promote a degree of intimacy that may present openings to recruitment. This "duality" ends only when a peace settlement is formalized— and perhaps not even then, if the government fears backsliding on the part of at least some members of the terrorist group.

As I've talked with intelligence professionals around the world during the past few years, I've often asked whether they would be willing to sit down and talk with Osama bin Laden and al Qaeda. Each one has salivated at the prospect. "Hell yes, I'd love to talk to OBL" is the typical response, and not because they harbor any illusions al Qaeda would ever be willing to abandon its grandiose dreams of a caliphate stretching across the Middle East. They want to talk to him because it would present a once-in-a-lifetime opportunity to gather intelligence on the most wanted man in the world and peer inside his organization.

THE INTEGRITY OF ENGAGEMENT

Given the political risks and mortal dangers involved in any outreach to terrorists, it is important that the government maintain the integrity of any engagement. Those entrusted with making the initial contacts with terrorists must present their findings to their superiors in unvarnished form. "The results must not be massaged to fit the prejudices or prevailing orthodoxies, or to avoid offending the prevailing political climate," writes David Omand, a senior British intelligence officer.[12] If an opportunity surfaces to start a peace process, that information must be conveyed accurately. Perhaps more important, if the time is not ripe for talking, that information must also be conveyed, even if it is inconvenient for elected politicians eager to appear as peacemakers to ingratiate themselves with voters. Any corruption in the process could severely damage public trust in the government and the state's intelligence services.

Threats to the integrity of the process may originate with the head of the government, as elected officials allow their egos to overwhelm their objectivity. These leaders may believe they have a special gift that will allow them to bring the terrorists to heel and end the conflict or may be angling for the next Nobel Peace

Prize. Some think that Spain's Socialist leader, José Luis Rodriguez Zapatero, had this weakness, which led him to announce (over)confidently in December 2006 that his government was on the verge of a breakthrough with ETA. The very next day, ETA detonated a massive car bomb at Madrid's Barajas airport.

Threats may also arise from lower-level intermediaries. According to firsthand accounts, the MI6 officer, Michael Oatley, led the IRA to believe during the 1974–75 peace talks that the British were willing to discuss withdrawing from Northern Ireland. Oatley's desire to maintain both the ceasefire and the negotiations caused him to raise false hopes about London's position. Any short-term benefits were outweighed by the longer-term consequences. After the IRA learned that withdrawal had never been on the table, it changed tactics, continuing the armed struggle while negotiating to maintain pressure on London. It demanded greater and greater concessions from London up front in future talks. In the end, these false hopes added burdens on future British prime ministers and the peace process.

The shadowy nature of intelligence work, which is sometimes more art than science, also threatens the integrity of the peace process. It is hardly possible to cross-check every message or run down every rumor. Garbles and ambiguous messages are inevitable. At other times, outright fraud may be at work, especially with third parties pursuing their own agendas. The John Major government did not quite know what to make of the "war is over" note it received in February 1993, allegedly from the IRA/Sinn Fein's Martin McGuinness. In this case, the fabrication (by members of the Derry backchannel wanting to jump-start the peace process) actually helped the two sides get back together, after the Major government responded to the note as if it accurately reflected the IRA's position.

More likely are overtures that send governments down rabbit holes. For example, "fake sheikhs" in Amman, Jordan, misled U.S. civilians and military officers during the summer of 2004 into believing that with American arms and money they could turn off the insurgency then raging across Anbar Province. Likewise, ETA's September 1998 announcement of an "indefinite" ceasefire raised hopes across Spain that the violent expression of Basque nationalism might be nearing an end. Prime Minister Aznar had little choice but to reverse his previous policy and engage with ETA. Yet all along, the Aznar government's political partner, the PNV, knew that the government was being deceived and chose to remain silent.

Or the threat to the integrity of the peace process may arise from inadequate preparations by one of the parties. For example, the Jaffna talks between the government of Sri Lanka and the Tamil Tigers during 1994 and 1995 were poorly conceived and structured from the start—as an exchange of formal letters rather than the give-and-take of a true negotiation. The two sides engaged in only a few days of direct talks spread out over almost six months. They gradually devoted more time to trying to shape domestic and world opinion than working through their disagreements. Also, Colombo's negotiators were inexperienced, with little knowledge of previous communications with Prabhakaran and little support from other government agencies. These talks revealed the government's lack of professionalism, sincerity, and commitment to a peace agreement.[13]

A government may deceive a terrorist group—they *are* terrorists, after all. But it should always ensure the integrity of its own process, motives, and intentions.

THE ROLE OF INTELLIGENCE

Once the government's forces have battled the terrorists to a standstill or better, and once the integrity of the engagement is assured, there remains the task of making contact with some of the most wanted men on the planet. This takes special talents and training. Needless to say, presidents, prime ministers, and other cabinet officers do not have them. A first-rate intelligence service is essential.

It is difficult to imagine a government having any serious interaction with terrorist groups without the benefit of a highly competent intelligence service. Terrorist groups by their very nature are secretive, duplicitous, and unaccountable, and these attributes confer on them special advantages over democratic governments and elected officials. Clandestine agents can help uncover their secrets, expose their lies, and hold them responsible for their actions so the government can have a more level playing field when it comes time to parley.

It takes good intelligence work to analyze a terrorist group and uncover its internal thinking. Does it want to talk to the government? Will it commit to a formal diplomatic framework that can lead to a genuine peace process? If so, is it willing to modify or abandon some of its long-standing goals? Is talking just a tactical ruse or is it a sincere attempt to end the conflict?

Even very good intelligence work comes with no guarantees. It cannot deliver certainty. But it can give the government greater confidence that it is worthwhile to engage, that there are benefits to keeping channels open, and that there may even be a chance for peace that can be seized. This can help create the space leaders need to make the politically risky decision to enter into talks. A government needs to know that if it publicly announces that it is willing to talk, bombs won't go off the next day.[14]

These assurances allowed prime ministers John Major and Tony Blair to publicly commit to engagement with the IRA/Sinn Fein. In Israel, the Mossad regularly examines statements and behavior by Hamas members "to see if they have had a change of heart," as a former senior officer for Mossad, Yoram Hessel, told me.

The importance of an intelligence service is perhaps best illustrated when it does not function very well. The U.S. military effort in Iraq was seriously handicapped by a shortage of interpreters and translators; it also lacked sufficient collection and analysis capabilities. "We only had 25 to 30 percent of what we needed as a bare minimum," commented a Marine intelligence officer on the 2003-to-2006 time period.[15] This situation did not change until General Petraeus took command in 2007.

The lack of good intelligence cost the American war effort in a variety of ways. It led the United States to meet with fake sheikhs in Amman, Jordan, who sold a story that they could turn off the insurgency. More significant, it led the United States to miss signals in 2004 and 2005 that some Anbar tribes were willing to join forces with the Americans to battle AQI. The Pentagon's frustration at its inability to get a good picture of the insurgency may have contributed to the abuse of prisoners at Abu Ghraib. Poor intelligence also meant that the Americans never fully understood the human terrain in Iraq, and this lack resulted in a greater number of American combat deaths and casualties.

This failure of intelligence is not as unusual as it might seem. Often intelligence services are initially unprepared to observe, analyze, and penetrate terrorist groups; they may also lack the legal authority they need to mount effective surveillance and counterterrorism operations. For example, Britain's intelligence system at the start of the Troubles was a disaster, with overlapping and competing responsibilities among a variety of government agencies and departments. Not until the Thatcher years was the problem finally sorted out. Post-Franco Spain faced a similar challenge, with almost a dozen secret intelligence services competing with one another in the absence of any permanent antiterrorist legislation.

The faster a government can successfully organize its intelligence efforts, the greater the chances that it can degrade and demoralize a terrorist movement, and perhaps even push it into negotiations.

In Search of Gerry Adams

A government's ability to degrade a terrorist organization, to decide to engage with terrorists, and to mobilize the intelligence community to navigate the first perilous steps with mortal enemies of the state are all necessary but not sufficient conditions for launching a peace process. It also needs a partner across the negotiating table. And not just any partner, but someone who can imagine an end to the armed struggle, who has the physical and moral courage to pursue that path, who has won the respect of his comrades in the movement, who can speak with authority and act with discretion, and perhaps most important, who can bring his people along, whether by persuasion, intimidation, or force. Without such a person, talks are doomed to fail.

The problem is that people with these qualities are few and are especially rare in terrorist groups. One or two figures may possess some of these attributes, like Arnaldo Otegi in the Basque region or Karuna Amman from the LTTE. But no such leader with *all* these qualities has ever existed in either of those organizations, or in Hamas or AQI.

Northern Ireland has been the exception. Whatever Gerry Adams's role in the Troubles or his long, strange journey to become a man of peace, he is an extraordinary figure of world importance because he has led a terrorist group away from the gun and into the corridors of political power.

Today, Adams has become the standard by which terrorist or insurgent leaders are measured, at least those who are engaged in a formal peace process or discussions with a government. In Anbar in April 2004, U.S. military intelligence officers were talking, unsuccessfully, with leading insurgents to see if any of them were willing to step forward, calm tensions, and help stabilize Fallujah. "We keep hoping they'll come up with a Gerry Adams," said one U.S. official. "But it just hasn't happened."[16] In Spain, a typical comment was that "ETA doesn't have anyone like Gerry Adams, no one who is capable of thinking politically and flexibly and who also controls the military."[17] It is difficult to think of any terrorist or insurgent conflict around the world that would not benefit from having someone with Adams's particular set of skills.

MITCHELL B. REISS

Adams had two advantages not often present in leaders of other terrorist groups. First, he was a senior leader in a rigidly hierarchical organization, one with exemplary military discipline and an order of battle. (The IRA was, after all, an *Army*.) This undoubtedly made it easier to halt the fighting and ensure that a political agreement would stick, with a minimum number of defections, once Adams was able to persuade the senior military leadership that the IRA needed to lay down its weapons and adopt a purely political way forward.

Karuna Amman, on the other hand, was only able to bring a minority of forces with him when he decided to break away from Prabhakaran in March 2004. And ETA leaders who have questioned and reconsidered the feasibility of their historic mission have only done so after being caught and imprisoned. Their appeals for an end to terror have gone unheeded. With Hamas, it is unclear who speaks for the movement. Its internal leadership, based in the Occupied Territories, and its external leadership, based in Syria and elsewhere in the region, have different priorities. And complicating matters further is that both leadership groups are subject to influence by Syria and Iran.

Second, Adams had the benefit of longevity. He did not starve himself to death in the Maze. He did not die in a shootout with British security forces or at the hands of Loyalist paramilitaries. He had become actively involved in the Republican cause as a teenager but, significantly, was only willing to consider an end to the armed struggle as he approached middle age. He morphed from the fiery young radical to the mature statesman willing to make very tough decisions on behalf of his community. As he grew older, his political views evolved as well. The Gerry Adams of the Good Friday Agreement and beyond was not the same Gerry Adams who attended the Cheyne Walk meeting, who reorganized the IRA's military structure and upgraded its operations in the late 1970s, and who pursued a strategy of both ballot and bullet throughout the 1980s and much of the 1990s. He needed this time—decades, it turned out—for a personal political evolution.

Abdul Sattar Albu Risha, the leader of the Anbar Awakening Council, is the closest example we have seen in this book to a leader like Adams. He had a checkered background (although no evidence emerged that he had ever attacked U.S. troops), the imagination to see that the Americans were not the Sunnis' enemy, the charisma to win others to his side, and the courage to defy AQI. With time, he may have blossomed into a national leader representing the Sunni community across Iraq. Unfortunately, he was assassinated by an IED outside his home in September 2007.

The actuarial odds are stacked too heavily against many terrorist leaders' living to middle age to allow even the possibility that their attitudes would change. Few governments are willing to remove the target from a terrorist leader's back in the hope that he might, years in the future, renounce violence and seek peace. Since September 2000, Israel has adopted a policy of targeted killings of terrorist leaders, even though evidence suggests that decapitation of a terrorist group does not make much difference in collapsing the group's resistance.[18] In the case of Hamas, "Those next in line for succession . . . add their names to Israel's target list, where life is Hobbesian: nasty, brutish, and short."[19] Decapitation of the movement's leaders translates to a deadly game of musical chairs.

Governments may also warehouse terrorist leaders in prison and await a change of heart. The gamble is that these men would retain the allegiance of their comrades on the outside while they moderate their views as they get older.

For any peace process to take off, every government needs what is euphemistically called a "partner for peace." It would be more accurate to say that every government facing a terrorist or insurgent threat needs a Gerry Adams.

PATIENCE IS NOT JUST A VIRTUE

When it comes to negotiations, amateurs talk about outcomes, professionals talk about process. There is no guarantee of success with any negotiation, much less one that poses as many risks as when governments sit down with terrorists. But unless the government is prepared to exercise patience, failure is guaranteed.

All engagements start slowly, in the shadows. At the time, violence is ongoing and passions are high, with people on both sides fighting and dying. Neither side knows if the other sincerely wants to engage or would prefer to embarrass the other side by leaking to the media that its adversary is suing for peace. Governments should take only small, tentative steps initially, until they have some confidence that the terrorist group wants to parley.

All engagements also start well below the level of senior officials, and are usually initiated by intelligence operatives unknown to the public at large. In Iraq, Colonel Derek Harvey and some CIA case officers surreptitiously made contact with leaders of the insurgency during 2003 and 2004. Britain used MI5 and MI6 agents to open and maintain channels to the IRA. The Spanish authorities used similar go-betweens to feel out ETA's intentions. Israel has sent mid-level intelligence officers when it has held indirect talks with Hamas.

Should these actions be exposed, the government could plausibly deny that any overtures to terrorists had been authorized at a senior level. Eliza Manningham-Buller, the former head of MI5, said: "You need to do this in a way that does not contaminate the politicians."[20] Lower-level officers could be thrown under the bus if they became embarrassments or liabilities to the government. (After the IRA leaked the July 1972 meeting, the secretary of state for Northern Ireland, William Whitelaw, feared that he would lose his job. In the end, he didn't, but no British elected official met with the IRA again for over two decades.)

Elected officials need to appreciate that these rhythms do not follow the political calendar. Results cannot automatically be delivered in time for the next election.

All engagements take far longer than originally anticipated, both the initial overtures to explore whether it is possible to move from the shadows and into public view, and the formal peace process itself. They will have pauses, setbacks, and reversals, and will need to be nurtured, developed, and encouraged if they are not to end in failure. It is not very glamorous work. It involves the long, hard, often tedious slog of parties meeting for hours a day, for weeks or for months on end.

For example, the González government labored for months to set up initial meetings with ETA representatives. The resulting talks in Algiers proved intensely frustrating, as the chief ETA negotiator insisted on repeatedly explaining the Basque country's special history and political situation. The Aznar government also needed months to establish its first meeting with ETA in May 1999. ETA would not agree to an agenda in advance of the meeting; they then revived old claims that were entirely unacceptable to Madrid.

From 2003 to 2006, CIA and American military officers spent days, weeks, and months courting danger to reach out to insurgents, with mixed success. It was only after AQI's inhuman violence combined with Shi'a death squads and ongoing American operations that some members of the "honorable resistance" decided to switch allegiances to the U.S. side. It then took a further surge of U.S. troops in early 2007 for the majority of the Sunni tribes in Anbar and the Sons of Iraq to decide to join the Americans. Perhaps the strongest argument for patience (as well as persistence) is provided by Britain's experience in Northern Ireland: It took six prime ministers and more than twenty-five years for the IRA to end its armed struggle.

A more patient approach is also said to be important for "building trust" between the parties. At best, this is a tired and overused cliché. It fundamentally mischaracterizes what happens during negotiations. Trust is never really established, not in the true meaning of the word: an unthinking, blind acceptance of the other party's word. During my years of working on the Northern Ireland peace process, I *never* trusted my counterparts from the Unionist, Republican, and Nationalist parties. To be frank, I sometimes had doubts about some of my British and Irish colleagues who were supposed to be on the same side of the table as me.

Rather, parties in a negotiation may be able to establish a sense of common purpose. This type of mutual understanding cannot be formed easily or fast. But it can sometimes be forged during patient, sustained, and intense negotiations, where the two parties come to see that their interests are not entirely antithetical and may, in places, even be mutual. It is called a peace *process* for a reason.

Governments face another problem: a terrorist group's "lack of capacity." The skill set that enables someone to rise to the head of a terrorist group—ruthlessness, charisma, organizational skills, and luck—is not the same one most in need at the negotiating table—critical thinking, poise, logical analysis, and empathy. It is not that terrorist leaders are necessarily stupid. But they may be ignorant about the wider world. Many are unlikely to have much formal education. They have not been exposed to competing views of history, identity, and politics. They may have spent much of their lives in the bush or may have become indoctrinated by their own propaganda. Living in a culture of violence and constant danger may have made them intolerant of dissenting perspectives.

For example, Martin McGuinness pleaded youth and inexperience when we revisited some of the "rookie mistakes" the IRA had made during its early meetings with the British: "I was only twenty-two at the time!"[21] (It wasn't just McGuinness—the entire IRA delegation had no negotiating experience.) During the 1974–75 peace talks, the IRA swallowed uncritically Oatley's vague assurances that the British might consider withdrawing from Northern Ireland. They proved fast learners after these experiences, but it still took over twenty more years of frustrating on-again, off-again negotiations before they were willing to commit fully to a peace process.

ETA was worse. The group did not have the competence or experience to initiate a peace process, never mind sustain it over time. It proposed unacceptable ideas on the venue and the agenda. It constantly lectured on its interpretation of Spanish history and Basque grievances. It humiliated the most conciliatory prime minister it ever had, José Luis Rodriguez Zapatero, by detonating a bomb at the Madrid airport the day after he announced to the country his hopes for substantial progress in peace talks. ETA members behaved no better in their dealings with the Basque nationalist party, the PNV, placing their revolvers on the table during discussions, refusing to allow any changes to documents they had drafted, and proposing that the PNV commit political suicide by leaving the Basque parliament and joining a virtual assembly of ETA's imagination.

And ETA did not improve its performance over time. According to Juan Manuel Eguiagaray, the González administration's lead negotiator during the Algiers talks, "I have always wondered at their ability to think politically. Their capability to admit reality is very small. They live in a very isolated manner and have not understood the changes in the world."[22] A decade later, Javier Zarzalejos talked with ETA as a member of the Aznar government and leveled similar charges: "It was very difficult to talk to these people. They were out of touch with reality, living clandestinely, living in a world of their own."

Moreover, terrorist groups usually have a very shallow talent pool. At best, there may be one (or two) members of the delegation who have the ability to represent the group and go head-to-head in talks with the government's officials.

The Sri Lankan government faced this problem with the LTTE. The Tamil Tigers designated a former journalist, Anton Balasingham, to lead its delegation from the Thimpu talks in 1985 to the first round of the Geneva talks held in February 2006. An American official closely involved in the peace process commented that "if he was the best they could do, they were in trouble."[23] And after Balasingham, the quality of the delegation fell off even more dramatically. At one point, G. L. Peiris, Colombo's chief negotiator, decided he needed to bring in outside expertise to provide the competence, knowledge, and sophistication the LTTE delegation lacked.[24] Making a tough negotiating environment more difficult, the Norwegians divided the peace process into smaller working groups or subcommittees. The result was that the LTTE's responsibilities multiplied, overwhelming members of the delegation with demands they were not equipped to meet.

Obviously, governments cannot choose the terrorist groups they negotiate with. But they can choose the pace at which the negotiation unfolds. The lack of capacity of most terrorist groups argues for a methodical, step-by-step approach, rather than an accelerated or expedited tempo. A party that tips its hand that it wants (or worse, that it needs) to get a deal done quickly will fail. Even novice negotiators know enough to take advantage of an adversary that seems more eager than they are to reach a deal.

This also means avoiding the temptation offered by a single "grand bargain," where all differences are placed on the table to be resolved in one go. To be sure, the grand bargain approach appears to have the advantage of one-stop shopping. The hope is that you can quickly strike a deal and be home in time for dinner with the family. But it overestimates the capacity of these groups to assimilate complex, life-and-death issues, draft timely and coherent replies, and understand how one relates to another strategically. They cannot rely on a chancellery, foreign ministry, or intelligence service back home to do the heavy lifting. They are on their own. Trying to force the issue is unlikely to succeed, and it will needlessly aggravate personal relations and poison the talks.

Along with power, patience rules. As a senior British intelligence officer, one with years of experience tracking terrorist groups and other unsavory characters around the world, remarked, "It takes time for the unthinkable to become the inevitable."

ALL NEGOTIATIONS ARE LOCAL

All negotiations with terrorist groups present a government with domestic challenges it needs to manage if it wants to give the talks a chance of success. The most treacherous moment for any government is when it decides to move from the shadows to the light—when it has enough confidence that the terrorist group is willing and able to help institutionalize a peace process that will be publicly acknowledged. Ideally, the peace process should have support across a broad political spectrum, with a consistent line by all political parties to ensure that the terror group cannot split or play one off against the other. Important constituencies—such as the military, security, and police forces—should publicly support engagement, whatever their private reservations. Astute governments will develop a public relations strategy that explains to domestic audiences why they have decided to negotiate.

Governments often fall well short of these goals. Sri Lanka did a particularly poor job of shaping domestic perceptions. After the government's experiences with the LTTE at Thimpu, with the Indo–Sri Lanka Accord, and from Ranasinghe Premadasa's backchannel dealings, it was evident that Prabhakaran could not be trusted as a partner for peace. The unity of Sri Lanka and Prabhakaran's vision of an independent Eelam were fundamentally and forever incompatible. In this case, the government needed to explain to the people that a peaceful resolution was not possible. Yet rather than explain this harsh truth to the electorate and take all measures necessary to defeat the LTTE, subsequent political leaders tried to outdo one another in promising an exhausted population a negotiated peace settlement with this murderous psychopath. Chandrika Kumaratunga and Ranil Wickremasinghe placed their own personal political fortunes ahead of the country's national security.

In Spain, President José Maria Aznar was skeptical of negotiations under almost any circumstances. Yet his government reversed its hard-line approach after ETA announced a "general and indefinite" ceasefire in September 1998. "Personally, I never believed them," he later told me. "But my problem was public opinion. The government had to be responsible. The government had to test ETA."[25] His national security advisers concurred, maintaining that the president had to respond to a changed mood in the country and the public's expectations, whatever his private reservations.

By contrast, in Britain there was little domestic political pressure to engage with the IRA. For British political leaders, few votes appeared to be at stake whether they talked or not. The bottom line, instead, was whether bombs were exploding on the mainland. When that threat receded after the Good Friday Agreement, the general public was complacent, ignorant, or mystified about why Prime Minister Tony Blair devoted a massive amount of time, energy, and sheer physical effort to trying to sort out Northern Ireland rather than attending to more pressing matters of state.[26] I personally witnessed the extent of this devotion during intense negotiations on Northern Ireland at the October 2006 summit meeting at St. Andrews, Scotland. The prime minister's chief of the General Staff, Sir Richard Dannatt, had just announced that the British army's presence in Iraq was jeopardizing the country's security and interests worldwide and that Britain needed to leave Iraq "soon." Blair left the negotiations to deal with the fallout, but a few hours and a press statement later, he was back at the table with the

Northern Ireland political parties, discussing the finer points of the devolution of power.

Israel has avoided most domestic complications simply by refusing to talk with Hamas, except for humanitarian reasons, and then only through third parties. As with Britain, there is little domestic pressure on any Israeli government to engage with Hamas. Rather, there is pressure *not* to negotiate. Any change in this policy would strain and probably split the coalition led by Prime Minister Bibi Netanyahu and his Likud Party. In Israel, domestic politics and public opinion have acted as brakes on engagement with Hamas.

Governments will have a difficult enough time negotiating with terrorist groups. They need to ensure that domestic political factors don't further complicate their job.

RED LINES, BRIGHT LINES, AND STOP SIGNS

Governments usually expend a good deal of time, a great deal of effort, and the investment of significant political capital to bring a terrorist group to the negotiating table in the first place. Under these circumstances, officials often find it difficult to walk away from the table for fear of having all their hard work come undone, for fear that it will be even more difficult the next time to entice the terrorists to return to the talks, and for fear of the domestic political fallout, where opponents may accuse the government of misjudging the moment or fumbling the chance for peace. The longer the talks go on, the greater the government's investment and the more the government has to lose should they stop. For all these reasons, negotiations have their own self-perpetuating momentum, like an undertow, that tugs the diplomats along until they discover, too late, that they're adrift and out to sea.[27]

Any government contemplating talks with a terrorist group therefore needs to determine, in advance, when it will walk away from the table, whether because the talks have reached an impasse or because of especially egregious behavior. In September 1996, in the middle of my negotiating nuclear issues with the North Koreans, a North Korean spy submarine ran aground on the east coast of South Korea, with its crew scrambling ashore. (The resulting manhunt lasted forty-nine days and involved 40,000 South Korean soldiers.) I suspended the talks immediately—not a hard call.

Negotiators often call this setting out bright lines or drawing red lines. Delineating some of these red lines, such as acts of major violence, are obvious. Interestingly, though, the length of time engagement is suspended has varied from only a few days (after the LTTE's assassination of the Sri Lankan presidential candidate Gamini Dissanayake and most of his party's senior leadership) to years (after the IRA's October 1984 bombing of the Grand Hotel in Brighton, which narrowly missed killing Prime Minister Margaret Thatcher). When setting the time period for any time-outs, each government will need to weigh carefully its own credibility, public opinion, and the views of any alliance partners.

The relatively more difficult red lines to identify before the talks start are the political ones.

Here the government faces a choice. Which ground must the government defend at all costs throughout the length of the negotiations? For the British, it was the principle that the future of Northern Ireland would be determined by the consent of the majority. For Spain, no government could allow an independent Basque homeland or any process, no matter how theoretical, that might lead to ETA's realizing its historic mission. Governments in Sri Lanka, too, could never contemplate anything but preserving the integrity of a unified state. An independent homeland for the Tamil people was out of the question. Israel refuses to even meet with Hamas until it has fulfilled three preconditions: recognize Israel, renounce violence, and accept all previous Israeli-Palestinian agreements.

Alternatively, what ground is the government willing to concede, if it absolutely has to? The British government wobbled and eventually relented over whether the IRA/Sinn Fein had to agree to a permanent ceasefire and decommission all of its weapons before it could enter the peace process. Sri Lankan governments appeared to have a policy of infinite patience over LTTE violations of the 2002 Cease-Fire Agreement. None of these prompted Colombo to withdraw from the deal, until President Mahinda Rajapaksa took the decision to do so in January 2008.

Governments need to set out clear lines they will not cross—for internal guidance during the negotiations, for reassuring public opinion, and for warning terrorist groups what issues are nonnegotiable.

Moral Hazards

Every negotiation with terrorists presents political traps and legal obstacles. But it also raises a profound moral dilemma about how best to contain and counter evil behavior. How can a government justify sitting down with people who have blood on their hands?

Many argue that governments should not do so. A meeting may appear to reward despicable behavior and legitimize a terrorist group.[28] It may demoralize foreign allies who have taken risks, committed resources, and lost people in counterterrorism efforts. It may allow the terrorist group to rest, rearm, and reorganize its forces. It may expose the government to charges from domestic opponents that it is jeopardizing public safety and national security. And it may make the government vulnerable to spoilers inside terror groups who can use violence to embarrass and undermine the government. This is a particularly sensitive problem for American administrations, given the leading U.S. role in the fight against terror.

Of course, though, talking may also bring important benefits to the state. Any assessment for determining whether to sit down with terrorists needs to weigh the benefits of engagement against the liabilities.

A complication here is that the balance sheet is skewed. Once the government publicly announces a negotiation, the negative aspects of talking are almost always booked immediately. And because no one knows at the start if the talks will ultimately prove successful, any future benefits are still unrealized gains. The government is betting that the benefits will outweigh the liabilities, but a full and accurate accounting may not be possible for many years. In the meantime, it has to reassure the public that the risks are worth taking.

So how does a government keep faith with its public when it sits down with terrorists? What is the morality of talking to these types of men?

I posed these questions to elected officials, career civil servants, senior intelligence agents, military officers, and counterterrorism experts as I traveled over the world these past few years. Some of them had clearly thought long and deeply about the subject beforehand, and struggled to hold simultaneously two conflicting thoughts: Terrorists are evil *and* they may be part of the solution.

These individuals explained that context matters, and that different societies have different thresholds for when government officials could publicly sit down with men who had blood on their hands. But except for a few outliers, their views coalesced around a variety of pragmatic and utilitarian arguments favoring engagement: The moral taint of dealing with terrorists, which none denied, was outweighed by the chance to end violence and achieve the greatest good for the greatest number of people.

For example, Eliza Manningham-Buller, the former head of MI5, explained that you need to "recognize that the world is untidy, cruel, and messy," but that your job is to deal with reality. Talking was "a tactical compromise for a strategic prize: the greater good."[29] A member of the CIA's clandestine service commented, "Everyone has blood on their hands, if they matter. If you want to talk to people without blood on their hands, then they don't matter."[30] A senior British intelligence official stated that making this moral compromise "is the price you have to pay" to stop the killing. The former Northern Ireland secretary of state, Peter Brooke, explained that he believed that his not talking to the IRA/Sinn Fein "wasn't being fair. I wasn't keeping faith with the Army and the RUC, if they were keeping the ring open and the politicians were sitting on their hands."[31]

Bertie Ahern, the former Irish prime minister, echoed these thoughts. Over tea and scones in the drawing room of his Dublin constituency office, he said, "You ask yourself, 'Can I stop the killing for the next decade?' I can't stop the killing of the last decade. . . . There's one acid test: Are these people willing, if circumstances were different, to move into a political process? The reward is that there aren't so many funerals."[32] Father Alec Reid, who toiled for years to advance the Northern Ireland peace process, agreed, saying that in his negotiations with the IRA/Sinn Fein, "We represented the next person who is going to be killed or injured in the conflict."[33] Ami Ayalon, the former head of Shin Bet, Israel's domestic intelligence service, maintained, "Anything you can do to shorten the war is ethical."[34]

Saving lives in the future is clearly a greater good for a greater number than bearing grudges forever. And yet a narrowly defined utilitarian approach has some drawbacks.

First, it may shortchange democratic values and conflict with notions of "justice as fairness." The goal in any negotiation is not just to end the terror by reaching an agreement. After all, capitulation and surrender can accomplish that. The goal is also to establish stability, security, and respect for law and order across society. The government must ensure that the benefits of the peace are shared by all of the country's citizens, who should be "equally counted as moral persons," as the political philosopher John Rawls has expressed it.[35]

Some peace settlements, however, may privilege group rights over individual rights. To end the killing and allow the greatest good for the greatest number of its citizens, a government may be tempted to consign a minority to a more marginalized status. As the price of reaching an agreement, the government may feel compelled to abandon democratic principles and make concessions that would jeopardize the rights of those people living in areas still controlled by the terrorist group.

On more than one occasion, this type of bargain was on offer in Northern Ireland. Some senior British and Irish officials appeared unwilling to insist that the IRA/Sinn Fein support policing and justice, the foundation of the rule of law in any society, for fear that this would impede efforts to reach a peace agreement.[36]

Similar calculations occurred in Sri Lanka. There multiple governments were willing to enshrine Prabhakaran's de facto monopoly on political power in the northern and eastern provinces in a manner that placed at risk basic democratic freedoms and human rights for the local Tamils, Sinhalese, and Muslims. These examples were an abdication of moral leadership and a failure to maintain the social contract between the state and all of its citizens.

Yet that may be too harsh a judgment and, frankly, far easier to make for someone not on the front lines than those leaders responsible for stewarding their country's future. Finding a moral compass that points "true north" when dealing with terrorist groups is not as straightforward as it may seem. A government often has to choose between different shades of gray in a less-than-perfect world. Yes, it can insist on the universality of democratic principles, but it runs the risk that the terrorist groups may resist. The two sides might then be unable to reach an agreement that would end the killing. Under this scenario, neither group rights nor individual rights would be favored over the other and the minority would not be relatively disadvantaged compared with the majority. But would justice and fairness have been served? The unhappy reality is that the population as a whole would still be mired in a war against terror. So, then, would society be better off?

On the other hand, a peace agreement, even if imperfect, would provide greater security and stability to at least some of the population. Would this be morally more defensible for the government if those forced to live with fewer civil rights were relatively small in number? And how small would be small enough?

When I served as the president's special envoy to the Northern Ireland peace process, I argued for a justice-as-fairness approach to resolving the Troubles. I strongly opposed those in the British and Irish governments who were willing to treat people differently in Northern Ireland by not just acquiescing to but actually blessing the IRA/Sinn Fein's refusal to support the rule of law. At the time, I was absolutely certain this was the right and honorable thing to do. And, fortunately, the peace process had a happy outcome when the IRA decommissioned its weapons, Sinn Fein endorsed policing and justice, and the political parties agreed to work together and assume joint responsibility for managing Northern Ireland. Today, the people of Northern Ireland are counted equally as moral persons.

But would I feel the same way if we had not achieved peace? If the IRA/Sinn Fein had refused to accept these demands and the fighting and killing had continued? Would I regret our missed opportunity to improve the lives of the vast majority of people in Northern Ireland? How would the principles of justice, equality, and fairness stack up against rising casualties from an ongoing war on terror? When, if ever, would it make sense to sacrifice a modicum of democratic values because an inflexible adherence to principle might cause further pain, anguish, and loss for a great many people?

These are some of the moral dilemmas that officials need to appreciate and consider when they decide to sit down with terrorists. There are no easy answers. Each person will have to search his conscience, use his best judgment, and then simply pray that history will show that he has chosen correctly.

CONCLUSION

As we proceed through the early part of the twenty-first century, wars between states and terrorist groups are increasingly likely. Many of these groups will have to be defeated militarily, their leaders killed or captured. But others may be willing to abandon their violence in return for partial satisfaction of their grievances and other benefits that the state might confer, such as amnesty and social reintegration.

Political leaders have an obligation to engage a terrorist group if it could enhance public safety and improve national security. But they need to think clearly and systematically about when it makes sense to engage terrorists and when it does not. Extending an open hand to all these groups, indiscriminately, is an attitude, not a strategy. Open-ended offers to parley may be interpreted by terrorists as signs of weakness and desperation, lead to more violence, demoralize allies, and undermine domestic support for conducting the war on terror.

Properly conceived and patiently implemented contacts with terrorists may produce a different result. Such engagements may yield greater insights into the motivations and ambitions of the terrorist group and support a sustainable dialogue. Over time, they may lead to a diplomatic process that defeats terrorism and ends the conflict.

While the whole notion of negotiating with terrorists remains politically charged, in the United States and elsewhere, it is clear that when it is informed by past precedents and hard-won experience, the benefits can outweigh the costs. It is possible to sit down and negotiate with evil and emerge with peace, justice, and honor.

A Note on Terms

Terrorism has a long history, dating back at least to when the Jewish Zealots rose up against the Romans in the first century AD Numerous texts have been written about specific terrorist movements down through the years and others have surveyed a general history of terrorism. Yet no commonly accepted definition of terrorism prevails in the field; by some accounts, there are well over a hundred definitions. There is not even a common vocabulary, as scholars wrestle over the varied and elusive meanings of "terrorist," "insurgent," "revolutionary," "guerrilla," "separatist," and "freedom fighter." Even the U.S. government does not have a common definition among its different agencies and departments. This definitional challenge is not limited to the United States. One expert has observed that "The evolving Western consensus about the essence of terrorism is probably not shared by the majority of people on earth."[1] No surprise then that the United Nations has never been able to define terrorism, despite many attempts to do so.

However, some common elements seem to characterize the many definitions of terrorism, including (1) the use of violence per se, (2) the use of violence for political objectives, and (3) the use of violence with the intention to create "far-reaching psychological effects" in the target population.[2] But even these elements are overly broad and do not help very much in distinguishing between terrorism and other forms of violence, such as guerrilla war or even some forms of conventional warfare.

This book does not attempt to referee among these competing definitions or propose a new one. Rather, the rule of thumb used here is whether a state's own leaders and legislation have labeled a group or organization as terrorists. This seems sensible. Not only does it avoid fruitless debate over terminology, but it places appropriate emphasis on the challenge before the state—and highlights the distance the state has to travel to engage with these groups and organizations.

There is a second challenge: the differences between terrorists and insurgents. It is not always clear where one ends and the other begins. The U.S. State Department has commented that "the line between insurgency and terrorism has become increasingly blurred as attacks on civilian targets have become more common." Many scholars and military officers acknowledge that terrorism can assume the characteristics of an insurgency and that insurgents use terrorist tactics from time to time. Official statements and publications often use the two terms interchangeably. While acknowledging this complexity, for the sake of simplicity the book will almost always use the term "terrorist group" or "terrorist" in place of "insurgency" or "insurgent."

A final challenge exists with the word "negotiating." For many, the term connotes images of dark-suited men in a mahogany-paneled room sitting somberly across a table from one another. It can mean that, of course, but it can also mean other things. It can range from presidential visits with 21-gun salutes to private citizens meeting in seedy bars in foreign countries and passing notes written by others. It can mean meetings where the parties only exchange honeyed words or where they warn, threaten, concede, or capitulate. The parties themselves can be diplomats, intelligence operatives, military officers, or private citizens.

"Negotiating" is therefore an imprecise term that masks what might be called a "communications continuum" along which different levels of official commitment can be plotted. At one end of the continuum, a government can plausibly deny that it ever had any interaction with terrorists. At the other end, the same government can be seen signing a peace agreement with (former) terrorists in front of the world's media. The cases in this book include these two end points, but it most often portrays the shadowboxing, meetings, arguments, and setbacks that take place between these extremes.

List of Interviews

For chapter 1

Gerry Adams, leader of Sinn Fein

Bertie Ahern, prime minister of Ireland, 1997–2008

Dermot Ahern, minister of justice and law reform,
former minister of foreign affairs

Sean Aylward, senior civil servant, Dublin

John Bew, deputy director of the International Centre for the Study of Radi-
calisation and lecturer, Department of War Studies, King's College, London

Paul Bew, historian, member of the House of Lords

Kenneth Bloomfield, former head of the Northern Ireland Civil Service

Denis Bradley, a member of the Derry backchannel to the IRA

Peter Brooke, secretary of state for Northern Ireland, 1989–92

Noel Dorr, former Ministry of Foreign Affairs official, Dublin

Brendan Duddy, leader of the Derry backchannel to the IRA

Garret FitzGerald, foreign affairs minister of Ireland, 1973–77; prime minister,
1981–82 and 1982–87

Martyn Frampton, research fellow, Peterhouse, Cambridge University

Dermot Gallagher, Ministry of Foreign Affairs official, Dublin

Douglas Hurd, secretary of state for Northern Ireland, 1984–85; secretary of state for foreign and commonwealth affairs, 1989–95

Tom King, secretary of state for Northern Ireland, 1985–89

Eliza Manningham-Buller, director general of MI5, 2002–07

Martin Mansergh, civil servant, Dublin

Martin McGuinness, leader of Sinn Fein, deputy first minister, Stormont Assembly

Ed Moloney, leading investigative journalist of the IRA

Kathleen M. O'Toole, chief inspector of the Garda Síochána Inspectorate

Charles Powell, former civil servant, London

Father Alec Reid, a Belfast-based priest who tried to assist the peace process

Albert Reynolds, prime minister of Ireland, 1992–94

David Trimble, former leader of the Ulster Unionist Party, First Minister of Northern Ireland, 1998–2001 and 2001–2

Shaun Woodward, secretary of state for Northern Ireland, 2007–10

FOR CHAPTER 2

Rogelio Alonso, expert on ETA and the IRA who teaches at the University Rey Juan Carlos, Madrid

Xavier Arzallus, longtime leader of the PNV

José Maria Aznar, prime minister, 1996–2004

Rafael Bardaji, Aznar's national security adviser

José Maria Benegas, a former leader of the Basque Socialist Party

Florencio Dominguez, leading journalist investigating ETA

Joseba Egibar, main PNV negotiator with ETA during talks, 1997–2000

Juan Manuel Eguiagaray, a Basque Socialist politician and negotiator with ETA

Gorka Espiau, heavily involved in the peace process

Eugenio Etxebeste, ETA's negotiator in Algiers

Inigo Gurruchaga, journalist for *El Correo* based in London

Juan Gutierrez, NGO mediator

Rodolfo Martin Villa, minister of interior under Suárez

Jaime Mayor Oreja, minister of interior under Aznar

Arnaldo Otegi, a leader of ETA's political wing

Fernando Reinares, professor of political science and security studies at Universidad Rey Juan Carlos, Madrid

Teo Uriarte, member of ETA in the 1960s and 1970s, now a member of the Socialist Party

Rafael Vera, Spain's director of state security and interior minister under González

Javier Zarzalejos, close adviser to Aznar

José Luis Zubizarreta, a Basque nationalist politician

FOR CHAPTER 3

Asoka Bandarage, professor, Georgetown University

Robert Blake, former U.S. ambassador to Sri Lanka

Austin Fernando, former secretary of defense

Nanda Godage, former senior Foreign Ministry official

John Gooneratne, former member of the Secretariat for Coordinating the Peace Process

Bernard Goonetilleke, former senior Foreign Ministry official involved in the peace process

Rohan Gunaratna, head of the International Centre for Political Violence and Terrorism Research (ICPVTR) at Nanyang Technological University, Singapore

Tore Hattrem, Norway's ambassador to Sri Lanka

Kapila Hendawitharana, head of Sri Lanka's intelligence service

Shanaka Jayasekera, former member of the Secretariat for Coordinating the Peace Process

Karuna Amman, former military commander of the LTTE

Palitha Kohona, former special adviser to President Mahinda Rajapaksa

C. Mahendran, former senior Foreign Ministry official

Milinda Moragoda, Cabinet minister under both Ranil Wickremasinghe and Mahinda Rajapaksa

H.M.G.S. Palihakkara, former senior Foreign Ministry official involved in the peace process

G. L. Peiris, lead government negotiator under the Wickremasinghe administration

Muttukrishna Sarvananthan, NGO activist

Bradman Weerakoon, retired civil servant, Colombo

For chapter 4

Dani Arditi, former national security adviser

Ami Ayalon, former head of Shin Bet

Efraim Halevy, former director of Mossad

Yoram Hessel, former head of Mossad's Global Operations, Intelligence and Foreign Relations

Dan Meridor, current deputy prime minister

Shaul Mofaz, former minister of defense, former chief of the General Staff of the Israel Defense Forces, and currently a member of the Knesset

Uri Ne'eman, former head of Mossad's Research and Analysis Unit

David Roet, Ministry of Foreign Affairs, Jerusalem

Gerald Steinberg, professor of political science, Bar-Ilan University

FOR CHAPTER 5

John R. Allen, deputy commander, U.S. CENTCOM

Ben Connable, former Marine intelligence officer

Ryan Crocker, former U.S. ambassador to Iraq

Anthony E. Deane, Army lieutenant colonel in Ramadi, 2006–7

Ray Gerber, Marine intelligence officer

Derek Harvey, former senior Army intelligence officer

Sterling Jensen, interpreter in Iraq from March 2006 to June 2007

Sean MacFarland, U.S. Army colonel in Ramadi, 2006–7

James Mattis, commander, U.S. Joint Forces Command

John McCary, former Army human intelligence collector in Iraq

Monica Miller, Army lieutenant colonel, U.S. CENTCOM

Keith Mines, CPA official in Anbar, 2003–04

John Nagl, retired United States Army lieutenant colonel, leading counterinsurgency expert

Paul Newton, British general with experience in Iraq

David H. Petraeus, commander, International Security Assistance Force (ISAF) and Commander, U.S. Forces Afghanistan (USFOR-A)

Martin Stanton, a civil-military affairs officer in Iraq in 2003, chief of reconciliation and engagement for MNC-I, 2007–8

Rob Torres, intelligence chief for Marine Police Transition Team Delta, al-Qaim, 2006

ACKNOWLEDGMENTS

For the past three years, I have traveled around the world talking to government officials, intelligence analysts and operatives, military personnel, diplomats, politicians, experts on terrorism, and former terrorists. It has been an unusual experience—sometimes risky, often enjoyable, and always stimulating.

This intellectual adventure, and this book, would not have been possible without the extraordinary support of Stephen del Rosso and his boss at the Carnegie Corporation of New York, Vartan Gregorian, who saw the potential contribution this study could make to the public policy debate over "talking to terrorists" and did not flinch from its more controversial implications. I owe them a huge debt of thanks. I am also grateful to Richard Solomon and the U.S. Institute of Peace for their funding support for additional research on the Northern Ireland peace process, which contributed materially to the chapter on the IRA.

This book would also not have been possible without the time, energy, and assistance of numerous individuals in the United States and overseas, some of whom have asked that they not be named. But for those who can be named, it is my pleasure to thank them here.

The following people originally agreed to serve as consultants when this project was still in its infancy: Yonah Alexander, Cofer Black, Francis Ricciardone, Dennis Ross, Matthew Sherman, Richard Stolz, and Anthony Zinni. I am grateful to them all.

For the chapter on the IRA, Ambassador Michael Collins of the Republic of Ireland's embassy in Washington and Andy Pike of the British consulate general in New York helped in making initial contacts with diplomatic officials and political leaders. David Cooney at Iveagh House in Dublin helped me track down those Irish diplomats, now retired, who were involved in the Northern Ireland peace process in the early days. Sean Aylward happily took it upon himself to coordinate all my meetings in Dublin.

I am grateful the following people gave so freely of their time and expertise: In Dublin, the former taoiseachs Bertie Ahern, Garret FitzGerald, and Albert Reynolds; Dermot Ahern, Timothy Dalton, Noel Dorr, Dermot Gallagher, Martin Mansergh, Eunan O'Halpin, Kathy O'Toole, and Father Alec Reid.

In Belfast and Derry, Gerry Adams, John Alderdice, Kenneth Bloomfield, Denis Bradley, Brendan Duddy (and his family), John McConnell, Martin McGuinness, Hugh Orde, and Ross Moore of the Linen Hall Librarian (and Yvonne Murphy, who introduced us). The American consul general in Belfast, Susan Elliot, kindly hosted a dinner in my honor at Ardnavalley in May 2009, with the assistance of the incomparable Lorna McCaugherty.

In London, Eliza Manningham-Buller, Jonathan Evans, Peter Brooke, Douglas Hurd, Charles Powell, David Trimble, and Owen Paterson. A special word of thanks goes to Paul Bew, who masterfully scheduled my meetings with his fellow members in the House of Lords, and to the extraordinary investigative journalist Ed Moloney, who patiently answered my many questions about the intricacies of the IRA and the peace process.

John Bew expertly helped me organize a conference, "Revisiting the Troubles," which brought together in November 2009 some of the finest British and Irish historians on the Northern Ireland peace process. The event was graciously hosted by Dean Godson, the research director and driving force behind the Policy Exchange, and whose own work on Northern Ireland is standard reference material. John Bew, Martyn Frampton, and Ed Moloney all read early drafts of the chapter and provided helpful comments.

For the chapter on ETA, I had the best possible guide in Inigo Gurruchaga, who generously gave of his time and contacts in Spain and unstintingly shared his deep knowledge of ETA. He also introduced me to Arantxa Azurmendi, who expertly translated during my interviews and provided her own insights along the way. Hugh Clifton and his team at the U.S. embassy in Madrid were extremely helpful in arranging meetings. Fernando Reinares kindly hosted me at Elcano Real Instituto. Inigo and Fernando reviewed the chapter and offered very useful comments.

In Madrid, I met with Rogelio Alonso, Rafael Bardaji, José Maria Benegas, Juan Manuel Eguiagaray, Juan Guiterrez, Jaime Mayor Oreja, and Javier Zarzalejos. Rafael Vera kindly invited me to his home in Torrelodones. In Bilbao, I met with Xavier Arzallus, Florencio Dominguez, Gorka Espiau, Teo Uriarte, and José Luis Zubizarreta. In San Sebastián, I met with Joseba Egibar, Eugenio "Antxon" Etxebeste, Arnaldo Otegi, and Urko Aiartza Azurtza. And in Washington, D.C., I met with former Prime Minister José Maria Aznar. With Pilar Tena's persistence, I was able to speak by phone with Rodolfo Martin Villa.

I worked closely with John Nagl and his colleagues at the Center for a New American Security (CNAS) in organizing a conference in late January 2010, "The Sunni Awakening: An After Action Review," in Tampa, Florida, with the assistance and support of CENTCOM. Lieutenant General John Allen delivered a thoughtful keynote address, and John McCary, Brigadier General Sean MacFarland, Major Niel Smith, Major General Najim al-Jabouri, and Derek Harvey all made formal presentations. LCDR Henry Kim and especially Jodi Fisler ensured that the conference ran smoothly.

I benefited from the expert comments and insights of all the participants at the conference. Those who generously gave me additional time were Ben Connable, Derek Harvey, Marty Stanton, Matt Sherman, Sterling Jensen, and Tony Deane. I also want to thank General David Petraeus, General Paul Newton, General James Mattis, Ambassador Ryan Crocker, Rob Torres, and Ray Gerber for sharing their insights about Iraq. Ben Connable, Tony Deane, John McCary, and John Nagl provided very useful comments on the Anbar Awakening chapter.

In Israel, Yoram Hessel generously opened doors for me with his former colleagues. I am grateful to Knesset members Dan Meridor and Shaul Mofaz, and also to Gerald Steinberg, Efraim Halevy, Uri Ne'eman, Dani Arditi, Ami Ayalon and Ambassador James Cunningham and his colleagues at the U.S. embassy in Tel Aviv. Ambassador Michael Oren and his staff at the Israeli embassy in Washington and David Roet and his staff at the Ministry of Foreign Affairs helped make introductions and arrange meetings in Israel. Charles and Michele Dunne each reviewed earlier drafts of the chapter.

I had the great benefit and privilege of working with Rohan Gunaratna in organizing an international conference in Colombo, Sri Lanka: "Engaging the

Tamil Tigers: Lessons from a Failed Peace Process." Rohan, Shanaka Jayasekara, Ambassador Bernard Goonetilleke, former defense secretary Austin Fernando, Minister Milinda Moragoda, Bradman Weerakoon, Minister Karuna Amman, and current defense secretary Gotabhaya Rajapaksa presented papers or delivered formal remarks. They also made time to answer my additional questions. While in Colombo, I met with Professor G. L. Peiris, S. L. Gunasekara, Muttukrishna Sarvananthan, Norway's ambassador Tore Hattrem, Ambassador H. M. G. S. Palihakkara, Ambassador C. Mahendran, and the Chief of National Intelligence, General Kapila Hendawitharana.

In preparing for my trip to Sri Lanka, Evan Feigenbaum, the State Department's Robert Blake and Anthony Renzulli, and Jack Gill recommended people for me to meet and otherwise provided helpful advice. Ambassador Palitha T.B. Kohona met with me at Sri Lanka's Permanent Mission to the United Nations, where we discussed the CFA and the 2002–04 peace talks. Rich Armitage shared with me his experience as the U.S. member of the Donors Group. Georgetown University professor Asoka Bandarage was an extraordinary guide through the complexities of the conflict and Sri Lanka's internal politics. John Gooneratne patiently shared with me his insights in an extensive e-mail correspondence after the conference and commented on a draft of the chapter, as did Bernard Goonetilleke, Bradman Weerakoon, Rohan Gunaratna, and Asoka Bandarage.

I had originally intended to visit the Philippines to explore the cases of the Moro Liberation Fronts, but this plan had to be scrapped at the last moment. Nonetheless, a number of people had offered to assist me, for which I remain grateful. They are Jennifer Keister, Susan Niblock, and Scott Thompson.

A number of other people provided assistance in a variety of ways: Mark Allen, Ken Campbell, Kurt Campbell, John Connorton, Jim Dobbins, Richard Harvey, Michael Holtzman, Edward Lacey, Robert Litwak, Regis Matlak, Timothy McWilliams, William Milam, Aaron David Miller, Michael O'Hanlon, David Omand, Ted Perlmutter, Christina Rocca, and Benjamin Runkle.

I am indebted to my many colleagues and students at William & Mary, but especially to Mike Tierney, Dennis Smith, and the irreplaceable Ania Baltes. Taylor Reveley's commitment to the college's academic mission resulted in my having an ideal working environment; he is a model for other university presidents to emulate. Among my students, Sam Wheeler somehow found time among his own studies to serve as a superb and very responsive research assistant. Other students who provided research assistance along the way included Rachel Walsh, Elizabeth Owerback, Sam Shreck, Sarah Argodale, Ricky Trotman, and John Lee.

Of course, any errors of fact, interpretation, or inference are my responsibility alone.

To my colleagues at Open Road Integrated Media, I am indebted. Jane Friedman originally convinced me to publish my book in electronic form and has encouraged me at every step in the process. Brendan Cahill, Rachel Chou, Luke Parker Bowles, Lisa Weinert, Andrea Colvin, Mary Sorrick, and Josh Raffel have been a terrific team in bringing my book to multimedia markets. Jake Klisivitch has been a patient and diligent editor. Toni Rachiele was a detailed and thorough copy editor.

Finally, I would like to thank my mother and father, who have always encouraged me and supported my work. I hope that the lessons contained in this book will help ensure that my son, Mathew, and daughter, Michael, grow up in a more peaceful and just world. And to my wife and best friend, Elisabeth, I cannot fully express my admiration and appreciation for her supporting my travels overseas, tolerating my late nights at the office, and encouraging me as I worked through new ideas. It is to her that this book is dedicated.

Williamsburg, Virginia
June 2010

End Notes

Introduction

1. "The most sacred texts . . . resolution and peacemaking."
   See Donald W. Shriver, Jr., *An Ethic for Enemies: Forgiveness in Politics* (New York: Oxford University Press, 1995), esp. pp. 12–62.

2. "They each authorized . . . naval supplies as 'protection.'"
   See Ray W. Irwin, *The Diplomatic Relations of the United States with the Barbary Powers, 1776–1816* (Chapel Hill: University of North Carolina Press, 1931).

3. "'Perdicaris alive or . . . Raisuli's every demand."
   Barbara W. Tuchman, *Practicing History: Selected Essays* (New York: Alfred A. Knopf, 1981), pp. 104–17. The episode was memorialized in a film starring Sean Connery as Raisuli, *The Wind and the Lion*.

4. The resulting arms-for-hostages . . . brought down Reagan's presidency."
   On the Iran-Contra scandal, see Peter Kornbluh, *The Iran-Contra Scandal: The Declassified History*, edited by Malcolm Byrne (New York: New Press, 1993); and Gary Sick, *All Fall Down: America's Tragic Encounter with Iran* (New York: Penguin, 1986).

5. "Bill Clinton's administration . . . support the peace process."
   Khaled Hroub, *Hamas: Political Thought and Practice* (Washington, D.C.: Institute for Palestine Studies, 2000), pp. 195–96.

6. "Clinton administration also held . . . attacks on the United States."
   See "Taliban Met with U.S. Often: Talks Centered on Ways to Hand Over bin Laden," *Washington Post*, October 29, 2001.

7. "In his January 2002 . . . October 2006 nuclear test."
   Earlier, the Bush administration talked to Iran during the Bonn conference in late 2001 to reestablish the state of Afghanistan after the American invasion that ended twenty-plus years of civil war.

8. "During a conflict . . . broker an end to them."
   See Paul Gordon Lauren, "Coercive Diplomacy and Ultimata: Theory and Practice in History,"

in Alexander L. George and William E. Simons, eds., *The Limits of Coercive Diplomacy*, (Boulder: Westview Press, 1994), 2nd ed., 23–50.

9.   "'And it enables us . . . best chance for peace.'"
James A. Baker, with Thomas M. DeFrank, *The Politics of Diplomacy: Revolution, War and Peace, 1989–1992* (New York: Putnam, 1995), p. 352.

10.   "In other words, it . . . 'balance' against it."
The first scholar to use the term "bandwagon" was Quincy Wright, *A Study of War*, (Chicago: University of Chicago Press, 1942), p. 136.

11.   "Britain, he declared . . . whichever nation he led'."
Winston Churchill, *The Gathering Storm* (Boston: Houghton Mifflin, 1948), p. 208.

12.   "The long-term cost savings . . . life of the agreement."
Congressional Budget Office, *The START Treaty and Beyond* (Washington, D.C.: USGPO, 1991), pp. 72–73.

13.   "Egyptian President Anwar Sadat . . . signing a peace treaty."
See Anwar el-Sadat, *In Search of Identity: An Autobiography* (New York: Harper & Row, 1977), p. 308.

14.   "Appeasement can invite further aggression . . . the Second World War."
Stephen R. Rock, *Appeasement in International Politics* (Lexington: University Press of Kentucky, 2000), p. 4.
       Winston Churchill has written, "The subjugation of Czechoslovakia robbed the Allies of the Czech Army of twenty-one regular divisions, fifteen or sixteen second-line divisions already mobilized, and also their mountain fortress line which, in the days of Munich, had required the deployment of thirty German divisions, or the main strength of the mobile and fully trained German Army, . . . besides this, the Skoda Works, the second most important arsenal in Central Europe . . . was made to change sides adversely." *The Gathering Storm*, pp. 336–37.

15.   "Then–vice president Dick Cheney . . . We defeat it.'"
Quoted in Warren Strobel, "US Acting Tough with N. Korea," *Philadelphia Inquirer*, December 21, 2003, p. A2; see also Glen Kessler, "Cheney Wields Power with Few Fingerprints," *Washington Post*, October 5, 2004, p. A7.

16.   "'This interval was spent . . . paying no attention to them.'"
Thucydides, *The History of the Peloponnesian Wars*, translated by Rex Warner (New York: Penguin, 1954), p. 82.

17.   "Transparency, accountability, constitutional checks . . . in non-democracies."
Kissinger strongly criticized this rationale for not talking to the Soviet Union during the Cold War. See Henry A. Kissinger, *White House Years*, (New York: Little, Brown, 1979) pp. 59–62.

18.   "The result is one-sided . . . not the other."
Fred Charles Ikle, "After Detection—What?" *Foreign Affairs*, January 1961, pp. 208–20

19.   "For example, Osama bin Laden . . . regimes like Saudi Arabia."
For an interesting and concise account of Osama bin Laden and al Qaeda, see Abdel Bari Atwan, *The Secret History of al Qaeda* (Berkeley: University of California Press, 2006).

20.   "One leading historian, Yale's . . . over seventy years."
"The Tradition of Appeasement in British Foreign Policy, 1865–1939," in Kennedy, *Strategy and Diplomacy: 1870–1945: Eight Studies* (London: Allen & Unwin, 1983), pp. 15–39.

21.   "Indeed, there are no . . . seized political power."
See Walter Laqueur, *Terrorism* (London: Abacus, 1980), p. 266.

22.   It concluded that terrorism . . . unprofitable coercive instrument."
Max Abrahms, "Why Terrorism Does Not Work," *International Security*, vol. 31, no. 2 (Fall 2006), p. 52.

MITCHELL B. REISS

23. "Although terrorist groups have . . . people killed by lightning."
John Mueller, "Six Rather Unusual Propositions About Terrorism," *Terrorism and Political Violence*, vol. 17, p. 488.
Lightning and acts of terrorism (including 9/11) have each been responsible for the deaths of roughly 3,600 Americans over the past forty years.

24. "As one member of the House . . . having them meet the Queen.'"
Personal interview, London, May 2009. Decades earlier, Hugh Gaitskill, the former British Labor Party leader, said, "All terrorists, at the invitation of the government, end up with drinks at the Dorchester." Quoted in Phil Rees, *Dining with Terrorists: Meeting with the World's Most Wanted Militants* (London: Pan Books, 2006), p. 6.

25. "In this moral universe . . . for engaging terrorists."
See, for example, David Frum and Richard Perle, *How to Win the War on Terror* (New York: Random House, 2003).

26. "'He is humiliated . . . self-respect are violated.'"
Lacqueur, *Terrorism*, pp. 272–73.

27. "'We are especially not . . . of the Third Reich.'"
Quoted in "Excerpts from the President's Address Accusing Nations of 'Acts of War.'" *The New York Times*, July 9, 1985.

28. "Indeed, in all the years since 9/11 . . . its entire history."
See Seth G. Jones and Martin C. Libicki, *How Terrorist Groups End: Lessons for Countering al Qaeda* (Santa Monica: RAND, 2008), pp. 103–20. This statistic excludes attacks in Iraq and Afghanistan.

29. "The 2004 report spoke . . . into the world economy.'"
National Intelligence Council, Mapping the Global Future (Washington, D.C.: USGPO, 2004), p. 81.

30. "The 2008 report warned . . . into terrorist groups.'"
National Intelligence Council, Global Trends 2025 (Washington, D.C.: USGPO, 2008), p. 68.

31. "'If this trend continues . . . increasing attacks worldwide.'"
Declassified Key Judgments of the National Intelligence Estimate, *Trends in Global Terrorism: Implications for the United States* (April 2006), www.dni.gov/press_releases/Declassified_NIE_Key_Judgments.pdf.

32. "According to the 2009 . . . the age of twenty-five."
Arab Human Development Report 2009 (New York: UNDP, 2009), www.arab-hdr.org/publications/other/ahdr/ahdr2009e.pdf, p. 3.

33. "His key indicator . . . percent of the population."
Heinsohn's most important work, *Söhne und Weltmacht* ("Sons and World Power: Terror in the Rise and Fall of Nations") (Zürich: Orell Füssli Verlag, 2003) has not been translated from the original German. But see Heinsohn, "Population, Conquest and Terror in the 21st Century" (August 2005), www.geocities.com/funnyguy_35/HeinsohnPopulation.PDF and "Islamism and War: the Demographics of Rage," July 16, 2007, www.opendemocracy.net/conflicts/democracy_terror/islamism_war_demographics_rage.

34. "Congress in February 2004 . . . terrorist groups are thriving.'"
George J. Tenet, "The Worldwide Threat 2004: Challenges in a Changing Global Context," testimony before the Senate Select Committee on Intelligence, February 24, 2004, www.cia.gov/cia/public_affairs/speeches/2004/dci_speech_02142004.html.

35. "But in the meantime . . . recognition to terrorist groups."
On whether to work with the elected representatives of Hezbollah, see Secretary of State Hillary Clinton's "Remarks After Meeting with Lebanese President Michel Sleiman," Beirut, Lebanon,

April 26, 2009, *www.state.gov/secretary/rm/2009a/04/122223.htm*. See also "U.S. Wants to Build Up Hezbollah Moderates: Adviser," *Reuters*, May 18, 2010.

36. "Only a few months after . . . deadly against American troops."
See Thomas E. Ricks, *Fiasco: The American Military Adventure in Iraq* (London: Penguin, 2006), pp. 217–21.

37. "The CIA's 2006 National . . . sought by jihadist groups.'"
Declassified Key Judgments of the National Intelligence Estimate, *Trends in Global Terrorism: Implications for the United States* (April 2006), *www.dni.gov/press_releases/Declassified_NIE_Key_Judgments.pdf*.

38. "Some more pessimistic ones . . . more likely than not.'"
See Graham Allison, *Nuclear Terrorism: The Ultimate Preventable Catastrophe* (New York: Times Books, 2004). We now have less than four years before Allison's prediction is proven either correct or not.

39. "'To say that a movement . . . dictate the political agenda.'"
Adam Roberts, "The War on Terror in Historical Perspective," *Survival*, vol. 47, no. 2 (Summer 2005), p. 109.

40. "One academic study . . . local or limited grievances."
Robert F. Trager and Dessislava P. Zagorcheva, "Deterring Terrorism: It Can Be Done," *International Security*, vol. 30, no. 3 (Winter 2005/06), p. 99.

41. "'Some are more or less . . . more or less enemies.'"
CIA Director Michael Hayden, "State of al Qaeda Today," speech before the Atlantic Council, November 13, 2008, *www.acus.org/http:/%252Fwww.acus.org/event_blog/cia-director-event-transcript*.

42. "Military force has rarely . . . terrorist group's demise."
The precise numbers are that 43 percent joined the political process, whereas only 7 percent were defeated militarily. See Seth G. Jones and Martin C. Libicki, *How Terrorist Groups End*, pp. 9–43.

43. "The military understands that . . . where and how to fight."
See John A. Nagl and Brian M. Burton, "Dirty Windows and Burning Houses: Setting the Record Straight on Irregular Warfare," *The Washington Quarterly*, vol. 32, no. 2 (April 2009), p. 97.

44. "'Violent extremist groups . . . exploit our vulnerabilities.'"
U.S. Department of Defense, Quadrennial Defense Review Report, February 2010, *www.defense.gov/qdr/QDR%20as%20of%2029JAN10%201600.pdf*, p. 20.

45. "One of the most thoughtful . . . cannot be solved militarily."
Rupert Smith, *The Utility of Force: The Art of War in the Modern World* (New York: Vintage, 2008).

46. "The best way is . . . to win their allegiance."
David Kilcullen, *The Accidental Guerrilla: Fighting Small Wars in the Midst of a Big One* (New York: Oxford University Press, 2009). See also, T.X. Hammes, *The Sling and the Stone: On War in the 21st Century* (Osceola, Wisconsin: Zenith Press, 2004) and John A. Nagl, *Learning to Eat Soup with a Knife: Counterinsurgency Lessons from Malaya and Vietnam* (Chicago: University of Chicago Press, 2005).

47. "'The enemies we face . . . many years to come.'"
The Quadrennial Defense Review, p. 9. The "Long War" concept was reemphasized in the June 2008 "National Defense Strategy." See Department of Defense, "National Defense Strategy," June 2008 *www.defenselink.mil/news/2008%20national%20defense%20strategy.pdf*.

48. "It also implied talking . . . State Department's budget."
The Landon Lecture, Kansas State University, Manhattan, Kansas, November 26, 2007, *www.defenselink.mil/speeches/speech.aspx?speechid=1199*

49. "The transition from . . . Britain's domestic intelligence unit."
Interview, Eliza Manningham-Buller, London, May 21, 2009.

50. "They contain a wide . . . socio-pathological personality."
For a study involving Basque terrorists, see Fernando Reinares, *Patriotas de la muerte: Quienes han militado en ETA y por que* ("Patriots of Death: Who Joined ETA and Why") (Madrid: Taurus, 2001); see also, Reinares, "Who Are the Terrorists? Analyzing Changes in Sociological Profile Among Members of ETA," *Studies in Conflict and Terrorism,* vol. 27 (2004), pp. 465–488. For a study of Egyptian extremists, see Gilles Keppel, *Muslim Extremism I Egypt: The Prophet and Pharoah* (Berkeley: University of California Press, 1986) See also, Marc Sageman, *Understanding Terror Networks* (Philadelphia: University of Pennsylvania Press, 2004); and Louise Richardson, *What Terrorists Want: Understanding the Enemy, Containing the Threat* (New York: Random House, 2007).

51. "In March 2009 . . . stabilize and secure Afghanistan."
"Obama Ponders Outreach to Elements of the Taliban," *The New York Times,* March 8, 2008; see also Helene Cooper, "Dreaming of Splitting the Taliban," *The New York Times,* March 8, 2009. During the previous six months, General David Petraeus, Defense Secretary Robert Gates, and UN Ambassador Zalmay Khalilzad had all raised the prospect of the U.S. talking to the Taliban. See David Ignatius, "Tea With the Taliban?" *Washington Post,* October 26, 2008.

52. "Yet only a few days . . . going to locate them."
Holbrooke was quoted as saying, "I am deeply, deeply dissatisfied with the degree of knowledge that the United States government and our friends and allies have on this subject." See Robert Burns, "Envoy Laments Weak US Knowledge About Taliban," AP, April 7, 2009. On this general topic, see Fotini Christia and Michael Semple, "Flipping the Taliban: How to Win in Afghanistan," *Foreign Affairs,* vol. 88, no. 4 (July/August 2009), pp. 34–45.
In his December 1, 2009, speech explaining his new Afghanistan policy, President Obama repeated his desire for the Afghan government to reach out to those Taliban who were willing to "abandon violence." See "Remarks by the President to the Nation on the Way Forward in Afghanistan," United States Military Academy, West Point, New York, December 1, 2009, *www.whitehouse.gov/blog/2009/12/01/new-way-forward-presidents-address*

53. "To reverse some . . . months, by July 2011."
See the White House, "Remarks by the President in Address to the Nation on the Way Forward in Afghanistan and Pakistan," December 1, 2009, *www.whitehouse.gov/the-press-office/remarks-president-address-nation- way-forward-afghanistan-and-pakistan.*

54. "The United States military . . . termed 'reintegration.'"
See Gen. Stanley McChrystal, NATO/ISAF, R:\1800-F-RIC\Initial Guidance, *Initial Guidance on Reintegration,* October 25, 2009; see also, "Afghans Offer Jobs to Taliban If They Defect," *The New York Times,* November 28, 2009; "Empty Promises Mar Afghan Offers to Insurgents," *Washington Post,* December 14, 2009.

55. "In these circumstances . . . killing all of its members."
The U.S. Army and Marine Corps *Counterinsurgency Field Manual* is succinct on this point: "True extremists are unlikely to be reconciled to any other outcome than the one they seek; therefore, they must be killed or captured." *U.S. Army Field Manual* No. 3–24, *Marine Corps Warfighting Publication* No. 3–33.5 (Chicago: University of Chicago Press, 2007), p. 17.

56. "The include examples where . . . to enter into negotiations."
In social science jargon, the chapter on Israel's decision not to meet with Hamas is an attempt to control for "selection bias." This allows us to know whether a factor identified as a reason for states to talk to terrorists is also present in cases when a state decides not to talk to terrorists. In short, this will give us greater confidence that a certain factor can truly be said to vary the outcome. See Barbara Geddes, *Paradigms and Sand Castles: Theory Building and Research Design in Comparative Politics* (Ann Arbor: University of Michigan Press, 2003), pp. 89–129.

I. The Irish Republican Army (IRA)

1. "The Irish Free State . . . United Kingdom as Northern Ireland."
    For the best single-volume history on this general subject, see Paul Bew, *Ireland: The Politics of Enmity, 1789–2006* (Oxford: Oxford University Press, 2007).

2. "In the words of one observer . . . 'Catholic hopes and Protestant fears,'"
    Adrian Guelke, *The Age of Terrorism and the International Political System* (London: I. B. Tauris, 1995), p. 107.

3. "Starting in 1969 . . . wounded during the Troubles."
    The UVF actually killed two Catholics and a Protestant in 1966, but there were no sectarian deaths in 1967 and 1968. See "Northern Ireland: The Troubles, 1963 to 1985," *www.bbc.co.uk/history/recent/troubles/the_troubles_article_02.shtml.*

4. "If majorities in both north . . . join the Republic of Ireland."
    See George J. Mitchell, *Making Peace* (Berkeley: University of California Press, 1999).

5. "The haphazard jailing of Catholics . . . IRA operatives on the run."
    Ed Moloney, *A Secret History of the IRA,* 2d ed. (London: Penguin, 2007), p. 101.

6. "The mouthpiece of the IRA . . . 'the Year of Victory.'"
    Cited in Richard English, *Armed Struggle: The History of the IRA* (London: Pan, 2004), p. 144.

7. "Accounts differ as to . . . hospital, all Catholics."
    The long-awaited official report on the events of Bloody Sunday was finally released on June 15, 2010. See *http://report.bloody-sunday-inquiry.org/.*

8. "After four hours . . . planets apart."
    Joe Haines, *The Politics of Power* (London: Jonathan Cape, 1977), p. 128. Haines was Wilson's press secretary. See also Merlyn Rees, *Northern Ireland: A Personal Perspective* (London: Methuen, 1985), pp. 13–16; see also, Brendan Anderson, *Joe Cahill: A Life in the IRA* (Dublin: O'Brien Press, 2002), pp. 245–46.

9. "'It was just a talking shop, really.'"
    Anderson, *Joe Cahill,* p. 248.

10. "Public records reveal that . . . a more formal meeting."
    Document reference: FCO 87/5, 9 February 1972, *http://cain.ulst.ac.uk/publicrecords/1972/index.html.* The IRA had declared a three-day ceasefire in March to provide political cover for Wilson's trip to Dublin.

11. "Heath could have . . . end to the violence."
    The meeting soon become public, as the IRA leaked it to the press in Dublin a few days later, angry that Whitelaw had not done more to preserve the ceasefire. Anderson, *Joe Cahill,* pp. 251–52. Wilson wanted to defend himself before Parliament by announcing that he had told Heath of his plans in advance. Heath denied that Wilson had done so and told him he would publicly deny it. In the end, Wilson disclosed the meeting anyway and did not suffer much criticism. Haines, *The Politics of Power,* p. 129.

12. "This secret plan . . . share power with the Nationalists."
    See BBC News, "Wilson Had NI 'Doomsday' Plan," September 11, 2008, *http://newsvote.bbc.co.uk/mpapps/pagetools/print/news.bbc.co.uk/2/hi/uk_news/politics/7.*

13. "The real British interest . . . closer to the United Kingdom."
    Document reference: PREM 15/1004, Prime Minister PM/72/10, March 13, 1972, *http://cain.ulst.ac.uk/publicrecords/1972/index.html.*

14. "With the end of . . . violence quickly resumed."
    Moloney, *A Secret History of the IRA,* 2d ed., p. 112.

15. "While the fall of Stormont . . . negotiate with the British."
Moloney, *A Secret History of the IRA*. A rival group, the Official IRA, declared a ceasefire on May 29, thereby placing additional pressure on the Provisional IRA to follow suit.

16. "Whitelaw refused . . . shooting British troops."
Cited in English, *Armed Struggle*, p. 157. He repeated this position to his Cabinet colleagues two days later. See Document reference: CAB 128/48, June 15, 1972.

17. "Whitelaw never explained . . . political leader from Derry."
Hume was the leader of the largest Nationalist political party at the time, the Social Democratic Labour Party (SDLP). Reportedly, he and another SDLP leader, Paddy Devlin, persuaded Whitelaw to accept the IRA's offer. See Peter Taylor, *Behind the Mask: The IRA and Sinn Fein* (New York: TV Books, 1997), p. 162.

18. "The two sides eventually agreed on a ten-day testing period."
Document reference: PREM 15/1009, June 21, 1972.

19. "And the United States . . . once the fighting had stopped."
William Whitelaw, *The Whitelaw Memoirs* (London: Aurum Press, 1989), p. 99.

20. "Whitelaw also judged that . . . Catholic community in the north."
Whitelaw, *The Whitelaw Memoirs*, p. 100.

21. "The IRA also demanded . . . and wanted persons."
Frank Steele, quoted in Taylor, *Behind the Mask*, p. 169.

22. "As Moloney has pointed out . . . when the 1972 cease fire was called.'"
Moloney, *A Secret History of the IRA*, p. 116.

23. "The IRA had also not anticipated . . . which the IRA accepted."
See "Note of a Meeting with the Provisional IRA," June 21, 1972, PREM 15/1009, *http://cain.ulst.ac.uk/publicrecords/1972/index.html*.

24. "'You will get fed up and go away.'"
Cited in Taylor, *Behind the Mask*, p. 170. The IRA actually believed it could quantify in terms of a body count the number of soldiers it needed to kill before the British would leave, and looked at the experience of former colonies such as Aden for guidance and inspiration. See Maria McGuire, *To Take Arms: My Year with the I.R.A. Provisionals* (New York: Viking, 1973). I am indebted to Martyn Frampton for bringing this point to my attention.

25. "'was the motive for talking.'"
Personal interview, Martin McGuinness, Belfast, May 26, 2009. This interview took place in the deputy first minister's cavernous office at Stormont, which McGuinness now occupied. The historical irony was not lost on him.
   Denis Bradley, who assisted Brendan Duddy with the Derry backchannel, observed, "There was no real IRA strategy at this time, no real debate. . . . It was only 'We have the right to use violence and armed struggle against the British.' The goal was to get the Brits to admit that they will one day leave Ireland and ideally to put a date on it. . . . The IRA had only one strategy and that was that they would make themselves such a nuisance that they would finish what was begun in 1916. They envisioned that a British civil servant would walk into a room and hand them a piece of paper saying that the Brits would get out. The IRA deposited all of its hopes and dreams at this time into this very narrow strategy." Personal interview, Denis Bradley, Derry, May 23, 2009.

26. "When some of these miscues . . . 'I was only twenty-two at the time!'"
Interview, Martin McGuinness, Stormont Assembly, Belfast, May 26, 2009. One member of the IRA delegation, Ivor Bell, threatened to wear his combat fatigues to the Cheyne Walk meeting, arguing that "history had taught him that British politicians would try to make the Irish feel ill at ease. He was going to wear this gear to put *them* ill at ease." Cited in Taylor, *Behind the Mask*, p. 164. In the end, Bell did not wear his fatigues to the meeting.

27. "Its captured members should . . . not as criminals or terrorists."
See Whitelaw, *The Whitelaw Memoirs*, p. 94; Kenneth Bloomfield, *A Tragedy of Errors: The Gov-*

ernment and Misgovernment of Northern Ireland (Liverpool: Liverpool University Press, 2007), pp. 37–38. This status was granted to Loyalist paramilitaries as well. Whitelaw admitted that this "seemed a fairly innocuous concession" at the time, but turned out to be a "misguided decision."

28. "Talking had led to more bloodshed, not less."
 Bew and Frampton emphasize this point in John Bew, Martyn Frampton and Inigo Gurruchaga, *Talking to Terrorists: Making Peace in Northern Ireland and the Basque Country* (London: Hurst, 2009), p. 43.

29. "Years later, Steele . . . preferred to go back to war."
 Cited in Taylor, *Behind the Mask*, p. 174. Harold Wilson had tried later in July 1972 to revive the ceasefire, this time meeting with the IRA at his country home. The effort failed.

30. "It placed 'military forts' . . . to infiltrate the organization."
 See Moloney, *A Secret History of the IRA*, 2d ed., p. 117, 126.

31. "The Irish government . . . isolate the IRA over time."
 Garret FitzGerald, *All in a Life: An Autobiography* (London: Macmillan, 1991), p. 199.

32. "But according to Garret FitzGerald . . . eventually negotiate a settlement with them.'"
 Quoted in David McKittrick and David McVea, *Making Sense of the Troubles: The Story of the Conflict in Northern Ireland* (Chicago: New Amsterdam Press, 2002), p. 85.

33. "'We would have . . . a complete disaster.'"
 Personal interview, Noel Dorr, Dublin, May 29, 2009.

34. "'They could destroy us.'"
 Personal interview, Garret FitzGerald, Dublin, May 29, 2009. As foreign minister during this time, FitzGerald made these worries known not only to the British, but also to Secretary of State Henry Kissinger in Washington, who was asked to convince London not to start down a path with the IRA that would lead to withdrawal.
  Loyalist paramilitaries were also vexed by the British overtures to the IRA. These paramilitary groups already existed, but they now gathered momentum and grew more violent. If the British government and local politicians would no longer defend their territory, rights and identity, then they would take matters into their own hands.' See David W. Miller, *Queen's Rebels: Ulster Loyalism in Historical Perspective* (New York: Harper & Row, 1978), esp. pp. 142–66.

35. "Over the next twenty years . . . key link between the British and the IRA."
 Duddy had previously assisted the local police in persuading the IRA to get its guns off the street for the January 30, 1972, NICRA march (what turned out to be Bloody Sunday); they were deposited in his home, where the IRA collected them afterward. Personal interview, Brendan Duddy, Derry, May 24, 2009. Duddy had also assisted in calming the local community during Operation Motorman in Derry. See Jonathan Powell, *Great Hatred, Little Room: Making Peace in Northern Ireland* (London: The Bodley Head, 2008), p. 67.

36. "Whenever Duddy hosted . . . local police stayed away."
 It is interesting to speculate whether the British had cleverly placed Lagan in Derry to establish a backchannel, but I came across no evidence to support this.

37. "In face-to-face meetings with Oatley . . . even withdrawal."
 See Taylor, *Behind the Mask*, pp. 208–24.

38. "The truce was effectively over."
 Ibid., pp. 227–29. The IRA was also under pressure to end the ceasefire because of the spike in Loyalist paramilitary violence against Nationalists and Republicans during 1975.

39. "'Martin McGuiness had warned . . . We won't last.'"
 Quoted by Bradley, personal interview, Derry, May 23, 2009.

40. "Consistent with this approach . . . 'like a tub of toothpaste.'"
 Roy Mason, *Paying the Price* (London: Robert Hale, 1999), p. 199.

41. "It could not distinguish between . . . anytime in the foreseeable future."
 See Taylor, *Behind the Mask*, p. 211.

42. "Curiously, when the IRA . . . a remarkable omission."
Document reference: PREM 16/521/2, January 20, 1975. As close as this document comes is in demand #11: "Confirmation that discussions between representatives of the Republican movement and HMG will continue towards securing a *permanent ceasefire*" (emphasis added).

43. "In November 1974 . . . for another five years in Northern Ireland.'"
Quoted in English, *Armed Struggle*, p. 179.

44. "Bradley thought the Catholic Church . . . the Church refused to get involved."
Personal interview, Denis Bradley, Derry, May 23, 2009. Bradley unfavorably compared the Catholic Church's distance from these talks with the direct involvement of Protestant Church leaders at Feakle, County Clare.

45. "Oatley was new to the game . . . when he arrived."
BBC2, *The Secret Peacemaker*, March 2008.

46. "Duddy independently confirmed . . . 'in very vague terms.'"
Personal interview, Brendan Duddy, Derry, May 24, 2009. See also *The Secret Peacemaker*. In Oatley's defense, he may have gotten wind of Harold Wilson's "Doomsday" plan and thought to use the prime minister's vacillation to promote the talks.

47. "'I, Michael Oatley, will solve the Irish problem.'"
Personal interview, Denis Bradley, Derry, May 23, 2009.

48. "Then it would be harder to go back to war."
Personal interview, Martin McGuinness, Stormont Assembly, Belfast, May 26, 2009.

49. "After an official from the British embassy . . . in any way with the provisionals.'"
Document reference: PREM 16/515/1, January 20, 1975.

50. "The new secretary of state . . . the new security measures time to work."
Bew, Frampton, and Gurrachaga, *Talking to Terrorists*, pp. 71–72.

51. "With so many of its members . . . open up a second front."
The IRA also targeted prison officers, killing nineteen between 1976 and 1980. Cited in David McKittrick and David McVea, *Making Sense of the Troubles* (Chicago: New Amsterdam Books, 2002), p. 139.

52. "In October 1980 . . . lost through the protest."
Taylor, *Behind the Mask*, p. 267.

53. "The Government will never . . . criminal offenses in the province."
Cited in ibid., p. 271.

54. "In mid-December . . . to settle the protest."
The IRA's leadership had never been enthusiastic about the hunger strike, fearful it would deflect time and effort from the war, uncertain if they had sufficient community support, and dubious about whether they could force Thatcher to cave. Moloney, *A Secret History of the IRA*, 2d ed., p. 206; Taylor, *Behind the Mask*, p. 269.

55. "The hunger strike was called off."
The reasons for ending the first hunger strike may have varied somewhat from the conventional narrative. "The Northern Ireland Office had, at an earlier stage in the hunger strike, spoken to the hunger strikers in the jail and offered concessions which went a long way towards satisfying their demands. Wrangling over guaranteeing the offer delayed matters. The document which eventually appeared was a considerable retreat from that offer. Not only that, but the document did not come on to the scene until the hunger strike had ended. One of the hunger strikers, Sean McKenna, had told the protest leader Brendan Hughes that he didn't want to die. Hughes agreed to save his life. When McKenna went into a coma, Hughes made good on his word and the hunger strike was ended. Sometime after that, the document appeared. It is possible that surveillance had detected the exchange between Hughes and McKenna and the British accordingly tailored the document and its timing." Ed Moloney, personal correspondence with the author, November 22, 2009.

56. "The IRA's 'Commanding Officer' . . . 'could drive a bus through it.'"
Cited in Taylor, *Behind the Mask*, p. 274.

57. "The republican leadership . . . stand for the open seat."
There is a dispute as to how much credit Adams deserves for this move. What is undisputed is that after the electoral strategy proved successful, Adams moved to take ownership of it. I am indebted to Martyn Frampton for this point.

58. "More men died."
See David Beresford, *Ten Men Dead: The Story of the 1981 Irish Hunger Strike* (New York: Atlantic Monthly Press, 1987), pp. 225–28 and 249–52.

59. "Sinn Fein won again."
A controversy has arisen in the past few years surrounding the July offer by the British and this by-election. The IRA's "Public Relations Officer" in the Maze prison at the time, Richard O'Rawe, has accused Adams of sabotaging a settlement that the hunger strikers were willing to accept in July, thereby condemning an additional six men to their deaths. See Richard O'Rawe, *Blanketmen: An Untold Story of the H-Block Hunger Strike* (Dublin: New Island, 2005). After Sands's victory in April, the British had changed the rules to prevent prisoners from contesting parliamentary elections. Therefore, Adams could not nominate a hunger striker or other prisoner for Sands's seat. So he chose a party apparatchik, Owen Carron, to run on the Sinn Fein ticket. Still, Sinn Fein needed to prevent the SDLP from contesting this election and splitting the Nationalist vote. If the hunger strike continued, however, Sinn Fein could more easily persuade the SDLP to stand aside for the Sinn Fein candidate and appeal to the memory of Bobby Sands to rally popular support.

60. "'But will anyone object if . . . we take power in Ireland?'"
Cited in Rogelio Alonso, *The IRA and Armed Struggle* (London: Routledge, 2003), p. 116.

61. "Decades later . . . turning point for Sinn Fein."
Personal interviews, Belfast and Stormont, May 26, 2009.

62. "'Above all . . . would not be won by violence.'"
Margaret Thatcher, *The Downing Street Years* (London: HarperCollins, 1993), pp. 390, 392.

63. "She came under pressure . . . and the Reagan White House."
Concerned over the rising popularity rise of IRA/Sinn Fein at expense of moderate Nationalists both north and south of the border, Garret FitzGerald complained that "it would take years rather than months for the ground thus lost to the IRA by the SDLP and ourselves to be recovered" (*All in a Life*, p. 375).

64. "She would allow others . . . she did it when necessary."
Personal interviews, Charles Powell and Douglas Hurd, London, May 19 and 20, 2009. When asked why Thatcher's memoirs conveyed a more dogmatic approach during the strike, Hurd commented that Thatcher had "rowed back" the amount of her actual flexibility.

65. "The Maze's governor was removed as well."
See the Margaret Thatcher Foundation, "Extract from a Letter dated 8 July 1981, from 10 Downing Street to the Northern Ireland Office," *www.margaretthatcher.org/archive/displaydocument.asp?docid=111766* and "Extract from a Letter dated 18 July 1981, from 10 Downing Street to the Northern Ireland Office," *www.margaretthatcher.org/archive/displaydocument.asp?docid=11767*. See also Taylor, *Behind the Mask*, p. 289, and Beresford, *Ten Men Dead*, p. 334.

66. "Thatcher hoped that . . . dampen Sinn Fein's appeal."
Thatcher, *The Downing Street Years*, p. 391.

67. "She characteristically responded . . . did not give their victims."
Although Thatcher authorized continued low-level contacts between MI6 and the IRA, any chance of negotiating an end to the violence, or even another ceasefire, would have to wait until she was no longer in office. That moment almost arrived in October 1984, when the IRA narrowly

missed assassinating the prime minister in a bombing at Brighton's Grand Hotel during the Conservative Party's annual conference.

68. "Thatcher supported the deal . . . cross-border security."
Thatcher was disappointed on the security cooperation received from Dublin. For a thoughtful assessment of the Anglo-Irish Agreement, see Bew, Frampton, and Gurruchaga, *Talking to Terrorists*, pp. 97–105.

69. "Loyalist paramilitary violence . . . the following three years."
See McKittrick and McVea, *Making Sense of the Troubles*, p. 175; esp. their chart on p. 327.

70. "Not surprisingly, then, . . . through the end of the decade."
Alonso, *The IRA and Armed Struggle*, p. 66; see also Martyn Frampton, *The Long March: The Political Strategy of Sinn Fein, 1981–2007* (London: Palgrave Macmillan, 2009).

71. "Terrorist acts . . . compromised and prevented."
Jack Holland and Susan Phoenix, *Phoenix: Policing the Shadows: The Secret War Against Terrorism in Northern Ireland* (London, Hodder & Stoughton 1996), p. 391.

72. "Modern unionists . . . insisting on a united Ireland."
Bew, *Ireland: The Politics of Enmity*, pp. 539–40.

73. "A despondent Adams . . . Irish people killing each other.'"
Cited in Bew, Frampton, and Gurruchaga, *Talking to Terrorists*, p. 107.

74. "When I interviewed . . . but for decades.'"
Personal interview, Martin McGuinness, Stormont, May 26, 2009.

75. "For the remainder of the 1980s . . . and the SDLP."
Gerry Adams, *Hope and History: Making Peace in Ireland* (London: Brandon, 2003), pp. 31, 79. Adams was also assisted in his efforts by a Belfast-based priest named Father Alec Reid. They had first met when Adams was in prison. Reid knew Adams's family and was convinced that Adams "wanted a peaceful way out of the conflict." Reid had also mediated disputes between Republican factions during the 1970s, winning the trust of Adams. Personal interview, Father Alec Reid, Dublin, May 29, 2009. For more on Reid, see David Little, *Peacemakers in Action* (Cambridge: Cambridge University Press, 2007), pp. 429–49.

76. "The process could begin . . . went on ceasefire."
Adams's questions and the verbatim British response can be found in Moloney, *A Secret History of the IRA*, 2d ed., pp. 251–54. In a November 2009 interview, King denied ever participating in any secret exchanges with Reid or anyone else at this time or of even knowing of any type of backchannel communications between the IRA/Sinn Fein and British officials. Personal interview, Tom King, London, November 5, 2009. Yet in two earlier interviews, Ed Moloney, King told Moloney that he had participated in these exchanges. Moloney independently confirmed this with sources from the Northern Ireland Office. Author's communication with Ed Moloney, November 22, 2009. The King-Adams channel ended abruptly in August 1987, when IRA members were found on the grounds of King's Wiltshire estate and charged with attempted murder.

77. "Haughey . . . gunrunning to the IRA in 1969-70."
Haughey was finance minister at the time. He was acquitted of the charges. See Justin O'Brien, *The Arms Trial* (Dublin: Gill and MacMillan, 2000).

78. "Partly because Haughey . . . about halting the war."
Personal interview, Martin Mansergh, Dublin, May 28, 2009; personal interview, Bertie Ahern, Dublin, May 28, 2009; personal interview, Dermot Gallagher, Dublin, May 27, 2009. After the Enniskillen atrocity, Adams had said publicly that he was not sure if he could continue to support the Republican cause if there was a second Enniskillen; these comments reinforced a private communication Adams had sent to Haughey months before. See Moloney, *A Secret History of the IRA*, 2nd ed., p. 269.

79. "Haughey also realized . . . foreign investment and tourism."
Personal interview, Dermot Gallagher, Dublin, May 27, 2009; interview, Bertie Ahern, Dublin, May 28, 2009.

80. "As he remarked . . . by balancing books."
Personal interview, Sean Aylward, Dublin, May 28, 2009.

81. "When the official asked Haughey . . . You're on your own.'"
Personal interview, Dermot Ahern, Dublin, May 27, 2009. Ahern agreed to the assignment "because the Taoiseach asked" and because Ahern represented a constituency along the south-north border and so did not think his constituents would really object to his involvement if the news leaked out.

82. "They felt that Adams . . . Sinn Fein's political isolation."
Personal interview, Dermot Ahern, Dublin, May 27, 2009; personal interview, Martin Mansergh, Dublin, May 28, 2009.

83. "These meetings became . . . 1998 Novel Peace Prize."
"Hume. . . . for long afterward believed that his subsequent meetings with Adams marked the start of the peace process." See *A Secret History of the IRA*, 2d ed., pp. 277–78. Hume shared the 1998 Peace Prize with Unionist leader David Trimble.

84. "Some have argued . . . Adams has at times encouraged)"
Aside from Adams, see Moloney, *A Secret History of the IRA*.

85. "The weight of evidence . . . Martyn Frampton"
See Frampton, *The Long March*, esp. pp. 47–65 and 74–101.

86. "He described a . . . that the IRA would never get over."
Personal interview, Martin McGuinness, Stormont, May 26, 2009. King's successor as secretary of state for Northern Ireland, Peter Brooke, did not know of the Oatley channel until February 1991. Personal interview, Peter Brooke, London, May 20, 2009.

87. "Sinn Fein released a . . . 'Setting the Record Straight.'"
The bogus message can be found in "Setting the Record Straight: A Record of Communications Between Sinn Fein and the British Government, October 1990–November 1993" (January 1994), p. 24. Sinn Fein made no mention in this document of the pre-October 1990 communications between the two parties, perhaps to spare the IRA rank and file the shock that the organization had been talking to the Thatcher government.

88. "According to him . . . and we write the message.'"
Personal interview, Denis Bradley, Derry, May 23, 2009.

89. "Both sides became . . . the war being over."
Personal interview, senior intelligence official, London, May 2009.

90. "It then sent a message . . . its intent to withdraw."
Bew, Frampton, and Gurruchaga, *Talking to Terrorists*, pp. 118–19.

91. "According to two of the . . . to achieve what they wanted."
Ibid., p. 123.

92. "Still searching for a deal . . . well and truly over."
Ibid., pp. 122–23.

93. "One of Major's . . . detonating bombs."
Telephone interview, Charles Powell, September 28, 2009.

94. "Sinn Fein was left . . . obstacles to peace.'"
"Setting the Record Straight," p. 32.

95. "'It was at the end . . . Where else could I go?'"
All quotes are from my personal interview, Albert Reynolds, Dublin, May 29, 2009.

96. "One senior IRA official . . . past twenty-five years is for nothing'"
     Cited in Moloney, *A Secret History of the IRA*, 2d ed., p. 413.

97. "If Republicans walked away . . . Sinn Fein would lose support"
     See Bew, Frampton, and Gurruchaga, *Talking to Terrorists*, p. 128.

98. "The IRA would review the ceasefire after four months."
     Moloney, *A Secret History of the IRA*, 2d ed., p. 429. How Adams was able to maneuver—fool, re-
     ally—the IRA into continuing to support the ceasefire is told in Moloney, pp. 392–54. A group of
     Loyalist paramilitaries announced a ceasefire a few weeks after the IRA, on October 13, 1994.

99. This was not good enough . . . a negotiated settlement."
     Cited in Bew, Frampton, and Gurruchaga, *Talking to Terrorists*, p. 132.

100. "But the Mitchell Commission . . . replacing one precondition with six."
     See *Mitchell, Making Peace*, pp. 22–38. The Commission did state that the parties "should con-
     sider" decommissioning while the negotiations were taking place.

101. "He also made clear . . . to wait for you.'"
     See Bew, Frampton, and Gurruchaga, *Talking to Terrorists*, p. 139.

102. "The McCartney sisters' . . . captivated Irish America."
     The McCartneys had special resonance with Irish-America because they hailed from the Short
     Strand, a working-class Catholic neighborhood that was staunchly supportive of Sinn Fein. Cath-
     erine McCartney has written a moving account of her brother's murder and the family's ongoing
     efforts to seek justice. See *Walls of Silence* (Dublin: Gill and Macmillan, 2007).

103. "'Once you get a terrorist group . . . political solution to the conflict.'"
     Personal interview, Dublin, May 27, 2009.

104. "Reflecting back over . . . engage in a political process.'"
     Personal interview, Gerry Adams, Belfast, May 26, 2009.

105. "The Irish leader Garret FitzGerald . . . confusion and muddle.'"
     FitzGerald, *All in a Life*, p. 268.

106. "'We thought the British had a strategy . . . And that was shit!'"
     Personal interview, Denis Bradley, Derry, May 23, 2009. Bradley thinks that this perception lasted
     for the first ten to twelve years of the Troubles.

107. "Unfortunately for the British . . . British intelligence officer."
     Personal interview, intelligence official, London, 2009.

108. "Engaging with terrorists . . . according to the former head of MI5."
     Personal interview, Eliza Manningham-Buller, London, May 21, 2009.

109. "This was reportedly . . . legal political party."
     See Bew, Frampton, and Gurruchaga, *Talking to Terrorists*, p. 51.

110. "Gerry Adams conceded that . . . support his agenda."
     Personal interview, Gerry Adams, Belfast, May 26, 2009.

111. "'Would turn my stomach . . . We will not do it.'"
     See House of Commons *Hansard Debates*, November 1, 1993, *www.publications.parliament.uk/
     pa/cm199293/cmhansrd/1993-11-01/Debate-2.html*.

112. "To which Major allegedly replied . . . it would turn *yours*.'"
     Personal interview, British official, London, January 2005.

113. "'It is very hard for the man in the street to understand this.'"
     Personal interview, Brendan Duddy, Derry, May 24, 2009.

114. "Thatcher's foreign minister . . . to stop more killing.'"
     Personal interview, Douglas Hurd, London, May 20, 2009.

115. "'Our interests are eternal . . . our duty to follow.'"
     Lord Palmerston, House of Commons, March 1, 1848, cited in Anthony Jay, ed., *The Oxford
     Dictionary of Political Quotations* (London: Oxford University Press, 1996), p. 284.

116. "In the mid-1990s . . . in the last twenty years.'"
Quoted in Rogelio Alonso, "Pathways out of Terrorism in Northern Ireland and the Basque Country: The Misrepresentation of the Irish Model," *Terrorism and Political Violence*, vol. 16, no. 4 (Winter 2004), p. 702.

117. "A former member of the IRA . . . been fundamentalist for so long.'"
Rogelio, *The IRA and the Armed Struggle*, p. 119.

2. BASQUE HOMELAND AND FREEDOM (ETA)

1. "To preserve a Basque heritage . . . a blend of both."
"In terms of either biology or anthropological history, there is no scientific evidence for the concept of a 'Basque' race." Stanley G. Payne, *Basque Nationalism* (Reno: University of Nevada, 1974), p. 9.

2. "ETA would be willing . . . 'maximum program.'"
See Robert P. Clark, *Negotiating with ETA: Obstacles to Peace in the Basque Country, 1975–1988* (Reno: University of Nevada Press, 1990), pp. 79–83; Inigo Gurruchaga, in John Bew, Martyn Frampton, and Inigo Gurruchaga, Talking to *Terrorists: Making Peace in Northern Ireland and the Basque Country* (London: Hurst, 2009), p. 185.

3. "Nonetheless, according to . . . but all attempts have failed.'"
Florencio Dominguez, "ETA: A Terrorist Organization Within a Democratic Society," in *Presentation of the Political Reality in the Basque Country: From Defamation to Tragedy* (Fundación para la Libertad: Bilbao, 2008), p. 52.

4. "In the months before Franco . . . resumption of the Civil War."
See Robert P. Clark, *The Basques: The Franco Years and Beyond* (Reno: University of Nevada Press, 1979), p. 301.

5. "ETA answered by assassinating . . . idea of liberal democracy."
Clark, *Negotiating with ETA*, pp. 73–75.

6. "It could boast of . . . Spain could only envy."
See Javier Corcuera Atienza, "The Autonomy of the Basque Country" and José Ignacio Martinez Churiaque, "The Economic Situation in the Basque Country," in *Presentation of the Political Reality in the Basque Country: From Defamation to Tragedy* (Fundación para la Libertad: Bilbao, 2008), pp. 5–12 and 33–40, respectively.

7. As the country moved . . . ninety-six deaths in 1980."
See Goldie Shabad and Francisco Jose Llera Ramo, "Political Violence in a Democratic State: Basque Terrorism in Spain," in Martha Crenshaw, ed., *Terrorism in Context* (University Park, Pa.: Pennsylvania State University Press, 1995), pp. 441–43.

8. "A demographic youth bulge . . . eager to join the ETA."
See Gurruchaga, *Talking to Terrorists*, p. 217.

9. "By the start of 1976 . . . and coordinating their efforts.'"
Fernando Reinares, "The Political Conditioning of Collective Violence: Regime Change and Insurgent Terrorism in Spain," *Research on Democracy and Society*, vol. 3 (1996), p. 313.

10. "Eagerness to undo the years . . . efforts to combat ETA"
Clark, *Negotiating with ETA*, p. 38.

11. "According to Robert Clark . . . spilling over onto French territory.'"
Clark, *Negotiating with ETA*, p. 31.

12. "They had the same ultimate goal . . . and the Tupamaros in Uruguay."
Clark, *The Basques*, p. 278.

13. "The rivalry between the two branches . . . was under way."
Clark, *Negotiating with ETA*, p. 23.

14. "ETA refused to accept responsibility . . . who will support terrorism."
    Personal interview, Teo Uriarte, Bilbao, July 15, 2009. Uriarte had been sentenced to death at the 1970 Burgos trial and later became a leading influence within ETA-PM.

15. "'We knew that democracy is coming . . . process in the Basque country.'"
    Personal interview, Teo Uriarte, Bilbao, July 15, 2009.

16. "Issues that might be deemed tactical . . . could be addressed."
    Clark, *Negotiating with ETA*, pp. 90–91.

17. "'Talks' were used to describe . . . discussions could follow."
    I am indebted to Arantxa Azurmendi for explaining these nuances, Madrid, July 2009.

18. "In September 1982 . . . have now fulfilled their role.'"
    Cited in Clark, *Negotiating with ETA*, p. 112.

19. "The Spanish government . . . groups' other demands."
    Clark, *Negotiating with ETA*, p. 98. "[T]he decision to lay down their arms was spurred by deals securing them pardons and reprieves that were agreed to on a one-by-one basis between left-leaning Basque nationalist politicians and the then-centrist Spanish government." Fernando Reinares, "The Political Conditioning of Collective Violence," p. 309.

20. "Did his death really end . . . American academic expert phrased it?"
    Clark, *The Basque Insurgents*, p. 255.

21. ETA-M 'devoted more time to . . . the preparations were very complicated.'"
    Personal interviews, José Maria Benegas, Madrid, July 9 and 10, 2009.

22. Eventually, Martin Villa . . . representatives of a sovereign Basque country."
    Telephone interview, Rodolfo Martin Villa, November 6, 2009.

23. "That is all."
    Quoted in Clark, *Negotiating with ETA*, pp. 88–89.

24. "A 'conspiracy of silence' . . . Franco-style authoritarianism."
    Personal interview, Teo Uriarte, Bilbao, July 15, 2009.

25. "They had no intention of ending the war except on their own terms."
    Personal interview, José Maria Benegas, Madrid, July 9, 2009.

26. "ETA-M believed that . . . make concessions in return."
    Personal interview, Florencio Dominguez, Bilbao, July 16, 2009.

27. "According to Florencio Dominguez . . . infected by the same disease.'"
    Ibid.

28. "Teo Uriarte . . . history never repeats itself.'"
    Personal interview, Teo Uriarte, Bilbao, July 15, 2009.

29. "An insightful Basque observer . . . confrontation with the Spanish state."
    Gurruchaga, *Talking to Terrorists*, p. 190.

30. "Over the next few years . . . and wounding more than thirty others."
    With respect to GAL's attacks, "about one-third of their victims had no links whatsoever to ETA and resulted from mistakes in identifying targets or from decidedly arbitrary attacks." Fernando Reinares and Oscar Jaime-Jimenez, "Countering Terrorism in a New Democracy: the Case of Spain," in Reinares, ed., *European Democracies Against Terrorism: Governmental Policies and Inter-governmental Cooperation* (Aldershot: Ashgate, 2000, p. 136. On the GAL, see Paddy Wordworth, *Dirty War, Clean Hands: ETA, the GAL and Spanish Democracy* (Cork: Cork University Press, 2001). The friends and family of a victim murdered in France in 1987 blamed the GAL. A Spanish judge, Baltazar Garzon, investigated and closed the case without launching a prosecution.

31. "According to Rafael Vera . . . leaders started having bodyguards."
    Personal interview, Rafael Vera, Torrelodones, July 20, 2009. Vera was convicted and imprisoned after he was linked to the GAL and convicted of corruption charges.

32. "But ETA soon broke off . . . the violence resumed."
Personal interview, Rafael Vera, Torrelodones, July 20, 2009.

33. "Suffering from a series of reverses . . . with the Spanish authorities."
Gurruchaga, *Talking to Terrorists*, p. 209.

34. "According to Juan Manuel Eguiagaray . . . I was pessimistic."
Personal interview, Juan Manuel Eguiagaray, Madrid, July 21, 2009.

35. "Rafael Vera . . . Why bother?'"
Personal interview, Rafael Vera, Torrelodones, July 20, 2009.

36. "'This was a risk we could take.'"
Personal interview, Juan Manuel Eguiagaray, Madrid, July 21, 2009.

37. "ETA had no right to negotiate on behalf of the Basque people."
Gurruchaga, *Talking to Terrorists*, p. 211.

38. "'If this negotiation . . . help with rounding up ETA.'"
Personal interview, Rafael Vera, Torrelodones, July 20, 2009.

39. "On a different occasion . . . withdrew from the competition."
Ibid.

40. "The Algerians said . . . negotiate with ETA."
Ibid. Algeria had its own agenda: It wanted Spain to expel a group of antigovernment Algerians living in Spain and Madrid's help in resolving a conflict in the Western Sahara in its favor. Spain paid Algeria for the cost of hosting the negotiations and provided the planes for relocating the expelled ETA members.

41. "'Most of what we learned . . . recalled Vera.'"
Personal interview, Rafael Vera, Torrelodones, July 20, 2009.

42. "'This was my goal . . . they were in Spanish prisons.'"
Ibid.

43. "'But whatever we were interested in . . . not to negotiate with ETA'"
Ibid.

44. "'We stopped it . . . give publicity to plotters.'"
Ibid.

45. "Eguiagaray: 'We were suspicious . . . it was a real car crash.'"
Personal interview, Juan Manuel Eguiagaray, Madrid, July 21, 2009.

46. "Once the Spanish government . . . solve the armed conflict."
Personal interview, Eugenio Etxebeste, San Sebastián, July 13, 2009.

47. "'Then perhaps we could get . . . and return to violence.'"
Personal interview, Juan Manuel Eguiagaray, Madrid, July 21, 2009.

48. "'The government denied us legitimacy . . . to get us to surrender.'"
Personal interview, Etxebeste, San Sebastián, July 13, 2009.

49. "'We could not talk about autonomy for the Basque country.'"
All Etxebeste wanted to discuss was "a negotiated political settlement." In order to prolong the ceasefire, appease the French and Algerian governments, and continue to collect intelligence, Eguiagaray's discussions started to drift into political territory. "I was taking a risk by talking with them about the Spanish constitution, federalism, the Basque autonomy statute, etc. They assumed that since we were both on the 'left' politically, we would see things much the same. We would have a common interpretation of the transition period." Personal interview, Juan Manuel Eguiagaray, Madrid, July 21, 2009. Spain was also mindful of its domestic audience. "We didn't want the failure in the talks to be attributed to the government. We wanted to make it sound that if the talks failed, then no one could blame us. They would blame ETA." Personal interview, Rafael Vera, Torrelodones, July 20, 2009.

50. "Etxebeste: 'Perhaps . . . violence wasn't taking us anywhere.'"
    Personal interview, Etxebeste, San Sebastián, July 13, 2009.

51. "'But at the possibility of discussing . . . the government pulled back.'"
    Ibid.

52. "'No. I can explain . . . what he would have done.'"
    Ibid.

53. "'We offered a period . . . [i.e., political negotiations] in Algeria.'"
    Ibid.

54. "Etxebeste adoptd the advice as ETA's own."
    Personal interview, José Maria Benegas, Madrid, July 9 and 10, 2009.

55. Benegas explained the situation . . . break off the talks anyway."
    Ibid.

56. "The group had successfully . . . as not to credit ETA."
    Personal interview, Rafael Vera, Torrelodones, July 20, 2009.

57. "According to Vera . . . would not have time to regroup.'"
    Ibid.

58. "'I decided to put . . . against ETA, without exception.'"
    Personal interview, José Maria Aznar, Washington, D.C., Sept. 30, 2009.

59. "'On my first day in office . . . as with the Socialists.'"
    Personal interview, Rafael Bardaji, Washington, D.C., Sept. 30, 2009.

60. "'Only if a terrorist group . . . it renounces violence.'"
    Personal interview, José Maria Aznar, Washington, D.C., Sept. 30, 2009.

61. "According to former national security . . . could solve ETA by force.'"
    Personal interview, Rafael Bardaji, Madrid, July 20, 2009.

62. "Etxebeste no longer needed . . . had no intention of talking."
    Personal interview, Jaime Mayor Oreja, Madrid, July 10, 2009.

63. "ETA's motivation at this time . . . Basque nationalist parties."
    Personal interviews, Florencio Dominguez, Bilbao, July 16, 2009; Joseba Egibar, San Sebastián, July 14, 2009; and Xavier Arzalluz, Bilbao, July 17, 2009. ETA's political wing has used different names over the years, reinventing itself after being banned by the government. These names successively were Herri Batasuna, Euskal Herritarrok and Batasuna. In whatever guise, Batasuna "has always been a puppet for ETA, which has set the guidelines and taken the most important decisions for Batasuna." Florencio Dominguez, "ETA: A Terrorist Organization Within a Democratic Society," in *Presentation of the Political Reality in the Basque Country: From Defamation to Tragedy* (Fundación para la Libertad: Bilbao, 2008), p. 51.

64. "It also never believed . . . in the Basque country."
    Personal interview, José Luis Zubizarreta, Bilbao, July 16, 2009; personal interview, Xavier Arzallus, Bilbao, July 17, 2009.

65. "'ETA-PM gave up . . . some with ETA-M.'"
    Personal interview, Xavier Arzalluz, Bilbao, July 17, 2009. ETA and the PNV might have sensed that they also shared a common foe—the central authorities in Madrid. According to Arzalluz, "All the propaganda of the government is directed at attacking ETA, but really what they are doing is attacking [Basque] nationalism. It is true that a lot of people think that if ETA disappears, this will deal a blow to Basque nationalism. Don't ever forget the huge pain and trauma these people [the Basques] have suffered. I don't want to give satisfaction to my enemies [Madrid] by condemning ETA. Is the enemy of my enemy my enemy?"

66. "Also, the PNV . . . its supporters on the left."
    Shabad and Llera Ramo, "Political Violence in a Democratic State: Basque Terrorism in Spain," in Martha Crenshaw, ed., *Terrorism in Context*, p. 452.

67. "(For example . . . other regions across Spain)."
    See Javier Corcuera Atienza, "The Autonomy of the Basque Country" in *Presentation of the Political Reality in the Basque Country: From Defamation to Tragedy* (Fundación para la Lbertad: Bilbao, 2008), pp. 5–12.

68. "For all these reasons . . . 'conflict *and* collusion.'"
    Shabad and Llera Ramo, "Political Violence in a Democratic State: Basque Terrorism in Spain," in Martha Crenshaw, ed., Terrorism in Context, p. 468.

69. "It only learned of . . . mid-level official in Catalonia."
    Personal interview, Jaime Mayor Oreja, Madrid, July 10, 2009. Mayor: "When these talks later became public, former Prime Minister González criticized the government for not knowing. He was right."

70. "But Herri Batasuna did . . . dealing directly with ETA."
    Personal interview, Joseba Egibar, July 14, 2009.

71. "But ETA thought that . . . with Aznar and the Popular Party."
    Personal interview, José Luis Zubizarreta, Bilbao, July 16, 2009.

72. "It called for all the parties . . . a negotiated political solution."
    Personal interview, Joseba Egibar, San Sebastian, July 14, 2009. This would not be the last time Basque nationalists were to misunderstand the Northern Ireland peace process. See Rogelio Alonso, "Pathways Out of Terrorism in Northern Ireland and the Basque Country: The Misrepresentation of the Irish Model," in *Terrorism and Political Violence*, vol. 16, no. 4 (Winter 2004), pp. 695–713.

73. "The document called for . . . the historic Basque nation."
    Personal interview, Joseba Egibar, San Sebastián, July 14, 2009.

74. "The proposal was unacceptable . . . political suicide for the PNV.'"
    Ibid. Rogelio Alonso has termed the PNV's appeasement of ETA "the radicalization of constitutional nationalism."

75. "'We thought this was . . . a sea change in public opinion.'"
    Personal interview, Javier Zarzalejos, Madrid, July 8, 2009.

76. "'Personally, I never . . . my problem was public opinion.'"
    Personal interview, José Maria Aznar, Washington, D.C., September 30, 2009.

77. "'Aznar had to respond . . . its position not to talk.'"
    Personal interview, Javier Zarzalejos, Madrid, July 8, 2009.

78. "'No one [in Spain] . . . end the armed struggle.'"
    Personal interview, Jaime Mayor Oreja, Madrid, July 10, 2009.

79. "'The Guardia Civil . . . this was the end.'"
    Ibid. Mayor did not trust the assessment: "I never thought so . . . there was too much hatred per square meter for this to be ended so easily."

80. "The contradictory assessments could not be reconciled."
    Personal interview, former Spanish official, Madrid, July 2009.

81. "The PNV, which had been . . . misinterpreted ETA's announcement."
    Personal interview, Joseba Egibar, San Sebastián, July 14, 2009; personal interview, Xavier Arzallus, Bilbao, July 17, 2009.

82. "Needless to say . . . anger, and disappointment."
    As to why PNV members did not inform the government, Zarzalejos believes that Arzallus saw himself as the leader of the entire Basque nationalist movement and thought he could manage—manipulate really—the dialogue between the government and ETA over prisoner releases (which only the government controlled). Ideally, Arzallus wanted Madrid to delegate policymaking over prisoners to the PNV, which he could then use to lead ETA away from violence and into the legitimate Basque nationalist fold. Personal interview, Javier Zarzalejos, Madrid, November 2, 2009.

83. "'If this was the first time . . . test if this was possible.'"
Personal interview, Jaime Mayor Oreja, Madrid, July 10, 2009. As soon as Aznar approved the talks, Mayor selected a three-man delegation of Aznar's most trusted aides. For talks that were not supposed to be political, the three men were all political appointees: Javier Zarzelejos, Martin Fluxá, and Pedro Arriola.

84. "'I establish one public condition . . . I never authorized a ngotiation. Never, never.'"
Personal interview, José Maria Aznar, Washington, D.C., September 30, 2009.

85. "'There was some domestic . . . It was a shell game.'"
Ibid.

86. "Javier Zaralejos . . . relations management exercise.'"
Personal interview, Javier Zarzalejos, Madrid, July 8, 2009.

87. "ETA made dramatic and . . . join with the Basque region."
Ibid.

88. "The administration also . . . of the González years."
Personal interview, Rafael Bardaji, Madrid, July 20, 2009.
Despite the impasse in Geneva, the two sides had agreed to hold another meeting. It never took place. One can only speculate as to why ETA refused. ETA originally wanted to negotiate sensitive political issues. It may have assumed that the government could not publicly agree to this in advance because of domestic political considerations, but would agree confidentially after the talks started. It discovered in Geneva that it had miscalculated and may have concluded that further talks would be unproductive. After the May meeting and before a second one could be scheduled, local elections took place in the Basque country. The Basque nationalist parties did poorly, while Aznar's Popular Party gained seats at the expense of the PNV. ETA (or factions within ETA) realized that its pan-Basque alliance strategy wasn't a winner and started looking for excuses to break off the talks. Personal interview, Jaime Mayor Oreja, Madrid, July 10, 2009; personal interview, Xavier Arzallus, Bilbao, July 17, 2009.
There is another, less well-known possibility. According to Bardaji, "After the Geneva meeting, the Guardia Civil had intercepted a message from Vitoria [the Basque capital] between ETA and its political wing that indicated that ETA was already thinking about ending the ceasefire and returning to violence. We responded by sending the police and Guardia Civil back on the beat, and ETA might have reacted to this" by ending the ceasefire. Personal interview, Rafael Bardaji, Madrid, July 20, 2009.
Whatever its internal decision-making, ETA did not immediately signal that the ceasefire was officially over. That took another six months. The disappointing talks in Geneva, the poor showing of the Basque nationalist parties in the local elections, and the PNV's reluctance to leave the regional and national parliaments and join an imaginary one controlled by ETA probably caused a fundamental reassessment by ETA. After investing time and energy in dual approaches to the Basque nationalists and the Aznar government, ETA was now left with ashes. ETA may have needed time to develop a new narrative, figure out how to shift blame away from itself and onto the Basque nationalist parties, reconstitute its organization, and train its younger members for the battles to come. Personal interview, Javier Zarzalejos, Madrid, July 8, 2009; personal interview, Rafael Bardaji, Madrid, July 20, 2009.

89. "'This period marked . . . a lesson for the whole society.'"
Personal interview, Javier Zarzalejos, Madrid, July 8, 2009.

90. "The Spanish government . . . ETA's encrypted messages."
Personal interview, Rafael Bardaji, Madrid, July 20, 2009.

91. "All this would prove . . . under threat from ETA."
Gurruchaga, *Talking to Terrorists*, p. 227.

92. "The Aznar administration . . . sea in which ETA swims.'"
Personal interview, Javier Zarzalejos, Madrid, November 2, 2009.

93. "Now a Spanish judge . . . . the ETA support network."
Gurruchaga, *Talking to Terrorists*, p. 222. Falcone was assassinated by the Corleone family in 1992.

94. "Acting through the Cortes . . . Political Parties Act in June 2002."
Some viewed the Political Parties Act (PPA) as unconstitutional because it contained language eliminating any prospect of parole for ETA murderers. This contradicted previous penal legislation that was premised on the idea that prisoners could be rehabilitated. The Spanish Supreme Court later pronounced that the provisions of the PPA did not violate the constitution.

95. "When Basque parliamentarians refused, Garzon had them arrested."
The Batasuna parliamentary group was known at this time as Euskal Herritarrok.

96. This immediately shut down . . . support political parties."
Personal interview, Rafael Bardaji, Madrid, July 20, 2009.

97. "Later that year . . . in counterterrorism efforts."
Gurruchaga, *Talking to Terrorists*, p. 230.

98. "According to the former . . . close to putting an end to ETA.'"
Personal interview, Rafael Bardaji, Madrid, July 20, 2009.

99. "More objective observers concurred . . . capacity to kill.'"
Fernando Reinares and Rogelio Alonso, "Confronting Ethnonationalist Terrorism in Spain," in Robert J. Art and Louise Richardson, *Democracy and Counterterrorism: Lessons from the Past* (Washington, D.C.: USIP, 2007), p. 106.

100. "ETA's leadership formally . . . from the organization."
Gurruchaga, *Talking to Terrorists*, p. 232.

101. "The so-called Anoeta Declaration . . . 'demilitarization, prisoners, refugees and victims.'"
Ibid., p. 232.

102. "Zapatero declared that . . . the word 'indefinite in 1998)."
Ibid., pp. 233–35. In May 2006, ETA clarified that "permanent" did not mean "irreversible." See also Florencio Dominguez, *Josu Ternera: una vida en ETA* (Madrid: La Esfora, 2006).

103. "A prison at Santander . . . anticipation of this move."
Personal interview, José Maria Benegas, Madrid, July 10, 2009.

104. On December 29, Zapatero . . . better off than we are today.'"
Quoted in Elaine Sciolino, "Spanish Prime Minister Takes Political Heat After Airport Attack by Basque Group," *The New York Times*, January 14, 2007.

105. "ETA assumed responsibility . . . or divided lines of authority."
José Maria Benegas, who has been a key behind-the-scenes operative for numerous Socialist governments with ETA, has speculated that the ETA leadership misconstrued the December talks. For this meeting, ETA had replaced its lead negotiator with a new individual who didn't have any information on what had been discussed and agreed upon in previous talks. When he reported back, the ETA leadership misunderstood the government's position and this confusion may have contributed to ETA deciding to bomb Barajas airport. Personal interview, José Maria Benegas, Madrid, July 10, 2009.

106. "The leader of the opposition . . . fooled by a pack of murders.'"
The New York Times, January 16, 2007. Zapatero's hopes for reviving the peace process remained undaunted. In March 2007, in a nod to ETA the government floated the idea that an ETA prisoner convicted of twenty-five murders might be allowed to serve out the remainder of his sentence at home. A strong public backlash, including a protest march involving hundreds of thousands of people in Madrid, caused the Zapatero government to retreat. *The New York Times*, June 9, 2007.

107. The prime minister . . . defend the public's safety."
The New York Times, June 6, 2007.

108. "He though he had . . . the golden touch."
Personal interview, José Luis Zubizarreta, Bilbao, July 16, 2009.

109. "The former ETA-PM members . . . when they were down.'"
Personal interview, Teo Uriarte, Bilbao, July 15, 2009.

110. "When I raised . . . 'We've made many mistakes.'"
Personal interview, Arnaldo Ortegi, San Sebastian, July 14, 2009.

111. "It is instead dominated . . . longer-term strategy."
"ETA's history has shown that the young entrants are unmistakably more radical, more uncompromising and less interested in negotiating." Daniele Conversi, *The Basques, the Catalans and Spain: Alternative Routes to Nationalist Mobilization* (Reno: University of Nevada Press, 1997), p. 251.

112. "Not surprisingly . . . favored ETA's dismantlement."
José M. Ruiz Soroa, "The Nationalist Canon," in *Presentation of the Political Reality in the Basque Country: From Defamation to Tragedy* (Fundación para la Libertad: Bilbao, 2008), pp. 17, 19.

113. "For example, Aznar complained . . . to the French authorities."
Personal interview, José Maria Aznar, Washington, D.C., September 30, 2009.

114. "Observed a knowledgeable Basque commentator . . . continue to be located in France.'"
Gurruchaga, *Talking to Terrorists*, p. 238.

115. "According to Florencio Dominguez . . . the past thirty years.'"
Personal interview, Florencio Dominguez, Bilbao, July 16, 2009.

116. "According to the Basque PNV . . . authority to take this decision?'"
Personal interview, Joseba Egibar, San Sebastián, July 14, 2009.

117. Again Dominguez . . . who also controls the military.'"
Personal interview, Florencio Dominguez, Bilbao, July 16, 2009.

118. José Maria Benegas also noted . . . that this has to end.'"
Personal interview, José Maria Benegas, Madrid, July 10, 2009.

119. "'Why does ETA . . . are clearly impossible?'"
Clark, *The Basque Insurgents*, pp. 274–75.

120. "As it plainly stated . . . 'process of nation-building.'"
Quoted in Alonso, "Pathways out of Terrorism in Northern Ireland and the Basque Country," p. 697.

121. "When leaders are arrested, they are replaced."
On May 20, 2010, Spanish and French authorities arrested ETA's latest military commander, the sixth ETA leader to be arrested in Spain or France the past two years. See Raphael Minder, "Alleged Basque Rebel Leader Arrested," *New York Times*, May 20, 2010, http://www.nytimes.com/2010/05/21/world/europe/21spain.html.

122. "Calls by prisoners . . . are ignored."
In a 2009 letter from prison, one of ETA's toughest leaders, José Maria Matanzas, called on ETA to end the war and form a political party instead. "The law has choked us and let's see who is bold enough to say we are invincible," he wrote. "Let's stop kidding ourselves—stop acting from our guts, stop crying like children at what we couldn't defend as men. Let's face our future." *El Pais*, July 20, 2009.

123. "'After the Franco years . . . the more ETA kills.'"
Personal interview, José Maria Benegas, Madrid, July 9, 2009.

124. "'At the start, the problem is . . . violence now has no use.'"
Personal interview, Arnaldo Otegi, San Sebastián, July 14, 2009.

125. "'Inevitably, sooner or later . . . It will take both sides.'"
Personal interview, Eugenio Etxebeste, San Sebastián, July 13, 2009.

126. "The security and intelligence . . . he maintained."
Personal interview, José Maria Aznar, Washington, D.C., September 30, 2009.

3. The Liberation Tigers of Tamil Eelam (LTTE)

1. "The body was then burned and the ashes scattered."
   In March 2010 in Colombo, I was shown the LTTE's phone logs and photographs of Prabhakaran immediately after he had been killed. There is still some mystery as to how Prabhakaran died, whether by Sri Lankan forces, by his own men, or by his own hand. Karuna maintains that Prabhakaran shot himself with his Glock 17. Personal interview, Karuna Amman, Colombo, March 8, 2010.

2. "The FBI has stated . . . including Al Qaeda in Iraq.'"
   www.fbi.gov/page2/jan08/tamil_tigers011008.html.

3. "Ethnic conflict was . . . from the British in 1948."
   "The only other example of ethnic riots in [the twentieth] century—fueled by religious irritations and commercial competition—was the Sinhalese-Muslim riots of 1915, which the British stamped out with severity and some misguided actions." S. J. Tambiah, *Ethnic Fratricide and the Dismantling of Democracy* (Chicago: University of Chicago Press, 1991), p. 13.

4. "With political and legal . . . demands for a separate state."
   Under section 29 of the 1947 constitution, no law could confer favor on any ethnic community, but the Supreme Court ruled that the Sinhala Only Official Language Act of 1956 did not violate the constitution. I am indebted to Bradman Weerakoon for pointing this out to me. Personal correspondence with the author, April 8, 2010.

5. "In the eastern province . . . significantly outnumbered Tamils."
   The tendency to characterize the Sri Lankan civil war as simply an ethnic conflict has been challenged by a number of scholars. See Tambiah, *Ethnic Fratricide*; Jonathan Spencer, ed., *Sri Lanka: History and the Roots of the Conflict* (London: Routledge, 1990); and Asoka Bandarage, *The Separatist Conflict in Sri Lanka: Terrorism, Ethnicity, Political Economy* (London: Routledge, 2009).

6. "Estimates of those killed . . . made homeless."
   See Tambiah, *Ethnic Fratricide*, esp. pp. 13–64; and Bandarage, *The Separatist Conflict in Sri Lanka*, pp. 104–9. For a summary of ethnic violence in Sri Lanka since independence, see H. P. Chattopadhyay, *Ethnic Unrest in Modern Sri Lanka* (New Delhi: MD Publications, 1994).

7. "Empowering the militants . . . providing that leverage."
   Thomas Abraham, "The Emergence of the LTTE and the Indo–Sri Lanka Agreement of 1987," in Rupersinghe, ed., *Negotiating Peace in Sri Lanka*, vol. 1, pp. 12–13. For an explanation of Indian policy during this period, see J. N. Dixit, "Indian Involvement in Sri Lanka and the Indo–Sri Lanka Agreement of 1987: A Retrospective Evaluation," in Rupersinghe, ed., *Negotiating Peace in Sri Lanka*, vol. 1, pp. 23–39; and J. N. Dixit, *Assignment Colombo* (Delhi: Konark, 1998).

8. "With the influx of . . . with over 10,000 members."
   A main reason for its growth was that RAW privileged the LTTE over the other Tamil militant groups. See Rohan Gunaratna, *Indian Intervention in Sri Lanka: The Role of India's Intelligence Agencies* (Colombo: South Asian Network on Conflict Research, 1993). Also, India's role in creating a separate Bangladesh from Pakistan in 1971 had fired the imaginations of young Tamil recruits.

9. "For its own narrow purposes . . . of the Sri Lankan state."
   India's close attention to Sri Lanka was also linked to Delhi's desire to keep foreign powers from gaining influence in South Asia. Delhi was suspicious of Sri Lanka's tilt toward the West for development assistance and foreign investment, the U.S. interest in the deep-water harbor at Trincomalee, VOA broadcasting facilities on the island, and the leasing of an oil tank farm. See John Gooneratne, *A Decade of Confrontation*, pp. 100–117. The terms of the 1987 Indo–Sri Lankan Accord addressed India's concerns in these areas.

10. "The Sri Lankan delegation . . . independent Tamil state."
    On the fourth "principle," Colombo was open to giving citizenship to Indian Tamils. Bandarage

MITCHELL B. REISS

comments that the Thimpu principles were similar to previous Tamil demands, but for the phrase "Tamil Nation" replacing the earlier "Tamil-speaking peoples." This new formulation was designed to exclude Tamil-speaking Muslims living in the northern and eastern provinces. Bandarage, *The Separatist Conflict in Sri Lanka*, p. 126.

11. "A few weeks later . . . angering their Indian hosts."
For an appraisal of the Thimpu talks that is critical of both delegations, see Sumanasiri Liyanage, "Re-reading Thimpu Principles: An Integrative Perspective," in Kumar Rupesinghe, ed., *Negotiating Peace in Sri Lanka: Efforts, Failures and Lessons*, vol. 1, 2d ed. (Colombo: Foundation for Co-Existence, 2006), pp. 1–8.

12. "The LTTE used this . . . the military camps."
Personal interview, former Sri Lankan security adviser, Colombo, March 8, 2010.

13. "Their refusal exposed . . . of a separate Tamil state."
"[India] hoped to create a 'coalition of willing parties' inclined to a negotiated solution . . . to try and ensure that the militant factions were kept in line so that they could be prevailed upon later to participate in negotiations." M. K. Narayan, "Role of Intelligence and Security Agencies," in Rupesinghe, ed., *Negotiating Peace in Sri Lanka*, vol. 1, p. 107.

14. "The next day . . . disregarding Sri Lanka's sovereignty."
See John Gooneratne, *A Decade of Confrontation: Sri Lanka and India in the 1980s* (Colombo: Stamford Lake, 2000); and M. R. Narayan Swamy, *Tigers of Lanka: From Boys to Guerrillas*, 8th ed. (Colombo: Vijitha Yapa Publications, 2008) pp. 199–246.

15. "The accord provoked . . . of the country's sovereignty."
At this time, the Janatha Vimukthi Peramuna (JVP), a Marxist Sinhalese political party, reemerged, and an offshoot, the Deshapremi Janatha Viyaparaya (DJV), emerged. Both were Sinhalese nationalist parties, strongly opposed to Indian intervention and the Sri Lankan government. See Rohan Gunaratna, *Sri Lanka: A Lost Revolution? The Inside Story of the JVP* (Kandy: Institute of Fundamental Studies, 1990).

16. "A joint Indo-Sri Lankan . . . help enforce the ceasefire."
The Accord also angered Sinhalese nationalists for both procedural and substantive reasons. President Jayewardene signed it without seeking the approval of his cabinet or parliament. The Accord also subordinated Sri Lanka's sovereignty over foreign policy to India's strategic interests. In an exchange of letters associated with the Accord, India made clear that it would determine aspects of Colombo's foreign policy relating to the use of Trincomalee harbor and the use of Sri Lanka for foreign broadcasting. It also entered into a joint lease arrangement with Sri Lanka for the Trincomalee oil tanker farm. These terms were seen as an attempt to "reduce the country to a client state, to Sikkimise it." Gooneratne, *A Decade of Confrontation*, p. 172. On the faltering efforts to implement the Accord's merger of the northern and eastern provinces, see Ketheshwaran Loganathan, "Indo–Sri Lanka Accord and the Ethnic Question: Lessons and Experiences," in Rupesinghe, ed., *Negotiating Peace in Sri Lanka*, vol. 1, pp. 65–97.

17. "The Indo-Sri Lankan Accord was a failure in almost every way."
An exception was that the IPKF allowed Colombo to shift its military forces to the south, where it was facing an insurrection by the JVP and DJV.

18. "At the meeting . . . represented on the council."
See Gooneratne, *A Decade of Confrontation*, pp. 157–62.

19. "Gandhi may have had . . . reneged on his word."
Ibid., p. 160. The LTTE only ever made a token surrender of weapons.

20. "Sure enough . . . state of Tamil Eelam."
Swamy, *Tigers of Lanka*, p. 244; Swamy, *Inside an Elusive Mind: Prabhakaran*, 6th ed. (Colombo: Vijitha Yapa Publications, 2008.), pp. 150–64.

21. "More important . . . Tamil National Army."
See Bradman Weerakoon, "Government of Sri Lanka-LTTE Peace Negotiations, 1989/1990," in

282

Rupesinghe, ed., *Negotiating Peace in Sri Lanka*, vol. 1, pp. 111–27; Weerakoon, *Rendering unto Caesar* (Colombo: Vijitha Yapa Publications, 2006), pp. 282–90; Dayan Jayatilleke, "The Prema-dasa-LTTE Talks: Why They Failed and What Really Happened," in Rupesinghe, ed., *Negotiating Peace in Sri Lanka*, vol. 1, pp. 141–55; Cyril Ranatunga, "Negotiating Peace in Sri Lanka: The Role of the Military," in Rupesinghe, ed., *Negotiating Peace in Sri Lanka* (London: International Alert, 1998), pp. 136–39 [this essay was left out of the subsequent two-volume publication]; and Swamy, *Inside an Elusive Mind*, pp. 207–9. Weerakoon describes Premadasa's reasoning as "convoluted thinking for the high-risk venture he had embarked upon." See Weerakoon, *Rendering unto Caesar*, p. 287.

22. "He could now claim . . . largest army in the world.'"
The LTTE, with help from the diaspora, extolled Prabhakaran and the LTTE's resistance in a two-volume book on the Indian military intervention, called *The Satanic Force*.

23. "After the IPKF left . . . confined to barracks."
David Little, "Sri Lanka: The Invention of Enmity," (Washington, D.C.: USIP, 1994), p. 8. The government had engaged in "no clear thinking about who was to fill the vacuum: the Army, the LTTE or was there to be some type of joint control?" Bradman Weerakoon, "Government of Sri Lanka-LTTE Peace Negotiations, 1989/1990," in Rupesinghe, ed., *Negotiating Peace in Sri Lanka*, vol. 1, p. 122.

24. "It continued its . . . Tamil separate state."
Bandarage, *The Separatist Conflict in Sri Lanka*, p. 153.

25. "A suicide bomber . . . scheduled for late October."
Earlier, in September 1994, the LTTE had sunk the Sri Lankan navy's largest battleship. The LTTE also had discouraged people in areas under its control from voting in the November 1994 presidential elections.

26. "Committees were empowered to monitor the ceasefire."
The full text of the Declaration can be found in Anton Balasingham, *The Politics of Duplicity: Re-visiting the Jaffna Talks* (Surrey: Fairmax, 2000), pp. 64–66. Balasingham served as the LTTE's chief negotiator for the Jaffna talks.

27. "Underscoring that the country . . . Killing twenty-two sailors."
For an excellent analysis of the talks, see P. Rajanayagam, "Govt.-LTTE Negotiations 1994–1995: Another Lost Opportunity," in Rupesinghe, ed., *Negotiating Peace in Sri Lanka*, vol. 1, pp. 157–214. For a view sympathetic to the LTTE, see S. J. Emmanuel, "Kumaratunga-Prabhakaran Talks: A Northern View," in Rupesinghe, ed., *Negotiating Peace in Sri Lanka* (London: International Alert, 1998), pp. 271–85 [this essay was left out of the subsequent two-volume publication]. Balasingham reproduced the LTTE-Government of Sri Lanka correspondence in *The Politics of Duplicity*.

28. "The goal, she declared . . . the negotiating table."
Kumaratunga had further polished her peace credentials by promoting an unprecedented "devolution package" in July 1995 that would have provided "more extensive devolution decentralization of power from the center to the regions than previously proposed." Bandarage, *The Separatist Conflict in Sri Lanka*, pp. 156–57. Balasingham unsurprisingly saw this step, and the peace talks, as part of a larger plan to defeat the LTTE. "In our case we confronted a cleverly devised trap. It was a peace trap for a long-term war. The central aim behind the government's strategy was to gain national and international support for a massive war effort to invade the north. Such support could only be obtained on proven grounds that the Tigers were not amenable to a peaceful political resolution of the conflict." Balasingham, *The Politics of Duplicity*, p. 2.

29. "Human rights groups . . . summary executions."
See Bandarage, *The Separatist Conflict in Sri Lanka*, pp. 163–64.

30. "According to an American military analyst . . . killed over 1,400 soldiers."
John H. Gill, "Tigers in the Trenches," presentation at the International Studies Association, New Orleans, February 16, 2010.

31. "In 2000, an estimated . . . military officers."
    See Bandarage, *The Separatist Conflict in Sri Lanka*, p. 169.

32. "She once called him 'the most corrupt man in my government.'"
    Personal interview, Ambassador C. Mahendran, Colombo, March 9, 2010. Corruption appeared to be a persistent problem among the senior military. During the George W. Bush administration, the United States offered to gift a retiring naval vessel to help the Sri Lankan navy interdict LTTE arms shipments. The offer of a free ship was originally refused. The reason given was that Colombo did not want a "used" ship. Telephone interview, former senior U.S. government official, March 25, 2010. A free ship would not offer the military the chance to reap "commissions" that the purchase of a new ship would. Ultimately, Colombo took the ship and used it effectively against the LTTE.

33. "During late 1999 . . . route to the mainland."
    According to Nanda Godage, a former senior Sri Lankan official, the civilian and military authorities had advance warning of the vulnerability of the military positions at Elephant Pass and in the Vanni but did not act in time. Personal interview, Colombo, March 7, 2010.

34. "Sri Lanka contracted . . . help end the conflict"
    Personal interview, G. L. Peiris, Colombo, March 11, 2010.

35. "Prabhakaran immediately requested . . . that favored he LTTE."
    The LTTE used ceasefire offers to demonstrate internationally that it was committed to peace and to avoid confrontation with the armed forces when it needed to bring in shiploads of military equipment. Personal correspondence, Bernard Goonetilleke, March 9, 2010.

36. "Ranil Wickremasinghe became the prime minister."
    Cited in Jayadeva Uyangoda, "Government-LTTE Negotiation Attempt of 2000 Through Norwegian Facilitation: Context, Complexities and Lessons," in Rupesinghe, ed., *Negotiating Peace in Sri Lanka*, vol. 1, p. 238. By the time of the election, over 21,000 members of the security forces and over 26,000 civilians had died. Bradman Weerakoon, "Initiating and Sustaining the Peace Process: Origins and Challenges," in Rupesinghe, ed., *Negotiating Peace in Sri Lanka*, vol. 2 (Colombo: Foundation for Co-existence, 2006), p. 32.

37. "Prabhakaran and Wickremasinghe . . . before the month was out."
    The two sides had been in communication via the Norwegians prior to the December 2001 elections. Personal interview, Ambassador. C. Mahendran, Colombo, March 9, 2010. According to General Kapila Hendawitharana, then the head of military intelligence, the security forces could have finished off the LTTE by early 2002. "We could've definitely defeated the LTTE at that time." The LTTE was down to 2,000 cadres, it was taking casualties, its frontline troops were down to a day's rations, and there was infighting between cadres from the northern and eastern provinces. "The ground reality was that Prabhakaran wanted a cease fire to buy time." When the general briefed the prime minister on the military situation, Wickremasinghe ridiculed what he called a flawed analysis and told the military to pull back their forces. The briefing was then described as a "half-baked" intelligence report in a leak to the press. Personal interview, General Kapila Hendawitharana, Colombo, March 9, 2010. Karuna Amman endorsed this view in his untitled presentation, at the conference "Engaging the Tamil Tigers: Lessons from a Failed Peace Process," Colombo, March 8, 2010.

38. "With Norway's assistance . . . in February 2002."
    The text of the CFA can be found in BBC News, February 22, 2002, *http://news.bbc.co.uk/2/hi/south_asia/1836198.stm*. For a detailed analysis of the CFA and its implementation, see Austin Fernando, *My Belly Is White* (Colombo: Vijitha Yapa, 2008). Fernando was Sri Lanka's defense secretary during this period.

39. "The Sri Lankan . . . agreement went forward."
    See John Gooneratne, *Negotiating with the Tigers (LTTE) (2002–2005): A View from the Second Row* (Colombo: Stamford Lake, 2007), pp. 10–12. During this time, Gooneratne was a senior member of the government's Secretariat for Coordinating the Peace Process (SCOPP). It was later

reported that the Indians had helped draft the CFA. Austin Fernando, presentation, conference on "Engaging the Tamil Tigers: Lessons from a Failed Peace Process," Colombo, March 8, 2010.

40. "In practice . . . Norway's faxes to the LTTE."
This information has been confirmed separately by two individuals with personal knowledge of these intercepts. Personal communication with the author, April 2010.

41. "It should have resisted more strongly."
See the interview, Erik Solheim, in Rupesinghe, ed., *Negotiating Peace in Sri Lanka*, vol. 2, p. 339. For a balanced assessment of the SLMM, see Priyan Seneviratne and Dinidu Endaragalle, "The Ceasefire Agreement—Violations, Violence and the Role of the SLMM," in Rupesinghe, ed., *Negotiating Peace in Sri Lanka*, vol. 2, pp. 115–47.

42. "The mistrust and dysfunction . . . peace efforts with the LTTE."
Anton Balasingham used this phrase during the negotiations to describe the Sri Lankan government. Personal interview, G. L. Peiris, Colombo, March 11, 2010. Balasingham would sometimes taunt his government counterpart, asking whether he would be able to win the president's approval if Balasingham agreed with his position. Personal correspondence, former senior government official directly involved in the peace talks, March 20, 2010.

43. "At an international media event . . . independent Tamil homeland."
See Bandarage, *The Separatist Conflict in Sri Lanka*, p. 184.

44. "Starting in September 2002 . . . Norway, Germany and Japan."
A record of the six rounds, complete with formal statements and press conferences, can be found at *www.peaceinsrilanka.org/*. Under Sri Lanka's Prevention of Terrorism Act, it was a crime for any Sri Lankan to engage in any sort of activity with members of the LTTE. Consequently, the government amended the Act in September 2002 before the first round of talks. An insider's account is provided by Gooneratne, *Negotiating with the Tigers*.
   Curiously, the LTTE agreed quickly to the CFA, yet was unwilling to commit to a formal peace process until seven more months had passed. This suggests that Prabhakaran tried to use the political calendar to his advantage. By waiting until only a few months remained before the end of Wickremasinghe's first year in office, he may have tried to take advantage of the prime minister's eagerness for a peace deal before President Kumaratunga could threaten to bring down his government. I am indebted to Shanaka Jayasekara for this point. Personal correspondence with the author, April 11, 2010.

45. "At the first round . . . 'the democratic, political mainstream.'"
The tenor of Balasingham's remarks were undercut at the same press conference by his threatening to kill one of the reporters who asked him about the conflict between his pledge to have the LTTE enter the democratic process and the LTTE's reported death threats against Sri Lanka citizens.

46. "In his annual Heroes Day . . . within a single state."
Prabhakaran had stated, "We are prepared to consider favorably a political framework that that offers substantial regional autonomy and self-government in our homeland on the basis of our right to internal self-determination." Cited in Gooneratne, *Negotiating with the Tigers,* pp. 27–28.

47. "His role subsequently . . . LTTE's negotiating strategy."
Gooneratne, *Negotiating with the Tigers*, p. 45; personal interview, G. L. Peiris, Colombo, March 11, 2010; Bernard Goonetilleke, "A Critical Assessment of the Norwegian-Brokered Peace Process," paper presented at the conference "Engaging the Tamil Tigers: Lessons from a Failed Peace Process," Colombo, March 8, 2010, p. 42.

48. "Whatever the true reason . . . talks in Colombo's favor."
Anton Balasingham, *War and Peace: Armed Struggle and the Peace Efforts of Liberation Tigers* (Surrey: Fairmax, 2004), p. 434. See also K. Venkataramanan, "Dilemmas of External Actors," in *Sri Lanka: Peace Without Process*, ed. by B. Raman, N. Sathiya Moorthy, and Kalpana Chittaranjan (New Delhi: Samskriti, 2006), pp. 216–17.

49. "The timing of the walkout . . . pledged by the Donors."
Fifty-one countries and twenty international institutions participated in the June 2003 Tokyo Donors Conference. Pledges totaled $4.5 billion. Distribution of funds was conditioned on the LTTE's renouncing terror and a final settlement that enshrined human rights, the rule of law, and democratic principles.

50. "The LTTE rejected them all."
See Gooneratne, *Negotiating with the Tigers*, pp. 78–89.

51. "The ISGA was a blueprint . . . power-sharing within a single state."
See Goonetilleke, "A Critical Assessment of the Norwegian-Brokered Peace Process," p. 36. The Sri Lankan government had established the Peace Secretariat in January 2002 to backstop the negotiations.

52. "She had long believed . . . regroup and rearm."
The LTTE had tried to assassinate Kumaratunga in December 1999, but ended up blinding her in one eye. During a National Security Council debate, the defense minister explained that sometimes it was necessary to turn a blind eye to LTTE violations of the CFA. The president upbraided the defense minister, saying that she was better equipped to make that judgment. Bradman Weerakoon, "Initiating and Sustaining the Peace Process: Origins and Challenges," in Rupesinghe, ed., *Negotiating Peace in Sri Lanka*, vol. 2, p. 7.

53. "Influential members of the . . . subscribed to this same assumption."
See Gill, "Tigers in the Trenches," presentation at the International Studies Association, New Orleans, February 16, 2010.

54. "As the government's chief negotiator . . . two sides of the same coin.'"
G. L. Peiris, "The Ceasefire Agreement: Problems and Prospects," in Rupesinghe, ed., *Negotiating Peace in Sri Lanka*, vol. 2, p. 109.

55. "Only one soldier died . . . LTTE forward defense zone."
See Austin Fernando, *My Belly Is White*, p. 49. The LTTE killed twenty-four intelligence agents during this period, however, and continued to murder and intimidate its Tamil, Muslim, and Sinhalese opponents and rivals.

56. "The LTTE appeared to . . . positive and constructive atmosphere."
There is one more argument made by proponents of the peace process: it led to the defection of Colonel Karuna, which seriously eroded the LTTE's military capability and image as the sole representative of the Tamil people. Under this interpretation, the peace process exposed Karuna to a world far from the jungle that opened his eyes to a different future. He was therefore more willing to back the Oslo communiqué's formula and to later break with Prabhakaran and the LTTE. A different take on the Karuna defection was that the peace talks allowed Prabhakaran the ability to focus on issues other than the day-to-day prosecution of the war, such as the organization's finances. This enabled him to discover Karuna's embezzlement, which led to threats to kill him. Either way, according to Milinda Moragoda, a member of the government's negotiating team, "Karuna was a product of the peace process." Remarks, the conference "Engaging the Tamil Tigers: Lessons from a Failed Peace Process," Colombo, March 8, 2010.

57. "According to the lead negotiator . . . even at a basic level.'"
G. L. Peiris, in Rupesinghe, ed., *Negotiating Peace in Sri Lanka*, vol. 2, p. 102.

58. "Their rivalry distorted . . . impossible to implement any."
Personal correspondence, former senior government official directly involved in the peace talks, March 20, 2010.

59. "His chief negotiator believed . . . decision on what to do.'"
Personal interview, G. L. Peiris, Colombo, March 11, 2010.

60. "Whenever he transgressed . . . confronted him head on."
Ibid. Kumar Rupesinghe, one of the most articulate liberal voices for peace in Sri Lanka, has writ-

ten, "It is assumed that through a process of *constructive engagement* that the LTTE will change its character and transform itself into a democratic entity. This assumption is based on experiences elsewhere, where guerrilla movements have entered the democratic mainstream.... It is assumed that transitions from war to peace and war weariness can create the conditions for a change of attitudes." Kumar Rupesinghe, "Introduction: Evaluating the Peace Process," in Rupesinghe, ed., *Negotiating Peace in Sri Lanka*, vol. 2, p. xvii (emphasis in original). He wrote this in 2006.

61. "Another senior government official . . . from militancy and terrorism.'"
Personal interview, Colombo, March 12, 2010.

62. "There was an effort . . . from being inflamed."
Personal interview, G. L. Peiris, Colombo, March 11, 2010.

63. "Although some violations . . . the government 351."
See Bandarage, *The Separatist Conflict in Sri Lanka*, p. 191.

64. "According to one of the government's negotiators . . . appease the Tigers."
Goonetilleke, "A Critical Assessment of the Norwegian-Brokered Peace Process," p. 17.

65. "A member of the government's . . . contained in the CFA."
Gooneratne, *Negotiating with the Tigers*, p. 114.

66. "It didn't really stand up . . . very well analytically."
Personal interview, G. L. Peiris, Colombo, March 11, 2010.

67. "Karuna also confirmed . . . LTTE built up its arms."
Personal interview, Karuna Amman, Colombo, March 7, 2010; see also *http://www.peaceinsrilanka.org/negotiations/ceasefire-agreement-20028*.

68. "So perhaps it is not . . . never on their agenda.'"
Personal interview, G. L. Peiris, Colombo, March 11, 2010.

69. "'Norway, knowing the roadblocks, resisted.'"
Bernard Goonetilleke, personal correspondence, March 9, 2010. See also Goonetilleke, "A Critical Assessment of the Norwegian-Brokered Peace Process," pp. 13–14.

70. "One of the negotiators . . . toward the deep end.'"
Remarks by Milinda Moragoda, conference "Engaging the Tamil Tigers: Lessons from a Failed Peace Process," Colombo, March 8, 2010.

71. "With only 70 personnel . . . violations of the CFA.'"
Goonetilleke, "A Critical Assessment of the Norwegian-Brokered Peace Process," p. 21.

72. "A march 2003 . . . 95 percent of Tamils."
Cited in K. Alan Kronstadt, "Sri Lanka: Background and U.S. Relations," *CRS Report for Congress*, January 22, 2008, p. 14. Terrorist or insurgent groups rarely have the same type of constituent pressure as governments.

73. "In June 2001 . . . facilitation efforts."
See "LTTE accuses Norway of breaching neutrality," *The Island* (June 12, 2001), *www.island.lk/2001/06/12/news01.html*.

74. "It meant that neither . . . 'diplomatic immunity.'"
Under this parity-of-status approach, the LTTE believed it should be allowed to import weapons, since Colombo was doing so. At a conference on the peace process in Colombo in March 2010, Karuna was asked point blank if LTTE members had used international travel to the peace talks as an opportunity to buy weapons. Karuna cheerfully said yes, and then gave specific examples, like smuggling sniper scopes back into Sri Lanka in the LTTE delegation's luggage. At this same conference, the former defense secretary Austin Fernando and other former officials stated that both the military and the government knew of these actions at the time. Remarks, conference "Engaging the Tamil Tigers: Lessons from a Failed Peace Process," Colombo, March 8, 2010. Karuna claimed that on at least one occasion he used prostitutes as cover to walk by security and leave the Novotel

Hotel in Bangkok so he could meet with LTTE weapons dealers. Personal interview, Karuna Amman, Colombo, March 8, 2010. The LTTE's preferred method of smuggling weapons was by sea.

75. "At its most extreme . . . the Sri Lankan navy."
The Norwegian author of this proposal was later sent home by President Kumaratunga after he allegedly tipped off the LTTE that one of its boats was under government surveillance. See Austin Fernando, *My Belly Is White*, pp. 611–18. Norway should have been aware that India was also concerned about the rise of a "third navy" in the Indian Ocean. For other complaints about Norway's behavior, see Shanaka Jayesekara, "The Role of Norwegian Facilitation in the Sri Lankan Peace Process," presentation at the conference "Engaging the Tamil Tigers: Lessons from a Failed Peace Process," Colombo, March 8, 2010.

76. "One of her own officials . . . 'water off a duck's back.'"
Gooneratne, *Negotiating with the Tigers*, p. 116.

77. "'In defecting from the LTTE . . . and spoken for them.'"
Bandarage, *The Separatist Conflict in Sri Lanka*, p. 195.

78. "When I talked with him . . . provided the terror.'"
Personal interview, Karuna Amman, Colombo, March 7, 2010.

79. "Karuna and his senior officers . . . meet the media."
Personal interview, General Kapila Hendawitharana, Colombo, March 9, 2010. The LTTE subsequently demanded that the government disarm Karuna and his men under Article 1.8 of the CFA.

80. "Rajapaksa's slim margin . . . vote for Wickremasinghe."
According to Karuna, Prabhakaran opposed Wickremasinghe because he feared that Wickremasinghe would revive the "international safety net" to try to trap the LTTE. Personal interview, Karuna Amman, Colombo, March 8, 2010.

81. "A few months later . . . government negotiators."
According to Palitha Kohona, who was a special adviser to the president on the peace process at this time and a member of the government's delegation to these meetings, the LTTE walked out of the Geneva meeting after the government insisted that the issue of child soldiers be discussed. He did not know why the LTTE refused to meet with the government delegation in Oslo. Personal interview, Palitha Kohona, New York, April 22, 2010. Bradman Weerakoon has said that the LTTE, in both Geneva and Oslo, wanted Colombo to stop supporting Karuna and his paramilitary organization, which it maintained was a violation of the CFA. The government parried that the CFA's language only referred to non-LTTE paramilitaries. Personal communication with the author, April 13, 2010.

82. "And most important . . . international pressure."
See Don Wijewardana, *How LTTE Lost the Eelam War* (Colombo: Stamford Lake, 2010), pp. 112–40.

83. "After being contacted . . . International Committee of the Red Cross."
Personal interview, Tore Hattrem, Colombo, March 10, 2010. Hattrem's account was independently confirmed by knowledgeable American sources. Telephone interview, March 16, 2010. Hattrem and the American ambassador in Colombo at this time, Robert Blake, have been accused of meeting with KP to try to find a way to extract Prabhakaran, his family, and his senior military men from the north and bring them to a third country as the government's forces slowly tightened the cordon around them. I found no evidence to support this very serious allegation. In fact, I learned that each diplomat used the media during this period to explain that the LTTE was shooting Tamil civilians so that the Tamil diaspora would halt its support for the LTTE.

84. "The deaths of Prabhakaran . . . 'has crippled the organization.'"
International Crisis Group, *Sri Lanka: A Bitter Peace* (January 11, 2010), p. 14. A subsequent International Crisis Group report has charged Sri Lanka, during the January-to-May 2009 time period, with killing "tens of thousands of Tamil civilian men, women, children and the elderly,"

with more wounded and "hundreds of thousands deprived of adequate food and medical care." See *War Crimes in Sri Lanka*, Asia Report No. 191, May 17, 2010, *www.crisisgroup.org/en/regions/ asia/south-asia/sri-lanka/191-war-crimes-in-sri-lanka.aspx*. An authoritative, objective source in Sri Lanka has estimated the death toll at 7,000 to 8,000 from January through the end of April 2009. Personal interview with the author, Colombo, March 2010.

85. "It's a tribal system . . . dealing with the LTTE.'"
Personal interview, Milinda Moragoda, Colombo, March 9, 2010; Moragoda remarks, conference "Engaging the Tamil Tigers: Lessons from a Failed Peace Process," Colombo, March 8, 2010.

86. "For example, many . . . were in government."
Austin Fernando is emphatic on this point, in *My Belly Is White*, passim; and in his paper "Revisiting the Peace Process of the United National Front Government (Security Issues)," presented at the conference "Engaging the Tamil Tigers: Lessons from a Failed Peace Process," Colombo, March 8, 2010.

87. "'Cessation of the suffering . . . would make them unbeatable.'"
Personal interview, Bradman Weerakoon, Colombo, March 11, 2010.

4. THE ISLAMIC RESISTANCE MOVEMENT (HAMAS)

1. "While it also engages in . . . social and terrorist leadership.'"
See Matthew Levitt, *Hamas: Politics, Charity, and Terrorism in the Service of Jihad* (New Haven: Yale University Press, 2006), pp. 2, 34.

2. "It engages in a wide array . . . Occupied Territories."
See Khaled Hroub, *Hamas: Political Thought and Practice* (Washington, D.C.: Institute for Palestine Studies, 2000).

3. "The rise of Hamas . . . cause from Arab priorities."
Most references state that Hamas was founded in 1987. In a recent book, however, the son of one of the founders states emphatically that Hamas was founded in 1986. See Mosab Hassan Yousef, *Son of Hamas* (Carol Stream, Ill.: Saltriver, 2010), p. 19.

4. "This wave of Islamic fervor . . . Hamas's agenda."
Hroub, *Hamas: Political Thought and Practice*, p. 38.

5. "According to two Israeli scholars . . . luxurious lifestyle."
Shaul Mishal and Avraham Sela, *The Palestinian Hamas: Vision, Violence, and Coexistence* (New York: Columbia University Press, 2000), p. 89. This comment really aims at the distinction between Arafat's PLO crowd in Tunis and Hamas in the territories. Local Fatah functionaries in the West Bank were equally taken aback by the Tunis crowd and felt shoved aside when they arrived in 1994. As veteran Middle East negotiator Dennis Ross has commented, Hamas provided hope to the Palestinian people. "Before Arafat's death, Hamas registered higher levels of public support than Fatah by a total of 32 percent to 29 percent. [After Arafat's death] Hamas's standing had dropped below 20 percent and Fatah's had risen above 40 percent. . . . When there is no hope, Hamas's standing is bound to increase." Ross, *The Missing Peace: The Inside Story of the Fight for Middle East Peace* (New York: Farrar, Straus and Giroux, 2004), p. 802.

6. "From 1993 to 2002 . . . nine separate ceasefires."
Seth Wikas, *The Hamas Ceasefire: Historical Background, Future Foretold?*, Peace Watch #357, The Washington Institute for Near East Policy, January 3, 2002, *www.ciaonet.org/pbei/winep/ peace_2002/2002_357.html*.

7. "Yassin conditioned this offer . . . release all Palestinians prisoners."
Mishal and Sela, *The Palestinian Hamas*, pp. 71–72, 105–12. A *hudna* is different from a *tahdi'ah*, which is more like a declaration of nonbelligerence or a "calming" of the situation.

8. "Hamas could accept . . . from the occupied territories."
Hroub, *Hamas: Political Thought and Practice*, pp. 69–86. Another way of looking at this 1993 offer was that Hamas's starting point for peace talks with Israel was the PLO's end point.

9. "An additional element . . . political agreements with Israel."
See Paul Scham and Osama Abu-Irshaid, *Hamas: Ideological Rigidity and Political Flexibility*, U.S. Institute of Peace Special Report 224, Washington, D.C. (June 2009), *http://www.usip.org/files/resources/Special%20Report%20224_Hamas.pdf;* and Hroub, pp. 73–74.

10. "The idea of Hamas . . . repeated in subsequent years."
See, esp. the so-called Prisoners' Document, *www.jmcc.org/documents/prisoners.html*, which was a joint effort by jailed members of Hamas, Fatah, Islamic Jihad, PFLP, and the Democratic Front for the Liberation of Palestine (DFLP), issued in May 2006; and in the paper presented by Hamas to former president Jimmy Carter in April 2008. Ethan Bronner, "After Meeting Leaders, Carter Says Hamas and Syria Are Open to Peace with Israel," *The New York Times*, April 22, 2008; and Jimmy Carter, "Pariah Diplomacy," *The New York Times*, April 28, 2008.

11. "Hamas thus became . . . opposed to the peace process."
Jeroen Gunning, *Hamas in Politics* (New York: Columbia University Press, 2008), p. 39.

12. "In response, Yassin declared . . . 'crime against Islam.'"
Wikas, *The Hamas Ceasefire.*

13. "But if it supported the . . . of its historic mission."
See Mishal and Sela, *The Palestinian Hamas*, p. 103.

14. "Khalid Mesh'al, who assumed . . . an attempt to contain it.'"
Cited in Azzam-Tamimi, *Hamas: Unwritten Chapters* (London: Hurst and Co., 2009), p. 187.

15. "Its members received . . . $15 million per month."
The $15 million per-month figure is cited in McGeough, *Kill Khalid*, p. 366. Lesser amounts are cited in Levitt, pp. 172–78. Hamas has also received state support for its different activities from a number of Arab states, including Saudi Arabia, Lebanon, Syria, Qatar, Libya, and Yemen.

16. "It has not attacked Israeli . . . anywhere in the world."
Levitt believes that Hamas has planned attacks in North America. See Levitt, *Hamas: Politics, Charity, and Terrorism in the Service of Jihad*, pp. 207–10.

17. "In 2008, over 3,200 . . . to the threat."
See "Summary of Rocket Fire and Mortar Shelling in 2008," Intelligence and Terrorism Information Center, *www.terrorism-info.org.il/malam_multimedia/English/eng_n/pdf/ipc_e007.pdf.*

18. "In February 2006 . . . Israel and the United States."
Reported in *People's Daily Online, http://english.people.com.cn/200602/16/eng20060216_243064.html* February 16, 2006. Hamas representatives denied the overture had taken place.

19. "In editorials in American . . . possibility of a *hunda*."
See Khalid Mesh'al, "We Will Not Sell Our People or Principles for Foreign Aid," *The Guardian*, March 31, 2006; Musa Abu Marzuq, "What Hamas Is Seeking," *Washington Post*, January 31, 2006.

20. "Less than 12 percent . . . its political agenda."
Jerusalem Media & Communication Center (JMCC), "Palestinian Attitudes Towards the Results of the PLC Elections Held on January 25, 2006," Poll no. 57, February 2006, *www.jmcc.org/public-poll/results/2006/no57.pdf*. On Hamas's approach to elections during the 2004-to-2006 period, see Gunning, *Hamas in Politics*, pp. 143–94. It is worth noting that the secular Palestinian movement was represented by multiple parties that split the vote and that Fatah in particular ran a poor campaign characterized by internal squabbling so that multiple candidates from Fatah often ran against each other in the same district, leaving the Hamas candidate with a plurality.

21. "It appeared to succeed . . . the following month."
For a discussion of the Mecca Agreement and the developments that led up to it, see International Crisis Group, *After Mecca: Engaging Hamas*, Middle East Report No. 62 (February 28, 2007).

22. "According to Efraim Halevy . . . dissolved and disintegrated."
Personal interview, Efraim Halevy, Tel Aviv, January 27, 2010. See also Halevy, *Man in the Shadows*, pp. xiv–xv.

23. "The PA leader . . . dissolved the unity government."
For an excellent discussion of the Hamas takeover of Gaza, and the events preceding it, see International Crisis Group, *After Gaza*, Middle East Report No. 68 (August 2, 2007).

24. "Israel placed an economic . . . under a Hamas government."
See International Crisis Group, *Ruling Palestine I: Gaza Under Hamas*, Middle East Report No. 73 (March 19, 2008).

25. "General Dani Arditi . . . responsibility for the breakdown."
Personal interview, Dani Arditi, Tel Aviv, January 28, 2010. See also, Jim Zanotti, et al., "Israel and Hamas: Conflict in Gaza (2008–2009)," CRS Report for Congress, February 19, 2009, *http://assets.opencrs.com/rpts/R40101_20090219.pdf*; and Daoud Kuttab, "Has Israel Revived Hamas?" *Washington Post*, December 30, 2008.

26. "And estimated 46,000 Gaza residents were displaced."
United Nations Office for the Coordination of Humanitarian Affairs Field Update on Gaza, January 19, 2009. Available online at *www.ochaopt.org/gazacrisis/admin/output/files/ocha_opt_gaza_humanitarian_situation_report_2009_01_19_english.pdf*. The UN's Human Right's Council appointed Richard Goldstone, a South African jurist, to head an official investigation into the Gaza conflict. The Goldstone Report charged Israel with violating international law. See *http://www2.ohchr.org/english/bodies/hrcouncil/docs/12session/A-HRC-12-48.pdf*. Israel denied the charges. See Israel Ministry of Foreign Affairs, "MFA Briefing to the Foreign Press on the Goldstone Report," October 1, 2009, *www.mfa.gov.il/MFA/Government/Speeches+by+Israeli+leaders/2009/MFA_briefing_foreign_press_Goldstone_Report_1-Oct-2009.htm*. See also Moshe Halbertal, "The Goldstone Illusion," *The New Republic*, November 6, 2009.

27. "It preserved an irreducible . . . against the Jewish state."
The results of a public opinion poll conducted by the Jerusalem Media and Communications Center (JMCC) immediately after Operation Cast Lead showed that almost half of all Palestinians believed that Hamas had won the war, compared with less than 10 percent who said that Israel had won. The war had also contributed to an increase in Palestinian support for military action against Israel, with those who believed that locally made rockets helped achieve Palestinian national goals rising 10 points, to over 50 percent, from just a few months earlier. JMCC, "Palestinians' Opinions after the Gaza War," Poll no. 67, January 2009, *www.jmcc.org/publicpoll/results/2009/67_jan_english.pdf*. This is consistent with polling data that showed Palestinians believing that violence was responsible for Israel's unilateral withdrawal from Gaza in 2005, with many crediting Hamas for forcing out the Israelis.

28. "Palestinian nationalists . . . with littler interference."
See Gunning, *Hamas in Politics*, pp. 33–34; Levitt, *Hamas: Politics, Charity, and Terrorism in the Service of Jihad*, p. 10; Zaki Chehab, *Inside Hamas: The Untold Story of the Militant Islamic Movement* (New York: Nations Books, 207), p. 212.

29. "'We didn't understand . . . that Hamas could pose.'"
Personal interview, Ami Ayalon, Tel Aviv, January 28, 2010.

30. "'We supported the Muslim Brotherhood . . . It was divide and rule.'"
Personal interview, Uri Ne'eman, Tel Aviv, January 28, 2010. Another reason for Israel not worrying about empowering Hamas at this time was, according to Ne'eman, that Hamas was an outgrowth of the Muslim Brotherhood in Egypt. Cairo had kept this group weak and under tight control for years, so there was no obvious reason why Israel should worry about the Muslim Brotherhood in Palestine.

31. "As Ne'eman has explained . . . the enemies of our partners."
Personal interview, Uri Ne'eman, Tel Aviv, January 28, 2010.

32. "Hamas has now seen . . . weapon against the PLO."
The concepts of total and limited spoilers are taken from Stephen John Stedman, "Spoiler Problems in Peace Processes," *International Security*, vol. 22, no. 2 (1997), pp. 5–53; see also the discussion in Gunning, *Hamas in Politics*, pp. 195–240.

33. "Israeli officials attempted to . . . formally into the peace process."
Another motive may have been to gain bargaining leverage over the PLO by suggesting that Israel could talk to other Palestinian groups. See Hroub, *Hamas: Political Thought and Practice*, p. 206.

34. "In early 1994 . . . talking with Hamas."
See Hroub, *Hamas: Political Thought and Practice*, pp. 204–06. U.S. officials, with an agenda similar to the Israelis', had met with Hamas in Amman, Jordan, in January and February 1993. The United States broke off the talks soon after the World Trade Center bombing in February 1993. Two months later, the State Department labeled Hamas a "terrorist organization" in its annual report on terrorism and shut down its Springfield, Virginia, headquarters.

35. "During this time, Israel . . . their colleagues and supporters."
According to Ami Ayalon, Israel's outreach at this time was not about talking to Hamas specifically; it was about promoting the democratic process. With the end of the Cold War, Saddam Hussein's defeat in the First Gulf War, and the signing of the Oslo Accords, Israel's leaders thought they could now place relations with the Arab world on a new footing that would emphasize democracy and economic development. Personal interview, Ami Ayalon, Tel Aviv, January 28, 2010. See also Shimon Peres, with Arye Naor, *The New Middle East* (New York: Holt, 1993).

36. "Hamas rejected all overtures . . . negotiations, concessions, or capitulations.'"
Cited in Hroub, *Hamas: Political Thought and Practice*, p. 207.

37. "But also, as the price . . . of two Israeli soldiers."
Israeli agents had sprayed Mesh'al with a slow-acting poison that would kill him within a day or so. But their act was observed by Mesh'al's bodyguards and the agents were pursued through the streets of Amman. Two were apprehended; the others retreated to the Israeli embassy, which was surrounded by Jordanian security forces. The best account of this episode is Paul McGeough, *Kill Khalid: The Failed Mossad Assassination of Khalid Mesh'al and the Rise of Hamas* (New York: New Press, 2009). See also Efraim Halevy, *Man in the Shadows: Inside the Middle East Crisis with a Man Who Led Mossad* (New York: St. Martin's Press, 2006), pp. 164–177. Halevy writes that the *hudna* offer only reached the prime minister's desk after the Mossad operation was over. Halevy, *Man in the Shadows*, p. 166.

38. "Israeli officials are . . . side-by-side in peace."
Personal interviews, current and former Israeli officials, Tel Aviv and Jerusalem, January 2010.

39. "In October 2009 . . . female Palestinian prisoners."
Telephone interview, German Foreign Ministry official, December 30, 2009. The mediation effort is taking place in the Middle East, not Germany. The BND had previously mediated between Israel and Hezbollah over the return of Israeli soldiers' remains. BND stands for Bundesnachrichtendienst.

40. "Indeed, the case has . . . serves in the military."
Israel has long experience negotiating with terrorist groups over the release of its soldiers. It negotiated with Hamas for the return of Sergeant Nachshon Wachsman before launching a rescue operation in which he was killed in October 1994. In July 2008, in a case that divided the country, Israel exchanged five prisoners, including the notorious terrorist Samir Kuntar, along with the remains of 199 terrorists, for the bodies of two Israeli soldiers. The controversy stemmed from the bloodthirsty nature of Kuntar's crime, which contained echoes of the Holocaust because it involved an Israeli mother smothering her baby to death in an attic to prevent the cries revealing their whereabouts, and the fact that Kuntar's release was seen by some as too high a price to pay for the return of soldiers who were not alive.

41. "'We need to convince . . . It is a balancing approach.'"
Personal interview, Shaul Mofaz, Tel Aviv, January 26, 2010.

42. "Interestingly, Israel does not . . . terrorist organization."
Personal interviews, Dan Meridor, Jerusalem, January 25, 2010; Uri Ne'eman, Tel Aviv, January 28, 2010; Dani Arditi, Tel Aviv, January 28, 2010.

43. "'Hamas doesn't want to . . . a passing accident of history.'"
Personal interview, Dan Meridor, Jerusalem, January 25, 2010.

44. "That distinction is crucial . . . sake of this obliteration."
"PM Netanyahu addresses the Foreign Press Association in Israel," January 20, 2010, *www.mfa. gov.il/MFA/Government/Speeches+by+Israeli+leaders/2010/PM_Netanyahu_addresses_FPA_20-Jan-2010.html*.

45. "The country would therefore . . . most generous patron."
Following Hamas's surprise victory in the Legislative Council elections, Bibi Netanyahu declared that "Hamastan has been formed, a proxy of Iran in the image of the Taliban." Laurie Copans, "Netanyahu Stands to Gain in Israeli Election Campaign after Hamas Win," *Associated Press*, January 30, 2006. Efraim Halevy asserts that Hamas is neither a proxy nor a pawn of Tehran. "Hamas receives funds, support, equipment, and training from Iran, but is not subservient to Tehran. A serious effort to dialogue indirectly with [Hamas] could ultimately drive a wedge between them." *Mother Jones*, February 19, 2008. *www.motherjones.com/washington_dispatch/2008/02/israel-mossad-out-of-the-shadows.html*.

46. "Again, Meridor . . . God never compromises.'"
Personal interview, Dan Meridor, Jerusalem, January 25, 2010.

47. "Abbas and the PA . . . stay away from Hamas."
See, for example, "PA Warns EU Against Legitimizing Hamas Through Dialogue," *Jerusalem Post*, January 24, 2010; and International Crisis Report, *After Gaza*, pp. 16, 30–31.

48. "But these calls . . . weapons into Gaza."
Personal interview, Gerald Steinberg, Jerusalem, January 27, 2010.

49. "According to Shin Bet . . . suicide attacks inside Israel."
See *http://www.ynetnews.com/articles/0,7340,L-3827600,00.html*.

50. "Some fraying around the edges. . . Hamas's leadership-in-exile."
Earlier, British diplomats met with Hamas officials in 2005 and 2007. France also has engaged in what it described as "contacts" with Hamas. See Mark Oliver, "Straw Confirms British Contact with Hamas," June 7, 2005, *www.guardian.co.uk/politics/2005/jun/07/foreignpolicy.israel*, and "European Envoy Meets Hamas Official," April 6, 2007, *http://query.nytimes.com/gst/fullpage.html ?res=9F0DEEDC173FF935A35757C0A9619C8B63&partner=rssnyt&emc=rss*; Steven Erlanger, "France Acknowledges Contacts with Hamas Leaders," *New York Times*, May 20, 2008; Molly Moore, "France Discloses 'Contacts' With Hamas," *Washington Post*, May 20, 2008. Prominent former American officials, such as Colin Powell, Brent Scowcroft, and Zbigniew Brzezinski have recommended talking to Hamas. See also House of Commons Foreign Affairs Committee, "Global Security: Israel and the Occupied Palestinian Territories," Fifth Report of Session 2008–09, July 15, 2009, p. 5; Glenn Kessler, "Mideast Players Differ on Approach to Hamas," *Washington Post*, March 16, 2008.

51. "This process is . . . PLO under Yasser Arafat."
Shaul Mishal, quoted in *Haaretz*, April 27, 2008. "Hamas has been carefully and consciously adjusting its political program for years and has sent repeated signals that it is ready to begin a process of coexisting with Israel . . . it may be possible for Israel to deal with Hamas." Scham and Abu-Irshaid, *Hamas: Ideological Rigidity and Political Flexibility*, p. 4.

52. "Yassin was now . . . Islam's ultimate victory."
Personal interview, Ami Ayalon, Tel Aviv, Jan. 28, 2010.

53. "'Provisional until when? . . . they do not know.'"
Efraim Halevy, *Yedioth Ahronoth*, December 22, 2008.

54. "'He'd be middle-aged, with children and grandchildren.'"
Personal interview, Tel Aviv, January 27, 2010. To underscore his argument, Halevy added, "Muslims reached the gates of Vienna and declared a *hudna* that has now lasted over 350 years." A Hamas official has expressed differently what would happen when the *hudna* expires. "What would happen at the truce's expiration, they say, will be up to future generations. By then, they will have learned to live under different, more normal conditions. Who knows what they will decide?," International Crisis Group, *After Mecca: Engaging Hamas*, p. 30.

55. "Its militancy has . . . avoid the tough decisions."
Personal interview, Dani Arditi, Tel Aviv, January 28, 2010. Interestingly, the "left" in Israel may be more reluctant to engage with Hamas than the right because they would see it as betraying Fatah, the key partner for peace and the repository of hopes for a final peace settlement. ICG, *After Gaza*, p. 27, footnote 236.

56. "'So there is no need . . . a change of heart.'"
Personal interview, Yoram Hessel, Tel Aviv, January 25, 2010.

5. THE ANBAR AWAKENING (SAH'WA AL-ANBAR)

1. "This tribal movement . . . militarily 'lost' province."
See Thomas E. Ricks, "Situation Called Dire in West Iraq," *Washington Post*, September 11, 2006, www.washingtonpost.com/wp-dyn/content/article/2006/09/10/AR2006091001204.html.

2. " According to the official U.S . . . and poorly coordinated."
Donald P. Wright and Colonel Timothy R. Reese, *On Point II: Transition to the New Campaign: The United States Army in Operation Iraqi Freedom, May 2003–January 2005* (Fort Leavenworth, Kan.: Combined Studies Institute Press, 2008) (hereafter referred to as *On Point II*), p. 80. According to the U.S. Army, Phase I is Deter/Engage. Phase II is Seize the Initiative. Phase III is Decisive Operations. And Phase IV is Transition. "Phase IV is critical to military campaigns because it is during this period military success is used to finalize the achievement of national goals that that serve as the overall objectives of the campaign." *On Point II*, p. 66.

3. "And fourth . . . down state-run industries."
For an authoritative examination of the CPA, see James Dobbins, Seth G. Jones, Benjamin Runkle, and Siddharth Mohandas, *Occupying Iraq: A History of the Coalition Provisional Authority* (Santa Monica: RAND, 2009).

4. "The first two orders . . . other dependents was great."
Thomas Ricks, *Fiasco: The American Military Adventure in Iraq* (London: Penguin, 2007), pp. 161–65. There has been some controversy over whether senior members of the Bush administration knew of these decisions before Bremer announced them. According to RAND's CPA study, Bremer had briefed these issues to the president and his senior advisers, and Rumsfeld had approved the decision. See Dobbins, et al, *Occupying Iraq*, p. xv.

5. "As Jay Garner recalls . . . face on the government.'"
George Packer, *The Assassin's Gate: America in Iraq* (New York: Farrar, Straus and Giroux, 2005), p. 191. Bremer's decision to delay the transition to an Iraqi government had a greater negative impact because the United States had previously raised expectations of a far quicker handover of power to the Iraqis.

6. "We were on top . . . Curse them."
Quoted in Ali A. Allawi, *The Occupation of Iraq: Winning the War, Losing the Peace* (New Haven: Yale University Press, 2007), p. 240.

7. "For the first time . . . ascendant power *as a community.*'"
Ibid., p. 135 (emphasis in original). Six years later, Sheikh Majed Abd al-Razzaq Ali al-Sulayman, an influential Anbari sheikh, still became upset at the memory of Bremer's actions: "What he did is just like putting a bomb in this room, and the bomb explodes the whole room. He decimated everything." *Al-Anbar Awakening,* vol. 2: *Iraqi Perspectives,* Gary W. Montgomery and Timothy S. McWilliams, eds. (Quantico: Marine Corps University Press, 2009) (hereafter referred to as *Al-Anbar Awakening,* vol. 2), p. 127.

8. "'The United States upset . . . you lose for generations.'"
Personal interview, Derek Harvey, Tampa, Florida, March 29, 2010.

9. "Before the war . . . by launching an insurgency."
Packer, *The Assassin's Gate,* p. 298.

10. "The means were easily available . . . over 10,000 caches."
Allawi, *The Occupation of Iraq,* p.140. After the First Gulf War, fifteen of Iraq's eighteen provinces rose up against Saddam's rule. The Republican Guard suppressed the revolt, party with the use of chemical weapons. As contingency planning against any future internal uprisings, Saddam prepositioned weapons, ammunition, food, and forged documents in secret locations around Baghdad. After the U.S. invasion, he now used these assets to fuel the insurgency. Personal interview, Derek Harvey, Tampa, January 19, 2010.

11. "The disorder and chaos . . . provided the opportunity."
In fact, the military was planning to reduce U.S. forces in Iraq at this time. The senior commander, General Tommy Franks, told subordinates in Baghdad in mid-April to be prepared to deploy troops back home by September 2003. Later that same month, Franks recommended to Secretary of Defense Donald Rumsfeld that the First Cavalry Division, then readying for deployment to Iraq, be kept stateside. *On Point II,* p. 27.

12. "It was largely a Sunni Arab phenomenon."
Derek Harvey, "A 'Red Team' Perspective on the Insurgency in Iraq," in John J. McGrath, ed., *An Army at War: Change in the Midst of Conflict* (Fort Leavenworth, Kan.: Combat Studies Institute Press, 2005), p. 192.

13. "With unemployment at . . . way to make money."
For an excellent discussion of the insurgents' motives, see Ahmed S. Hashim, *Insurgency and Counterinsurgency in Iraq* (Ithaca: Cornell University Press, 2006), pp. 59–124. Reconstruction funds were supposed to employ idle men and dampen their interest in joining the resistance. The CPA's inability to account for $9 billion in reconstruction funding did not help matters. See Packer, *The Assassin's Gate,* p. 243. See also, Allawi, *The Occupation of Iraq,* pp. 348–69; *On Point II,* pp. 385–91.

14. "The bounty for attacking . . . vehicle was disabled."
See Dobbins, et al., *Occupying Iraq,* p. 60; and Bruce Hoffman, *Insurgency and Counterinsurgency in Iraq* (Santa Monica: RAND, 2004), p. 12. The prices increased more than fourfold in 2004.

15. "Although Saddam had welcomed . . . fraction of the insurgents."
"The impact of foreign jihadis grew over time, but during the early stages of the insurgency it appears to have been negligible, and al Qaeda in particular was absent, claiming none of the spectacular attacks orchestrated in 2003." International Crisis Group, *In Their Own Words: Reading the Iraqi Insurgency,* Middle East Report No. 50, February 15, 2006, p. 6.

16. "Most of the violence . . . 'anemic and uncoordinated.'"
On Point II, p. 32. There is an unresolved debate over whether Saddam was directing the insurgency. Before his capture in December 2003, he was on the run from American forces and meeting in cars with his former senior security and intelligence officials to activate and direct the resistance. Personal interview, Derek Harvey, Tampa, January 19, 2010. See also Joe Klein, "Saddam's Revenge," *Time,* September 18, 2005.

17. "The resistance . . . techniques and procedures.'"
    See DoD News Briefing, July 16, 2003, *www.globalsecurity.org/wmd/library/news/iraq/2003/07/iraq-030716-dod01.htm.*

18. "The violence intensified . . . UN headquarters."
    The United Nations withdrew all but a skeleton crew from Iraq. Later in August, the moderate Shi'a leader Ayatollah Mohammed Baqir al-Hakim was assassinated, along with eighty-four others, by a car bomb outside the Imam Ali Mosque in Najaf. A Gallup poll the following month showed that 94 percent of people living in Baghdad thought that the city was more dangerous after the U.S. occupation than under Saddam. Seventy percent were afraid to go out of their home during the day; 80 percent afraid to go out at night. See Dobbins, et al., *Occupying Iraq*, p. 96.

19. "In November . . . support among the people."
    See Jonathan S. Landay, "CIA Has a Bleak Analysis of Iraq," *Philadelphia Inquirer*, November 12, 2003. *http://www.globalpolicy.org/component/content/article/168/37280.html.*

20. "It was like swatting bees."
    Bing West, *The Strongest Tribe: War, Politics, and the Endgame in Iraq* (New York: Random House, 2008), p. 10.

21. "The violence and insecurity . . . further hampered their effectiveness."
    See Allawi, *The Occupation of Iraq*, p. 179; Dobbins, et al., *Occupying Iraq*, pp. 98–99; Hoffman, *Insurgency and Counter-Insurgency in Iraq*, pp. 10–11.

22. "We only had 25 . . . a bare minimum."
    Personal interview, Ben Connable, Williamsburg, Virginia, February 27, 2010. Connable alone managed all the translators and interpreters in Anbar province for the first half of 2004.

23. "As more soldiers died . . . than they were regenerating."
    Vernon Loeb, "Rumsfeld Seeks Better Intelligence on Iraqi Insurgents," *Washington Post*, December 11, 2003. Some military officers believed that this pressure to gather intelligence led directly to the abuses at Abu Ghraib prison. See Thomas E. Ricks, *The Gamble: General David Petraeus and the American Military Adventure in Iraq, 2006–2008* (New York: Penguin, 2009), p. 39.

24. "The Iraqi commander . . . U.S. troops into the cities."
    Al-Anbar Awakening, vol. 2, pp. 45, 195–96. See also Allawi, *The Occupation of Iraq*, p. 90.

25. "Complicating stability and security . . . seen as a sideshow."
    Keith Mines, personal manuscript provided to the author, March 2010. From August 2003 to February 2004, Mines served as the governance coordinator for the CPA in Al Anbar. The Pentagon had decided in January 2003 to delete a division from the invasion force that would have been assigned to control Anbar. Ricks, *Fiasco*, p. 84.

26. "It had two police trainers . . . one CPA representative."
    West, *The Strongest Tribe*, p. 21. The number of CPA officers jumped to three the following year.

27. "Making a complex situation . . . engage with the locals."
    Practical problems with unity of civilian and military chains of command between CJFT-7 and CPA, three different Coalition military commands, and four separate campaign plans to direct the military from May 2003 to January 2005 may account for some of this strategic confusion. See *On Point II*, pp. 161–64, 571–72.

28. "'We had no idea . . . as we went along.'"
    Personal interview, Ben Connable, Williamsburg, Virginia, February 27, 2010.

29. "They were more comfortable with kinetic operations."
    Ibid.

30. Even as the violence . . . back to military service."
    Personal interview, Martin Stanton, Tampa, January 19, 2010. Colonel Stanton was a civil-military affairs officer in 2003 and then chief of reconciliation and engagement for the Multinational Corps–Iraq from January 2007 to summer 2008.

31. "'many of the tribal elite . . . laws were confusing them.'"
Najim Abed Al-Jabouri and Sterling Jensen, "The Iraqi and AQI Roles in the Awakening," paper presented at the conference "The Anbar Awakening: An After Action Review," Tampa, Florida, January 21–22, 2010, p. 4.

32. "The result, according to John McCary . . . happening on the ground."
John McCary, "Sparks Before the Fire: What Tribal Engagement in Iraq Can Teach Us About Winning Allies in Afghanistan," paper presented at the conference "The Anbar Awakening: An After Action Review," Tampa, Florida, January 21–22, 2010. Some of these initiatives were quite creative. The 3rd Armored Cavalry Regiment had established a provincial council in Ramadi consisting largely of tribal leaders, along with a police academy, where it was rehiring former police and training new ones. The Commander's Emergency Response Program (CERP) used funds to grease the skids with reconstruction projects, elicit greater cooperation, and keep peace on the streets. Keith Mines, the lone CPA official in Anbar, proposed that tribal leaders convene the Iraqi equivalent of a *loya jirga*, a grand assembly of respected elders, which he had witnessed on an earlier tour in Afghanistan. Those who came forward would be rewarded with weapons and funding; the cost would be $3 million.

33. "In response to requests . . . in a democratic Iraq.'"
Joe Klein, "Saddam's Revenge," *Time*, September 18, 2005. Bremer's memoirs of his time as CPA head, *My Year in Iraq: The Struggle to Build a Future of Hope*, doesn't even list Anbar in the index. I am indebted to Keith Mines for bringing this to my attention.

34. "There were always rebuffed . . . CIA's old pals.'"
George Tenet, *At the Center of the Storm: My Years in the CIA* (New York: HarperCollins, 2007), p. 441. Tenet writes, "The reasons are not entirely clear to me, but some elements of the administration were obviously concerned that long-standing animus between the Agency and the INC [Iraqi National Congress] would stand in the way of the political advancement of Chalabi." p. 441.

35. "'The CPA wanted . . .authority of the federal government.'"
McCary, "Sparks Before the Fire," p. 6. The CPA opposed similar efforts outside of Anbar as well. In September 2003, Derek Harvey had contacted Grand Ayatollah Sayyad Ali al-Sistani's son to help organize a conference in Hilla before Ramadan to discuss joint security cooperation with U.S. forces during Ramadan and the creation of local Iraqi defense groups with U.S. support. Bremer and CPA shut it down before it got started.
Harvey was particularly fearless in his efforts to engage directly with insurgent leaders, leaving the Green Zone late at night with minimal force protection. His excursions were so dangerous that fellow officers sometimes refused to accompany him. Personal interview, Martin Stanton, Tampa, January 19, 2010.

36. "The NSC initiative went no further."
Telephone interview, April 14, 2010. The CIA officer reported the CPA's response back to Langley, but does not know how it was handled from there,

37. "'[General] Abizaid and I . . . adamantly refused to do so.'"
Ricardo Sanchez, *Wiser in Battle: A Soldier's Story* (New York: HarperCollins, 2008), p. 238.

38. "According to two senior . . . staff, budget and support."
Personal interview, Martin Stanton, Tampa, January 19, 2010; personal interview, Derek Harvey, Tampa, January 19, 2010. CPA created the Office of Provincial Outreach on December 4, 2003.

39. "Cammanders . . . becoming public or widespread."
McCary, "Sparks Before the Fire," pp. 4–5.

40. "'They were trying to work it . . . com in under was.'"
Ibid., p. 5.

41. "In a press conference . . . 'on a glide path towards success.'"
"82nd Airborne Division Commanding General's Briefing from Iraq," January 6, 2004,

http://merln.ndu.edu/MERLN/PFIraq/archive/dod/tr20040106-1103.pdf. The following month, Swannack and Abizaid were nearly assassinated when their convoy was attacked in Fallujah with rocket-propelled grenades.

42. "President Bush personally decided . . . firepower would be diminished."
The United States was faced with only poor choices: (1) bomb a city of 200,000 people, (2) conduct an urban assault, (3) do nothing, or (4) try to cut a deal with the insurgents. Even a military victory would represent a political defeat. Hashim, *Insurgency and Counterinsurgency in Iraq*, p. 36.

43. "The decision was not discussed . . . Iraqi Governing Council."
Remarks at the conference "The Anbar Awakening: An After Action Review," Tampa, Florida, January 21–22, 2010.

44. "CPA feared that . . . at the end of June."
Lakhdar Brahimi, the UN representative helping CPA form a new Iraqi government, also threatened to leave the country unless the Marines halted their advance. See Sanchez, *Wiser in Battle: A Soldier's Story*, pp. 350–57. The best account of the battle for Fallujah is Bing West, *No True Glory: A Frontline Account of the Battle for Fallujah* (New York: Bantam, 2005). See also the interview, Lieutenant General James T. Conway, in *Al-Anbar Awakening*, vol. 1: *American Perspectives*, Timothy S. McWilliams and Kurtis P. Wheeler, eds. (Quantico: Marine Corps University Press, 2009) (hereafter referred to as *Al-Anbar Awakening*, vol. 1), pp. 41–58.

45. "After Fallujah, a Marine . . . the tribes for some time.'"
Former Marine intelligence officer, remarks at the conference "The Anbar Awakening: An After Action Review," Tampa, Florida, January 21–22, 2010.

46. "To try to make the best . . . retreat from the city."
Ricks, *Fiasco*, p. 343.

47. "'Incident levels actually . . . clashed with coalition forces.'"
Carter Malkasian, "Did the Coalition Need More Forces in Iraq?: Evidence from al-Anbar," *Joint Forces Quarterly*, issue 46, 3d quarter (2007), p. 122.

48. "'By the end of June . . . Islamic government in the city.'"
Allawi, *The Occupation of Iraq*, p. 279.

49. "Others had none . . . Amman at the time.'"
For the Americans, it was difficult to parse the intricate hierarchy of minor and major tribes, the interpersonal relationships, and which ones Saddam had artificially promoted as "fake sheikhs" to better control the Anbar tribes. After the First Gulf War, Saddam had "created an Office of Tribal Affairs and required the sheikhs to register with it. Each sheikh was assigned a classification reflecting the measure of his influence, which gave Hussein the ability to manipulate the sheikhs by manipulating classifications and patronage. In effect, the sheikhs became officials of the state." *Al-Anbar Awakening*, vol. 2, p. 4.

50. "'It was tantalizing that . . . the insurgency was intoxicating.'"
Personal interview, Ben Connable, Williamsburg, Virginia, February 27, 2010.

51. "According to *Vanity Fair* . . . 'lost opportunity.'"
David Rose, "Heads in the Sand," *Vanity Fair*, May 12, 2009, *www.vanityfair.com/politics/features/2009/05/iraqi-insurgents200905*. See also Mark Perry, *Talking to Terrorists: Why America Must Engage with Its Enemies* (New York, Basic Books, 2009), pp. 33–83.

52. "As further confirmation that . . . the Awakening movement."
See Nibras Kazimi, "David Rose, *Vanity Fair* and the Hamdani Myth," May 15, 2009, *http://talismangate.blogspot.com/search?q=david+rose*. Kazimi's analysis was confirmed independently with four U.S. intelligence officers—two Army and two Marine Corps. Personal interviews, February and March 2010.

53. "The number of Americans . . . highest of the war."
Allawi, *The Occupation of Iraq*, p. 335.

54. "The deputy governor was kidnapped and killed."
Hashim, *Insurgency and Counterinsurgency in Iraq*, p. 40.

55. "In the ensuing chaos . . . rally around his leadership."
See Brian Fishman, "After Zarqawi: The Dilemmas and Future of Al Qaeda in Iraq," *The Washington Quarterly*, vol. 29, no. 4 (Autumn 2006), p. 23. Volumes have been written on the tensions between the Sunni and Shi'a. In Iraq, they were due to (1) religious differences over who properly inherited the mantle of legitimacy from the Prophet Muhammad, (2) Sunni repression of the Shi'a during Saddam's regime, and (3) a Sunni sense of entitlement due to their privileged status under Saddam.

56. "In return, Zarqawi gained . . . and propaganda support."
See *Al-Anbar Awakening*, vol. 2, p. 10.

57. "At this time, Zarqawi . . . larger number of Iraqis."
Estimates of the number of foreign fighters varied. Robert Earle, the senior civilian adviser to Ambassador John Negroponte, placed the number around 500. See Earle, *Nights in the Pink Motel: An American Strategist's Pursuit of Peace in Iraq* (Annapolis: Naval Institute Press, 2008), p. 57. Other sources placed the number slightly higher, but still less than 1,000. See *On Point II*, p. 110.

58. "Despite the relatively small . . . fear throughout the populace."
Harvey, "A 'Red Team' Perspective," p. 194.

59. "Zarqawi and AQI further complicated . . . opposed the U.S. presence?"
For analyses of the "insurgent landscape," see Amatzia Baram, *Who Are the Insurgents?: Sunni Arab Rebels in Iraq*, U.S. Institute of Peace, Special Report No. 134 (April 2005); and International Crisis Group, *In Their Own Words: Reading the Iraqi Insurgency*, Middle East Report No. 50 (February 15, 2006).

60. "After the Army intelligence officer . . . 'Is that guy a Democrat?'"
Personal interviews, Derek Harvey, Tampa, January 19, 2010, and April 20, 2010. Harvey was told of the president's reaction to his briefing by a senior Pentagon official who had remained in the room.

61. "From here on out . . . against the Sunnis."
See Allawi, *The Occupation of Iraq*, pp. 388–97. After the election, "SCIRI [Supreme Council for the Islamic Revolution in Iraq, a leading Shi'a political party] took over the Interior Ministry, allowing the Badr Corps [SCIRI's armed militia] to infiltrate its police and commando units. Soon Iraqis witnessed a steep rise in the killing of Sunnis that could not be explained by the fight against insurgents alone." International Crisis Group, *The Next Iraqi War?: Sectarianism and Civil Conflict*, Middle East Report No. 52 (February 27, 2006), p. 3. When the constitution's drafting committee was finally selected in May 2005, only two of its fifty-five members were Sunni Arabs.

62. "The Iraqi Security Forces . . . combatting the insurgents."
The Army's official history of the war commented that "as this study was prepared for publication [in 2008], the ISF was still not fully prepared to engage internal and external threats to their country." *On Point II*, p. 474.

63. "'We are Sunni . . . let's fight them together.'"
David Kilcullen, "Anatomy of a Tribal Revolt," *Small Wars Journal*, August 29, 2007, http://smallwarsjournal.com/blog/2007/08/anatomy-of-a-tribal-revolt/.

64. "'Out in the wild Western . . . and death by torture.'"
Ibid. AQI was "like a bulldog on a leash," remarked a U.S. official who studied the insurgency. "Every time anyone tries to control the beast, they end up getting bit themselves." Remarks at the conference "The Anbar Awakening: An After Action Review," Tampa, Florida, January 21–22, 2010.

65. "After a family was finally . . . with more wounded."
This story is recalled in *Al-Anbar Awakening*, vol. 2, p. 144. The volume contains numerous other tales of AQI's brutality.

66. "'I cannot describe the horror ... ghosts out of a cemetery.'"
    See interview, "Miriam" (a pseudonym) in *Al-Anbar Awakening,* vol. 2, p. 21.

67. "He would establish an ... across the Middle East."
    See Andrew Phillips, "How al Qaeda Lost Iraq," *Australian Journal of International Affairs,* vol. 63, no. 1 (March 2009), pp. 64–84; and International Crisis Group, *Iraq After the Surge I: The New Sunni Landscape,* Middle East Report No. 74 (April 30, 2008), pp. 3–9.

68. "Each tribe had a different ... free from AQI's embrace."
    "[W]e underestimated the impact of 30 years of Saddam's rule on that society, as far as undercutting basic values and the willingness of people to step up and try to make a change.... When one looks at what Saddam did to punish people when there were suspicions of treachery, or when some individuals just did not play ball with extortion or corruption schemes, or did not give what was asked to Uday, his son, the people who resisted that paid a price. Over time, this creates an atmosphere and a psychological outlook that keeps one from raising their head above the parapet, if you will." Harvey, "A 'Red Team' Perspective on the Insurgency in Iraq," p. 198.

69. "By 2005, these talks ... new Iraqi government."
    In June 2005, Secretary of Defense Rumsfeld publicly acknowledged on NBC's *Meet the Press* that the United States had been talking to the insurgents, but not to men who had "blood on their hands." See *www.msnbc.msn.com/id/8332675.* See also Dana Priest, "U.S. Talks with Iraqi Insurgents Confirmed," *Washington Post,* June 27, 2005, *www.washingtonpost.com/wp-dyn/content/article/2005/06/26/AR2005062600096.html.*

70. "Any deal stillborn."
    See West, *The Strongest Tribe,* pp. 75, 96.

71. "The first prominent example ... near the Syrian border."
    An argument can be made that the Albu Nimr tribe from the town of Hit, located on the Euphrates between Ramadi and al-Qaim, "awakened" first, in early 2004. Its men joined the local Iraqi National Guard unit and patrolled with the Marines. But in October 2004, the Marine battalion assigned to Hit was transferred to Fallujah; its replacement battalion was given responsibility for both Hit and Haditha. As AQI increased its attacks, there were soon not enough Marines to help the local Iraqi security forces. See Malkasian, "Did the Coalition Need More Forces in Iraq?," pp. 122–23.

72. "At that time, it appears ... control of the black market.'"
    Malkasian, "Did the Coalition Need More Forces in Iraq?," p. 123.

73. "The turning point was ... a member of the tribe."
    See the interview, Sheikh Sabah al-Sattam Effan Fahran al-Shurji al-Aziz, in *Al-Anbar Awakening,* vol. 2, p. 141.

74. "So in this way ... supporters around them."
    Al-Anbar Awakening, vol. 2, p. 141.

75. "Armed with greater numbers ... which fled the area."
    As AQI continued to persecute the Albu Mahal, the tribe's paramount sheikh (then in Jordan) called the minister of defense in August 2005 to ask for weapons, ammunition, and vehicles. With this support, the Albu Mahal created the "Desert Protectors," a militia of fewer than 400 men whose mission was to interdict foreign fighters coming over the Syrian border to join AQI.

76. "By the summer of 2006 ... the Albu Mahal tribe."
    Malkasian, "Did the Coalition Need More Forces in Iraq?," p. 124. Also, personal correspondence with John McCary, April 2010; and telephone interview, Sterling Jensen, April 12, 2010; Jensen was an interpreter in Iraq from March 2006 to June 2007, working with both the 1st Brigade, 1st Armored Division, and the 1st Brigade, 3rd Infantry Division. Telephone interview, Rob Torres, April 13, 2010. Torres was the intelligence chief for Marine PTT (Police Transition Team) Delta embedded with the local police in al-Qaim from January to July 2006.

77. "Some Sunnis had come . . . further marginalize their influence."
The sheikhs were also disgusted by Zarqawi's sending suicide bombers to attack three Western hotels in Amman, Jordan, the month before; all the victims were Muslims, including those attending a wedding party.

78. "When the Committee called . . . about seventy tribesman."
Many of the Iraqi wounded and nonwounded from this attack resumed their place in line to enlist in the police, suggesting to some American officers that there might be broader grassroots opposition to AQI than they had thought. Ben Connable, personal correspondence with the author, May 9, 2010.

79. "According to a Marine intelligence officer . . . al Qaeda in Iraq's arsenal.'"
Personal interview, Major Lester R. Gerber, Williamsburg, Virginia, April 19, 2010.

80. "The name caught on . . . adopted it as their own."
Personal correspondence, April 13, 2010. It is also possible that Joint Special Operations Command may have wanted to place an Iraqi face on its targeted killings of AQI commanders and bolster Sunni morale at the same time. See Bob Woodward, "Why Did Violence Plummet? It Wasn't Just the Surge," *Washington Post*, September 8, 2008, *www.washingtonpost.com/wp-dyn/content/article/2008/09/07/AR2008090701847.html.*
The Anbar Revolutionaries mimicked AQI's ruthless methods. The militia group appeared to originate in Fallujah, where some Sunnis started assassinating AQI members, and then spread outward to neighboring areas. Stories circulated that they infiltrated AQI cells and then used inside knowledge to target its members. Clerics started to support the Anbar Revolutionaries, identifying AQI men when they came to the mosques so that they later could be executed; one such operation netted twelve AQI members attending the Rahman Mosque in Ramadi. Using local knowledge, they would also conduct night raids, then leave corpses in the streets to be found the next morning with notes warning people that this is what happens to members of AQI. Telephone interview, Sterling Jensen, April 12, 2010; see also the interview, Staff General Haqi Isma'eel Ali Hameed, in *Al-Anbar Awakening*, vol. 2, pp. 230–31.

81. "Rather, they had the ability . . . strike back with a vengeance."
I am indebted to John McCary for this point.

82. "The rise of the Anbar Revolutionaries . . . Americans against AQI."
Telephone interview, U.S. civilian official with extensive experience in Iraq, April 2010.

83. "'We didn't recognize at this time . . . solve the insurgency.'"
Remarks at the conference "The Anbar Awakening: An After Action Review," Tampa, Florida, January 21–22, 2010.

84. "Other units knew . . . endorsed by senior commanders."
"At various levels of command and at various times, we had been 'burned' by tribal leaders who pledged their support and never delivered. A great deal of this push-back at MNF-West level and below was based on personal experience and disappointments." Ben Connable, personal correspondence with the author, May 9, 2010.

85. "The document was designated . . . Iraqi forces stood up."
The document was the first time the Bush administration had formally articulated its plan for winning in Iraq. See *http://georgewbush-whitehouse.archives.gov/infocus/iraq/iraq_national_strategy_20051130.pdf.* See also Ricks, *The Gamble*, pp. 13–14.

86. "By late 2005, the plan . . . be reduced to eight"
Ricks, *The Gamble*, p. 54. See also West, *The Strongest Tribe*, pp. 106–12. The United States had started consolidating bases earlier, but Casey accelerated the process.

87. "His decision to send home . . . 'we've won and we're done.'"
See "News Briefing with Gen. George Casey," U.S. Department of Defense, December 16, 2005, *www.globalsecurity.org/military/library/news/2005/12/mil-051216-dod02.htm.*

88. "None of Zarqawi's depredations . . . reprisals against the Sunni."
Until the Samarra bombing, most Shi'a had followed the guidance of the influential Grand Ayatollah Sistani, who had counseled restraint and not retaliation against the Sunnis. On Sistani and his waning influence after the Samarra bombing, see International Crisis Group, *The Next Iraqi War?*, pp. 24–25.

89. "Maples shared it with . . . including General Casey."
Personal interview, a senior U.S. official, 2010.

90. "Over the next sixteen months . . . fourteen to six brigades."
Michael Gordon, "U.S. General in Iraq Outlines Troop Cuts," *New York Times*, June 15, 2006,

91. "'The social and political situation . . . insurgency in al-Anbar.'"
Devlin's written brief is reprinted in full in Ricks, *The Gamble*, pp. 331–35. Even Zarqawi's death on June 7, 2006, after the United States dropped two 500-pound bombs on an AQI safe house (sic), could not temper the Devlin brief's somber analysis. Some Marine generals later complained that the assessment wasn't accurate. But it was consistent with the Army's assessment and had been endorsed by the DIA's General Maples. Personal interview, Derek Harvey, Tampa, March 29, 2010. All of the participants at the Tampa conference in January with whom I spoke agreed with Devlin's assessment.

92. "The Army and Marines had neglected . . . not yet been published."
"Although drafts were available as early as June of that year [2006], the members of the Ready First were too busy to read, process and apply new doctrine while fighting a raging insurgency. Additionally, the manual's theoretical bent would have been of little practical use in Ramadi." Niel Smith, "The Awakening in Ramadi: Misunderstandings and Myths," paper presented at the conference "The Anbar Awakening: An After Action Review," Tampa, January 21–22, 2010.

93. "Fewer tgb 1001 Iraqi police . . . go out on patrols."
See Niel Smith and Sean MacFarland, "Anbar Awakens: The Tipping Point," *The Military Review* (March–April 2008), pp. 41–42.

94. "Daily battles turned these . . . repulsed AQI's attacks."
Smith, "The Awakening in Ramadi: Misunderstandings and Myths," p. 11.

95. "'With new outposts established . . . from insurgents.'"
Smith and MacFarland, "Anbar Awakens: The Tipping Point," p. 46.

96. "'We had a 20 percent . . . Ramadi at the start.'"
Remarks at the conference "The Anbar Awakening: An After Action Review." See also MacFarland's interview in *Al-Anbar Awakening*, vol. 1, pp. 177–85.

97. "'They were willing to fight . . . how to harness them.'"
Personal correspondence with the author, February 15, 2010. See also Anthony E. Deane, "Providing Security Force Assistance in an Economy of Force Battle," *Military Review* (January–February 2010), pp. 80–90.

98. "Plus, given the low number . . . 500 new Iraqi policemen."
Personal correspondence with the author, February 15, 2010.

99. "'We didn't know Sattar . . . guy with a goatee.'"
Remarks at the conference "The Anbar Awakening: An After Action Review." "Prior to going all in with the sheikhs, I read every report that mentioned Sattar, and brought in the SEALS, CIA, and TF West. No one had anything on Sattar." Tony Deane, personal correspondence with the author, May 9, 2010.

100. "The religious leaders initially . . . not a religious person.'"
See *Al-Anbar Awakening*, vol. 2, p. 35.

101. "the right job for the right man . . . he had a bad record."
See interview, Sheikh Majed Abd al-Razzaq Ali al-Sulayman, in *Al-Anbar Awakening*, vol. 2, p. 133.

102. "Abdul Sattar was willing . . . sheikhs remained in the shadows."
Meanwhile, senior command had tweaked the policing system to make it easier to get buy-in from the sheikhs. After signing up, recruits now could head straight to the police training academy in Jordan so they could not be intimidated or killed by AQI while waiting to report. In addition, new police stations were located where they could protect the tribe's homes and families, which reassured the sheikhs about their personal safety. It was important that local recruits were allowed to serve locally, where they could protect their own tribe, rather than being posted to another part of Ramadi or Anbar. All these measures helped with recruitment, retention, and morale.

103. "There was lots of dissension . . . work with these guys."
Personal interview, Tampa, April 20, 2010.

104. "Deane refused."
Personal correspondence with the author, April 5, 2010. As late as February 2007, senior-level command harbored doubts about Abdul Sattar. Upon arriving in Iraq, Petraeus asked to meet the Awakening Council's leader. Major General Walter Gaskin advised against it, arguing that Abdul Sattar was not important enough for someone of Petraeus's stature. Petraeus met with him anyway.

105. "The awakening appeared seeks to expel Coalition forces.'"
"The Current Situation in Iraq and Afghanistan," General Michael V. Hayden, Statement for the Record, Senate Armed Services Committee, November 15, 2006, p. 5, *www.au.af.mil/au/awc/ awcgate/cia/hayden15nov06.pdf.*

106. "'the tribes were just . . . trying to survive.'"
Personal interview, Derek Harvey, Tampa, April 20, 2010.

107. "The Ready First gave . . . (CERP) funds."
Remarks at the conference "The Anbar Awakening: An After Action Review." See also Smith and MacFarland, "Anbar Awakens: The Tipping Point," p. 43.

108. "U.S. commanders also looked . . . police or auxiliary forces.'"
Personal interview, U.S. military officer with extensive experience in Iraq, April 2010.

109. "Said one sheikh . . . flee the area by themselves."
See the interview, Sheikh Jassim Mohammad Saleh al-Sudawadawi in *Anbar Awakening,* vol. 2, p. 77. AQI also had its own information operations campaign, labeling those who joined the Awakening as "betrayers of the faith."

110. "In addition, some Council . . . they would be killed."
Personal interview, U.S. military officer with extensive experience in Iraq, April 2010.

111. "The report recommended . . . to Iraqi control."
The Iraq Study Group Report (December 6, 2006), *http://media.usip.org/reports/iraq_study_group_ report.pdf,* pp. 27, 32.

112. "It judged that . . . Shi'a strongman, or anarchy."
National Intelligence Estimate, "Prospects for Iraq's Stability: A Challenging Road Ahead," (January 2007), *www.dni.gov/press_releases/20070202_release.pdf.*

113. "Despite the prevaling pessimism . . . combat forces."
The driving force behind this rethinking of U.S. military strategy was General Jack Keane, the former vice chief of staff of the Army. See Ricks, *The Gamble,* pp. 74–105; and Linda Robinson, *Tell Me How This Ends: General David Petraeus and the Search for a Way out of Iraq* (New York: Public Affairs, 2008), pp. 25–45. See also Frederick W. Kagan, "Choosing Victory: A Plan for Success in Iraq, Phase I Report" (January 5, 2007), *http://www.aei.org/docLib/20070111_ ChoosingVictoryupdated.pdf.*

114. "Critics thought . . . 'reinforcing failure.'"
Ricks, *The Gamble,* p. 150.

115. "According to Major General John Allen . . . violence in Anbar.'"
Quoted in *Al-Anbar Awakening,* vol. 1, p. 229. Allen was the deputy commanding general, II Marine Expeditionary Force (Forward) and MNF-West from January 2007 to February 2008.

116. AQI's many acts of . . . who had condemned AQI."
See Bill Roggio, "The Sunni Civil War," *Long War Journal*, March 27, 2007, *www.longwarjournal. org/archives/2007/03/the_sunni_civil_war.php.*

117. "He also set up . . . the insurgents and promote reconciliation."
F-SEC was led by Graeme Lamb, a British general with counterinsurgency experience from Northern Ireland. "The fundamental purpose guiding F-SEC operations was the idea that persuading select individuals from Iraqi insurgent groups (or those sympathetic to them) to engage in dialogue with the Iraqi government was more efficient than trying to destroy the groups with military force." Jeanne F. Hull, "Iraq: Strategic Reconciliation, Targeting, and Key Leader Engagement," (September 2009), p. 14, *www.strategicstudiesinstitute.army.mil/pdffiles/PUB938.pdf.* This article provides a good overview of the many challenges F-SEC faced in Iraq.

118. "Petraeus did not ask permission . . . from President Bush."
See Ricks, *The Gamble*, p. 202.

119. "Maliki could have cared less . . . that was fine by him.'"
Personal correspondence with an officer in Iraq at the time, April 2010. This officer added, "The government was much less concerned with Anbar until [the SOI] approached Baghdad. He [Maliki] got very anxious when it spread to Abu Ghraib," which was a western suburb of the city.

120. "'And when the Shi'a . . . ready to fight them.'"
Personal interview, Major Lester R. Gerber, Williamsburg, Virginia, April 19, 2010.

121. "Working with the Americans . . . obtain reconstruction contracts.'"
Najim Abed al-Jabouri and Sterling Jensen, "The Iraqi and AQI Roles in the Awakening," p. 16.

122. "'We are going to be . . . but that is the way forward.'"
Quoted in Ricks, *The Gamble*, p. 205. The military quickly ran into an unexpected problem: Its lawyers said it could not use CERP funds to pay the insurgents. Instead, they were paid to provide security for reconstruction contracts; in practice, they manned checkpoints.

123. "As for these men having belonged . . . blood on their hands?'"
Personal interview, May 21, 2009. By the end of 2007, 103,000 Iraqis had joined the Sons of Iraq. General Petraeus estimated that 20 percent of this number were Shi'a. Personal interview, David Petraeus, Tampa, April 20, 2010. On the Sons of Iraq program, see Robinson, *Tell Me How This Ends*, pp. 251–70; Ricks, *The Gamble*, pp. 202–16. Critics of the SOI argued that it solved a short-term problem while creating a longer-term one: The arming of Sunni militias might help defeat AQI but it would threaten the Maliki government once the AQI threat receded. Petraeus promised Maliki that U.S. forces would supervise the SOI closely; the SOI also had to pledge fealty to the Iraqi government. But whether the men in SOI posed a longer-term threat to the Iraqi government would ultimately depend on the efforts Baghdad would make on bringing these men into the police and ISF.

124. "In mid-April . . . not accomplishing anything.'"
See "Senator Reid on Iraq: 'This War Is Lost,'" CBS News (April 20, 2007), *www.cbsnews.com/ stories/2007/04/20/politics/main2709229.shtml.*

125. "'Today, it is a . . . Taliban-like ideology.'"
General David H. Petraeus, "Report to Congress on the Situation in Iraq," *http://www.defense.gov/ pubs/pdfs/Petraeus-Testimony20070910.pdf.*

126. "He said he intended to . . . end of 2011."
See Remarks of President Barack Obama, "Responsibly Ending the War in Iraq, "Camp Lejeune, North Carolina (February 27, 2009), *http://www.whitehouse.gov/the_press_office/Remarks-of-President-Barack-Obama-Responsibly-Ending-the-War-in-Iraq/.*

127. "'Sectarian violence didn't . . . We defeated it.'"
Personal interview, David Petraeus, Tampa, April 20, 2010.

128. "'Samarra took place and the Shi'a . . . senior military intelligence officer."
Personal interview, Derek Harvey, Tampa, March 29, 2010.

129. "'It's good when your enemy . . . can see the difference.'"
Personal correspondence, August 26, 2009.

130. "'I wake up every morning grateful for him.'"
Personal interview, Derek Harvey, Tampa, January 19, 2010. To be sure, AQI was a learning organization at the tactical level, but the point here speaks to the strategic level.

131. "'And then, later . . . dollars and reconstruction contracts.'"
Personal interview, David Petraeus, Tampa, April 20, 2010.

132. "The Sunnis, in turn . . . rejoin the government in mid-2008."
Personal interview, Ryan Crocker, Williamsburg, Virginia, April 26, 2010, and personal correspondence with the author, May 1, 2010.

133. "Keith Mines, the lone CPA . . . to seize that opportunity.'"
Keith Mines, personal manuscript provided to the author, March 2010.

134. "The official Army history . . . quick creat of new Iraq.'"
On Point II, p. 25.

135. "A blind man on a dark night . . . told me in April 2010."
Personal interview, David Petraeus, Tampa, April 20, 2010.

136. "'the opportunity was always there . . . in 2005 and 2006."
See *George Packer*, "The Lesson of Tal Afar: Is It Too Late for the Administration to Correct Its Course in Iraq?," April 10, 2006, *www.newyorker.com/archive/2006/04/10/060410fa_fact2*.

137. "And they weren't sure . . . protect them,' said Crocker."
Personal interview, Ryan Crocker, Williamsburg, Virginia, April 26, 2010.

138. "'They hadn't stood at . . . and looked into it.'"
Quoted in Dexter Filkins, "His Long War," *New York Times Sunday Magazine*, October 18, 2009, p. 45.

139. "'Sattar would not have been . . . Sattar was going to die.'"
Personal interview, Derek Harvey, Tampa, March 29, 2010. AQI assassinated Sattar anyway, with an IED planted outside his home, eight days after he met President Bush and almost a year to the day after he announced the Anbar Awakening Council. See "Bomb Kills a Key Sunni Ally of U.S.," *Washington Post*, September 14, 2007, *www.washingtonpost.com/wp-dyn/content/article/2007/09/13/AR2007091300490.html*.

140. "'we could have made . . . Chalabi approach and Bremer's actions.'"
Personal correspondence with the author, April 21, 2010. Concerning Tal'Afar, Harvey believes that McMaster's "efforts were commendable and the way to go, but that AOR [area of Responsibility] was unique in many respects."

141. "Iranian opposition to . . . rising Persian interference in Iraq."
See Najim Abed al-Jabouri and Sterling Jensen, "The Iraqi and AQI Roles in the Awakening," pp. 9–10.

142. "Prime Minister Nouri al-Maliki . . . commission in June 2007."
The name of the organization was the Iraqi Follow-Up Committee for National Reconciliation (IFCNR).

CONCLUSION: LESSONS EARNED

1. "'Either you are with us, or you are with the terrorists."
See *http://georgewbush-whitehouse.archives.gov/news/releases/2001/09/20010920-8.html*.

2. "Once a week, President Obama . . . developments and trends."
See Anne E. Kornblut, "For Obama, Weekly Tutorials in Terrorism," *Washington Post*, May 6, 2010.

3. "Gone is much of . . . 'bring 'em on.'"
President Bush made this statement on July 2, 2003. He later publicly regretted saying it.

4. "The special CIA unit . . . more urgent priorities."
See Mark Mazzetti, "C.I.A. Closes Unit Focused on Capture of bin Laden," *The New York Times*, July 4, 2006.

5. "In these cases, governments . . . aggressive information campaign."
The Obama administration has expanded upon the Bush administration's policy of military strikes against members of al Qaeda and other terrorist groups around the world. This "secret war" also includes training local counterterrorism forces and conducting joint operations with them. See Karen DeYoung and Greg Jaffe, "U.S. 'Secret War' Expands Globally," *Washington Post*, June 4, 2010.

6. "You have to be careful . . . make judgements over time."
Telephone interview, the author, April 2010.

7. "We saw a military stalemate . . . years, but for decades."
Personal interview, Martin McGuinness, May 26, 2009.

8. "Dialogue is essential . . . prepared to do that."
Personal interview, Gerry Adams, Belfast, May 26, 2009.

9. "Unsettled them tremendously . . . mistrust inside the organization."
Personal interview, London, May 22, 2009. Using negotiations as a counterterrorism device is especially useful given some recent trends that make it increasingly difficult to infiltrate terrorist movements. First, modern search engines make it almost impossible to set up cover stories for clandestine agents that can't be broken. Second, many of the bad guys today live in tribes and know one another. They test newcomers to the group by asking them to commit crimes such as murder or bank robbery. When newcomers resist, their lives are placed in jeopardy. Personal correspondence with Richard Stolz, June 2, 2010. A career CIA official, Stolz retired as deputy director for operations in September 1990.

10. "If part of a movement . . . vital tactical information.'"
Daniel Byman, "Talking with Insurgents: A Guide for the Perplexed," *The Washington Quarterly*, vol. 32, no. 2 (April 2009), p. 128.

11. "'performance . . . with a police objective.'"
Personal interview, Rafael Vera, Torrelodones, July 20, 2009.

12. "'The results must not be . . . senior British intelligence officer."
David Omand, "Ethical Guidelines in Using Secret Intelligence for Public Security," *Cambridge Review of International Affairs*, vol. 19, no. 4 (December 2006), p. 620. See also Omand, *Securing the State* (New York: Columbia University Press, 2010).

13. "These talks revealed . . . to a peace agreement."
The LTTE's chief negotiator, Anton Balasingham, gave his opinion of these talks in the title of his book: *The Politics of Duplicity: Re-Visiting the Jaffna Talks* (Surrey: Fairmax, 2000).

14. "A government needs to know . . . go off the next day."
Some observers of Northern Ireland have speculated that the British reached an informal agreement with the IRA to prevent a dedicated campaign of violence directed at maximizing civilian casualties. Under this "code of conduct," the IRA would allegedly refrain from attacking purely civilian targets. Or when it did attack such targets, such as Harrods department store in downtown London, it would phone in warnings ahead of time so that civilians could be evacuated. (If true, one can only speculate as to what the British had to "give" in order to "get.") Other explanations as to why the IRA did not attempt mass casualty attacks on the British mainland include religious, cultural, societal, and political factors. The full story must await further memoirs, historical investigations, and access to government files.

15. "'We only had 25 . . . 2003-to-2006 time period."
Personal interview, Ben Connable, Williamsburg, Virginia, February 27, 2010. Connable alone managed all the translators and interpreters in Anbar province for the first half of 2004.

16. "'We keep hoping they'll . . . just hasn't happened.'"
Quoted in Joel Klein, "Saddam's Revenge," *Time*, September 18, 2005.

17. "In Spain, a typical . . . who also controls the military.'"
Personal interview, Florencio Dominguez, Bilbao, July 16, 2009.

18. "Since September 2000 . . . collapsing the group's resistance."
See Jenna Jordan, "When Heads Roll: Assessing the Effectiveness of Leadership Decapitation," *Security Studies*, vol. 18, no. 4 (October–December 2009), pp. 719–55.

19. "In the case of . . . nasty, brutish, and short.'"
Gal Luft, "The Logic of Israel's Targeted Killing," *Middle East Quarterly* (Winter 2003), pp. 3–13, *www.meforum.org/515/the-logic-of-israels-targeted-killing*.

20. "Eliza Manningham-Buller . . . not contaminate the politicians.'"
Personal interview, Eliza Manningham-Buller, London, May 21, 2009.

21. "For example, Martin McGuiness . . . 'I was only twenty-two at the time!'"
Interview with Martin McGuinness, Stormont Assembly, Belfast, May 26, 2009. One member of the IRA delegation, Ivor Bell, threatened to wear his combat fatigues to the Cheyne Walk meeting, arguing that "history had taught him that British politicians would try to make the Irish feel ill at ease. He was going to wear this gear to put *them* ill at ease." Cited in Taylor, *Behind the Mask*, p. 164. In the end, Bell did not wear his fatigues to the meeting.

22. "They lived in a very . . . changes in the world."
Personal interview, Juan Manuel Eguiagaray, Madrid, July 21, 2009.

23. "An American official closely . . . they were in trouble.'"
Telephone interview, the author, March 25, 2010.

24. "At one point, G.L. . . . the LTTE delegation lacked."
Personal interview, G. L. Peiris, Colombo, March 11, 2010. Sri Lanka brought in the former premier of Ontario, Bob Rae, from the Forum on Foundations, to help the LTTE delegation understand the concept of federalism.

25. "'But my problem was . . . had to test ETA.'"
Personal interview, José Maria Aznar, Washington, D.C., September 30, 2009.

26. "When that threat receded . . . more pressing matters of state."
To get a sense of the Blair administration's investment in the Northern Ireland peace process, see Jonathan Powell, *Great Hatred, Little Room: Making Peace in Northern Ireland* (London: The Bodley Head, 2008).

27. "For all these reasons . . . adrift and out to sea."
The movie *Bridge on the River Kwai,* based loosely on a true World War II story, captures this idea perfectly. The British commander in charge of building a railway bridge in Thailand for the Japanese with POW laborers becomes so proud of his work that he tries to stop British commandoes from blowing it up. The movie was filmed in Sri Lanka.

28. "A meeting may appear . . . legitimize a terrorist group."
It is interesting to speculate as to what a terrorist group could lose if it agreed to engage with the United States: a devaluing of its ideological purity, a compromising of its revolutionary agenda, and an erosion of local support. It could appear as just another group of guys trying to cut a deal.

29. "Talking was 'a tactical . . . the greater good.'"
Personal interview, Eliza Manningham-Buller, London, May 21, 2009.

30. "'Everyone has blood on . . . then they don't matter.'"
Telephone interview, the author, April 2010.

31. "'wasn't being fair . . . sitting on their hands.'"
Personal interview, Peter Brooke, London, May 20, 2009.

32. "'You ask yourself . . . aren't so many funerals.'"
Personal interview, Bertie Ahern, Dublin, May 28, 2009.

33. "Father Alec Reid . . . injured in the conflict.'"
Personal interview, Father Alec Reid, Dublin, May 29, 2009.

34. "Ami Ayalon, the former . . . war is ethical.'"
Personal interview, Ami Ayalon, Tel Aviv, January 28, 2010.

35. "The government must ensure that . . . John Rawls has expressed it."
See John Rawls, *A Theory of Justice* (Cambridge, Mass.: Harvard University Press, 1971).

36. "Some senior British and Irish . . . reach a peace agreement"
See Mary-Alice C. Clancey, *Peace Without Consensus: Power Sharing Politics in Northern Ireland* (Surrey: Ashgate, 2010).

A Note on Terms

1. Ariel Merari, "Terrorism as a Strategy for Insurgency," in Gerard Chaliand and Arnaud Blin, eds., *The History of Terrorism: From Antiquity to Al Qaeda* (Berkeley: University of California Press, 2007), p. 14.

2. Ibid., pp. 14–15; and Bruce Hoffman, *Inside Terrorism* (New York: Columbia University Press, 2006), p. 40

Index

Breinigsville, PA USA
18 October 2010

247292BV00002BC/2/P